Dinnerware
OF THE 20TH CENTURY

THE TOP 500 PATTERNS

Wedgwood, Columbia Enamelled. *Photo courtesy of Wedgwood.*

Dinnerware

OF THE 20TH CENTURY

THE TOP 500 PATTERNS

Harry L. Rinker

HOUSE OF COLLECTIBLES • NEW YORK

Important Notice. All of the information, including valuations,
in this book has been compiled from the most reliable sources,
and every effort has been made to eliminate errors
and questionable data. Nevertheless, the possibility of error, in a work of such
immense scope, always exists. The publisher will not
be held responsible for losses that may occur in the purchase,
sale, or other transaction of items
because of information contained herein. Readers
who feel they have discovered errors are invited
to *write* and inform us, so they may be corrected in
subsequent editions. Those seeking further information
on the topics covered in this book are advised
to refer to the complete line of *Official Price Guides*
published by the House of Collectibles.

Copyright © 1997 by Rinker Enterprises, Inc.

All rights reserved under International and Pan-American Copyright Conventions.

HC This is a registered trademark of Random House, Inc.

Published by: House of Collectibles
201 East 50th Street
New York, NY 10022

Distributed by Ballantine Books, a division of Random House, Inc., New York,
and simultaneously in Canada by Random House of Canada Limited, Toronto.

http://www.randomhouse.com

Manufactured in the United States of America

ISSN: 1094-1193

ISBN: 0-676-60085-9

Text design by Debbie Glasserman

Cover design by Kristine V. Mills-Noble
Cover photo © George Kerrigan

First Edition: September 1997

10 9 8 7 6 5 4 3 2 1

Contents

Adams, Singapore Bird. *Photo courtesy of BC Design.*

Acknowledgments

This book would not have been possible without the cooperation of dozens of individuals.

Gary S. Corns, manager of the Imaging Services Design Team, served as project coordinator at Replacements, Ltd. Bob Page, Replacements, Ltd.'s founder, deserves the highest praise for his enthusiastic support and willingness to provide access to the Replacements, Ltd.'s database. Chris Kirkman, Nathan Atkins, and the curating staff guided and assisted me in finding the information I needed in Replacement, Ltd.'s extensive research library. Doug Anderson, Executive Vice President, Mark Klein, Director of Marketing, Mark Donahue, Media and Marketing Coordinator, Dale Frederiksen, and Todd Hall all lent their talents to this project. Special thanks to Pat Thompson of Greensboro, North Carolina, for her encouragement and support throughout this project.

Dena George at Rinker Enterprises, Inc., was responsible for the price listings, company histories, some text, and image management. Nancy Butt performed in-house research and worked with manufacturers and their public relations firms in the recruitment of information and images. Both were assisted by Dana Morykan, Kathy Williamson, Virginia Reinbold, and Richard Schmeltzle.

The cooperation received from manufacturers and their agents was most welcome. These include: Arabia of Finland/Hackman Tabletop, Inc., Linda Morse, Operations Assistant; Block China Corporation, Joseph Block, Vice President of Sales; Churchill Tableware, Ltd., Kate Briggs, Marketing; Denby Pottery Company Ltd. USA, Sherry Leahy, Marketing Coordinator; Hall China Company, Everson Hall, Historian; Herend/Martin's Herend Imports, Lisa Zwanziger, and Maureen Miklavic, Marketing Director; The Homer Laughlin China Company, J. David Conley, National Sales Manager Retail Markets; The Hutschenreuther Company, Barbara Fischer, Executive Assistant; International China Company, Inc., Joseph Young, Executive Vice President, Sales; Lenox Brands, Alice J. Kolator, Director, Public Relations, and Tracy Mitchell; Mikasa, Inc., Denise Ugaro; Nikko Ceramics, Inc., Grace J. Dul, Marketing; Noritake Co., Inc., Judy Stern, Public Relations Manager; The Pfaltzgraff Co., Holly Stetler and Lorri Privitera, Communications Specialist; Portmeirion USA, Carol Yachtis, National Marketing and Training Coordinator; Rosenthal USA Ltd., Chris Schapdick, Product Manager/PR; Royal Doulton, Dave Sansone, Public Relations; Syracuse China Co./Libbey Inc., Ruth Hancock, Archivist; *Tableware Today,* Amy Stavis, Editor/Publisher; Waterford/Wedgwood and BC Design Incorporated, Chie Riley and Bernadette Hoyt; Wedgwood USA, Stacey Lundy, Marketing Assistant; and, Josiah Wedgwood & Sons Limited, Lisa Alkins, Communications Department, and Clare Elsby.

The House of Collectibles staff, headed by Timothy J. Kochuba, is commended for its patience and fortitude in bringing this project to conclusion. Randy Ladenheim-Gil served as project coordinator and editor, Simon Vukelj directed the marketing efforts, and Alex Klapwald supervised production.

Inevitably, with a project of this size and nature, many individuals whose names do not appear here also helped assemble data, as well as performed other tasks that led to the publication and successful sale of this book. My thanks to all of these individuals—the talents they brought to the project are sincerely appreciated.

Finally, my thanks to you, the purchaser of this book. I trust you will find that it more than meets your expectations.

Introduction

Many of my fondest childhood memories are associated with the dining room of my childhood home in Hellertown, Pennsylvania. A wonderful Chippendale-style Colonial Revival dining room suite—a table and eight chairs, china cabinet, small buffet, and large buffet—took center stage.

While eating in the dining room was reserved for special occasions, it frequently was used several times a month. Sunday meals, shared meals with relatives (I had over thirty-six aunts and uncles and forty first cousins, all of whom lived within ten miles of our home), holidays, and entertaining friends accounted for the activity. Good cooking was a hallmark of my mother's family. There are no thin Prossers in my family. Perhaps this is why so many "family" meals took place in our dining room.

Eating in the dining room meant getting out the linen tablecloth and napkins. Placemats were a definite no-no. Next came the dinnerware, stemware, flatware, and tabletop accessories. I do not remember a meal without a centerpiece and candelabra.

My parents had two different sets of "dining room" dinnerware. A formal pattern service for six was used for very special occasions. I do not remember it. It was used for adult entertaining, an event that generally coincided with a visit by my brother and me to another house for the evening to visit with our cousins. When my parents died, I sold or gave the set away—I do not remember which. Memories are associated with use, not ownership.

I have my parents' second dinnerware service, Grindley's Scenes After Constable pattern. I still use it occasionally. In 1966 I helped organize and served as the first president of the Pennsylvania Canal Society. After becoming involved with canals and their history, imagine my delight when I discovered that the center motif on several forms of the Scenes After Constable pattern pictured canal locks.

The pattern apparently was quite popular in the 1930s. I extended the place setting count and added serving pieces over the years, as I discovered additional pieces at garage sales, flea markets, and antiques shows. Although the service has reached the point where it already is larger than I will ever need, I probably will continue to enlarge it well into the future. My memories are too strong to allow me to pass up a reasonably priced piece.

Whereas the dining room dinnerware was permanent, the kitchen dinnerware changed frequently. I vaguely remember a solid color service, possibly Fiesta. This was replaced early in my childhood by premium china, received as a result of purchasing groceries at Acme. A few short years later, a melamine plastic set appeared. By the time it arrived, an automatic dishwasher had been installed in the kitchen. Mother grew discontent with her melamine dinnerware when continual washing faded the colors. Before long, a set of inexpensive stoneware dinnerware appeared, Pfaltzgraff, if I remember correctly. I had married and was on my own by that time, hence, my memory is clouded.

Earlier I mentioned that I came from a large nucleated family. Aunt Ruth and Uncle Brownie lived two homes up in the row, right next to Aunt Jeanette and Uncle Bill. My grandfather and stepgrandmother lived a block away, next door to Uncle Earl and Aunt Peg and, later, Aunt Doris and Uncle Bud. Each home had a revolving door. I did not grow up in one home; I grew up in over a dozen. As a result, my dinnerware memories range from fine sets of Haviland to assembled sets of Stangl. Researching and working with the patterns in this book invoked more than one trip down memory lane.

From 1972 through early 1977 I served as executive director of The Historical Society of York County in York, Pennsylvania. Pfaltzgraff's headquarters, as well as one of its plants, is located in York. Louis J. Appell Jr., the company's president, served on the Society's board. The Bonham House, one of the Society's historic properties, was located right next to the Pfaltzgraff corporate offices. It should come as no surprise that several of my early everyday dinnerware patterns were made by Pfaltzgraff. I still use some of the survivors.

As a writer and appraiser of antiques and collectibles, I frequently am asked by individuals to value their dinnerware services and recommend someone, sometimes anyone, who might buy them. I always ask the individual if he or she asked their children if they would like the set. The stock answer is, "They do not want it."

My response is twofold. First, give it time. The nostalgia gene is a late bloomer. Many young adults who said no to their parents' queries in their thirties have deep-seated regrets by the time they reach their forties. Second, I suggest that parents invite their children to dinner and use the dinnerware service in question. Surprise, surprise. After a few great meals, attitudes do change.

The true value of things is not monetary, but the memories associated with them. Use creates memories. Dinnerware, stemware, and flatware were not created to be displayed in a china cabinet or stored in a buffet. They were made and sold to be used. It is a lesson that I plan never to forget. I hope you will not either.

Dinnerware of the 20th Century: The Top 500 Patterns is designed to serve a number of purposes. There is a great deal more to this book than a list of forms and their values. Use the book to its full potential.

First, the book provides the basic guidelines needed to select, use, and care for dinnerware. There is an old adage that the more one knows about something, the more one appreciates it. This book offers the opportunity to learn about dinnerware—how dinnerware and the fine art of dining has evolved, the manufacturers that are involved, and the unique design history of some patterns.

Second, this book shows the tremendous variety of patterns that are readily available to a decorator or person who wishes to acquire a new dinnerware service. There are dozens of choices for most decorating styles. Every pattern is illustrated. Take a few minutes, flip through the pages, and marvel at the ingenuity of pattern designers and manufacturers.

Third, the checklist approach identifies what forms are available within each pattern, based upon available information. Not everyone needs a pattern that contains dozens of serving and accessory pieces. However, those who do will appreciate knowing which patterns to consider and which to avoid. The checklist also provides the user with a hunting list. Many individuals will be surprised to learn how many forms are available in their particular pattern.

Fourth, this book answers the question: about how much will I have to pay to replace a piece or expand my dinnerware service? The pricing is retail and realistic. Most individuals buy with a budget in mind; realistic prices allow the user to determine which patterns are affordable and which are not.

Dinnerware of the 20th Century is one title from a series of three books that focus on tableware. If you find it helpful and informative, you may also be interested in its companion titles—*Stemware of the 20th Century* and *Silverware of the 20th Century*.

I

GUIDELINES FOR SELECTING, USING, AND CARING FOR DINNERWARE

Wedgwood, Napoleon Ivy. *Photo courtesy of Wedgwood.*

CHAPTER ONE

A Brief History of Dinnerware

The first step in understanding ceramic dinnerware is to divide it into three groups—pottery, stoneware, and porcelain. Pottery is fired at low temperatures and is not translucent or vitrified. It has a porous body. Stoneware has a partially vitrified ceramic body that is dense, extremely hard, and varies in color from blue-gray to brown. Stoneware is fired at a higher temperature than pottery. Porcelain is a hard, nonporous, vitrified, translucent ware. Hard paste porcelain is made from kaolin and china stone or petuntse. Soft paste porcelain combines white clay and ground glass and is fired at a lower temperature than hard paste porcelain.

Today's dinnerware owes much of its development to advances made in body and glaze formulas, decorative methods, and manufacturing techniques that occurred in England's Staffordshire pottery district between 1750 and 1850. English pottery manufacturers set the standards for the rest of the world, a position they still enjoy.

In the mid-1720s, Astbury, a Staffordshire potter, developed the formulas for a cream-colored ware. Previously, potters whitened their wares by adding tin oxide to the lead glaze covering the plate. Building on Astbury's success, Josiah Wedgwood improved the glaze formula and the body composition, the latter through the incorporation of Cornish china clay and china stone. Initially, Wedgwood's creamware was buff-colored. By 1768, it achieved its white body. Wedgwood's refinements were so monumental that scholars credit him as the true creator of cream-colored wares.

In 1765, Josiah Wedgwood received the patronage of Queen Charlotte, the wife of George III. Wedgwood changed the name of his "ivory" creamware to Queen's ware. Today, Wedgwood's creamware and colored bodies are still known as Queen's ware. Further, Queen's ware has become a generic term for all creamware, regardless of who manufactures it.

By the late 1790s, Wedgwood's Queen's ware gave the company a near monopoly in the earthenware tableware trade. During the latter half of the eighteenth century, European pottery manufacturers devoted much of their efforts to copying Wedgwood's Queen's ware. They did not achieve a high level of success until the beginning of the nineteenth century, however. Queen's ware is known in France as *faience-fine*, *faience anglais*, and *terre de pipe anlaise*, in Germany as *Steingut*, in Italy as *terraglia*, and in Scandinavia as *flint porslin*.

Creamware decoration was and continues to be achieved through a variety of methods—painting, use of colored glazes, transfer printing, molding, and piercing. Enamels were used on early painted pieces. In 1750, John Sadler, a partner in Sadler and Green in Liverpool, invented transfer printing. The concept also was developed independently by John Brooks in London in 1753. The Bow Porcelain Factory and Battersea Enamel Works were employing the technique by the mid-1750s. By 1756, it was used in Worcester. Sadler and Green were decorators, applying their technique to large quantities of creamwares sent to Liverpool by Wedgwood for that purpose.

The search for strong, durable tableware bodies did not end with Wedgwood's development of Queen's ware. Much of the eighteenth century was devoted to developing a porcelain body that matched the ceramics from China's Yüan dynasty. Porcelain is a hard, nonporous, vitrified translucent ware, a compound of refractory refined clay, a fusible rock, and the addition of a small quantity of flux to assist in the fusion. The key to porcelain development in England was finding the right clay and fusible rock.

J. F. Böttger and von Tschirnhaus produced the first European porcelain at Meissen around 1709. By the mid-1750s, Louis XV's Sèvres plant was producing an excellent porcelain body. The first English porcelain was produced at Chelsea in the late 1740s. Bow and Worcester soon followed. In 1768, William Cookworthy, a chemist in Plymouth, received a patent for a porcelain body made from Cornish materials. Richard Champion, manager of Bristol, bought the patent in 1775 and moved production from Plymouth to Bristol. After Champion's patent expired in 1796, numerous English and European manufacturers were producing porcelain tableware. English manufacturers were aided in their efforts by a high tariff imposed on imported ceramics in 1794.

Turner and Company, a Lane End potter, developed stone china, a dense, hard porcellanous ware around 1800. Spode used the formula for its "Stone China" and "New China," beginning in 1805. Wedgwood produced stone china wares between 1820 and 1861.

Josiah Spode II is frequently credited with the development of bone china, a porcelain body that includes clay, feldspathic rock, and about 50 percent calcined cattle bones, around 1799. Actually, the use of bone ash in china production was established by the mid-eighteenth century. Spode's contribution involved significantly increasing the amount of bone ash added to the mix. Josiah Wedgwood II began the production of bone china at Etruria in the early 1810s, but discontinued it in the early 1820s. Wedgwood resumed production of bone china in 1878.

Bone china offers significant advantages over feldspathic porcelain. It is whiter in color, less brittle, and lighter in weight. A wider range of colors can be used in its decoration. Bone china continues to be made almost exclusively in England. A few Scandinavian and American factories have made it successfully. The Japanese are continually experimenting with the body.

In 1813, Charles James Mason patented "Ironstone China." Mason's Ironstone greatly advanced the use of earthenware bodies in tableware. Mason's Ironstone had a harder body than other "ironstone" chinas and was thinner. He also introduced a small amount of cobalt blue into the glaze, giving the pieces a much whiter look. Mason's Ironstone was so successful that virtually every potter made a version of it between 1830 and 1880.

Dinnerware shapes and decoration range from one-of-a-kind designs created for private individuals to exclusive designs for a specific department store or distributor to mass-produced pieces. Wedgwood's Queen's shape describes the hexafoil lobed rim plate pattern that dates back to Queen Charlotte's period service. The Willow Pattern owes its origin to a transfer design engraved by Thomas Minton for Thomas Turner around 1780. This "Chinese" scene is an English invention. Hundreds of manufacturers have utilized it through the years. The Spode Museum at its plant in

Stoke-on-Trent, England, contains several dinnerware pattern books documenting the rim design of services made for members of the royal family, English aristocracy, and other customers.

The Victorian dining room was regal and formal. Tables were carefully laid. Victorians were proud of their china, glassware, and flatware services. Dinnerware quickly divided into two basic groups—services made for the wealthy and services made for the middle class, much of the latter ironstone. Services made by Coalport, Spode, and Haviland were viewed differently than services made by Adams, Johnson Brothers, and Mason. Favored decorative motifs included Flow Blue patterns, Oriental, naturalistic patterns featuring florals and foliage, and, as the Victorian era ended, stylized Art Nouveau.

Formal Victorian dining required a staggering number of service pieces, depending on the menu. China was changed for every course. In the mid-nineteenth century, servants served from the sideboard, thus leaving ample room to set the table with a myriad of objects. There was a plate, cup, or service dish for every occasion. A three o'clock tea or coffee cup differed in size and shape from a five o'clock cup. Oyster plates were used to serve oysters. Asparagus was served in a service dish made exclusively for that purpose. A large service had six or more platters. Few people today recognize a pancake server or a pepper pot.

Ellen Hill's *Mulberry Ironstone: Flow Blue's Best Kept Little Secret* (Madison, N.J.: Ellen Hill: 1993) contains a detailed listing of the pieces found in late nineteenth-century tea, dinner, dessert, and breakfast sets. A typical tea set contained two teapots (use was determined by the number of people attending or use of the smaller one for a hot water pitcher), a cream pitcher, a covered sugar bowl, a waste bowl, handleless cups, deep saucers, and cup plates (handled cups initially were used primarily for coffee), small individual plates, bread and butter plates, a coffeepot (optional), a milk pitcher, a water pitcher, honey and jam dishes, toddy plates, a small whiskey or spirits pitcher, and a covered jug.

By the 1870s in England and by 1900 in the United States, the mass production of inexpensive ceramic dinnerware made it possible for everyone, from factory worker to owner, to own one or more ceramic dinnerware services. Even in the poorest household, owning a set of good china, glassware, and flatware was a necessity. While ordinary earthenware dinnerware was acceptable for daily use, holidays and special occasions called for the best china.

Through the nineteenth century and the first decades of the twentieth century, Americans exhibited a buying preference for English-, French-, and German-made dinnerware for their best china. Haviland & Co. traces its origin to David and Daniel Haviland, two brothers who went to Limoges, France, searching for china to import. David remained in France, initially supervising the purchasing, designing, and decorating of stock for export. In 1865, he acquired a Limoges factory and produced his own china. Marriages and family disputes eventually led to the formation of several different "Haviland" companies, each of which added to the legend of the Haviland name.

Lenox, Inc., founded in 1889 by Jonathan Coxon Sr. and Walter Scott Lenox, rose to challenge English and European manufacturers in the better china market. The company discovered that superior tableware could be made from the same clay it used to make its Belleek-type wares. Tiffany and Company in New York displayed Lenox's first complete set of dinnerware in 1917. The company received recognition when President Wilson ordered a 1,700-piece dinnerware service for the White House that same year. Franklin Roosevelt (1932), Harry Truman (1951), and Ronald

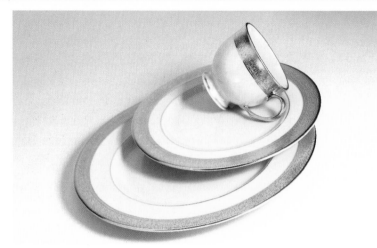

From Lenox: The Westchester pattern, from the Presidential Collection. *Photo courtesy of Lenox.*

Reagan (1981) are among the other American presidents who ordered White House dinnerware services from Lenox.

By the 1930s, Lenox, Inc. played a major role in the American dinnerware market, making translucent ivory-toned china, translucent white-bone china, and a casual line with the strength of stoneware. Frank G. Holmes, who designed the Wilson White House service, was responsible for many of the company's modern patterns.

American's use of ceramic dinnerware, especially on a daily basis, achieved popular status at the turn of the twentieth century. In 1903, the Larkin Soap Company established the Buffalo Pottery to produce premiums for its mail-order business. Semi-vitreous china dinnerware was an extremely popular premium. Low production costs, an advanced transportation system, and new marketing techniques, for example, the mail-order catalog, provided American potters with the opportunity to become major players in the ceramic dinnerware market.

Everyday dinnerware came from American pottery manufacturers, especially those located in and around East Liverpool, Ohio. A partial list of manufacturers includes Colonial Pottery, Crooksville China, Dresden Pottery, W. S. George Pottery, Hall, Harker Pottery Company, Hull, Edwin M. Knowles China Company, Knowles, Taylor, and Knowles, Limoges China Company, Homer Laughlin China Company, Royal China, Saxon (French-Saxon) China Company, Shawnee, and Sterling. Fiesta, perhaps the most popular American dinnerware pattern, is a Homer Laughlin product.

Not all American dinnerware pottery production occurred in Ohio. Several other leading firms produced extremely popular utilitarian household patterns: Red Wing Pottery's (Red Wing, Minnesota) Bob White and Capistrano patterns, Southern Potteries' (Erwin, Tennessee) Blue Ridge dinnerware patterns, and Stangl's (Flemington, New Jersey) Bittersweet and Golden Harvest patterns are just some examples. In California, Gladding, McBean and Company (Glendale and Los Angeles) manufactured Franciscan dinnerware, and Vernon Kilns (Vernon) offered its popular Gingham and Organdie patterned wares.

The use of dinnerware as a premium was introduced as an incentive. Larkin offered Noritake's Azalea pattern china for the first time in its 1924 catalog. By 1931, Larkin identified it as "Our Most Popular Pattern." Hall developed its Autumn Leaf pattern as a premium for Jewel Tea and its Blue Bouquet for the Standard Coffee Company of New Orleans. During the Depression, dinnerware premiums were used as enticements to shop and do business at a wide variety of commercial establishments, from movie theaters to banks. Large-chain grocery stores continued this tradition in the decades following World War II. Dinnerware was one of many products available when redeeming premium stamps, for example, S&H Green Stamps.

Formal dinnerware services decreased in size in the period between 1920 and 1940. Many accessory pieces such as butter dishes, bone dishes, and master and individual salts were no longer made in many patterns. Instead of services containing four to six platters, the number was reduced to two or three. However, few brides began their married life without one or two full dinnerware services.

This period also witnessed the increased importation of inexpensive Japanese table services. Noritake garnered a significant market share. Although the Depression finalized the demise of many American pottery manufacturers, many manufacturers were experiencing financial difficulties due to inexpensive imports as early as the mid-1920s. The flooding of the American market with inexpensive Japanese imported dinnerware following the end of World War II contributed to this demise. By the mid-1970s, Japanese dinnerware manufacturers directly challenged English and European manufacturers for dominance of the American market.

The formal dining bastion fell in the late 1950s, when Americans became enamored with the concept of casual dining. Dinnerware suppliers touted Melmac and other melamine dinnerware as the epitome of "casual elegance." Twenty-five percent of dinnerware sold in the late 1950s was made of plastic. The patio and kitchen became the household's primary evening dining locations. The dining room now was reserved for holidays and special occasions. In many suburban homes built in the 1960s, the living room and dining room were combined into a single room.

The impact of television on American dining habits was profound. Television (TV) trays and TV dinners ended the "gather around the table" dinner in many families. As more mothers entered the work place, less time was available for the preparation of an elaborate evening dinner. The role of fast food has been revolutionary. Schedule juggling by suburban families for after-school sport and social activities has practically eliminated a fixed dinner time when a family can sit down together for a meal. Little wonder that dinnerware has been reduced to the bare essentials!

Through the mid-1960s, fine dinnerware was marketed through department, jewelry, and specialty stores. A 1950s "jewelry" store offered dinnerware, stemware, flatware, leather goods and luggage, figurines, and tabletop accessories, in addition to jewelry, clocks, watches, and repair services. Large catalog mail-order firms such as Montgomery Ward and Sears, Roebuck and Company also continued to play a key marketing role.

Beginning in the late 1960s, things changed dramatically. The arrival of the shopping mall and chain stores created demand for inexpensive dinnerware services. Corning developed and offered Corelle as an alternative to ceramic and plastic dinnerware. The arrival of the dishwasher brought demands that dinnerware be dishwasher-safe.

Many manufacturers began to sell direct, through outlet shops and catalogs. By the mid-1980s, shopping by catalog became a viable option. In the 1990s, television home shopping poses an immediate challenge to mail-order catalog shopping. Several manufacturers already have marketing sites on the World Wide Web.

These new sales approaches have limited the number of patterns and service sizes. To escape having a dinnerware service identical to one's neighbor, many individuals have rediscovered their grandparents' and parents' china services. Once again, these services are appearing on the table on a regular basis. Dinnerware believed worthless a decade ago is once again a treasured possession.

CHAPTER TWO

Dinnerware Finesse—Selecting and Using the Dinnerware That Is Right for You

Most individuals own several sets of dinnerware—everyday, family, and best. Given the diversity of dining requirements, this makes perfect sense. Everyday dinnerware is used on a daily basis. Its patterns are casual and colorful. Family dinnerware is used on weekends, holidays, and when the extended family comes for a meal. This dinnerware service frequently includes place settings for twelve or more. The table is set with the best dinnerware when special guests are invited to dine. The service is porcelain, the pattern more formal.

Different dining experiences require different types and patterns of dinnerware. The durability of stoneware/ironstone body dinnerware with its bright colors and high glaze makes it ideal for breakfast, lunch, and daily dining. As it is inexpensive compared to porcelain, owners are content to use it, knowing that replacing a broken piece is easy and relatively inexpensive. Porcelain is the dinnerware of choice for formal dining. It exudes elegance through its translucency, hardness, thinness, and endless variety of designs.

THE DINING ROOM

The dining room is back. Much of its warmth and special charm was lost in the decades immediately following World War II, when many suburban homes were built with a combination living and dining room or no dining room at all. Today's new homes usually include a separate dining room. Further, the room is large, containing ample space for a table that comfortably seats eight to twelve individuals, a serving buffet, a china cabinet, and one or two additional furniture pieces.

The return of the dining room has sparked a renewed interest in semi-formal and formal dining. While today's family still eats many of its evening meals at a nook, table, or counter in the kitchen, the dining room is finding more and more use on weekends and for entertainment purposes. Americans have rediscovered the joys of sitting down at a linen-covered table set with fine dinnerware, stemware, and flatware that is decorated in an imaginative, pleasant decor.

What is responsible for the re-emergence of the dining room? The economic revival of the mid-1990s deserves some of the credit. As society has become more affluent, lifestyle expectations have

Casual dining has been the rule for many years. Pictured, the Iris on Grey pattern by Lenox. *Photo courtesy of Lenox.*

The dining room is back! Pictured, the Castle Garden pattern from Lenox's Chinatown Collection. *Photo courtesey of Lenox.*

risen. Decorating styles have shifted from the informal Country styles that dominated the mid-1970s to a more traditional, formal style. Finally, individuals again recognize the link between fine dining and the atmosphere in which it occurs.

What is fine dining? Fine dining is a combination of good food, good conversation, and pleasant surroundings. The last is viewed as a table attractively set with coordinated dinnerware, stemware, flatware, linens, and decorative accessories. While most individuals associate fine dining with an evening meal in a dining room, the concept is immune from time and place. An elegant breakfast on the patio or a gracious outdoor picnic also constitutes fine dining.

Fine dining does not require servants or an unlimited budget. It occurs with the creative use of available material and the host's or hostess's imagination. The dinnerware chosen for the meal is an important ingredient in the mix.

SELECTING YOUR DINNERWARE

You are the most important person your dinnerware needs to please. Properly chosen, it provides a sense of excitement and pride each time you use it.

Select carefully. Do not rush. Take your time. If you are typical of most people, you will live with your choice for several decades, if not your lifetime. Study what is available in a wide range of marketplaces, from the local department store to replacement services. When you find a pattern with which you can live, but which is not exactly what you want, keep looking.

How will you know when you find the right pattern? The answer is simple. You will fall in love with it. The pattern will appear perfect to you. Chances are it will be love at first sight. Trust your heart. There is no need for a prolonged courtship.

When selecting dinnerware, consider these four criteria—use, cost, quality, and quantity. Whether selecting a pattern for everyday or best use, the key is versatility. Consider how and where the dinnerware will be used. Your everyday pattern must be durable enough to withstand daily use. If you plan to put your best service in a dishwasher, avoid any pattern with a gold or platinum trim or other decoration.

If you have young children and/or a lifestyle in which pieces are likely to be broken or stacked for an extended period, consider purchasing an inexpensive, easy-to-replace dinnerware pattern. Nothing is gained by purchasing an expensive pattern and harassing your children constantly about how they are using it. The right dinnerware pattern makes everyone comfortable.

A versatile dinnerware pattern is one that is at home in a variety of color settings and decorative motifs. Test the pattern's appearance on a wide variety of background colors. An entirely new dining room decor can be achieved by changing the color of a table's linens. An ideal pattern is one that works as well in a formal setting as it does in an informal one.

A dinnerware pattern should blend with the decorating decor of the setting and room in which it will be used. A pattern with an overall intricate design is inconsistent with a pastel floral patterned tablecloth. A blue pattern works much better in a room whose color scheme is off-white or red than it does in a room dominated by greens or yellows.

Buy the best you can afford. A manufacturer offering several dozen dinnerware patterns does not have a different price for each pattern. Instead, the manufacturer groups the patterns into four to eight different price ranges. These ranges are designed to correspond to the budgets of prospective buyers.

It is a mistake to settle for your second or third pattern choice because you cannot afford your first choice. Most dinnerware services are not the result of a one-time purchase but are assembled over a period of time. Many a service for twelve began initially as a service for two. If you are willing to add to your dinnerware as you can afford it, you can afford your first-choice pattern.

There are many measures of quality—from the design of the pattern and shape line of the dinnerware to the reputation of the manufacturer and the retailer from whom it is purchased. Make pattern design and shape your initial selection focus. Select a pattern design that is attractive and appealing. When a design motif is popular, it usually is found in several variations, the result of its interpretation by different manufacturers. Make sure you have seen all of these variations before making your final selection.

Do not select a pattern until you have seen the entire shape line. While the pattern design may be extremely appealing on the dinner plate, it may lose its appeal on hollowware pieces such as the creamer and sugar or coffeepot. Looking at the pattern in its totality involves seeing it in a full table setting for eight with all of the accessory pieces.

The number of patterns greatly exceeds the number of shape lines. A typical manufacturer will offer a dozen or more patterns utilizing the same shape line. In some instances, the shape line of the flat pieces within a dinnerware pattern is different from the form line used for the hollowware pieces in the same pattern—another reason why it is important to see the entire shape line before making your final selection.

When selecting your best pattern, consider how it will look when displayed. Chances are you are going to house it in your china cabinet in open view, not hide it away behind a buffet's doors. Do not be embarrassed to show off your best dinnerware.

Quantity involves the number of individual forms available within the shape line. Every pattern

Your choice of a specific dinnerware pattern is extremely important in creating the exact ambience you want in your dining room. Choices abound. Throughout this book you will find pattern groupings designed to assist you in the selection process. These suggestions are intended to be the first stage in the process. Review all of the patterns in the book and add or subtract additional patterns as you deem appropriate. Once you have assembled your working list, it is easy to choose the pattern that works best for you.

As you review the patterns, you will note that some appear to be quite similar, for example, the Japanese Blue Danube, Johnson Brothers' Blue Nordic, and Meakin's Blue Nordic. Popular patterns were offered with slight variations by a number of different manufacturers. Only one variation, with the exception of Blue Willow in the Oriental listings, appears in a listing. Hopefully, you will agree that it is the variant that best complements the other selections in the list.

You will note a wide variety of pattern interpretations within a single theme, which is why dinnerware is so exciting and offers so much. There is a pattern that is right for everyone's taste.

Many of these group listings could easily be expanded to include a dozen or more patterns. Since the desire to limit is implicit in the process, five was selected as the ideal working number. The Chintz listing includes only four patterns because there are only four Chintz patterns in the book.

There is no right or wrong choice. The choice that counts is the one that pleases you. Further, who said you had to limit your choice to one? Many hosts or hostesses have three or more dinnerware services, selecting the one that best suits their needs at the moment.

offers a typical five-piece place setting—dinner plate, salad plate, butter plate, and cup and saucer. However, some patterns offer one or two platter sizes, while others offer five or six. Some patterns offer a deep soup, while others offer a choice of a soup cup or a deep soup or both.

As the twentieth century progressed, the number of forms available within a shape line decreased, one reason why older patterns are currently so popular with today's younger users. They offer a wider variety of serving accessories than found in contemporary patterns.

"Buy new" was a rallying cry of the generation of young adults who grew up from the 1960s through the 1980s. As members of this generation turned forty, they began to see the value in collectibles from previous generations. Suddenly grandmother's and mother's dinnerware service was not something to be avoided like the plague, but it was considered a treasured heirloom of the past. A fair number of young adults setting up housekeeping in the 1990s share these sentiments.

Today, the family and sentimental value inherent in grandmother's or mother's dinnerware service and the pleasure that comes from using it far outweigh any concern that the pattern is not one the present owner would have chosen if given a choice. Further, these heirloom dinnerware services are not residing unused in buffets and china cabinets. They are too good to sit on the shelf and are a vital part of the modern family's entertainment agenda. As a result, owners are constantly seeking to enlarge them or to replace damaged pieces.

USING YOUR DINNERWARE

Use your dinnerware. Use it, but do not abuse it. Given today's emphasis on casual living, everyday dinnerware is designed to withstand daily use. However, all dinnerware will break when dropped or if handled carelessly.

Be respectful when handling and using dinnerware. Follow the suggestions found in chapter 3. Once you are in the habit of doing this, it becomes second nature.

In an age when time is a precious commodity, is the use of ceramic dinnerware worth the extra effort when glass, plastic, and paper dinnerware is available? The answer is an unqualified yes. Ceramic dinnerware more closely represents the style and pace of life most individuals prefer. It adds an aura of quality even in a highly informal setting. Its use sends an "I'm worth it" message.

Do not hesitate to change your dinnerware service. As your personal tastes change, your dinnerware pattern may no longer reflect those tastes. When that occurs, consider buying a new dinnerware service.

But what about the cost? Let's put the issue into perspective. How much do you spend every three to five years for a new car or every ten years for a new television set? These costs can easily exceed the cost of a new dinnerware service. Further, consider what percentage of the original purchase price you receive when you trade in or sell your five-year-old car? The depreciation in value of your dinnerware service, assuming you purchased it new, is likely to be less. Your old set of dinnerware has value, a value that is often more than monetary.

Since today's dinnerware is designed to serve several generations, do not discard your old service. Recycle it. Consider passing it along to your children or a friend's children as a starter set. If no one wants it, place it at auction or sell it to a replacement service. Remember, dinnerware is something that is *too good to throw out*. Apply the concept.

CHAPTER THREE

Caring for Your Dinnerware

The best way to care for a dinnerware service, whether a family heirloom, bridal gifts nurtured into a complete table setting, or a pattern acquired to complement your current room decor, is to use it. Each use renews the joy and excitement associated with owning fine dinnerware and enhances the love you feel for the pattern and the pieces comprising it. After all, do we not exercise the most care toward the things we cherish the most?

Although they may appear delicate, twentieth-century ceramics are tough and durable, designed to withstand heavy use. Are they breakable? Absolutely. Does this mean they have to be handled with kid gloves? Absolutely not.

The survival key is reasonable care. Initially, you may have to systematically practice care techniques. However, within a short period of time, they become automatic. You will do them without thinking about them. Remember the information in this chapter at some point in the future when you are getting out or putting away your dinnerware and you'll think to yourself, "Isn't it amazing how easy and enjoyable it is to use fine dinnerware on a regular basis."

PROPERLY STORING DINNERWARE

There are two steps to properly storing dinnerware. The first is a thorough analysis of the area in which you intend to store or display your dinnerware. The second is the storage and display method.

Analyzing Your Storage Area

Carefully examining and analyzing the storage area is the first step in properly storing dinnerware. Take a moment and consider a few worst-case scenarios. Design your storage area so it has a back-up system in place to counter any potential danger.

If your storage unit is a hanging cupboard, make sure it is securely bolted to the wall. The same applies to shelves. All too often, hanging cupboards and shelves are secured only at two locations, which is not enough. If one bolt or screw fails, the cabinet will tilt or fall. Most hanging cabinets and shelves are not designed to hold their positions with only one bolt or screw in place.

The solution is to use three to six securing bolts or screws. Instead of securing a shelf with only braces placed slightly in from the left and right ends, consider one to two separate braces in the middle. Always secure a hanging cupboard with a minimum of three bolts or screws at the top and one or two bottom "L" braces. If you are going to err, err on the side of too much, not too little support.

Carefully check the weight-bearing potential of all interior shelving. Far too many built-in kitchen cabinets and china closets contain shelves whose support rests only on small quarter-inch triangular metal clips at each of the four corners. If any one of these fails, the shelf will collapse. Damage is often several shelves deep.

Do the shelves in your kitchen cabinet sag in the middle? You would be surprised how many do. When stacked, ceramic dinnerware proves a heavy load. Consider strengthening the load-bearing capacities of your shelves with one or two supporting rods or block columns. Usually a column located in the center, an equal distance from the sides and front and back, is sufficient. However, if the shelf is long, use two columns located at the one-third and two-third points of the shelf's length.

Be extra careful when determining each column's length. Each should fit snugly between shelves, but should not raise the top shelf or depress the bottom shelf even slightly. The purpose is to assist load bearing, not take over the responsibility from the end brackets.

Most storage cabinets consist of multiple shelves. When inserting additional support columns, line them up directly on top of each other. When offset, they do not have the same load-sharing capabilities as when aligned.

Go to a hardware store and buy a line level, the kind contractors use to make sure a chalk line is level. Use it twice a year to check the level of your shelves. When you find that a shelf, whether glass or wood, is no longer level across its entire surface, replace it. Once wood or glass develops a bend, it is cheaper to replace it than to straighten it out.

How deep are your shelves? Far too many pieces of dinnerware are broken each year by individuals reaching for a piece located on the back of a shelf and, in doing so, knocking off or striking a piece in front. While common sense dictates that you should remove any dinnerware pieces in front before removing any from the back, few individuals actually practice this safety measure.

What is the ideal shelf size? This is not an easy question to answer. One solution for determining shelf depth is to measure the width of your largest serving plate and add an extra inch or two. If you are able to store your serving platters and large hollowware pieces on bottom shelves, then follow the procedure described above using the depth of the largest serving piece. If you are fortunate enough to work with a kitchen cabinet designer, perhaps a stepped shelf series is the answer.

A viable working shelf height is far more important an issue than shelf depth. Most kitchen cabinets are too high. Users need to stand on their tiptoes or on a kitchen stool to reach the upper shelves. This method of storage considerably increases the risk of damage to dinnerware. You need to be able to see what you are doing and to have solid footing when handling your dinnerware, which is why many individuals prefer to store their dinnerware in china closets. However, just as storage shelves can be too high, they also can be too low. The ideal dinnerware storage level is knee-to-shoulder height. Dining room buffets, Colonial Revival china cabinets featuring a cabinet area above a one-drawer and extended leg base, and open hutches are excellent furniture forms for achieving proper storage goals. A shallow floor-to-ceiling cabinet unit in a kitchen is another viable unit.

Check the heating and lighting conditions in your storage area. Rapid changes in temperature can damage dinnerware. Do not store your dinnerware in cabinets that are attached to or rest against an outside wall of your home. Some comfortable winter evening at home, place your hand on one of your home's outside walls. You will be surprised to find how cold it is.

Pictured, Churchill's Blue Willow pattern. *Photo courtesy of Churchill Tableware, Ltd.*

Keep dinnerware storage units away from heating sources. A buffet or china cabinet located directly above or beside a heating source is an invitation to disaster. Wood and ceramics have few problems adjusting to gradual changes in temperature. When the change is rapid, something has to give.

Likewise, be careful of direct sunlight exposure, especially if dinnerware is housed inside a closed storage unit. Remember getting into your car on a sunny winter day and being surprised how warm it was? The sun heats up the inside of a closed storage unit in exactly the same way.

Sunlight also acts as a bleach. While the color dyes used on most twentieth-century dinnerware resist fading caused by sunlight and heat, why take chances? If the decoration on your dinnerware is above the glaze, you need to be extra cautious.

Storage and Display Methods

An ideal storage goal is to develop a storage method where no two ceramic surfaces touch each other—either from placing pieces on top, inside, or alongside each other. Avoid any contact that can cause chipping, hairline cracks, or damage to surface decoration.

When stacking flat ceramic pieces on top of each other, do not create a stack that weighs more than you can comfortably handle; better to have two stacks of six than one stack of twelve. If your storage shelf shows the slightest sign of bowing, the stack is too large.

There is a wide range of materials you can insert between flat ceramic pieces to separate the glazed surfaces. Lace doilies, napkins, paper towels, thin bubble wrap, thickly folded tissues, and commercial or homemade round cloth mats are examples.

If using paper or Styrofoam plates, a commonly made suggestion, be sure to use a thin plate with flexible edges. Divider plates with a fixed shape or rim create an unstable stack unless the shape conforms exactly to the ceramic plates placed between them. Avoid using plates with a slippery surface, as ceramic plates in the middle of the stack can pop out unexpectedly.

When stacking plates, stack only like plates together. Do not put a stack of smaller plates on top of a stack of larger plates. Plates are not designed to carry large weight loads, although you may not think so, based on the helpings some individuals place on them. Yes, multiple stacking saves space, but it may not save the plates. Obviously, never stack a larger plate on top of a smaller one.

The best method for stacking plates is to stand them straight up. There are a number of commercially made plate racks that are ideal. Find one that is right for your storage area and consider using it.

If possible, do not stack cups. Most cup designs make this a risky proposition, even when the stack includes only two or three cups. Inserting one object into another subjects the inserted piece to surface wear at the point of contact. Further, cup handles are delicate. While you may think you are placing the cups gently inside each other, you may be using enough force to break off the handle or weaken the juncture of the handle with the cup.

The best way to store cups is to hang them on individual hooks. Use curved rather than square hooks. If available, select hooks that have a plastic sleeve over them. The plastic sleeve softens the surface; however, plastic does deteriorate over time, so watch for cracking in the sleeve. Cracked plastic edges are sharp. Replace any hook with cracked plastic immediately.

To be on the safe side, replace all hooks every eight to ten years, even if there are no signs of major wear. When replacing a hook, do not insert it into the screw hole from the previous hook. Unless the screw threading is the same size or larger, the screw may not bite properly. Create a new hole for each new hook.

Mail-order catalogs, department stores, jewelry shops, and other places that sell fine dinnerware frequently offer protector cases for dinnerware plates, cups, and soups. A typical storage unit holds twelve pieces. One company offers an ensemble set with storage space for twelve five-piece place settings, a platter, and a vegetable. Most cases have foam dividers and a zipper for easy access and most come with cloth pads for insertion between pieces.

A china cabinet is essentially open storage. Arrange your dinnerware so it is attractively displayed. Consider displaying a place setting as a focal point. A vertical display of one or more platters or a row of dinner plates behind hollowware pieces is certain to catch visitors' eyes.

When standing a plate or platter in an upright position, be sure you have a stand that will adequately support its weight. Most individuals underestimate the stand strength needed. If you err, err on the side of too much support.

Metal stands can cause chips and nicks in plate rims, and their use is not recommended. Wooden stands are fine; however, make certain there is no wood roughness at any point where the plate or platter comes into contact with the stand. Metal stands coated or covered with a plastic sleeve are another viable alternative. Clear plastic stands are a third choice. Be sure that they have a large base and a high back extension bar.

If a stand slips, the results can be tragic. Many china cabinets have glass shelves, which are slippery, especially when covered with a fine layer of dust. Often merely the act of walking by a china cabinet or a large truck rumbling past the house can provide enough vibration to cause a stand to move. Your stand should have a gripping agent on the base to hold it in place.

PROPERLY WASHING DINNERWARE

You essentially have two choices—washing by hand or using a dishwasher. Connoisseurs argue that the only safe method is by hand. This is not true. There are patterns and circumstances where hand washing is the only appropriate approach and other instances where using the dishwasher is

DISASTER-PROOFING YOUR DINNERWARE

If you live in an area subject to earthquakes, tornadoes, or floods, consider the following tips from Scott M. Haskins's *How To Save Your Stuff From a Disaster*, published by Preservation Help Publications, P. O. Box 1206, Santa Barbara, CA 93102.

Scientists working with representatives of the Getty Museum have developed a product called Quake Wax *(Editor's note: Quake Wax is now being sold under the brand name Be Still My Art—Museum Mounting Wax)*. "Quake Wax is a sticky synthetic wax that can be used between the base of a small to medium object and a table top or shelf to anchor it down. The object can be picked up at any time and Quake Wax will not stain the furniture surface. Other materials, like Plastellina or other 'fixing' materials, which contain oil should be avoided as they can stain furniture and objects alike. Use [Quake Wax] on decorative plates, curios, and porcelain statues in hutches, to make sure they don't rattle around and break against each other during the shake. . . .

• Install clasps or hooks on cabinet doors. They usually pop open, even during a moderate shake, and let everything inside fall to the floor.

• A lip on the front of a shelf will help keep objects in their place. They will have a harder time 'walking' off as everything vibrates.

• Replace glass shelves in curio cabinets (which break and crash down on other items . . . they are heavy too) with Lucite or Plexiglas shelves. They can be made to order at your local glass shop. Help to hold them in place with Quake Wax."

perfectly acceptable. However, even in the latter case, an occasional hand washing enhances the overall appearance of the dinnerware.

Washing By Hand

Ideally, each piece of dinnerware should be washed and wiped separately. Why? When glazed ceramics are wet, they can easily scratch one other when rubbed together with any force. The glaze finish on ceramics is essentially glass, and all glass behaves in this fashion.

Rinse dinnerware to remove excess food and other grime prior to washing. Make washing the final, not the only, cleaning process. Do not scrape off stubborn material with a sharp knife or any pointed object. Soak to loosen stubborn dirt.

If your dinnerware is an unglazed earthenware pattern, you need to take a few extra precautions. Do not soak unglazed earthenware dinnerware for an extended period of time. Earthenware will absorb water and swell. Some leaching of components also may occur if soaking is prolonged. Finally, dirt and other food and chemical deposits in dirty water may leave marks or stains. Do not hesitate to change water during the washing process, if necessary.

When washing by hand, place a rubber mat or towel in the bottom of the sink as a cushioning device. This helps prevent damage if a piece slips from your hand during the washing process. Also consider providing similar cushioning underneath the area where you will be drying the dishes.

Do not use abrasives of any kind, from dishwashing liquid with abrasives or powder to a scouring pad. Avoid using steel wool. A mild household detergent works best, especially if the rinsing process was done effectively.

Use water that is hot to the touch but not scalding. Washing pieces individually will require that you insert your hands into the water dozens of time. When the water feels cool, consider emptying the sink and refilling it.

Always wash ceramics separately from cutlery, pots and pans, and silverware. The reasons are self-evident. Be especially careful around aluminum. Contact with aluminum can result in gray, pencil-like lines.

A soft brush is a helpful tool when washing fluted china, vases, and figures. Again, scrub lightly and gently. Hot water and detergent will loosen the dirt. All you are doing is assisting its departure.

Dry dinnerware with a soft cloth. Air drying is fine. However, do this only if you have sufficient space to stack dinnerware pieces so they do not come into contact with each other. A stacked and overloaded dish drainer is asking for trouble.

Gold or platinum gilding on dinnerware is above the glaze. Hand washing is mandatory for patterns dating before 1970 and should be considered for all patterns. Rub gold or platinum surfaces gently. Incorrect washing will result in gilding loss. Replacing lost gilding is extremely expensive, in fact, prohibitive.

If your dinnerware pattern features above-the-glaze decoration in any color, the best approach is hand washing. Not all colors can be used for under-glaze decoration. A chemical reaction causes gold to turn brown and platinum to turn a dowdy gray if fired under the glaze. Adopting an under-the-glaze-only approach severely limits a manufacturer's choice of colors. There are too many exquisite effects that can be achieved with over-the-glaze decoration to eliminate it from consideration.

To Use or Not to Use the Dishwasher — That Is the Question

Is your ceramic dinnerware dishwasher-safe? Many manufacturers make this claim for contemporary patterns. While they would not make the claim if it were not true, a little skepticism is a good thing. If it does not say "dishwasher-safe" on the back of the piece, assume that it isn't.

Dishwasher controls have reached the point where they can be programmed to perform a myriad of differing tasks. Wash and rinse temperatures should never exceed those recommended by the manufacturer of the machine being used. Carefully read and reread the machine's instruction manual.

It is critical to select the correct washing agent and water temperature. While some washing agents and rinse aids are practically harmless when used at reasonable temperatures, they can do a lot of damage when used at high temperatures. Several manufacturers recommend Cascade, Dishwasher ALL, and Calgonite for U.S. and Canadian users.

Evaporation in a hot atmosphere is the process used for drying in dishwashers. Occasionally, this process leaves a deposit on dinnerware, the result of some of the washing agent being allowed to dry on the dinnerware before the rinse cycle starts. The fault rests with the dishwasher, not your dinnerware. If this scum is allowed to build up, it becomes difficult to remove. The minute you see a problem, call the dishwasher's local service agent and request that your dishwasher be serviced.

Dishwasher vibration can cause pieces to strike each other. As indicated earlier, ceramic glazes are highly susceptible to scratching when wet. Most modern dishwashers have plastic covered racks that prevent movement of dishes and eliminate this contact.

The key to safe dishwasher use is to resist the temptation to overload the dishwasher so the dishes are washed in one, not two loads. Overloading is an invitation to trouble. In this case, it is the user, not the dishwasher, that is responsible for any damage.

Solving Stains and Other Marking Problems

Dinnerware can stain. Leaving fruit acids or vinegar in a ceramic piece overnight is one way this happens. What is the solution? Rinse dinnerware immediately after use. Postpone washing, but never postpone rinsing.

Borax or common salt applied to a soft cloth is one method used to remove tea and coffee stains. Other methods include soaking in a solution of detergent and water or boiling briefly in a large pot of water.

Soft metal flatware can leave metal markings on plates, especially those with a matte finish. The surface of the plate is not damaged. Such marks often can be removed by boiling the plate in a solution of detergent and water or by rubbing gently with a metal polish.

Glazes crack. The end result is known as crazing or crackling. In many cases, it is simply the result of age. Crazing is visible because dirt has worked its way into the cracks. Sometimes the dirt can be leeched out by soaking the dinnerware in a solution of 20-volume hydrogen peroxide. Be sure to thoroughly wash and rinse any piece of dinnerware subjected to this treatment prior to use.

USING DINNERWARE

Hostesses or hosts often like to warm their china on warming racks before placing it on the table for a meal. This presents no problem, provided the warming is done gradually and at a modest temperature. However, avoid exposure to the direct heat of a naked flame or any rapid temperature rise.

Heat transfers. Avoid placing dinnerware on a cold or wet surface immediately after placing extremely hot food or liquid into it. The temperature contrast may be enough to cause the piece to crack.

Most dinnerware is not freezer-safe. Even for those patterns that are, it is not wise to freeze food that has a liquid consistency in a deep ceramic dish. Freezing causes the liquid to expand, which may crack the piece.

IN PERSPECTIVE

A late 1950s or early 1960s Syracuse China pamphlet entitled *Look what you can do with Syracuse china: Twenty-eight pages of entertaining ideas* offers the following insights into washing dinnerware in a dishwasher:

"But all is not black. There are exceptions that always prove the rule. Fortunately, in this case, many of them. For the most popular china colors today are pastels—and the lighter the colors, the less the danger! Also—gold, because it can be applied more thickly, stands up far better than platinum. Ergo: the many gold decorated patterns are safer! With proper care—the right detergent used in the prescribed amount with correct water temperature and coated racks—many fine patterns will survive years of machine washing."

Just as you would put only dinnerware marked "dishwasher-safe" in a dishwasher, follow the same logic for the microwave. If it is not marked "microwave-safe," assume it is not. Further, never put dinnerware with metallic banding in the microwave. You do not need this type of fireworks.

Dust ceramics with a very soft cloth. A terry cloth towel is not soft enough. If the cloth feels smooth to the touch, it probably is safe. Always use a clean cloth, and never use dusting spray. Make sure any cloth used has not been previously sprayed.

Use care when handling dinnerware. "Two hands" is a good rule. Always support hollowware with one hand on the bottom. This is critical when picking up any hollowware piece that is filled with liquid. Handles are great, but extra support helps lessen the load. Pick up plates, platters, and other flat dinnerware pieces from beneath, not by the rim.

PROPERLY TRANSPORTING DINNERWARE

If you are moving, it is best to leave the packing of your fine dinnerware to specialists. They have the skill and experience to do the job right. They will wrap each piece separately and surround each within a box or barrel with excelsior or plastic peanuts to prevent the packages from coming into contact with each other. Check the moving company's insurance policy to ensure that it provides replacement cost coverage for any damaged pieces.

If you insist on packing and moving your dinnerware on your own, follow these simple rules:

1. Pack in uniform-sized boxes. This makes stacking the boxes during the moving process easier.
2. Use medium-sized boxes. The final packing weight per box should not exceed twenty to twenty-five pounds.
3. Reinforce the bottoms of all boxes with an extra piece of cardboard or foam before packing anything in the box.
4. Wrap each piece separately, first with soft white tissue paper and then with bubble wrap, using $1/2$" to 1" size bubbles.
5. When placing pieces in a box, ensure that there is cushioning around all sides of the wrapped unit. Do not make the mistake of assuming that a box with dividers provides adequate protection for individual pieces. If the piece is free to move, it is not properly packed.
6. Do not forget to add padding on the top before closing and sealing the box.
7. Mark the box with a detailed list of its contents.
8. Call your insurance agent and make sure your homeowner's insurance policy covers your dinnerware while in transit.
9. Say a prayer that everything arrives undamaged! This is why the use of professional movers is recommended.

IN SUMMARY

Your dinnerware service is not a museum piece. It was designed and manufactured to be used. Treat it with the respect it deserves and it will last for generations.

Fine dinnerware, especially when it is a family heirloom, adds an aura of elegance to even the simplest of meals. It is always appropriate and welcome.

CHAPTER FOUR

Expanding or Replacing Pieces from Your Dinnerware Service

Are you thinking of expanding your dinnerware service from eight to twelve? After using your dinnerware several times, you may find that an extra platter or vegetable dish would have greatly aided in serving the meals. Or perhaps you or a guest may have accidentally broken a cup or plate. What should you do? The answer is simple. Take advantage of the wide range of opportunities, from antiques and collectibles periodicals to replacement services, which are available for expanding or replacing your dinnerware.

There is a direct correlation between the amount you will pay per piece and the time you are willing to spend in the hunt. However, the hunt is not without its costs. If you spend two or three hours of your time and several dollars in postage and telephone calls to save only five dollars on a piece, rethink your approach. Even though the cost may be slightly higher, finding a source that can supply you with the pieces you need is often the most economical approach.

DOCUMENTING YOUR PATTERN

You already know the manufacturer, the name of your pattern, and exactly what it looks like. Many of the people you contact will know the manufacturer and pattern name but will not be able to visualize it. You will need to help them.

Photocopying is one method of documenting your pattern. Place a piece of flatware, for example, a dinner plate or bread and butter plate, on a photocopy machine. Place a piece of white tissue around it to ensure that the photocopy has a white background. Carefully lower the top. Avoid putting any pressure on the plate. Why add another piece to your "need" list?

Make a copy of the front and back of the flatware piece. The front view provides information about the pattern and shape. The back shows the mark, which often contains information about the maker and pattern. If the photocopy is black and white, add information about the colors used in the pattern.

If you have access to a good 35mm camera, consider taking a series of photographs showing the front and back of a flatware piece and the side view and bottom of a hollowware (three-dimensional) piece. When photographing the flatware piece, take the picture from a position directly above it. Any angle distorts the image. Photograph the hollowware piece from an angle that shows its depth, usually about ten degrees above its center. Also consider taking a photograph with the camera directly facing the surface.

It is critical that the picture be in focus. Photograph details with a close-up or telephoto lens. Make sure you have enough depth of field when photographing hollowware pieces. If you cannot take a close-up of the mark, make a rough sketch or do a tracing.

Beware of reflected light. If you do not have proper lighting, take the pictures in a shaded area, which eliminates shadows. Bracket your exposure a half stop in either direction.

Use a solid-color backdrop. Check that the color is not reflected in the glaze, thus distorting the color of the piece on the finished photograph. Place a ruler beside the piece to provide size information.

Include a card with your name, address, and telephone number with the photograph. This enables individuals who are searching on your behalf to know who to contact upon finding a match.

KNOW EXACTLY WHAT YOU ARE SEEKING

Lack of adequate information is one of the primary reasons that individuals do not respond to "want" requests. You must be specific. The two key elements are the exact name of the form and its size. When seeking a flat serving piece, it is important to designate whether you are looking for a rectangular or oval platter or a round chop plate. Dinnerware plates vary slightly in size. You must specify whether you are looking only for a 10″ dinner plate or are willing to purchase one that measures 9 $7/8$″ or 10 $1/8$.″

If you wish to expand your service, consider sending the person a list of the pieces that you already own, as well as a list of those you desire. The seller may have pieces that are not on your list, and you certainly want to know about these.

Clearly indicate the condition level at which you wish to buy. If you want the piece in excellent condition, that is, virtually free of any defects, state this specifically. The more emphasis you place on condition, the more difficult it will be to locate the pieces you desire. Consider compromising, especially on hard-to-find hollowware forms.

The standard approach is to ask for quotes. Some individuals prefer to indicate on their list what they are willing to pay. Usually they note that this is a maximum price and that they hope to receive lower quotes. The reality is that virtually every quote is at the willing-to-pay price.

Indicate your full name, address, and day and evening telephone numbers on any request you distribute. Today, sellers are far more likely to telephone than to write.

BUYING OPTIONS

You have more buying options than you realize. Utilizing a replacement service is the most obvious choice. However, before exploring that sales venue, here are seven additional possibilities. Using your imagination, you probably can add to the list.

Garage sale circuit. This is not as crazy as it sounds, especially if you have one of the more popular patterns and frequently attend garage sales. This is the cheapest buying source you will find.

In most cases, the seller wants to sell the pieces as a lot, rather than individually. Buy them all. The spare pieces provide an inexpensive backup in case you break one of your pieces. If you try to buy only a few pieces, do not be surprised if the seller asks a price almost equal to the entire lot. Sellers know that what remains will be worth considerably less because it has been split.

Do not be afraid to hand out your list of "wants" to individuals who appear to be garage sale regulars. You cannot be everywhere at once. Dozens of eyes searching on your behalf are better than two eyes.

Friends and neighbors. If you have a friend or neighbor who has a dinnerware set that matches your pattern, do not hesitate to say, "If you ever tire of that set and want to get rid of it, call me." Never underestimate the power of positive suggestion.

When using your dinnerware for a party or family gathering, mention your desire to expand your service or find replacement pieces. You will be amazed at what people remember. Again, your chances for success increase proportionally to the number of people searching on your behalf.

Post your "want" list on church, grocery store, or service club bulletin boards. Be sure to attach a photograph to the list. You need something to catch an individual's attention.

Antiques malls. Antiques malls are becoming increasingly aware of the importance of securing want lists and passing them on to their dealers. Many have bulletin boards and are more than willing to post buyers' want lists.

Many antiques malls allow their dealers to place business cards in their booths. As you walk through the mall, collect the cards of those dealers who feature dinnerware services for sale, and send them a copy of your want list. If the booth is devoted to replacement dinnerware, consider calling the dealer and talking with him or her directly.

Antiques shows. While it is far more common to find a flatware or glassware replacement specialist at an antiques show, many do feature dinnerware replacement dealers. Take the time to talk with them and discuss your specific needs.

Talk with generalist dealers offering only one or two services. Antiques show dealers bring only a small portion of their merchandise to the show. They may have exactly what you are seeking at home. Practice the old adage, "It never hurts to ask."

Antiques and collectibles trade periodicals. Most antiques and collectibles trade periodicals have a classified advertisement section. Many also offer business card classifieds, an advertisement measuring 3 1/2" x 2", the standard business card size. Follow a traditional business card approach when designing your advertisement.

You will place a "want" or "seeker" advertisement. Keep it short and simple, for example, "WANTED. Quotes on Noritake's Barrymore pattern dinnerware. Name, telephone number, with area code." You should have no difficulty limiting your request to twenty words or less.

There are over fifty antiques and collectibles trade periodicals. In addition to using a regional paper with a strong circulation, consider placing your advertisement in one or more of the following national publications:

The Daze, P. O. Box 57, Otisville, MI 48463
Antique Week, P. O. Box 90, Knightstown, IN 46148
Warman's Today's Collector, 700 East State Street, Iola, WI 54990
Antique Trader Weekly, P. O. Box 1050, Dubuque, IA 52004
Maine Antique Digest, P. O. Box 1429, Waldoboro, ME 04572
Collectors News, 506 Second Street, Grundy Center, IA 50638

Manufacturer. Some patterns remain in production for decades. Before assuming that the pattern you inherited or purchased is discontinued, check with the manufacturer. While some shapes may no longer be available, others may.

Some manufacturers maintain a small inventory of out-of-production pieces so they can fulfill replacement demands. A few, alas their number is small, maintain a file of individuals who are looking for specific pieces, should they be contacted by individuals wishing to sell discontinued items back to the manufacturer.

Mail-order catalogs. If your pattern is still in production, the manufacturer does not sell direct, and you cannot find a source within reasonable driving distance, consider contacting a mail-order catalog firm specializing in the sale of dinnerware and home decor items. Barrons (P. O. Box 994, Novi, MI 48376) and Ross-Simons (9 Ross-Simons Drive, Cranston, RI 02920) are two examples.

Mail-order catalogs generally sell at full retail. In addition, you pay a shipping and handling charge. Surprisingly, many replacement services sell current production material at a slight discount. Do comparison shopping before ordering.

REPLACEMENT SERVICES

Ordering from a replacement service is the quickest and easiest way to expand or replace an item from your dinnerware service. Today's replacement services are very customer-oriented.

Most replacement services have a staff of skilled researchers who are more than willing to assist you in identifying any dinnerware pattern. Send them a set of photocopies or photographs, as described earlier. Within a few weeks, you will receive a letter providing you with the name of the pattern and a list of pieces available. If the research efforts prove negative, you will be informed of this as well.

Many replacement services automatically add your name to their records. If they do not have the pieces you need, they will contact you when they find them. A few services offer a "call collect" program. You provide a number that can be called collect within a few hours after they enter a piece in their sales inventory.

Replacement services acquire material in a variety of conditions. When reviewing a quote, pay close attention to the condition of the piece being offered. If you are uncertain about a piece's condition, call for clarification.

You may find the same piece in identical condition listed at two separate prices. When you find a bargain price, take advantage of it.

Many replacement services also offer repair services. If a piece is chipped or not badly broken, especially a hollowware piece, consider having it repaired. Repairs are done with the assumption that the piece will be reused. The restoration cost may be less than buying a replacement piece. Also, if the piece is scarce, you will be able to use the piece until an unbroken one is available.

Finally, order only from a replacement service that offers a money-back guarantee, no questions asked. This is the most important aspect of doing business by mail. If you have a problem, call immediately.

Replacements, Ltd. (P. O. Box 26029, Greensboro, NC 27420 / 1-800-737-5223) worked closely with the House of Collectibles and me in preparing the information for this book. I have visited its warehouse and used its curating library and strongly recommend contacting Replacements, Ltd. whenever you are exploring replacement service options.

SALLY JESSY RAPHAEL ON USING A REPLACEMENT SERVICE

Talk show host extraordinaire Sally Jessy Raphael has some wonderful stories about her use of Replacements, Ltd., and other replacement services. She bought her first dinnerware, Harebell by Shelley Bone China, when she was living in Puerto Rico.

"Most people from Puerto Rico at that time would go to St. Thomas, which is only ten minutes away by airplane, to buy china because it was duty free. The shop was very—to me—quite la-di-da. At that time we had almost no money, and what we had we were going to spend on china. I hoped I asked the intelligent, right questions, although I was a kid. I said to the man who was waiting on me, 'Will this be open stock?' In other words, will I be able to buy a couple of place settings now and then be able to continue. And he looked down his nose at me and said, 'Madam, Shelley Bone China has been in business for four hundred years. What makes you think that because you deigned to buy one of their patterns they would discontinue operation?' I was greatly chastened, but not chastened enough not to take the two or three place settings I could afford, and we went on our way.

"Well, one year later, Shelley Bone China, four hundred years old, went bankrupt. Unfortunately, it was still my favorite pattern, and what could I do? Well, I would pick up a piece or two at a flea market, or whatever. Then I read an ad for Replacements about ten years ago. And here I sat with my few pieces of Shelley and I told them about it, and they have been able to provide me with the whole set of china. Now I'm rich. I have more dinner plates than you'd ever want in your entire life.

"We are china freaks at our house. Carl [my husband] has three china patterns. And I have three. And we use our china frequently. Every day. If it breaks, then Replacements or somebody replaces it. We spend a lot of time on setting a table. It's a hobby of ours. It's very important to us. I do something that I don't know if other people do. Rather than worry who I'm going to leave the china to, I buy enough for each child. So there's no fighting, no arguing. Everybody gets the same china they grew up with. People have wonderful memories of the china and silver they grew up with. My theory is that everyone hates what they grew up with for a long period of time and then they come back around to it."

FINDING A REPLACEMENT SERVICE

You will find advertisements for replacement services in a wide range of periodicals, from magazines such as *Family Circle* to antiques and collectibles trade newspapers such as *Antique Week* (P. O. Box 90, Knightstown, IN 46148). Check several publications, and begin your search with a list of a half dozen or more possibilities.

Read a replacement service advertisement carefully. Some specialize in patterns from only one or two companies. Others offer an extremely wide range of replacement services that also may include stemware, flatware, tabletop accessories, and contemporary collectibles.

David J. Maloney Jr.'s *Maloney's Antiques & Collectibles Resource Directory, 3rd Edition* (Dubuque, IA: Antique Trader Books: 1995) contains the most comprehensive list of replacement (matching) services available. Look under his Dinnerware, Glass, and Flatware general headings. Maloney provides a full mailing address, telephone number, and brief description of each firm's specialties. He also provides a list of firms that repair dinnerware.

Do not hesitate to ask family or friends who have used a replacement service about their experiences. Personal recommendations often are the best.

CHAPTER FIVE

Keys to Using This Book

This book has three specific goals: (1) To offer the assistance needed to select and care for the dinnerware patterns that are right for you; (2) To provide a checklist of forms that were manufactured as part of those dinnerware patterns; and (3) To enhance your appreciation of your selections by providing historical information about the manufacturer and, occasionally, about the pattern itself.

Do not ignore this book's opening chapters as they contain a wealth of information. Chapter 3 is a "must read." Even the most experienced dinnerware user will learn something new.

ORGANIZATION

The heart of this book is an alphabetical listing—first by manufacturer and then by pattern—of the 500 most-requested patterns from replacement services. In a few instances, the exact manufacturer of a pattern is unknown. These patterns are generically grouped by country or region of origin. When available, a brief history introduces the manufacturer.

Pattern names correspond to those used by the manufacturer. To maintain consistency, the dinner plate has been selected as the form of choice for illustration. Illustrations contain the details necessary for pattern identification.

An alphabetical approach also is used within the listings. Listings are by form. Shape is a qualifying adjective of a form. All plates, including chop plates and cake plates, are round, unless otherwise noted.

A pattern name index is provided. The same pattern name was used by different manufacturers. Of course, the pattern designs differed. If you own a pattern, know its name, and want to locate it quickly, use the pattern name index.

UNDERSTANDING THE CHECKLIST FORMAT

Pattern listings are based on a checklist approach. The goal is to provide the user with a complete list of forms and shapes made in the pattern. Although all basic forms and shapes are included, some that had limited production and do not appear regularly for sale in the marketplace are missing. Checklists are built over time. The checklists in this book represent a strong start.

Not all manufacturers use the same terminology for the same form. This book does. The same form terms are used consistently from pattern to pattern.

Understanding the method used for listing forms is essential when locating the correct price. Some forms were manufactured with variations. For example, a vegetable dish was often designed with or without a lid. The following system was used for listing variations. A vegetable bowl with a lid is listed as "Vegetable, covered." A vegetable bowl that originally had a lid that is now missing is "Vegetable, covered, no lid." Finally, a vegetable bowl that was designed to be "open" (never had a lid) is described simply as "Vegetable." An orphan lid will be listed as "Lid, vegetable."

Forms may be found individually priced, such as "Cup" or "Saucer," or as a unit, "Cup and Saucer." Discrepancies sometimes exist between the price of the set and the sum of its pieces. As a rule, it is less expensive to buy as a set than as individual pieces.

The dinnerware industry has generous manufacturing tolerances. A 10" plate can range in size from 9 ³/₄" to 10 ¹/₄". Because many individuals wish to purchase exact replacement matches for their dinnerware, known size variations are listed separately. In most instances, there is no difference in price, nor should there be. The issue is not value, but knowing the degree of variation within the form.

The size of each piece has been included when available. Sizes included in this book are measured in either diameter/length or height. The following chart will help determine which dimension applies:

Size in Diameter/Length		Size in Height	
Ashtray	Dish	Candlestick	Mug
Augratin	Plate	Coffeepot	Pitcher
Baker	Platter	Compote	Shaker
Bonbon	Relish	Creamer	Sugar Bowl
Bowl	Soufflé	Cup	Teapot
Butter Pat	Tray	Jar	Tumbler
Casserole	Vegetable	Jug	Vase
Coaster			

Two exceptions would be the sizes included with lids and saucers. A size listed with a lid is the size of the piece to which the lid belongs. A size listed with a saucer is the size of the cup that goes with the saucer.

UNDERSTANDING DINNERWARE SERVICE SIZES

What pieces constitute a dinnerware service set? Dinnerware is sold in setting sizes. The size and selection of shapes of a service varies from country to country, depending on its traditions. In Great Britain, where afternoon tea is a national tradition, no hostess or host would be without a tea set. Therefore, British standard dinner sets do not include tea cups and saucers.

Some suggested settings follow.

UNITED STATES

5-Piece Individual Place Setting
1 Dinner Plate
1 Tea or Salad Plate
1 Bread and Butter Plate
1 Tea Cup and Saucer

5-Piece Completer Set
Platter
Vegetable Bowl
Creamer and Covered Sugar

29-Piece Tea Set
8 Plates
8 Tea Cups and Saucers
Covered Teapot
Creamer and Covered Sugar

45-Piece Dinner Set
8 Dinner Plates
8 Salad Plates
8 Bread and Butter Plates
8 Tea Cups and Saucers
Platter
Vegetable Bowl
Creamer and Covered Sugar

20-Piece Starter Set
4 Dinner Plates
4 Tea or Salad Plates
4 Bread and Butter Plates
4 Tea Cups and Saucers

7-Piece Hostess Set
Vegetable Bowl
Gravy Boat and Underplate
Covered Butter Dish
Salt and Pepper Shakers

96-Piece Dinner Set
12 Dinner Plates
12 Salad Plates
12 Bread and Butter Plates
12 Tea Cups and Saucers
12 Soup Bowls
12 Fruit Bowls
2 Platters
2 Vegetable Bowls
Creamer and Covered Sugar
Gravy Boat and Underplate
Salt and Pepper Shakers
Coffeepot

GREAT BRITAIN

5-Piece Individual Place Setting
Dinner Plate
Dessert Plate
Butter Plate
Tea Cup and Saucer

25-Piece Dinner Set
6 Dinner Plates
6 Salad Plates
6 Butter Plates
Medium Oval Dish
2 Covered Vegetable Dishes
Sauce Boat and Stand

22-Piece Tea Set
6 Tea Cups and Saucers
6 Butter Plates
Cake Plate
Creamer and Covered Sugar

38-Piece Dinner Set
6 Dinner Plates
6 Salad Plates
6 Butter Plates
6 Cream Soup Cups and Stands
Large Oval Dish
Medium Oval Dish
2 Covered Vegetable Dishes
Sauce Boat and Stand

SEEKING A PRECISE PATTERN MATCH

Close does not count when seeking replacement or additional pieces for a dinnerware pattern. The match must be exact.

Although the Willow pattern from several different manufacturers appears identical at a glance, there are numerous differences upon close examination. There has to be, as designs are patented and an exact copy would represent a patent infringement. Eventually, design patents do expire. Even when this happens, however, manufacturers have far too much pride to allow themselves to be accused of blatant copying.

But when a pattern design is hand-painted, as many of the patterns included in this book are, some latitude is acceptable. In most cases, the differences will be unnoticeable, except to an expert eye. Slight variations in color tone will be far more evident than design liberties. Use the arm length test. If you do not notice any difference when identical forms are held at arm's length, all is well.

PRICING NOTES

The prices that appear in this book are based on what you would pay to purchase a specific piece of dinnerware from a seller specializing in dinnerware replacement. They are price guidelines, not price absolutes. Price is of the moment, contingent on supply and demand and a host of other variables.

Prices are based on the assumption that a piece is in fine condition, that is, it shows no visible damage at arm's length and only minor defects upon close inspection. Visible defects such as chips and knife marks lower a piece's value significantly, often 50 percent or more.

The dinnerware patterns that appear in this book are mass-produced. As a result, it pays to comparison shop. Replacement services are price-competitive. Further, each brings its own interpretation of value to the patterns sold. The interpretation can differ significantly from seller to seller.

Over two dozen of the patterns listed in this book are currently in production. They are available for sale at authorized sales centers and via mail-order catalogs, usually at the manufacturer's suggested retail price. Before buying from these sources, check prices for these patterns from replacement services. In many instances, replacement service prices are substantially discounted from the manufacturer's suggested retail prices. Replacement services buy their inventory on the secondary market, often at favorable prices, then pass along these savings to their customers.

Replacement service prices for pieces currently in production tend to be lower than those at traditional retail sales sources. However, replacement services charge premium prices for pieces from discontinued patterns or discontinued forms from a current production pattern.

Individuals who remember or have sales receipts or price lists showing what they paid initially for their pieces sometimes have difficulty justifying the price quotes they receive from replacement services. While they may desire only one or two pieces, the replacement service probably had to buy an entire service to be in a position to make these pieces available. When considered in this light, replacement service prices are not out of line.

A REQUEST FOR YOUR HELP

As much as I would like it to be, this book is not comprehensive. Dinnerware manufacturers do not maintain reference archives. Last year's advertisements, catalogs, and price lists are discarded when this year's sales materials arrive. Design and production records are kept for a few years and then trashed. Historical records are lost when one company acquires another. Contemporary manufacturers focus on the future, not the past.

Over a decade ago, Replacements, Ltd., Greensboro, North Carolina, began assembling a dinnerware, stemware, flatware, and collectibles reference library. Today, its holdings are the best research source on the subject in the United States. Replacements, Ltd. generously made its library available. However, even in this great collection, there are gaps.

You can help fill the gaps. If you have additional information about a pattern, please share it. Here are a few possibilities: (1) promotional literature about your pattern, for example, a pamphlet describing how it was made, its designer, and/or its special features; (2) a brochure and/or price list of available forms and shapes; (3) pieces in your service that do not appear on the checklist; and (4) manufacturers' promotional literature from how to care for your dinnerware to how to run a successful dinner party.

While I would love having the original copy, it is advisable to send me a photocopy. First, appropriate information will be incorporated into a future edition of this book. Second, I will make a duplicate copy and send it to the Replacements, Ltd. library. Finally, although I tried to make this book error-free, I am certain some slipped through the cracks. I cannot correct them if you do not point them out to me.

Send any information you have that expands my research database and any comments, positive or negative, to: Dinnerware Pattern Research, Rinker Enterprises, Inc., 5093 Vera Cruz Road, Emmaus, PA 18049. Your assistance will be most appreciated.

CHAPTER SIX

Dinnerware Glossary

This glossary is designed to help you understand the terminology used to describe the shapes, methods of decoration, types of dinnerware bodies, and manufacturing and aging terms encountered when talking about dinnerware. Take a few minutes and review it.

Terminology and the meaning of terms change over time. Today, a *nappy* is an open, shallow, flat-bottomed serving dish. In the 1940s, it was most often a round or heart-shaped candy dish with an applied oval handle. A term such as *baker* has more meaning to manufacturers and wholesalers than it does to the general public.

Applied Decoration   Molded decorations applied with slip to a ceramic piece before firing.

Art Pottery   Ornamental ware made by hand in limited quantities around the turn of the century. Today it is used as a general term to describe much of twentieth-century decorative ware.

Baker   Open, oval serving dish. *Also called a vegetable dish.*

Bone China   A vitrified, translucent porcelain containing animal bone ash.

Bouillon Cup   A two-handled cup used for serving clear soups. It is similar in shape and size to a teacup.

Bread and Butter Plate   A plate for holding cake, bread or rolls, and butter, usually 6″ to 6 1/2″ in diameter.

Casserole   A round or oval-covered dish.

Ceramic   A mineral-based material that can be fired at a high temperature to a hard state.

Cereal Dish   A shallow dish for serving cereal, usually 6″ to 6 1/2″ in diameter. *Also called an Oatmeal.*

China   Another name for porcelain. Today it is used as a general term for dinnerware.

Chop Plate   A large serving tray, usually round in shape and 12″ to 16″ in diameter.

Compote   A long-stemmed dish for serving candy, fruit, or nuts.

Coupe   A flat shape that does not have a rim and is rolled slightly at the edges. Usually used to describe the shape of plates, platters, and soup bowls.

Crazing   Surface cracks in the glaze of pottery resulting from the differences in contraction between the body and the glaze.

Cream-colored Ware   A cheap grade of pottery similar to white granite but with a creamier color. Many American potteries produced cream-colored ware between 1850 and 1900.

Cream Soup and Saucer   A low, two-handled cup used for serving bisque or cream soups. The cup is shorter and wider than a bouillon cup, and the saucer is generally slightly larger than a tea saucer.

Decal   A transfer decoration applied to a piece before firing. The decal's plastic film burns out during firing, leaving the design melted into the glaze. *Also called Decalcomania.*

Demitasse   A small cup and saucer.

Dinner Plate   A plate for serving the main course, usually 8″ to 10″ in diameter.

Dinnerware   Items used during a meal. Pieces are usually divided into two categories—flatware and hollowware.

Earthenware   A slightly porous, opaque ware with a clear glaze that is fired at a relatively low temperature.

Eggcup   A small cup with no handle, similar to a custard cup. A double eggcup is an hourglass-shaped double cup with two different cup sizes.

Embossed   A raised design formed when the piece is molded or shaped, as opposed to being applied separately. *Also called relief.*

Fine China   Top-quality clay fired at high temperatures to produce a hard, nonporous body that is thin, translucent, and delicate, yet strong.

Firing   The process of heating a ceramic body in an oven or a kiln until it is hard.

Flatware   Dinnerware that is nearly flat in shape, such as plates and platters.

Foot   An extension on the bottom of a cup or dish upon which it rests.

Glaze   A transparent or colored mixture of water, clay, and mineral substances applied to the body of a piece before firing. A glaze can be used to seal a porous surface to make it nonporous, or, in the case of a colored glaze, it can be applied as decoration.

Granite Ware   A type of stoneware with a speckled appearance.

Gravy Boat   A low, oval bowl with a spout and handle. *Also called a sauce boat.*

Greenware   An unfired piece that has been removed from the mold and smoothed of rough spots and seams.

Grill Plate   A dinner-sized plate divided into sections.

Ground   The basic body on which decorations are applied.

Hand Painting   Decoration painted by hand and usually covered with a clear glaze.

Hollowware   Dinnerware pieces with raised sides, such as bowls, pitchers, cups, creamers, sugars, and teapots.

Hotelware   Dinnerware that is generally thicker and sturdier than that produced for home use.

Ironstone   A hard, vitrified, opaque, nonporous ware containing ground stone that is stronger than earthenware.

Jumbo Cup and Saucer   A large coffee cup and saucer. *Also referred to as oversized.*

Kaolin   A fine, white clay used in porcelain production that fires to a pure white.

Lug Handle   A pierced or solid tablike handle found on bowls that is generally parallel to the tabletop.

Luncheon Plate   A plate for serving the main course at breakfast or lunch, usually 7″ to 8″ in diameter.

Luster   A deep metallic-colored glaze applied to earthenware to give it an iridescent appearance.

Matte   A dull, nonreflective glaze or surface finish.

Nappy   An open, shallow, flat-bottomed serving dish.

Overglaze   Decorations applied after the glaze has been fired. This process is used to decorate with colors that would fade in the intense heat used in firing the glaze. The piece is usually fired a second time at a cooler temperature to set the decoration.

Platter   A large serving tray, usually oval in shape and 12″ to 18″ in length.

Porcelain   A hard, nonporous, vitrified translucent ware.

Pottery   A general term for ceramics made from clay or clay mixtures, or the factory where they are produced.

Ramekin   A flat-bottomed dish with raised vertical sides and a narrow rim for baking and serving individual food portions. It is often accompanied by a plate.

Redware   A porous, coarse earthenware made from clay with a high ferrous oxide content that gives it a rose-pink to dark reddish-brown color when fired.

Rim   The raised upper edge or lip of a plate or bowl.

Salt Glaze   A finish produced by throwing salt into the kiln during firing, which vaporizes and combines with the silica in the stoneware body to form a shiny, slightly coarse glaze.

Semiporcelain   A slightly porous glazed earthenware that is less shiny and translucent than true porcelain.

Shaped Rim   A rim that has a patterned rather than a smooth outer profile.

Slip   Clay and water mixed to the consistency of cream, used in either molding or decorating.

Snack Plate   A plate with a cup ring near the edge.

Spongeware   Ware that is decorated by dabbing color on a body with a sponge or rag to produce a mottled effect.

Stoneware   A high-temperature-fired, partially vitrified ceramic body of great density and hardness varying in color from blue-gray to brown. Stoneware is often finished with a salt glaze. *Also called ironstone or white granite.*

Terra Cotta   A hard, reddish-brown, unglazed earthenware.

Transfer Printing   The process of decorating dinnerware whereby a design is created on a copper or steel plate; a heated mixture of coloring oxide and oil is applied to the plate and wiped off; a sheet of wet tissue is laid on top and the impression is transferred; the paper with the design is applied to a glazed ceramic surface and gently rubbed; the paper is dissolved in water; and the piece is re-fired in a muffle or enameling kiln.

Translucent   The quality whereby light and shadows can be seen through a piece.

Underglaze   Designs or colors applied before a piece is glazed and fired.

Underplate   An oval platter accompanying a gravy boat or tureen.

Vitrified   Fused by firing at high temperatures to create a glasslike, nonporous body or surface.

White Ware   White earthenware and ironstone.

Yellow Ware   A hard earthenware body made from a naturally occurring yellowish clay that is fired at a high temperature to a deep yellow-to-cream color.

COMMONLY USED CERAMIC MATERIALS IN DINNERWARE

In everyday language dinnerware is referred to as "china" or "porcelain." However, more specifically, dinnerware is available primarily in four materials, each with its own properties:

• **Feldspar Porcelain:** Consists of 50 percent kaolin, 25 percent feldspar, 20 percent quartz, and 5 percent clay. The finished product is translucent and white. The pieces have been fired with a glassy substance (vitrification), which makes the surface dense and durable.

• **Bone China:** Consists of 50 percent animal bone ash, 30 percent kaolin, and 20 percent feldspar. It is very translucent and strong (vitrified). The glaze may contain lead.

• **Earthenware:** Consists of 35 percent quartz, 25 percent clay, 25 percent kaolin, and 15 percent feldspar. The quality of earthenware differs. Some are quite porous and not very chip-resistant.

• **Stoneware:** Consists of 5 to 25 percent clay, 50 percent kaolin, 25 percent feldspar, 0 to 25 percent quartz, and 0 to 25 percent aluminum oxide. It is very chip-resistant and not translucent.

(Courtesy of Hackman Tabletop, Inc., 777 Summer Street, Suite 402, Stamford, CT 06901.)

II

DINNERWARE PATTERNS

Adams, Verushka. *Photo courtesy of BC Design Incorporated*

CHAPTER SEVEN

The Patterns

WILLIAM ADAMS & SONS, LTD.

John Adams of Burslem established the Brick-House Works in North Staffordshire, England, in 1657. It is the oldest private firm of potters in the United Kingdom. Several generations of the Adams family worked the pottery until the late 1770s, when William Adams built the larger potteries at Cobridge.

In 1819, William Adams entered into partnership with his four sons. By the end of the eighteenth century, there were four separate potteries at Stoke-on-Trent, working under the name of William Adams & Sons, along with one at Greenfield Tunstall. Following William Adams's death in 1863, all production was moved to Tunstall.

One of the leading earthenware manufacturers in the United Kingdom, William Adams joined the Wedgwood Group in 1966. Although there is no longer an Adams manufacturing unit, the Adams backstamp is used by the Wedgwood Group today.

William Adams & Sons developed several outstanding shapes—Ceres, Empress, Elgin, and Crown. Complete dinnerware sets are produced in Ceres and Empress. The Elgin and Crown shapes are used in accessory pieces.

Calyx tableware patterns are the best known of Adams's work. The blue-to-green shading of the Calyx glaze, exemplified in patterns like Ming Jade and Singapore Bird, is reminiscent of the celadon glaze of the Chinese Sung dynasty A.D. 960–1279. These distinctly Oriental patterns met with great success when introduced and are popular to this day.

Adams also produced Micratex Ironstone, a pure white Ironstone combining strength, durability, and attractiveness. Ironstone designs range from bold, hand-painted Pennsylvania Dutch patterns to detailed, precise British prints.

William Adams & Sons, LTD., Brentwood, Empress Shape, blue design

Coffeepot, covered	$180.00
Creamer	55.00
Cup, oversized, 2 3/4 x 4″	45.00
Cup and Saucer, demitasse	45.00
Cup and Saucer, flat, 2 1/2″	45.00
Eggcup, double, 4″	50.00
Gravy Boat, attached underplate	150.00
Lid, teapot	90.00
Plate, bread and butter, 6 1/4″	15.00

Plate, dinner	45.00		Platter, oval, 11 3/4″	60.00
Plate, salad	30.00		Saucer	10.00
Platter, octagonal, 11 1/2″	110.00		Saucer, demitasse	5.00
Platter, oval, 11 5/8″	110.00		Sugar Bowl, covered	45.00
Sugar Bowl, covered	70.00		Sugar Bowl, covered, no lid	35.00
Vegetable, covered, octagonal	215.00		Teapot, covered	100.00
Vegetable, covered, no lid	165.00		Tureen Underplate	70.00
Vegetable, octagonal, 9 3/4″	110.00		Vegetable, covered, oval	140.00
Vegetable, oval, 9″	95.00		Vegetable, octagonal, 9 1/2″	45.00
			Vegetable, oval, 9 1/8″	45.00
			Vegetable, round, 9″	70.00

**William Adams & Sons, LTD.,
Empress White, Empress Shape**

Ashtray, 4″	$15.00
Bowl, cereal, flat, 6 1/2″	20.00
Bowl, fruit, 5 3/8″	15.00
Bowl, fruit, flat, 5 3/8″	15.00
Bowl, soup, flat, 8″	30.00
Chop Plate, 12 1/2″	95.00
Coffeepot, covered, 6 1/2″	100.00
Cream Soup Saucer	20.00
Creamer	30.00
Creamer, mini	20.00
Cup, demitasse	15.00
Cup, Irish coffee, 4″	20.00
Cup and Saucer, demitasse	20.00
Cup and Saucer, flat, 2 1/2″	25.00
Cup and Saucer, Irish coffee, 4″	25.00
Gravy Boat Underplate	25.00
Lid, coffeepot	50.00
Lid, sugar bowl	20.00
Lid, tureen	120.00
Lid, vegetable, oval	70.00
Pepper Shaker, 4″	30.00
Pitcher, 5 3/4″	30.00
Pitcher, 6 5/8″	50.00
Plate, bread and butter, 6 1/4″	10.00
Plate, dinner, 10 1/8″	25.00
Plate, luncheon, 9″	30.00
Plate, salad, 8 1/8″	15.00
Platter, octagonal, 11 1/2″	60.00

**William Adams & Sons, LTD., Lancaster,
Hexagon/Chinese Shape, floral border**

Ashtray, 5 1/8″	$10.00
Bowl, fruit, 5 3/4″	15.00
Bowl, soup, flat, 7 7/8″	20.00
Cachepot, 5 1/4″	35.00
Casserole, covered, round, 6 3/4″	110.00
Coffeepot, covered	85.00
Cream Soup and Saucer	25.00
Cream Soup Saucer	10.00
Cup, breakfast, 2 3/4″	25.00
Cup, flat, 2 5/8″	15.00
Cup and Saucer, flat, 2 5/8″	20.00
Eggcup, double, 3 3/4″	40.00
Gravy Boat, attached underplate	70.00
Gravy Boat and Underplate	80.00
Mug, 3 3/8″	25.00
Napkin Ring	10.00
Plate, bread and butter, 6 1/8″	10.00
Plate, dessert, 7 1/8″	10.00
Plate, dinner, 10 3/8″	15.00
Plate, luncheon, 9″	20.00
Plate, salad, 8 1/4″	10.00
Platter, oval, 12 1/4″	55.00
Platter, oval, 14 1/4″	70.00
Sauce Pan, covered, 4 7/8″	60.00
Saucer	5.00
Saucer, demitasse	5.00

Sugar Bowl, covered	40.00
Tray, sandwich, 15 3/8″	40.00
Vegetable, covered, round	130.00
Vegetable, oval, 9 7/8″	35.00

William Adams & Sons, LTD., Lowestoft, Hexagon/Chinese Shape, newer design

Bowl, soup, flat	$50.00
Coffeepot, covered	190.00
Cream Soup and Saucer, 2 1/8″	85.00
Cream Soup Bowl, 2 1/8″	80.00
Creamer	60.00
Cup, flat, 2 1/2″	40.00
Cup and Saucer, demitasse	35.00
Cup and Saucer, flat, 2 1/2″	45.00
Gravy Boat Underplate	80.00
Lid, coffeepot	95.00
Lid, teapot	95.00
Lid, vegetable, octagonal	185.00
Plate, bread and butter, 6 1/8″	20.00
Plate, dinner	50.00
Plate, salad	30.00
Platter, oval, 12 3/8″	130.00
Saucer, demitasse	10.00
Vegetable, covered, octagonal	235.00

William Adams & Sons, LTD., Ming Jade, Hexagon/Chinese Shape, shaped rim

Bowl, soup, flat	$50.00
Cream Soup and Saucer	85.00
Creamer	60.00
Cup, flat, 2 1/2″	40.00
Cup and Saucer, flat, 2 1/2″	45.00
Gravy Boat, attached underplate	150.00
Lid, coffeepot	100.00
Lid, sugar bowl	35.00
Plate, bread and butter, 6 1/8″	20.00
Plate, dinner, 10 1/4″	50.00
Plate, salad, 8 1/4″	30.00
Saucer, demitasse	15.00
Vegetable, covered, octagonal	200.00
Vegetable, oval, 9 3/4″	90.00

William Adams & Sons, LTD., Singapore Bird, Hexagon/Chinese Shape, newer design

Bowl, soup, flat, 7 3/4″	$50.00
Coffeepot, covered	170.00
Cream Soup and Saucer	75.00
Creamer, 3 1/4″	50.00

**THE TOP FIVE PATTERNS
COLOR SCHEME—
GREEN**

■

ADAMS, WM. & SONS, LOWESTOFT
FRANCISCAN, IVY
METLOX POTTERY, CALIFORNIA IVY
NORITAKE, PARADISE
WEDGWOOD, CHINESE TIGERS

Cup and Saucer, demitasse, 2 1/4"	40.00	Eggcup, double, 3 3/4"	50.00
Cup and Saucer, flat, 2 5/8"	45.00	Gravy Boat, attached underplate	130.00
Eggcup, double, 4"	50.00	Lid, sauce boat	65.00
Eggcup, single, 2 1/2"	40.00	Lid, vegetable, octagonal	100.00
Gravy Boat, attached underplate	130.00	Plate, bread and butter	15.00
Gravy Boat and Underplate	130.00	Plate, dinner	50.00
Gravy Boat, no underplate	100.00	Plate, salad	25.00
Lid, coffeepot	85.00	Platter, oval, 11 3/4"	110.00
Lid, sugar bowl	30.00	Platter, oval, 12 1/8"	120.00
Lid, vegetable	100.00	Platter, oval, 13 3/4"	145.00
Plate, bread and butter, 6 1/8"	15.00	Platter, oval, 14 1/8"	150.00
Plate, dinner	50.00	Saucer, 2 1/2"	15.00
Plate, luncheon, 9"	40.00	Saucer, oversized	20.00
Plate, salad, 8 1/8"	25.00	Sugar Bowl, covered	60.00
Platter, oval, 12"	120.00	Sugar Bowl, covered, no lid	50.00
Saucer, demitasse	15.00	Vegetable, covered, octagonal	200.00
Sugar Bowl, covered	60.00	Vegetable, oval, 8 3/4"	75.00
Tureen, covered, no lid	295.00	Vegetable, oval, 9 1/8"	80.00
Vegetable, oval, 9 7/8"	80.00		

William Adams & Sons, LTD., Singapore Bird, Hexagon/Chinese Shape, older design

Bowl, melon, 7"	$65.00
Bowl, soup, flat, 7 3/4"	50.00
Bowl, soup, flat, 9"	50.00
Creamer	50.00
Cup and Saucer, demitasse	40.00
Cup and Saucer, flat, 2 1/2"	45.00
Cup and Saucer, oversized, 2 3/4"	55.00
Dish, leaf-shaped, 5 3/8"	25.00

William Adams & Sons, LTD., Veruschka, blue and red

Creamer	$40.00
Cup and Saucer, flat, 2 1/2"	35.00
Lid, vegetable	95.00
Plate, bread and butter, 6"	15.00
Plate, dinner	35.00
Plate, salad	20.00
Sugar Bowl, covered	60.00
Vegetable, oval, 9 7/8"	70.00

The Arabia factory was founded in 1873 in Helsinki, Finland. The company's name is derived from the land on which it was built. Rorstrand, a Swedish porcelain manufacturer, built the factory on land belonging to a manor, where the pastures had been given historical names (Arabia, Canaan, etc.).

Arabia was founded to satisfy the demand of Finland's expanding domestic market. Its location provided easy access to the Russian market, where one-third of the company's products were sold.

Following Finland's independence from Russia in 1917, Rorstrand sold the company to a Finnish investor. The Arabia factory expanded quickly. By World War II it had undergone several expansions and had become the country's largest manufacturer of ceramic goods.

The Arabia factory moved to its present location in 1947. In 1990, the Finnish conglomerate, Hackman, acquired Arabia. While Arabia originally manufactured earthenware, production efforts have concentrated on stoneware since the 1970s. Today, all Arabia items sold in the United States are made of vitrified stoneware.

Anemone by Arabia of Finland.
Photo courtesy of Hacksman Tabletop, Inc.

The Anemone pattern was originally produced from 1962 to 1985. It was reintroduced in the late 1980s, and remained in production until December 31, 1996.

Anemone was designed by Ulla Procopé, known as "The Mother of the Arabia Classics." She worked with Arabia from 1948 until her death in 1968. Ulla Procopé received many awards for her designs. Her works are displayed in the Museum of Industrial Arts in Copenhagen, the Victoria & Albert Museum in London, and the Stedelijk Museum in Amsterdam.

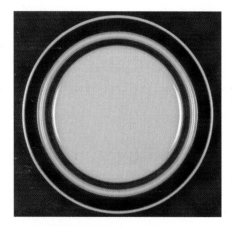

Arabia of Finland, Anemone,
S Shape, blue bands

Bowl, cereal, coupe, 6 1/4"	$20.00
Bowl, cereal, lug, 6 1/4"	25.00

Bowl, soup, flat	20.00
Casserole, covered, round, 5 5/8", no lid	125.00
Chop Plate, 13 1/4"	70.00
Coffeepot, covered	120.00
Creamer	50.00
Cup, demitasse	25.00
Cup and Saucer, demitasse, 1 3/4"	35.00
Cup and Saucer, flat, 2 1/4"	25.00
Cup and Saucer, flat, 3 1/2"	25.00
Mug, 3 1/2"	20.00
Plate, bread and butter, 6"	15.00
Plate, dinner, 10 1/8"	25.00
Plate, salad, 8"	15.00
Saucer, 2 1/4"	10.00
Saucer, 3 1/2"	10.00
Sugar Bowl, covered	50.00
Teapot, covered	120.00
Vegetable, covered, no lid	100.00
Vegetable, round, 9 1/8"	60.00

ARCADIAN

Arcadian Fine China is a mark found on china produced by Jackson China, Inc., of Falls Creek, Pennsylvania. The Jackson China Company traces its origins to the Bohemian Pottery Company, a pottery that produced crocks and flower pots from 1910 to 1917, when it was purchased by Harry W. Jackson and Emanuel A. Fischel. The name was then changed to Jackson Vitrified China Company.

In the mid-1920s, a disgruntled former employee of the Bohemian Pottery murdered Jackson and his associate, Mr. Darden. Fischel continued to operate the factory, now known as the Jackson China Company, from 1923 to 1946, when it was purchased by Philip R. Distillator. Distillator modernized and expanded the factory, doubled the work force, and began producing household dinnerware. A decorating plant operated in Newark, New York, until it was destroyed by fire in 1967.

Competition from foreign manufacturers forced Jackson China Company out of the dinnerware business and, in 1976, the company was purchased by Andrew Greystake. The name was changed to Jackson China, Inc., and the product line was switched to institutional china for restaurants and hotels.

Jackson China, Inc. was recently acquired by Newman Industries of Bristol, England. Newman Industries is a multinational company involved in ceramics, engineering, and electric motors.

Arcadian, Old Rose, small roses, shaped rim

Bowl, fruit, 5 1/4″	$25.00
Bowl, soup, flat, 8 1/8″	30.00
Creamer	60.00
Cup and Saucer	55.00
Gravy Boat, attached underplate	130.00
Plate, bread and butter, 6 1/4″	20.00
Plate, dinner	45.00
Plate, salad	30.00
Platter, oval, 13 3/4″	120.00
Platter, oval, 15 5/8″	150.00
Sugar Bowl, covered	75.00
Vegetable, covered, oval	200.00
Vegetable, oval, 10 1/4″	100.00

JOHN AYNSLEY & SONS

John Aynsley & Sons was founded by John Aynsley in Longton, Staffordshire, England, in the 1860s, for the production of porcelain and bone china. Aynsley was a four-time mayor of Longton and a descendant of John Aynsley, one of the first manufacturers of porcelain in Lane End, England.

John Aynsley & Sons, Cottage Garden, Portland Shape

Ashtray, 4 $^5/_8$″	$15.00
Avocado, 5 $^5/_8$″	40.00
Bell	35.00
Bowl, cereal, coupe, 6 $^3/_4$″	20.00
Bowl, salad, serving, 9 $^1/_4$″	55.00
Bowl, soup, flat, 8″	20.00
Bowl, soup, flat, 9 $^1/_2$″	25.00
Box, covered, duck, large	40.00
Box, covered, duck, small	30.00
Box, covered, elephant, small	30.00
Box, covered, horse, large	40.00
Box, covered, horse, small	30.00
Box, covered, pig, large	40.00
Bud Vase, 7″	30.00
Bud Vase, mini	15.00
Cake Plate, square, handled, 10 $^1/_2$″	25.00
Chop Plate, 12″	80.00
Coffeepot, covered	80.00
Cream Soup and Saucer	40.00
Cream Soup Saucer	15.00
Creamer	30.00
Cup and Saucer	25.00
Cup and Saucer, demitasse	20.00
Ginger Jar, covered, 7″	125.00
Ginger Jar, covered, hexagonal, 6 $^7/_8$″	90.00

Jug, 5 $^1/_2$″	50.00
Lid, casserole, oval, 10″	35.00
Lid, vegetable, round	80.00
Pickle Dish, 8″	20.00
Plate, bread and butter, 6 $^3/_8$″	10.00
Plate, dessert, 7″	15.00
Plate, dinner, 10 $^1/_2$″	25.00
Plate, luncheon, 9 $^1/_8$″	20.00
Plate, salad, 8 $^1/_4$″	15.00
Platter, oval, 13 $^1/_2$″	70.00
Platter, oval, 13 $^3/_4$″	70.00
Platter, oval, 16″	110.00
Saucer	10.00
Spice Jar, covered	30.00
Sugar Bowl, covered	45.00
Sugar Bowl, covered, no lid	40.00
Sugar Bowl, open	30.00
Sugar Bowl, open, mini	30.00
Teapot, covered	80.00
Vase, 3 $^1/_8$″	35.00
Vegetable, covered, round	140.00
Vegetable, oval, 10 $^3/_4$″	45.00

John Aynsley & Sons, Famille Rose, gold trim

Ashtray, 8 $^1/_2$″	$70.00
Biscuit Barrel	210.00

Bud Vase, 3 1/4″	80.00	Cup, demitasse	20.00
Bud Vase, 3 3/4″	80.00	Cup, footed, 2 5/8″	25.00
Bud Vase, 4 3/4″	80.00	Cup and Saucer	35.00
Cigarette Holder	50.00	Cup and Saucer, demitasse	25.00
Coaster, 3 1/2″	30.00	Lid, teapot	55.00
Coaster, 4 1/4″	30.00	Plate, bread and butter	15.00
Compote, 5 3/4″	100.00	Plate, dinner, 10 5/8″	30.00
Creamer, 4″	100.00	Plate, luncheon, 9″	30.00
Creamer, mini	65.00	Plate, salad	20.00
Cup, demitasse	50.00	Plate, salad, crescent, 8 1/2″	40.00
Cup, flat, 2 3/8″	70.00	Platter, oval, 13 1/2″	100.00
Cup and Saucer, demitasse	60.00	Saucer	10.00
Cup and Saucer, flat, 2 3/8″	80.00	Tureen, covered	350.00
Ginger Jar, covered	200.00	Vegetable, covered, 7 1/2″, no lid	160.00
Ginger Jar, covered, 7″, no lid	150.00	Vegetable, covered, round	180.00
Gravy Boat and Underplate	250.00		
Napkin Ring	40.00		
Pitcher, 5 3/8″	140.00		
Plate, bread and butter	35.00		
Plate, dinner	75.00		
Plate, salad	50.00		
Salt and Pepper Shakers, pair	145.00		
Sugar Bowl, open	100.00		
Sugar Bowl, open, mini	65.00		
Tea Caddy, covered	125.00		
Tea Caddy, covered, no lid	80.00		
Tray, mint, 8 1/4″	70.00		

John Aynsley & Sons, Pembroke, York Shape, shaped rim, gold trim

Avocado, 5 3/4″	$40.00
Bell	40.00
Bonbon, 4 3/8″	35.00
Bonbon, 6 5/8″	35.00
Bowl, cereal, coupe, 6 5/8″	20.00

John Aynsley & Sons, Leighton Cobalt, York Shape, blue band

Bowl, cereal, coupe, 6 1/2″	$25.00
Bowl, salad, serving, 9 3/8″	75.00
Bowl, soup, flat, 8″	30.00
Bowl, soup, flat, 9 1/2″	30.00
Cake Plate, square, handled, 10 1/2″	35.00
Chop Plate, 12 1/4″	85.00
Coffeepot, covered	90.00
Cream Soup and Saucer	45.00
Creamer	35.00

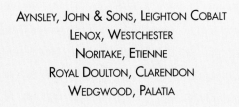

THE TOP FIVE PATTERNS PERIOD LOOK—FORMAL (BLUE/GOLD)

AYNSLEY, JOHN & SONS, LEIGHTON COBALT
LENOX, WESTCHESTER
NORITAKE, ETIENNE
ROYAL DOULTON, CLARENDON
WEDGWOOD, PALATIA

Bowl, fruit, 5 1/8"	15.00	Cup and Saucer, footed, 2 5/8"	30.00
Bowl, salad, serving, 9 3/8"	90.00	Gravy Boat Underplate	30.00
Bowl, soup, flat, 8"	25.00	Lid, teapot	40.00
Box, covered, duck, large	40.00	Lid, vegetable, round	85.00
Box, covered, pig, large	40.00	Pickle Dish, 8"	30.00
Bud Vase, 3 1/4"	30.00	Pitcher, 5 3/8"	90.00
Bud Vase, 3 5/8"	30.00	Plate, bread and butter	15.00
Bud Vase, 4 5/8"	30.00	Plate, cookie, 8 1/4"	30.00
Bud Vase, 7 1/8"	30.00	Plate, dessert, 7 1/8"	20.00
Butter Pat, 3 1/2"	15.00	Plate, dinner	30.00
Cake Plate, square, handled, 10 1/2"	30.00	Plate, luncheon, 9 1/8"	25.00
Cigarette Holder, 2 1/4"	30.00	Plate, salad, 8 1/4"	20.00
Cigarette Holder, 3 1/8"	30.00	Plate, salad, crescent, 8 1/2"	30.00
Coffeepot, covered	80.00	Platter, oval, 13 5/8"	75.00
Cream Soup and Saucer	40.00	Relish, 8 1/4"	30.00
Cream Soup Saucer	15.00	Ring Holder	30.00
Creamer, 3 1/4"	30.00	Saucer, demitasse	5.00
Creamer, mini	25.00	Saucer, smooth	10.00
Cup and Saucer, demitasse	20.00	Spill Vase, 3 1/2"	40.00
Cup and Saucer, flat, 2 3/8"	30.00	Sugar Bowl, covered	50.00

Block China was founded in New York in 1960 by Jay L. Block and Robert C. Block. Block China's philosophy is to bring new, innovative ideas and looks to the tabletop market by offering high-quality merchandise at affordable prices. Block China distributes to the best department and specialty stores across the country.

In 1996 the company was acquired by Salton Maxim, a housewares company located in Mount Prospect, Illinois. The company still has family ties, as evidenced by its president, Robert Block, and his nephew, Joseph Block, who is the vice president of sales.

Poinsettia by Block. *Photo courtesy of Block China Corporation.*

Each of the patterns in the Watercolors line begins as an original watercolor painting from nature by Mary Lou Goertzen. Goertzen was born and raised in a Mennonite community in Kansas. She has carried forward into her life and art the fundamental simplicity and values of her upbringing. The mother of three and wife of Ernest Goertzen, she lives in a converted one-room schoolhouse in the coastal mountain community of Deadwood, Oregon. Goertzen says of her work, "One of my central themes is simplicity. In this sense I feel I am reflecting my Mennonite heritage in a real way."

The Watercolors line is produced on pure white porcelain manufactured by SPAL of Alcobaca, Portugal. The eight Watercolors patterns include Trillium, Western Rose, Geranium, Hillside, Daffodil, Hydrangea, Poppy, and Poinsettia. According to Block China, Poinsettia, introduced in 1984, is their longest-running and most successful Christmas pattern.

**Block China Corporation,
Poinsettia, Watercolors**

Bowl, cereal, coupe, 5 ⅞"	$15.00
Bowl, soup, flat, 8 ¾"	15.00
Candlelight, white	20.00

Chip and Dip, no bowl	130.00
Chop Plate, 12"	35.00
Coffeepot, covered	50.00
Creamer	25.00
Cup and Saucer, demitasse	15.00
Cup and Saucer, flat, 2 ½"	15.00
Cup and Saucer, oversized, 2 ¾"	20.00
Jam	35.00
Lid, coffeepot	25.00
Plate, bread and butter	5.00
Plate, dinner, 10 ½"	15.00
Plate, salad, 8"	10.00
Platter, oval, 15 ¾"	90.00
Saucer	5.00
Saucer, demitasse	5.00
Sugar Bowl, covered	30.00
Teapot, covered	50.00
Vegetable, round, 7 ¾"	40.00
Water Can	30.00

Platter, oval, 13 3/8"	140.00
Saucer	15.00
Sugar Bowl, covered	90.00
Vegetable, covered, round	300.00
Vegetable, covered, no lid	200.00

**Castleton China Co., Dolly Madison,
shaped rim**

Bowl, fruit, 5 5/8"	$40.00
Bowl, soup, flat, 8"	50.00
Cream Soup and Saucer	100.00
Creamer, 2 1/2"	95.00
Creamer, 2 7/8"	95.00
Cup and Saucer, demitasse	60.00
Cup and Saucer, footed, 2 1/4"	70.00
Gravy Boat, attached underplate	220.00
Lid, teapot	160.00
Lid, vegetable, round	230.00
Plate, bread and butter, 6 1/2"	30.00
Plate, dinner, 10 3/4"	55.00
Plate, salad, 8"	40.00
Platter, oval, 16"	283.00
Saucer	25.00
Saucer, demitasse	20.00
Sugar Bowl, covered, 2 3/4"	120.00
Sugar Bowl, covered, 3 1/4"	120.00
Sugar Bowl, covered, 3 1/4", no lid	85.00
Vegetable, covered, round	455.00
Vegetable, oval, 10 1/8"	150.00
Vegetable, oval, 11 1/8"	150.00

**Castleton China Co., Gloria,
shaped rim, gold trim**

Bowl, fruit, 5 3/4"	$30.00
Coaster, 4 1/8"	25.00
Cream Soup and Saucer	60.00

Cream Soup Bowl	55.00
Creamer, 2 7/8"	70.00
Cup, demitasse	35.00
Cup and Saucer, demitasse	40.00
Cup and Saucer, footed, 2 1/4"	50.00
Gravy Boat, attached underplate	150.00
Lid, coffeepot	150.00
Lid, teapot	150.00
Lid, vegetable, round	165.00
Plate, bread and butter, 6 1/2"	20.00
Plate, dinner, 10 3/4"	40.00
Plate, luncheon, 9 3/8"	30.00
Plate, salad, 8"	25.00
Platter, oval, 13 1/2"	130.00
Platter, oval, 16"	200.00
Platter, oval, 19"	300.00
Saucer	15.00
Snack Plate	30.00
Snack Plate and Cup	50.00
Sugar Bowl, covered, 3 1/8"	80.00

**Castleton China Co., Lace,
shaped rim, platinum trim**

Creamer	$90.00
Cup and Saucer, footed, 2 1/4"	60.00

Lid, sugar bowl   60.00
Plate, bread and butter, 6 ³/₈″   30.00
Plate, dinner, 10 ³/₄″   55.00
Plate, salad, 8 ³/₈″   40.00
Saucer   20.00

Castleton China Co., Laurel, shaped
rim, gold trim

Bowl, soup, flat, 8″ $40.00
Cream Soup and Saucer   70.00
Cream Soup Saucer   25.00
Creamer   75.00
Cup and Saucer, demitasse   40.00
Cup and Saucer, footed, 2 ¼″   55.00
Lid, sugar bowl, 2 ³/₄″   45.00
Lid, vegetable   175.00
Plate, bread and butter, 6 ½″   20.00
Plate, dinner, 10 ³/₄″   50.00
Plate, salad   30.00
Platter, oval, 13 ³/₈″   160.00
Saucer, demitasse   15.00
Sugar Bowl, covered, 2 ³/₄″   90.00
Sugar Bowl, covered, 3 ¼″   90.00
Vegetable, covered, round   350.00

Castleton China Co., Lyric,
shaped rim, platinum trim

Cup, footed, 2 ¼″ $55.00
Cup and Saucer, demitasse   50.00
Cup and Saucer, footed, 2 ¼″   60.00
Gravy Boat, attached underplate   230.00
Lid, sugar bowl   50.00
Plate, bread and butter, 6 ³/₈″   30.00
Plate, dinner, 10 ⁷/₈″   55.00
Plate, salad   35.00
Saucer, demitasse   15.00
Sugar Bowl, covered   100.00

Castleton China Co., Ma Lin,
shaped rim, gold trim

Bowl, fruit, 5 ½″ $40.00
Bowl, soup, flat, 8″   60.00
Cream Soup Bowl   75.00
Creamer, 2 ³/₄″   80.00
Creamer, 3 ¼″   80.00
Cup and Saucer, demitasse   50.00
Cup and Saucer, footed, 2 ¼″   50.00
Gravy Boat, attached underplate   180.00
Lid, sugar bowl, 3 ½″   50.00
Lid, teapot   190.00

Lid, vegetable	200.00
Plate, bread and butter, 6 3/8″	25.00
Plate, dinner	55.00
Plate, luncheon, 9 1/8″	45.00
Plate, salad, 8 3/8″	30.00
Platter, oval, 13 3/8″	180.00
Platter, oval, 15 3/8″	230.00
Saucer	15.00
Saucer, demitasse	15.00
Sugar Bowl, covered, 3 1/2″	100.00
Teapot, covered	380.00
Vegetable, covered, round	400.00
Vegetable, oval, 10″	160.00
Vegetable, oval, 11 1/4″	170.00

Castleton China Co., Sunnybrooke, gold trim

Bowl, fruit, 5 1/2″	$30.00
Cream Soup and Saucer	70.00
Cream Soup Bowl	60.00
Creamer	70.00
Cup, demitasse, 2 1/4″	35.00
Cup, footed, 2 1/8″	45.00
Cup and Saucer, demitasse, 2 1/4″	40.00
Cup and Saucer, footed, 2 1/8″	50.00
Gravy Boat, attached underplate	170.00
Lid, teapot	150.00
Lid, vegetable	165.00
Plate, bread and butter, 6 1/4″	20.00
Plate, dinner, 10 3/4″	45.00
Plate, luncheon, 9″	35.00
Plate, salad, 8 1/4″	25.00
Saucer	15.00
Saucer, demitasse, 2 3/8″	15.00
Sugar Bowl, covered	90.00
Vegetable, covered, round	330.00
Vegetable, oval, 11″	130.00

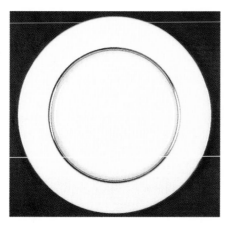

Castleton China Co., Severn, shaped rim, platinum trim

Chop Plate, 13 1/4″	$190.00
Coffeepot, covered	330.00
Cream Soup and Saucer	80.00
Creamer	80.00
Cup and Saucer, demitasse	45.00
Cup and Saucer, footed, 2 1/4″	55.00
Lid, sugar bowl	45.00
Plate, bread and butter, 6 1/4″	20.00
Plate, dinner, 10 3/4″	50.00
Plate, luncheon	45.00
Plate, salad, 8 1/2″	30.00
Platter, oval, 13 1/4″	180.00
Platter, oval, 15 3/8″	200.00
Saucer	20.00
Sugar Bowl, covered	90.00
Teapot, covered	330.00
Vegetable, covered, round	380.00
Vegetable, oval, 10″	150.00
Vegetable, oval, 11 1/4″	160.00
Vegetable, round, 10″	195.00

Castleton China Co., Sunnyvale

Bowl, soup, flat, 8″	$55.00
Chop Plate, 12 3/4″	265.00

Cream Soup and Saucer	100.00	Platter, oval, 13 1/2″	200.00
Cream Soup Saucer	35.00	Platter, oval, 15 7/8″	290.00
Creamer	50.00	Platter, oval, 16″	290.00
Cup and Saucer, footed, 2 1/4″	70.00	Saucer	25.00
Gravy Boat, attached underplate	220.00	Saucer, demitasse	15.00
Plate, bread and butter, 6 1/2″	30.00	Sugar Bowl, covered, 3 1/8″	120.00
Plate, dinner, 10 7/8″	55.00	Vegetable, covered, round	470.00
Plate, luncheon, 9 1/2″	45.00	Vegetable, oval, 10 1/4″	150.00
Plate, salad, 8″	40.00	Vegetable, oval, 11 1/4″	170.00

Churchill originated as a group of small potteries in the Staffordshire District of England. The oldest was Bridgwoods, which was established in Lane End in 1795 and moved to Longton in 1853. The second oldest was Broadhursts of Lane End, which was established in 1847 and moved to the Portland Pottery in Fenton in 1870. Both potteries prospered with the production of earthenwares and bone china. The success of these potteries and others in the Staffordshire District led to the establishment of the Clarence Works in Longton, the Alexander Works at Cobridge, and the Marlborough Works at Tunstall, three potteries that would eventually become part of the Churchill Group.

The Roper family has successfully led the company for the last four generations. Edward Roper took over Broadhursts in the 1920s. His son Peter joined the firm in 1928 and remained until his death in 1991. In 1979, Broadhursts acquired the Sandyford Works in Tunstall from Myott-Meakin Ltd.

Later, in 1979, the company built a new office and showroom at the Anchor Works, Longton. At this point the company consisted of three main firms: Broadhursts, producing tableware at the Portland Pottery; Bridgwoods, producing hotelware at the Anchor Works; and Churchill China, producing mugs, figurines, and ceramics at the former Clarence Works, now the Crown Clarence Works.

In 1984, the company adopted Churchill Group as its name. Other subsidiaries acquired since 1979 include Stratford Bone China, W. Moorcroft, Wessex Ceramics, and Staffordshire Crystal.

In 1992, the Churchill Group registered as a public limited company, and was renamed Churchill China PLC. The companies were divided into two divisions: Tableware, including the Marlborough Works at Tunstall, the Alexander Works at Cobridge, and the Crown Clarence Works at Longton; and Hotelware at the Anchor Pottery in Longton.

Churchill currently ranks fourth among British tableware suppliers, after Doulton, Wedgwood, and Staffordshire Tableware.

The Willow pattern is the English interpretation of the hand-painted blue-and-white Chinese porcelain that was imported to England in the sixteenth century. It is generally accepted that Thomas Minton engraved the first Willow pattern at his Caughley Pottery in Staffordshire in the 1780s. Early versions varied, but by 1810 a pattern created by Josiah Spode was considered the "true" Willow pattern.

> **The standard Willow pattern can be identified by the following rhyme:**
>
> Two pigeons flying high,
> Chinese vessels sailing by,
> Weeping willows hanging o'er,
> Bridge with three men, if
>   not four.
> Chinese temple, there it stands,
> Seems to take up all the land.
> Apple tree with apples on,
> A pretty fence to end my song.

Churchill China, Blue Willow

Bowl, cereal, coupe, 6″	$7.50	Butter Dish, covered, ¼ lb.	30.00
Bowl, soup, coupe, 8″	10.00	Casserole, covered, round, 6″	70.00
		Chop Plate, 12 ³/₄″	25.00
		Clock, plate	45.00
		Coffeepot, covered	50.00
		Creamer	15.00
		Cup and Saucer, flat, 2 ½″	10.00
		Cup and Saucer, flat, 2 ⅞″	10.00
		Gravy Boat	30.00
		Lid, casserole, 6″	20.00
		Mug, 4 ¼″	7.50
		Mug, soup, 3 x 4″	5.00
		Plate, bread and butter	7.50
		Plate, dinner, 10 ³/₈″	7.50
		Plate, salad, 8 ⅛″	7.50
		Platter, oval, 14 ½″	50.00
		Salt and Pepper Shakers, pair	20.00
		Vegetable, round, 8 ⅞″	15.00

COALPORT

The origin of Coalport began with the establishment of Caughley China Works in 1750 by Squire Edward Browne, who lived at Caughley Hall, Shropshire, located on the opposite bank of the river Severn from the village of Coalport. Upon the death of Squire Browne in 1753, his nephew, Ambrose Gallimore, took over operations. He was joined in 1772 by Thomas Turner, the reputed originator of the Blue Willow pattern.

In 1798, Turner retired and the company was sold to John Rose and Edward Blakely, who had established a ceramic manufactory at Coalport. The operations at Caughley were moved to Coalport in 1814. This year also saw the acquisition of Anstice, Horton and Rose, another Coalport pottery, and the South Wales potteries at Swansea and Nantgarw. The business traded under the name of John Rose & Company.

Following John Rose's death in 1841, production at Coalport continued under the direction of his son Thomas Rose, his nephew W. F. Rose, and William Pugh. They were commissioned by Queen Victoria to create a dessert service that she presented to Czar Nicholas I of Russia after it was displayed at the Great Exhibition in 1851.

The Coalport Works was purchased by Peter Schuyler Bruff in 1885 and renamed Coalport China Company in 1889.

After World War I business declined, and in 1923 the Coalport firm was sold to Cauldon Potteries Ltd. The operation and many of the workers were moved to the pottery district of Stoke-on-Trent in 1926. By 1936, the Crescent Potteries of George Jones & Sons Limited had acquired both the Coalport and Cauldon businesses.

The conclusion of World War II found the company struggling once again. The 1950s saw a name change to Coalport China Limited, and in 1958, E. Brain and Company Ltd., whose Foley China Works had been established in 1850, bought Coalport China. The new management made a concerted effort to re-create a demand for Coalport China, retaining its separate identity, and by 1963 the company was producing nothing else.

Coalport China Limited became part of the Wedgwood Group in 1967.

Coalport, Athlone, blue, gold trim

Bowl, fruit, 5"	$50.00
Coffeepot, covered	350.00
Cup, demitasse	50.00
Cup, flat, 2 1/4"	75.00
Cup and Saucer, demitasse	70.00
Cup and Saucer, footed, 3"	80.00
Lid, teapot	175.00
Lid, vegetable, round	255.00
Plate, bread and butter, 6 1/8"	30.00
Plate, dinner	75.00
Plate, salad	45.00
Saucer, 3" cup	25.00

Sugar Bowl, covered	135.00
Teapot, covered	350.00

Coalport, Ming Rose, gold trim

Ashtray, 3 $^1/_8$″	$35.00	Creamer, 3 $^3/_4$″	95.00
Ashtray, 4″	35.00	Cup, demitasse, 2 $^3/_8$″	75.00
Ashtray, 4 $^1/_8$″	35.00	Cup, footed, 3″	70.00
Ashtray, 5 $^1/_4$″	35.00	Cup and Saucer, flat, 2 $^1/_4$″	75.00
Bell, 3 $^7/_8$″	80.00	Cup and Saucer, footed, 3″	75.00
Bonbon, 7 $^5/_8$″	70.00	Egg Box, covered, medium	80.00
Bonbon, 8 $^3/_4$″	70.00	Egg Box, covered, small	60.00
Bonbon, 9 $^3/_4$″	70.00	Ginger Jar, covered, 3 $^3/_8$″	120.00
Bowl, fruit, 5″	45.00	Ginger Jar, covered, 4 $^1/_8$″	120.00
Box, covered, round, 4 $^1/_4$″	60.00	Ginger Jar, covered, 5 $^5/_8$″	120.00
Bud Vase, 4″	95.00	Ginger Jar, covered, 6 $^1/_4$″	145.00
Bud Vase, 5 $^3/_4$″	95.00	Gravy Boat and Underplate, individual	75.00
Bud Vase, 6 $^1/_2$″	95.00	Jam	100.00
Cachepot, 4 $^3/_4$″	120.00	Lid, coffeepot	175.00
Cigarette Holder, 2 $^3/_4$″	55.00	Lid, coffeepot, mini	165.00
Cream Soup Bowl	110.00	Lid, sugar bowl	60.00
		Lid, teapot	175.00
		Mug, 3 $^1/_4$″	55.00
		Mustard	100.00
		Pitcher, 5 $^1/_2$″	150.00
		Plate, bread and butter, 6 $^1/_4$″	30.00
		Plate, dinner, 10 $^7/_8$″	70.00
		Plate, salad, 8 $^1/_8$″	45.00
		Ring Holder	40.00
		Saucer, 2 $^1/_4$″	25.00
		Saucer, demitasse, 2 $^3/_8$″	25.00
		Spill Vase, 3 $^1/_2$″	30.00
		Sugar Bowl, covered	120.00
		Sugar Bowl, open, mini	65.00
		Tray, mint, 8 $^3/_4$″	70.00
		Tray, silver, 4 $^5/_8$″	30.00
		Trinket Box, covered	80.00
		Vase, 8 $^3/_4$″	170.00
		Vegetable, covered, round	500.00

CROWN DUCAL

Crown Ducal Ware was produced by A. G. Richardson & Company, Ltd. at the Gordon Pottery, Tunstall, Staffordshire, England. The pottery was founded in the early 1910s.

Crown Ducal, Bristol, pink

Cup and Saucer, oversized, 2 1/2″	$45.00
Gravy Boat, attached underplate	120.00
Plate, bread and butter, 5 7/8″	15.00
Plate, dinner	35.00
Plate, salad	20.00
Platter, oval, 12 1/4″	80.00
Saucer	15.00
Saucer, oversized	15.00

Vegetable, oval, 8 7/8″	60.00
Vegetable, oval, 9 1/8″	70.00
Vegetable, oval, 9 7/8″	70.00
Vegetable, round, 8 1/4″	70.00
Vegetable, round, 8 3/4″	70.00
Vegetable, round, 9″	75.00

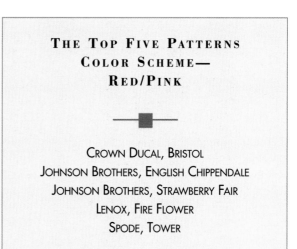

**THE TOP FIVE PATTERNS
COLOR SCHEME—
RED/PINK**

CROWN DUCAL, BRISTOL
JOHNSON BROTHERS, ENGLISH CHIPPENDALE
JOHNSON BROTHERS, STRAWBERRY FAIR
LENOX, FIRE FLOWER
SPODE, TOWER

CROWN VICTORIA

Crown Victoria is the thorn in my side. It is the one manufacturer or importer about which I could find no information. Obviously, Crown Victoria's "Lovelace" dinnerware pattern was well-received and continues to be a favorite among those using heirloom dinnerware.

It is time to ask for your help. If you have the name and address of the manufacturer or importer, sales or promotional literature, and/or a list of pieces available, please send a photocopy to: Rinker Enterprises, Inc., 5093 Vera Cruz Road, Emmaus, PA 18049.

**Crown Victoria, Lovelace,
shaped rim, platinum trim**

Augratin, 10 ³/₈″	$40.00
Baker, rectangular, 12 ¹/₂″	80.00
Bowl, fruit, 5 ¹/₂″	10.00
Bowl, soup, coupe, 7 ⁵/₈″	15.00
Butter Dish, covered, ¹/₄ lb.	35.00
Casserole, covered, individual	30.00
Casserole, covered, round, 8 ¹/₈″	80.00
Casserole, covered, round, 8 ¹/₈″, no lid	65.00
Coaster, 3 ⁵/₈″	5.00
Coffeepot, covered	65.00
Coffeepot, covered, no lid	45.00
Creamer	25.00
Cup, footed, 3″	15.00
Cup and Saucer, footed, 3″	20.00
Gravy Boat, attached underplate	60.00
Lid, casserole, individual	15.00
Lid, teapot	30.00
Lid, vegetable	45.00
Mug, 4 ¹/₂″	15.00
Pepper Shaker	12.50
Plate, bread and butter, 6 ¹/₄″	5.00
Plate, dinner, 10 ³/₈″	15.00
Plate, salad	15.00
Ramekin, 4″	15.00
Soufflé, 7 ¹/₂″	30.00
Sugar Bowl, covered	30.00
Teapot, covered	65.00
Vegetable, covered, round	90.00
Vegetable, oval, 10 ³/₈″	30.00
Vegetable, round, 9 ¹/₈″	40.00

THE DENBY POTTERY COMPANY LTD.

The Denby Pottery Company was established in 1809. William Bourne, owner of a nearby pottery, purchased the clay rights to land in rural Derbyshire, England, where stoneware clay had recently been discovered. He installed his son Joseph on the property. Joseph Bourne built the pottery at Denby, and it quickly became an integral part of Denby village life.

Upon Joseph's death in 1860, his son Joseph Harvey Bourne managed the pottery. Joseph Harvey Bourne outlived his father by only nine years. He left the pottery to his widow, Sara Elizabeth Bourne. Sara Elizabeth controlled the company until her death in 1898, when it was inherited by her nephews Joseph Bourne Wheeler and Joseph Henry Topham.

Under Wheeler's supervision, Denby diversified into giftware and tableware. Joseph was the last member of the Bourne family to be involved in the daily running of the pottery. He was responsible for Denby's modernization and the development of a new design direction.

These innovations began in the 1930s with the employment of designer Donald Gilbert and continued into the 1950s when designer Albert Colledge joined the firm. Albert's son, Glyn, joined his father in the 1960s. New patterns continued to be developed during the 1970s, most notably "Arabesque," "Troubadour," and "Gypsy."

In 1970, the company diversified, supplying cutlery, glass, and furniture, and in 1976 it was renamed Denby Tableware. Denby can now be found in almost thirty countries, including Canada, New Zealand, Australia, Italy, Norway, France, and the United States.

**The Denby Pottery Company LTD.,
Camelot, light green**

Baker, oval, 11 1/4″	$80.00
Bowl, cereal, coupe shape, 6 5/8″	20.00
Bowl, fruit, 5 7/8″	15.00
Bowl, soup, flat, 8 1/4″	20.00

Butter Dish, covered, 1/4 lb.	50.00
Casserole, covered, round, 5 1/2″	90.00
Casserole, covered, round, 6 3/4″	125.00
Coffeepot, covered	95.00
Creamer, 2 1/4″	20.00
Creamer, 3 1/8″	20.00
Cup and Saucer, flat, 2 1/2″	20.00
Gravy Boat	65.00
Mug, 3 1/2″	20.00
Mug, 4″	20.00
Pepper Shaker, 3 1/8″	20.00
Plate, bread and butter, 6 3/8″	15.00
Plate, dinner, 10 1/8″	20.00
Plate, salad, 8 3/4″	15.00
Platter, oval, 12 1/2″	55.00
Salt and Pepper Shakers, pair, 2 7/8″	45.00
Salt and Pepper Shakers, pair, 3 1/8″	45.00
Salt Shaker, 2 7/8″	20.00
Soup Server, covered, individual, 3 1/2″	40.00
Sugar Bowl, covered	25.00
Vegetable, round, 7 1/8″	50.00

The Denby Pottery Company LTD., Castile, blue, shaped rim

Creamer, 3 1/8″	$40.00
Cup, footed, 3 3/8″	20.00
Cup and Saucer, footed, 3 3/8″	20.00
Plate, bread and butter	17.50
Plate, dinner, 10 3/4″	25.00
Plate, salad, 9 1/8″	20.00
Sugar Bowl, open	40.00

The Denby Pottery Company LTD., Gypsy

Baker, oval, 10 1/4″	$85.00
Casserole, covered, round, 7 1/2″	150.00
Coffeepot, covered	105.00
Creamer	40.00
Cup and Saucer, flat, 2 1/2″	25.00
Lid, butter dish, 1/4 lb.	30.00
Lid, casserole, individual	20.00
Pepper Shaker	25.00
Plate, bread and butter, 6 5/8″	17.50
Plate, dinner	30.00
Plate, salad	20.00
Platter, oval, 12 1/2″	65.00
Salt and Pepper Shakers, pair	50.00
Saucer	10.00
Sugar Bowl, covered	45.00
Sugar Bowl, covered, no lid	30.00
Vegetable, oval, divided, 11 3/4″	90.00

FLINTRIDGE CHINA COMPANY

Thomas W. Hogan and Milton E. Mason established the Flintridge China Co. in Pasadena, California, in 1946. Former Gladding, McBean & Co. employees, their aim was to produce thinner china.

Their first products were demitasse cups, but before their second year they were producing full dinnerware services. Flintridge China Co. introduced the very successful silver trim (platinum) to the American public in 1952.

In 1970, the company was sold to Gorham Silver Company, a Division of Textron. Flintridge China Co. was dissolved at that time, though Gorham continued to supply the pattern matchings from the Flintridge line for many years.

Flintridge China Company, Miramar, platinum trim

Coffeepot, covered	$220.00
Cup and Saucer, flat	70.00
Cup and Saucer, footed	70.00
Plate, bread and butter, 6″	25.00
Plate, dinner, 10 ½″	50.00
Plate, salad, 8 ½″	35.00

FRANCISCAN

Charles Gladding, Peter McGill McBean, and George Chambers established Gladden-McBean & Company in Lincoln, Placer County, California, in 1875. After merging with the Los Angeles Pressed Brick Company in 1924, Gladden-McBean & Company consisted of plants in Los Angeles, Santa Monica, Alberhill, and Glendale.

Franciscan Ware was produced at the Glendale (later Los Angeles) plant, which began operating in 1902 as the Pacific Art Tile Company. Gladden-McBean chose the name "Franciscan" to be symbolic of California. They began producing Franciscan earthernware in brilliant glaze colors in 1934. Franciscan china was introduced in 1942.

A decline in sales, attributed to the import of inexpensive Japanese china, was a factor in Gladden-McBean's sale of its Franciscan plant to the Lock Joint Pipe Company in 1962. The merger resulted in the formation of the International Pipe and Ceramics Corporation, shortened to Interpace Corporation, in 1968. Interpace later sold Franciscan Ceramics to Josiah Wedgwood and Sons, Ltd. in 1979. Production of the Franciscan line was moved to Wedgwood's Stoke-on-Trent facility in 1984.

Franciscan, Apple (newer)

Ashtray, 4 1/2″	$20.00
Bowl, cereal, coupe, 6″	15.00
Bowl, fruit, 5 1/4″	12.50
Bowl, oatmeal, 5 1/2″	27.50
Butter Dish, covered, 1/4 lb.	50.00
Butter Dish, covered, 1/4 lb., no lid	25.00
Casserole, individual, 4″	50.00
Chop Plate, 12 3/8″	65.00
Chop Plate, 14″	145.00
Compote, 3 5/8″	80.00
Creamer, 3 1/4″	25.00
Creamer, individual, 2 3/4″	25.00

Cup and Saucer, flat, 2 3/4″	17.50
Gravy Boat, attached underplate	50.00
Jam, covered, no lid	115.00
Pitcher, 6 1/4″	75.00
Plate, bread and butter, 6 3/8″	7.50
Plate, dinner, 10 5/8″	20.00
Plate, luncheon, 9 5/8″	17.50
Plate, salad, 8″	15.00
Platter, oval, 12 5/8″	40.00
Platter, oval, 14 1/8″	50.00
Relish, 10 1/2″	40.00
Relish, 3 part, 11 7/8″	75.00
Salt and Pepper Shakers, pair	27.50
Salt Shaker	15.00
Saucer	5.00
Sherbet, 2 1/4″	22.50
Sugar Bowl, covered, 3″	35.00
Sugar Bowl, covered, 3″, no lid	22.50
Sugar, individual, 2 5/8″	40.00
Sugar, individual, covered, 2 5/8″, no lid	25.00
Teapot, covered, no lid	90.00
Vegetable, covered, round	100.00
Vegetable, covered, round, no lid	70.00
Vegetable, oval, divided, 10 3/4″	50.00
Vegetable, round, 7 5/8″	32.50
Vegetable, round, 8 1/2″	40.00
Vegetable, round, 9″	50.00

Franciscan, Apple (older)

Bank, pig	$32.50
Bowl, cereal, coupe, 6″	10.00
Bowl, fruit, 5 1/8″	7.50
Bowl, oatmeal, 5 1/2″	15.00
Bowl, soup, flat, 8 3/8″	15.00
Coffeepot, covered	65.00
Creamer	20.00
Cup and Saucer, flat, 2 3/4″	15.00
Gravy Boat, attached underplate	35.00
Mug, 2 7/8″	15.00
Napkin Ring	12.50
Pepper Shaker	10.00
Pie Server, stainless blade	15.00
Pitcher, 6 1/8″	35.00
Plate, bread and butter, 6 1/4″	10.00
Plate, dinner, 10 3/4″	15.00
Plate, luncheon, 9 3/8″	12.50
Plate, salad, 7 7/8″	10.00
Plate, salad, crescent, 7 7/8″	17.50
Platter, oval, 12 1/2″	35.00
Platter, oval, 14 1/4″	35.00
Salt and Pepper Shakers, pair	22.50
Saucer	5.00
Sherbet, 2 1/4″	15.00
Sugar Bowl, covered	30.00

Teapot, covered	60.00
Tray, two-tiered	55.00
Vegetable, covered, round	70.00
Vegetable, round, 7 7/8″	25.00
Vegetable, round, 8 5/8″	27.50
Vegetable, round, 9″	30.00

Franciscan, Carmel, platinum trim

Chop Plate, 13 3/8″	$140.00
Coffeepot, covered	180.00
Creamer	60.00
Cup, demitasse	40.00
Cup, flat, 1 5/8″	35.00
Cup and Saucer, flat, 1 5/8″	40.00
Gravy Boat	120.00
Lid, coffeepot	90.00
Plate, bread and butter, 6 3/8″	15.00
Plate, dinner, 10 1/2″	35.00
Plate, salad, 8 1/8″	25.00
Platter, oval, 12 1/2″	100.00
Sugar Bowl, covered	70.00
Sugar Bowl, covered, no lid	55.00
Vegetable, oval, 8 7/8″	70.00

FRANCISCAN, DESERT ROSE

The Desert Rose pattern was first manufactured in late 1941 or early 1942. It is the best-selling American dinnerware pattern in history.

Annette Honeywell, a freelance artist who sold several concept designs to Gladding, McBean & Company, is credited with the concept for the Desert Rose Pattern. Mary Jane Winans, a designer for the company, was responsible for the production design work.

The pattern was modeled after the Rosa Rugosa because the simplicity of the bloom was adaptable to hand painting. While this rose is primarily native to the Midwest and northern sections of the United States, it was named Desert Rose to connect it to California and the Franciscan Company. When the pattern was introduced, products labeled "California" were very popular.

Franciscan, Desert Rose (older). *Photo courtesy of BC Design Incorporated.*

Franciscan, Desert Rose (newer)

Ashtray, 3 1/2″	$20.00
Bowl, cereal, coupe, 5 7/8″	15.00
Bowl, fruit, 5 1/4″	12.50
Bowl, salad, serving, 10 1/4″	100.00
Bowl, soup, flat, 8 1/2″	20.00
Bud Vase, 5 7/8″	100.00
Butter Dish, covered, 1/4 lb.	50.00
Candlestick, single light, 3 1/2″	50.00
Child's Plate, 8 7/8″	65.00
Chop Plate, 11 3/4″	75.00
Chop Plate, 14″	165.00

Coffeepot, covered, no lid	90.00	Bowl, oatmeal, 5 1/2″	15.00
Compote, 4″	80.00	Bowl, salad, serving, 10″	70.00
Cookie Jar, 9″	275.00	Bowl, salad, serving, 11 3/8″	70.00
Creamer	25.00	Bowl, soup, flat, 8 1/4″	15.00
Cup, flat, 2 1/4″	15.00	Bud Vase, 5 3/4″	17.50
Cup and Saucer, flat, 2 1/4″	15.00	Bud Vase, 10 3/4″	17.50
Cup and Saucer, oversized, 3″	45.00	Butter Dish, covered, 1/4 lb.	35.00
Gravy Boat, attached underplate	60.00	Cake Plate and Server, 12 1/4″	45.00
Jam, covered, no lid	115.00	Candlestick, single light	40.00
Lid, butter dish, 1/4 lb.	35.00	Chop Plate, 13″	35.00
Mug, 2 3/4″	22.50	Clock, plate	45.00
Pitcher, 6 1/4″	75.00	Coffeepot, covered	65.00
Plate, bread and butter, 6 3/8″	7.50	Coffeepot, covered, no lid	45.00
Plate, dinner, 10 5/8″	17.50	Cookie Jar, 7 1/2″	50.00
Plate, luncheon, 9 1/2″	20.00	Creamer	20.00
Plate, salad, 8″	15.00	Cup and Saucer, flat, 2 1/4″	15.00
Platter, oval, 12 3/4″	40.00	Mug, 2 7/8″	15.00
Platter, oval, 14 1/4″	50.00	Mug, 3 1/2″	15.00
Relish, 10 3/4″	40.00	Napkin Ring	12.50
Relish, three-part, 12″	85.00	Pepper Shaker	10.00
Salt and Pepper Shakers, pair	32.50	Pitcher, 6 1/4″	35.00
Salt and Pepper Shakers,		Plate, bread and butter, 6 1/4″	10.00
oversized, pair, 6 1/4″	60.00	Plate, dessert, 7 1/4″	10.00
Salt Shaker	15.00	Plate, dinner, 10 5/8″	15.00
Sherbet, 2 1/2″	22.50	Plate, grill, 10 3/8″	50.00
Sugar Bowl, covered	40.00	Plate, luncheon, 9 1/4″	12.50
Sugar Bowl, covered, no lid	25.00	Plate, salad, 7 7/8″	10.00
Teapot, covered	120.00	Plate, salad, square, 7 1/2″	10.00
Tureen, covered, no lid	395.00	Platter, oval, 12 1/4″	35.00
Vegetable, covered, round, 6 3/4″	100.00	Platter, oval, 14 1/8″	35.00
Vegetable, covered, round, 6 3/4″, no lid	70.00	Salt and Pepper Shakers, pair	22.50
Vegetable, oval, divided, 10 3/4″	70.00	Sherbet, 2 1/2″	15.00
Vegetable, round, 8″	40.00	Spoon Holder	17.50
Vegetable, round, 9″	50.00	Sugar Bowl, covered	30.00
		Teapot, covered	60.00
		Teapot, covered, no lid	40.00
		Tray, 6 1/8″	17.50
		Tray, two-tiered	55.00
		Tumbler, 5 1/4″	15.00
		Tureen, covered	200.00
		Tureen, covered, no lid	140.00
		Utensil Holder, 6 3/4″	25.00
		Vase, 10 3/4″	35.00
		Vegetable, covered, round	70.00
		Vegetable, oval, divided, 10 5/8″	35.00
		Vegetable, oval, divided, 10 3/4″	35.00
		Vegetable, round, 8″	27.50
		Vegetable, round, 9″	30.00

Franciscan, Desert Rose (older)

Bank	$32.50
Bowl, cereal, coupe, 5 7/8″	10.00
Bowl, fruit, 5″	7.50

Franciscan, Floral

Ashtray, 8″	$12.50
Bowl, cereal, coupe, 7 1/8″	15.00
Butter Dish, covered, 1/4 lb.	45.00
Casserole, covered, round, 9 3/4″	120.00
Chip and Dip, no bowl	60.00
Coffeepot, covered	80.00
Creamer	20.00
Cup and Saucer, flat, 3 1/4″	15.00
Gravy Boat and Underplate, covered	50.00
Gravy Boat, covered, no underplate	35.00
Gravy Boat, covered, no underplate, no lid	25.00
Pitcher, 6 3/4″	45.00
Plate, bread and butter	10.00
Plate, dinner, 10 1/2″	20.00
Plate, salad, 8 1/2″	10.00
Platter, oval, 13 5/8″	50.00
Salt and Pepper Shakers, pair	25.00
Salt Shaker	12.50
Saucer	5.00
Sugar Bowl, covered	30.00
Sugar Bowl, covered, no lid	22.50
Vegetable, oval, divided, 10 3/8″	50.00
Vegetable, round, 7 3/4″	35.00
Vegetable, round, 9 3/8″	40.00

Mug, 2 7/8″	40.00
Pitcher, 6 1/4″	30.00
Plate, bread and butter, 6 1/4″	20.00
Plate, dinner, 10 3/4″	45.00
Plate, salad, 7 3/4″	25.00
Platter, oval, 14 1/8″	120.00
Platter, oval, 14 1/2″	120.00
Relish, 8″	35.00
Saucer	7.50
Saucer, oversized, 7 1/8″	12.50
Sugar Bowl, covered	50.00
Teapot, covered	120.00
Tray, two-tiered	125.00
Vegetable, covered, round	150.00
Vegetable, covered, 6 3/4″, no lid	95.00
Vegetable, round, 8 5/8″	65.00

Franciscan, Fresh Fruit, large fruit

Bowl, cereal, coupe, 6″	$22.50
Bowl, salad, serving, 10 1/4″	80.00
Bowl, soup, flat, 9 5/8″	45.00
Coffeepot, covered	120.00
Creamer	40.00
Cup, flat, 2 7/8″	20.00
Cup and Saucer, flat, 2 7/8″	22.50
Gravy Boat and Underplate	100.00
Gravy Boat Underplate	35.00

Franciscan, Hacienda Gold

Bowl, cereal, coupe, 6 3/8″	$15.00
Butter Dish, covered, 1/4 lb.	40.00
Casserole, covered, round, 8 5/8″	100.00
Coffeepot, covered	70.00
Creamer	20.00
Cup and Saucer, flat, 2 5/8″	15.00
Gravy Boat, attached underplate	50.00

Lid, casserole, round, 8 5/8″	50.00
Lid, coffeepot	35.00
Lid, teapot	35.00
Pitcher, 6″	40.00
Pitcher, 7 1/8″	45.00
Plate, bread and butter, 6 5/8″	7.50
Plate, dinner, 10 3/4″	17.50
Plate, salad, 8 1/4″	15.00
Platter, oval, 14″	45.00
Salt and Pepper Shakers, pair	25.00
Salt Shaker	12.50
Saucer	5.00
Sugar Bowl, covered	30.00
Teapot, covered	70.00
Vegetable, oval, divided, 11″	50.00
Vegetable, round, 9 3/8″	40.00

Teapot, covered	70.00
Teapot, covered, no lid	55.00
Vegetable, oval, divided, 11 1/8″	50.00
Vegetable, round, 9 3/8″	40.00

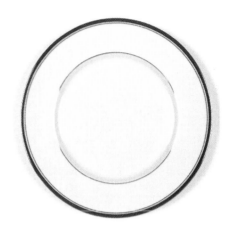

Franciscan, Huntington, shaped rim, platinum trim

Creamer	$65.00
Cup and Saucer, footed, 2 1/4″	50.00
Plate, bread and butter, 6 3/8″	20.00
Plate, dinner, 10 5/8″	45.00
Plate, salad	27.50
Platter, oval, 12 1/2″	120.00
Platter, oval, 16″	200.00

Franciscan, Hacienda Green

Bowl, cereal, coupe, 6 1/4″	$15.00
Butter Dish, covered, 1/4 lb.	40.00
Butter Dish, covered, 1/4 lb., no lid	30.00
Casserole, covered, round, 8 5/8″	100.00
Coffeepot, covered	70.00
Creamer	20.00
Cup and Saucer, flat, 2 1/2″	15.00
Gravy Boat, attached underplate	50.00
Lid, casserole, round, 8 5/8″	50.00
Lid, coffeepot	35.00
Pepper Shaker	12.50
Pitcher, 6″	40.00
Pitcher, 7″	45.00
Plate, bread and butter, 6 5/8″	5.00
Plate, dinner, 10 1/2″	17.50
Plate, salad, 8 3/8″	10.00
Platter, oval, 11 1/2″	40.00
Platter, oval, 14″	45.00
Salt and Pepper Shakers, pair	24.00
Saucer	5.00
Sugar Bowl, covered	30.00

Franciscan, Huntington Rose, platinum trim

Bowl, fruit, flat, 6 3/8″	$32.50
Cup and Saucer, footed, 2 1/4″	50.00
Plate, bread and butter, 6 3/8″	20.00
Plate, dinner	45.00
Plate, salad	27.50
Saucer	15.00
Saucer, demitasse	15.00

Franciscan, Indigo, Coupe Shape, platinum trim

Cup and Saucer, footed, 2 3/4"	$50.00
Lid, coffeepot	115.00
Lid, sugar bowl	45.00
Plate, bread and butter, 6 1/4"	22.50
Plate, dinner	50.00
Plate, salad, 8 1/4"	30.00
Platter, oval, 13"	170.00
Saucer	17.50

Franciscan, Ivy Earthenware

Ashtray, small, 4 3/8"	$25.00
Bowl, cereal, coupe, 6"	25.00
Bowl, fruit, 5 3/8"	20.00
Bowl, salad, serving, 11"	180.00
Butter Dish, covered, 1/4 lb.	80.00
Casserole, covered, round, 7 3/8"	145.00
Chop Plate, 11 3/4"	90.00
Chop Plate, 14"	180.00
Creamer, 3 3/4"	32.50
Cup and Saucer, flat, 2 5/8"	27.50
Cup and Saucer, footed, 2 5/8"	27.50
Gravy Boat, attached underplate	75.00
Lid, butter dish, 1/4 lb.	55.00
Lid, sugar bowl	20.00

Pepper Shaker	17.50
Plate, bread and butter, 6 3/8"	10.00
Plate, dinner, 10 3/8"	40.00
Plate, salad, 8 1/2"	25.00
Platter, oval, 11 1/4"	70.00
Platter, oval, 13"	70.00
Platter, oval, 18 3/8"	245.00
Relish, 10 1/2"	60.00
Salt and Pepper Shakers, pair	35.00
Saucer	10.00
Saucer, oversized	40.00
Sugar Bowl, covered	40.00
Tumbler, water, 5 1/8"	40.00
Vegetable, oval, divided, 12 3/8"	75.00
Vegetable, round, 7 1/4"	40.00
Vegetable, round, 8 1/8"	50.00

Franciscan, Madeira, shaped rim

Ashtray, large, 8 1/4"	$22.50
Bowl, cereal, coupe, 7"	15.00
Butter Dish, covered, 1/4 lb.	40.00
Candlestick, single light, 6 1/8"	17.50
Candlestick, three light	40.00
Casserole, covered, round, 9 3/4"	100.00
Chip and Dip, 13 5/8", no bowl	40.00
Coffeepot, covered	60.00
Creamer, 3 1/4"	20.00
Cup and Saucer, flat, 3 1/8"	17.50
Gravy Boat and Underplate, covered	50.00
Gravy Boat, covered, no underplate	40.00
Lid, casserole, round, 9 3/4"	50.00
Pitcher, 6 3/4"	45.00
Plate, bread and butter, 6 3/4"	7.50
Plate, dinner, 10 1/2"	17.50
Plate, salad, 8 1/2"	10.00
Platter, oval, 13 1/2"	45.00
Salt and Pepper Shakers, pair	25.00
Salt Shaker	12.50
Saucer	5.00

Sugar Bowl, covered	30.00
Sugar Bowl, covered, no lid	20.00
Teapot, covered	70.00
Vegetable, oval, divided, 10 3/8″	50.00
Vegetable, round, 7 7/8″	35.00
Vegetable, round, 9 1/2″	40.00

Cup and Saucer, flat, 2″	60.00
Gravy Boat Underplate	65.00
Lid, teapot	125.00
Plate, bread and butter, 6 1/4″	25.00
Plate, dinner	55.00
Plate, salad, 8 3/8″	35.00
Saucer	20.00
Sugar Bowl, covered	90.00

Franciscan, Mariposa, shaped rim, gold trim

Cream Soup Bowl	$100.00
Creamer	100.00
Cup, footed, 2 1/4″	65.00
Cup and Saucer, footed, 2 1/4″	70.00
Gravy Boat, attached underplate	240.00
Plate, bread and butter, 6 1/4″	30.00
Plate, dinner	65.00
Plate, salad, 8 1/4″	40.00
Platter, oval, 12 1/2″	190.00
Platter, oval, 16 1/8″	300.00
Saucer	22.50
Sugar Bowl, covered	120.00
Sugar Bowl, covered, no lid	85.00

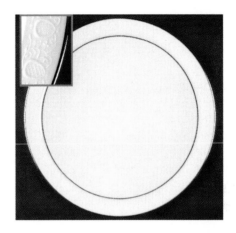

Franciscan, Moon Glow, platinum trim

Creamer	$80.00
Creamer, covered	90.00
Creamer, covered, no lid	70.00
Cup, flat, 2 1/8″	55.00
Cup and Saucer, flat, 2 1/8″	60.00
Gravy Boat Underplate	65.00
Lid, coffeepot	125.00
Lid, sugar bowl	45.00
Plate, bread and butter	25.00
Plate, dinner	55.00
Plate, salad	35.00
Sugar Bowl, covered	90.00

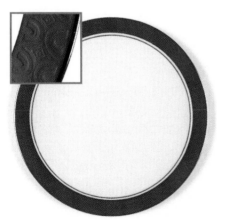

Franciscan, Midnight Mist, platinum trim

Creamer, covered	$90.00
Creamer, covered, no lid	70.00

**THE TOP FIVE PATTERNS
PERIOD LOOK—
POST-WAR MODERN**

FRANCISCAN, HACIENDA
FRANCISCAN, SILVER PINE
FRANCISCAN, STAR BURST
HOMER LAUGHLIN CHINA CO., FIESTA
ROYAL DOULTON, TAPESTRY

Plate, bread and butter, 6 3/8″	17.50
Plate, dinner	40.00
Plate, salad	25.00
Platter, oval, 12 5/8″	100.00
Saucer	12.50
Sugar Bowl, covered	60.00
Sugar Bowl, covered, no lid	45.00

Franciscan, October, brown trim

Baker, microwave, square, 9 5/8″	$145.00
Bowl, cereal, coupe, 7″	20.00
Bowl, fruit, 5 1/4″	20.00
Creamer	32.50
Cup and Saucer, flat, 3 3/8″	22.50
Gravy Boat, attached underplate	75.00
Pepper Shaker	22.50
Plate, bread and butter	15.00
Plate, dinner	35.00
Plate, salad, 8″	20.00
Platter, oval, 14″	80.00
Salt and Pepper Shakers, pair	45.00
Saucer	7.50
Sugar Bowl, covered	40.00
Sugar Bowl, covered, no lid	32.50
Tray, microwave, square, 8 1/4″	115.00
Vegetable, round, 8 3/4″	55.00

Franciscan, Renaissance Gold

Cream Soup and Saucer	$130.00
Cup and Saucer, footed, 2 1/2″	65.00
Plate, bread and butter, 6 1/4″	30.00
Plate, dinner	60.00
Plate, salad	40.00

Franciscan, Platinum Band

Cream Soup Saucer	$22.50
Creamer	50.00
Cup and Saucer, flat, 1 5/8″	40.00
Gravy Boat	130.00

Franciscan, Renaissance Grey

Cup and Saucer, footed, 2 3/8″	$50.00
Gravy Boat, attached underplate	180.00
Plate, bread and butter, 6 3/8″	20.00
Plate, dinner, 10 5/8″	40.00
Plate, salad, 8 1/4″	25.00
Saucer	17.50
Sugar Bowl, covered	90.00

Franciscan, Renaissance Platinum

Creamer	$75.00
Cup and Saucer, footed, 2 3/8″	50.00
Plate, bread and butter, 6 3/8″	25.00
Plate, dinner, 10 1/2″	45.00
Plate, salad, 8 3/8″	32.50
Saucer	15.00

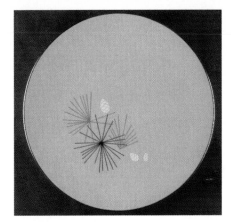

Franciscan, Silver Pine, platinum trim

Cream Soup Bowl	$60.00
Creamer	50.00
Cup and Saucer, flat, 1 3/4″	35.00
Gravy Boat	140.00
Plate, bread and butter, 6 3/8″	12.50
Plate, dinner, 10 1/2″	32.50
Plate, salad, 8 1/4″	20.00
Platter, oval, 16 1/8″	170.00
Saucer	12.50
Sugar Bowl, covered	70.00

Franciscan, Sea Sculptures

Casserole, covered, round, 9 1/4″	$200.00
Casserole, individual, 4 1/2″	50.00
Creamer	40.00
Cup and Saucer, flat, 2 3/4″	25.00
Lid, casserole, individual, 4 1/2″	25.00
Pepper Shaker	20.00
Plate, bread and butter	12.50
Plate, dinner, 10 3/4″	25.00
Plate, luncheon, 9 1/8″	20.00
Platter, oval, 12 3/4″	85.00
Salt and Pepper Shakers, pair	40.00
Saucer	7.50
Sugar Bowl, covered	50.00
Sugar Bowl, covered, no lid	35.00

Franciscan, Star Burst

Butter Dish, covered, 1/4 lb.	$45.00
Creamer	22.50
Cup and Saucer, flat, 2 1/4″	15.00
Gravy Boat, attached underplate	50.00
Gravy Ladle	40.00
Mustard, covered, no lid	60.00
Pitcher, 9 5/8″	120.00
Plate, bread and butter, 6 1/2″	5.00
Plate, dinner, 10 3/4″	15.00
Plate, luncheon, 9 1/2″	45.00
Plate, salad, 8″	17.50
Plate, salad, crescent, 9 1/2″	45.00

Platter, oval, 13 1/8″	40.00
Platter, oval, 15 1/8″	60.00
Saucer	5.00
Sugar Bowl, covered	30.00
Sugar Bowl, covered, no lid	20.00
Teapot, covered, no lid	150.00
Vegetable, covered, round	80.00
Vegetable, covered, round, no lid	65.00
Vegetable, round, divided, 8 3/8″	22.50
Vinegar	75.00

Franciscan, Woodside, gold trim

Bowl, fruit, flat, 6 1/4″	$27.50	Gravy Boat, attached underplate	150.00
Bowl, soup, flat, 8 1/4″	35.00	Plate, bread and butter, 6 3/8″	15.00
Coffeepot, covered	160.00	Plate, dinner, 10 1/2″	37.50
Cream Soup and Saucer	60.00	Plate, salad, 8 3/8″	25.00
Creamer	55.00	Platter, oval, 16″	180.00
Cup, demitasse	35.00	Salt and Pepper Shakers, pair	70.00
Cup and Saucer, footed, 2 1/4″	45.00	Saucer	15.00
		Sugar Bowl, covered	70.00
		Vegetable, oval, 9 3/4″	100.00

FRANCONIA

Christoph Krautheim founded the Krautheim & Adelberg Porcelain Factory in Selb, Bavaria, Germany, in 1884 as a decorating shop. In 1912, a factory for porcelain production was added. From 1912 to the present, Krautheim & Adelberg porcelain has been imported to the United States by Hermann C. Kupper, Inc. Franconia is an export mark used since 1945.

Franconia, Delphine, platinum trim

Franconia, Hawthorne, gold trim

Creamer	$60.00
Cup and Saucer, footed, 2 1/4″	50.00
Gravy Boat, attached underplate	160.00
Lid, coffeepot	100.00
Plate, bread and butter, 6 1/8″	20.00
Plate, dinner, 10″	50.00
Plate, luncheon, 9″	35.00
Plate, salad, 7 3/4″	25.00
Platter, oval, 12″	120.00
Platter, oval, 13 5/8″	130.00
Saucer	17.50
Saucer, demitasse	15.00
Sugar Bowl, covered	70.00
Sugar Bowl, covered, no lid	50.00
Vegetable, oval, 10″	110.00
Vegetable, round, 9 3/4″	110.00

Bowl, cereal, coupe, 6 1/4″	$35.00
Bowl, fruit, 5 1/8″	25.00
Bowl, soup, flat, 7 7/8″	40.00
Cake Plate, handled, 12 5/8″	110.00
Coffeepot, covered	200.00
Cream Soup and Saucer	60.00
Cream Soup Saucer	20.00
Creamer	50.00
Cup and Saucer, demitasse	40.00
Cup and Saucer, footed, 2 1/4″	50.00
Gravy Boat, attached underplate	140.00
Lid, sugar bowl	35.00
Lid, tureen	300.00
Lid, vegetable, round	100.00
Plate, bread and butter, 6 1/8″	15.00
Plate, dinner, 10 7/8″	40.00
Plate, luncheon, 9 1/8″	30.00
Plate, salad, 8 1/4″	22.50

Platter, oval, 12″	100.00
Platter, oval, 13 3/4″	110.00
Platter, oval, 15 3/8″	140.00
Saucer	15.00
Sugar Bowl, covered	70.00
Teapot, covered	200.00
Vegetable, covered, round	200.00
Vegetable, oval, 9 7/8″	80.00
Vegetable, round, 9 7/8″	90.00
Vegetable, round, 10 3/4″	110.00

Franconia, Millefleurs, gold trim

Bowl, fruit, 5 1/4″	$32.50	Plate, dinner, 10 7/8″	40.00
Bowl, soup, flat, 8″	40.00	Plate, luncheon, 9 1/8″	35.00
Cream Soup and Saucer	70.00	Plate, salad, 7 7/8″	25.00
Cream Soup Bowl	65.00	Platter, oval, 12″	100.00
Creamer	70.00	Platter, oval, 13 3/4″	110.00
Cup and Saucer, demitasse	40.00	Platter, oval, 15 3/8″	160.00
Cup and Saucer, footed, 2 3/8″	50.00	Saucer	15.00
Gravy Boat, attached underplate	160.00	Saucer, demitasse	15.00
Lid, vegetable, round	150.00	Sugar Bowl, covered	80.00
Plate, bread and butter, 6 1/8″	17.50	Vegetable, oval, 10″	100.00
		Vegetable, round, 9 3/4″	110.00

GORHAM COMPANY

Jabez Gorham established the Gorham Company in Providence, Rhode Island, in 1831 as a manufacturer of sterling flatware and silver hollowware. Jabez's son John was responsible for developing the techniques that enabled Gorham to become one of the world's leading silversmiths. Gorham became a division of Textron, Inc. of Providence in 1967 and began developing a total tabletop marketing approach.

In 1970, Gorham acquired the Flintridge China Company of Pasadena, California, a china manufacturer that originated in 1945 as a partnership of Thomas Hogan and Milton Mason. In the next eight years, Gorham more than doubled its china manufacturing capabilities. On December 31, 1984, Gorham ceased producing china.

Quiche Dish, 10 $\frac{1}{8}$"	70.00
Salt and Pepper Shakers, pair, 3 $\frac{1}{4}$"	45.00
Saucer	10.00
Soufflé, 7"	80.00
Vegetable, oval, 10 $\frac{1}{8}$"	100.00
Vegetable, round, 8 $\frac{3}{4}$"	60.00

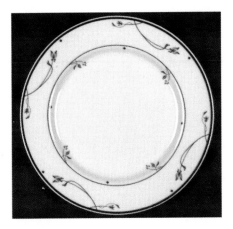

Gorham, Ariana, Standard Shape, Fine China

Augratin, individual, 8 $\frac{5}{8}$"	$30.00
Baker, oval, 12"	100.00
Baker, rectangular, 13"	160.00
Butter Dish, covered, $\frac{1}{4}$ lb.	70.00
Casserole, covered, round, 6 $\frac{1}{4}$"	180.00
Casserole, covered, round, 7"	100.00
Coffeepot, covered	170.00
Creamer	55.00
Cup and Saucer, flat, 2 $\frac{1}{4}$"	30.00
Lamp, hurricane, bottom only	30.00
Lid, casserole, round, 7"	50.00
Pie Plate, 10 $\frac{1}{4}$"	100.00
Pitcher, 6 $\frac{1}{2}$"	70.00
Plate, bread and butter	25.00
Plate, dinner	45.00
Plate, salad	30.00
Platter, oval, 14 $\frac{1}{2}$"	150.00
Platter, oval, 16 $\frac{1}{8}$"	200.00

**Gorham, Black Contessa, Coupe Shape,
Contessa Cup, Fine China**

Creamer, 3 $\frac{7}{8}$"	$85.00
Cup, footed, 2 $\frac{1}{2}$"	65.00
Cup and Saucer, footed, 2 $\frac{1}{2}$"	70.00
Plate, bread and butter, 6 $\frac{3}{8}$"	30.00
Plate, dinner	55.00
Plate, salad	40.00
Sugar Bowl, covered, no lid	75.00
Vegetable, round, 8 $\frac{1}{4}$"	130.00

Gorham, Rondelle, Standard Shape, platinum trim

Cream Soup	$80.00
Cup and Saucer, footed, 3″	60.00
Plate, bread and butter, 6 1/2″	30.00
Plate, dinner, 10 5/8″	60.00
Plate, salad, 8 3/8″	40.00
Saucer	20.00
Sugar Bowl, covered, 2 1/8″	95.00
Sugar Bowl, covered, 3″	95.00

HALL CHINA COMPANY

Robert Taggert Hall founded the Hall China Company in East Liverpool, Ohio, in 1903. Hall's ambition was to produce china using the single-fire process. For the next twelve years, Hall continued to experiment with the process while still producing enough whiteware to keep the company in business. In 1911, Hall China Company produced its first successful leadless glazed chinaware using the single-fire process.

Hall China grew rapidly and a second plant was acquired in 1919. A third plant was added in 1927, and a final move in 1930 consolidated the three separate plants into their present East Liverpool location.

Hall China Company produced Autumn Leaf for the Jewel Tea Company from 1933 to 1976. It is the most popular dinnerware pattern ever produced by Hall China.

Autumn Leaf was an exclusive line made for Jewel Tea and was sold only through the Jewel Companies. However, the decal for Autumn Leaf, produced by Commercial Decal Company of East Liverpool, Ohio, was not exclusive, and it was used by many other major dinnerware manufacturers in the early 1930s.

According to Emerson Hall, historian for the Hall China Company, Autumn Leaf was originally distributed door-to-door with laundry detergents and other household products by Jewel Tea. Jewel Tea went out of business in 1979, and Hall China has not produced original pieces since.

The Hall China Company produces Autumn Leaf commemorative pieces each year for the National Autumn Leaf Club, a collectors' club in Indianapolis, Indiana. The company also produces a few new pieces that are sold as limited editions by China Specialties of Strongsville, Ohio.

Hall China Company, Autumn Leaf, gold trim

Baker, round, 7 3/4″	$30.00
Bowl, fruit, flat, 5 1/2″	10.00
Bowl, salad, 9″	40.00
Cake Plate, 9 1/2″	40.00

Casserole, covered, round, 8″	60.00
Coffeepot, covered	75.00
Coffeepot, covered, no lid	55.00
Creamer	25.00
Cup and Saucer, flat, 2 1/4″	15.00
Custard Cup, 2 1/8″	10.00
Jug, 5 1/2″	35.00
Mixing Bowl, 6 1/4″	25.00
Pie Plate, 9 3/4″	50.00
Pitcher, 5 1/2″	50.00
Plate, bread and butter	7.50
Plate, dinner	25.00
Plate, luncheon, 9 1/8″	20.00
Plate, salad, 8 1/4″	17.50
Platter, oval, 13 5/8″	40.00
Ramekin, 4 1/8″	20.00
Vegetable, covered, oval	100.00
Vegetable, covered, oval, no lid	65.00
Vegetable, oval, 10 3/8″	40.00

HARMONY HOUSE CHINA

Harmony House is a trade name used by Sears Roebuck for products supplied by companies such as Hall China, Homer Laughlin, Laurel Potteries, Salem China, and Universal Potteries. This trademark may be the only mark found on some pieces, or it may be combined with a maker's mark.

Harmony House China, Wembley, gold trim

Bowl, fruit, 5 1/2″	$12.50
Bowl, soup, flat, 7 7/8″	20.00
Creamer	30.00
Cup and Saucer	30.00
Gravy Boat, attached underplate	70.00
Lid, vegetable, round	55.00
Plate, bread and butter, 6 3/8″	7.50
Plate, dinner, 10 1/8″	20.00
Plate, salad, 7 3/4″	12.50
Platter, oval, 12″	60.00
Platter, oval, 14 1/4″	70.00
Platter, oval, 16 1/8″	95.00
Saucer	10.00
Sugar Bowl, covered	40.00
Sugar Bowl, covered, no lid	25.00
Vegetable, covered, round	120.00
Vegetable, oval, 10 7/8″	50.00

Brothers David and Daniel Haviland established D. G. & D. Haviland, a china importing company, in New York in 1838. In 1842, David moved to Limoges, France, and in 1847 he began manufacturing and decorating china specifically for the American market. He revolutionized the French china industry by both manufacturing the whiteware blank and decorating it at the same site.

In 1852, Robert Haviland joined his brothers and D. G. & D. Haviland became Haviland and Company. The American Civil War caused the demand for Haviland china to fall, and the New York office was closed in 1863. Two years later, David's son Theodore came to the United States to market Haviland china. He met with great success, and in 1865 the factory in Limoges was expanded, with Theodore's brother, Charles Edward, taking over management. Theodore eventually found it impossible to work under his brother Charles, and on December 31, 1891, Haviland and Company was dissolved.

Charles Edward and his son George, established a new company on January 1, 1892, using the Haviland and Company name. Theodore opened a new factory in 1893, named the Theodore Haviland Company. He was joined by his son William in 1903.

Charles Edward's Haviland and Company prospered until the Great Depression, when the demand for fine porcelain plummeted. Haviland and Company ceased production in 1931.

In 1936, William Haviland's son Theodore established a porcelain factory in the United States, using the name Theodore Haviland. In 1941, William and Theodore bought all of the "designs, trademarks and rights" of the former Haviland and Company. They recombined both companies under the original name of Haviland and Company.

Theodore's brothers, Harold and Frederick, joined the company in the late 1950s. The family sold its interests in Haviland and Company in 1981.

Haviland, Appleblossom

Bowl, fruit, 5″	$35.00
Bowl, soup, flat, 7 7/8″	50.00

Cream Soup and Saucer	80.00
Creamer, 2 3/4″	80.00
Cup and Saucer, demitasse	50.00
Cup and Saucer, footed, 2 1/4″	55.00
Gravy Boat, attached underplate	200.00
Lid, coffeepot	150.00
Lid, vegetable, round	185.00
Plate, bread and butter, 6 1/2″	30.00
Plate, dinner, 10 3/4″	55.00
Plate, salad, 7 1/2″	35.00
Platter, oval, 11 5/8″	140.00
Platter, oval, 14″	190.00
Platter, oval, 16 1/4″	270.00
Saucer	20.00
Saucer, demitasse	15.00
Sugar Bowl, covered	100.00
Sugar Bowl, covered, no lid	70.00
Vegetable, covered, round	370.00

Vegetable, oval, 9 ⁵/₈″   150.00
Vegetable, round, 10 ¹/₄″   190.00

Haviland, Autumn Leaf, gold trim

Bowl, fruit, 5″	$30.00
Bowl, fruit, 5 ⁵/₈″	30.00
Bowl, soup, coupe, 7 ¹/₂″	40.00
Bowl, soup, flat, 7 ⁷/₈″	40.00
Coaster, 4 ¹/₂″	20.00
Cream Soup Saucer	25.00
Creamer, 2 ¹/₂″	80.00
Creamer, mini	55.00
Cup, flat, 2″	45.00
Cup and Saucer, footed, 2″	50.00
Gravy Boat, attached underplate	200.00
Lid, sugar bowl	45.00
Lid, teapot	125.00
Plate, bread and butter, 6 ³/₈″	25.00
Plate, dinner, 10 ¹/₄″	45.00
Plate, luncheon, 8 ⁵/₈″	35.00
Plate, salad, 7 ¹/₂″	30.00
Platter, oval, 11 ¹/₄″	120.00
Platter, oval, 13 ⁵/₈″	150.00
Platter, oval, 16″	200.00
Saucer, demitasse	15.00
Sugar Bowl, covered	100.00
Sugar Bowl, covered, mini	70.00
Vegetable, covered, round	330.00
Vegetable, oval, 9 ¹/₂″	120.00
Vegetable, round, 10 ³/₈″	150.00

Haviland, Bergere, France

Bowl, fruit, 5″	$ 45.00
Bowl, soup, coupe, 7 ¹/₂″	65.00
Creamer	100.00
Cup, flat, 2 ¹/₈″	50.00
Cup and Saucer, flat, 2 ¹/₈″	60.00
Plate, bread and butter, 6 ³/₈″	30.00
Plate, dinner, 10 ³/₈″	60.00
Plate, salad, 7 ⁵/₈″	40.00
Platter, oval, 13 ³/₈″	200.00
Platter, oval, 14″	210.00
Platter, oval, 15 ⁵/₈″	250.00
Sugar Bowl, covered	130.00
Sugar Bowl, covered, no lid	95.00
Vegetable, oval, 10 ⁵/₈″	165.00

Haviland, Clinton, New York, gold trim

Bowl, fruit, 5 ¹/₈″	$30.00
Bowl, soup, flat, 7 ⁷/₈″	45.00
Cream Soup and Saucer	70.00
Creamer	70.00

HOW TO SET A TABLE CORRECTLY

Setting a table correctly is not difficult if one combines common sense and a few basic rules. A standard dinner place setting includes: a dinner plate, salad plate, bread and butter plate, cup and saucer, dinner knife, fork, teaspoon, salad fork, soup spoon, and butter spreader, and a water goblet, wine glass, cordial, and sherbet.

Follow these popularly recognized rules for breakfast, lunch, or dinner place settings. Include only the setting pieces necessary for each meal. Keep in mind that all rules are meant to be broken, or at least bent a little on occasion.

- Allow at least 20″ of space for each place setting.
- China and silver are placed parallel, approximately 1″ from the edge of the table.
- Forks go on the left, knives and spoons on the right—from the outside in and in order of use. The exception is the cocktail fork, which goes on the right.
- All knife blades point inward.
- The bread and butter plate goes above the dinner fork, with the butter spreader laid horizontally across the top of the plate, or vertically beside it.
- The salad plate goes to the left of the forks.
- The cup and saucer go to the right of the spoons.
- The water goblet goes above the knife, with the wine glasses to the right of the goblet.

Breakfast   Lunch   Dinner

Cup and Saucer, demitasse	45.00
Cup and Saucer, footed, 2 1/4″	50.00
Gravy Boat, attached underplate	200.00
Lid, vegetable, round	135.00
Plate, bread and butter, 6 1/2″	20.00
Plate, dinner, 10 1/4″	45.00
Lid, coffeepot	150.00
Lid, sugar bowl	50.00
Plate, luncheon, 8 5/8″	40.00
Plate, salad, 7 1/2″	30.00
Platter, oval, 11 5/8″	100.00
Platter, oval, 14 1/8″	150.00
Platter, oval, 16 1/4″	200.00
Saucer	15.00
Saucer, demitasse	15.00
Sugar Bowl, covered	100.00
Vegetable, covered, round	270.00
Vegetable, oval, 9 5/8″	100.00

Haviland, Delaware, New York

| Bowl, fruit, 5 1/8″ | $25.00 |
| Bowl, soup, coupe, 7 5/8″ | 40.00 |

Cream Soup and Saucer	70.00
Creamer	70.00
Cup and Saucer, demitasse	45.00
Cup and Saucer, flat, 2 1/8″	50.00
Gravy Boat, attached underplate	200.00
Lid, teapot	150.00
Plate, bread and butter, 6 3/8″	20.00
Plate, dinner	45.00
Plate, luncheon, 8 3/4″	35.00
Plate, luncheon, square, 8″	45.00
Plate, salad, 7 1/2″	30.00
Platter, oval, 11 5/8″	100.00
Platter, oval, 14 1/8″	130.00
Platter, oval, 16 3/8″	200.00
Saucer	15.00
Saucer, demitasse	15.00
Sugar Bowl, covered	90.00
Vegetable, covered, round	300.00
Vegetable, covered, round, no lid	200.00
Vegetable, oval, 9 5/8″	100.00

Sugar Bowl, covered	115.00
Vegetable, covered, round	360.00
Vegetable, oval, 9 1/4″	135.00
Vegetable, oval, 10″	150.00
Vegetable, round, 9 1/8″	150.00
Vegetable, round 10 1/2″	165.00

Haviland, Ladore, France

Bowl, fruit, 5 1/8″	$45.00
Coaster, 4 1/2″	35.00
Coffeepot, covered	295.00
Cream Soup and Saucer	100.00
Cream Soup Bowl	90.00
Creamer	55.00
Cup, demitasse	55.00
Cup, flat, 2″	55.00
Cup and Saucer, flat, 2″	60.00
Lid, coffeepot	150.00
Plate, bread and butter, 6 3/8″	30.00
Plate, dinner, 10 3/8″	60.00
Plate, salad, 7 5/8″	40.00
Platter, oval, 13 3/8″	230.00
Sugar Bowl, covered	130.00
Sugar Bowl, covered, no lid	100.00
Vegetable, covered, oval	395.00

Haviland, Gloria

Bowl, cereal, coupe, 6 1/4″	$35.00
Bowl, fruit, 5″	35.00
Bowl, soup, coupe, 7 5/8″	45.00
Cup and Saucer, flat, 2″	60.00
Gravy Boat, attached underplate	240.00
Nut Dish	35.00
Plate, bread and butter, 6 1/4″	25.00
Plate, dinner, 9 3/4″	50.00
Plate, luncheon, 8 3/4″	40.00
Plate, salad, 7 1/2″	35.00
Platter, oval, 13 3/4″	175.00
Platter, oval, 16″	250.00
Relish, 8″	50.00
Saucer	20.00

Haviland, Montmery, France

Bowl, cereal, coupe, 6 1/4"	$35.00
Bowl, fruit, 5"	35.00
Bowl, soup, coupe, 7 1/2"	45.00
Butter Dish, covered, round	145.00
Butter Dish, covered, round, no lid	100.00
Cream Soup and Saucer	90.00
Creamer	90.00
Cup, bouillon	55.00
Cup and Saucer	60.00
Cup and Saucer, bouillon	60.00
Cup and Saucer, oversized, 2 1/4"	60.00
Gravy Boat, attached underplate	250.00
Lid, vegetable, oval	190.00
Plate, bread and butter, 6 3/8"	30.00
Plate, luncheon, 8 5/8"	40.00
Plate, dinner	50.00
Plate, salad, 7 1/2"	35.00
Platter, oval, 11 1/4"	145.00
Platter, oval, 15 7/8"	235.00
Saucer, 2"	20.00
Saucer, demitasse	20.00
Saucer, oversized, 2 1/4"	20.00
Sugar Bowl, covered	120.00
Teapot, covered, no lid	200.00
Vegetable, covered, oval	375.00
Vegetable, covered, round	375.00

Cup and Saucer, footed, 2 1/4"	50.00
Gravy Boat, attached underplate	200.00
Lid, coffeepot	120.00
Lid, sugar bowl	50.00
Lid, vegetable, round	150.00
Plate, bread and butter, 6 1/2"	20.00
Plate, dinner	40.00
Plate, salad, 7 5/8"	30.00
Platter, oval, 11 5/8"	120.00
Platter, oval, 14 1/8"	150.00
Platter, oval, 16 1/4"	200.00
Sugar Bowl, covered	100.00
Vegetable, covered, round	300.00
Vegetable, oval, 9 5/8"	110.00

Haviland, Pasadena, New York

Bowl, fruit, 5"	$30.00
Bowl, soup, flat, 7 7/8"	40.00
Coffeepot, covered	280.00
Cream Soup and Saucer	70.00
Cream Soup Saucer	25.00
Creamer	70.00
Cup, demitasse	42.00
Cup, footed, 2 1/4"	45.00
Cup and Saucer, demitasse	45.00

Haviland, Princess, France

Bowl, cranberry, 5 5/8"	$115.00
Bowl, fruit, flat, 5 1/8"	25.00
Bowl, soup, flat, 7 1/2"	45.00
Butter Dish, covered, round, no lid	100.00
Butter Pat, 3 1/8"	25.00
Cup and Saucer, bouillon	60.00
Cup and Saucer, demitasse, 2 1/4"	50.00
Cup and Saucer, flat, 2 1/8"	55.00
Gravy Boat, attached underplate	200.00

Lid, vegetable, round, for footed vegetable	150.00
Nut Dish, 5 ³/₄″	45.00
Plate, bread and butter, 6 ¹/₄″	25.00
Plate, dinner, 9 ³/₄″	50.00
Plate, luncheon, 8 ⁵/₈″	30.00
Plate, salad, 7 ¹/₂″	30.00
Platter, oval, 12 ¹/₈″	140.00
Platter, oval, 14 ¹/₈″	160.00
Platter, oval, 16 ¹/₄″	220.00
Relish, 7 ¹/₄″	60.00
Relish, 8 ¹/₂″	60.00
Saucer	20.00
Saucer, demitasse	15.00
Sugar Bowl, covered, 3 ¹/₈″	120.00
Sugar Bowl, covered, 4″	120.00
Vegetable, covered, oval	300.00
Vegetable, covered, round	300.00
Vegetable, covered, no lid	200.00
Vegetable, oval, 9 ⁷/₈″	120.00
Vegetable, round, 9″	160.00
Vegetable, round, 10 ¹/₈″	165.00

Saucer, 2″	10.00
Saucer, 2 ¹/₄″	10.00
Saucer, bouillon	10.00
Vegetable, covered, oval	260.00
Vegetable, covered, round	260.00
Vegetable, oval, 9 ¹/₄″	100.00
Vegetable, oval, 10″	110.00
Vegetable, round, 9 ⁵/₈″	110.00
Vegetable, round, 10 ¹/₄″	120.00

Haviland, Ranson, all white

Bowl, fruit, 5 ³/₄″	$25.00
Bowl, soup, coupe, 7 ³/₈″	40.00
Cup and Saucer, flat, 2″	45.00
Gravy Boat, attached underplate	160.00
Lid, vegetable, oval, for footed vegetable	125.00
Plate, bread and butter, 6 ¹/₄″	20.00
Plate, dinner	35.00
Plate, luncheon, 8 ⁵/₈″	30.00
Plate, salad	30.00
Platter, oval, 11 ⁵/₈″	100.00
Platter, oval, 13 ⁵/₈″	110.00
Platter, oval, 15 ³/₄″	165.00
Platter, oval, 16″	185.00
Platter, oval, 17 ⁵/₈″	200.00
Ramekin, 3 ⁵/₈″	40.00

Haviland, Rosalinde, France, gold trim

Bowl, fruit, 5″	$45.00
Bowl, soup, coupe, 7 ¹/₂″	50.00
Coffeepot, covered	295.00
Cream Soup Saucer	35.00
Creamer, 3 ¹/₄″	90.00
Cup, demitasse	60.00
Cup and Saucer, flat, 2″	65.00
Gravy Boat, attached underplate	290.00
Plate, bread and butter, 6 ¹/₂″	30.00
Plate, dinner, 10 ¹/₂″	60.00
Plate, salad, 7 ⁵/₈″	40.00
Platter, oval, 13 ³/₄″	200.00
Saucer	20.00
Sugar Bowl, covered	120.00
Vegetable, oval, 9 ¹/₂″	150.00

Haviland, Rosalinde, New York, gold trim

Bowl, fruit, 5 1/8″	$35.00
Bowl, soup, coupe, 7 1/2″	50.00
Coffeepot, covered, no lid	205.00
Creamer	80.00
Cup and Saucer, demitasse	55.00
Cup and Saucer, flat, 2″	60.00
Gravy Boat, attached underplate	200.00
Lid, sugar bowl	50.00
Plate, bread and butter, 6 1/2″	30.00
Plate, dinner, 10 1/2″	55.00
Plate, luncheon, 8 3/4″	45.00
Plate, salad, 7 1/2″	35.00
Platter, oval, 11 5/8″	140.00
Platter, oval, 14 1/8″	200.00
Platter, oval, 16 3/8″	230.00
Saucer	20.00
Saucer, demitasse	20.00
Sugar Bowl, covered	100.00
Vegetable, covered, round	350.00
Vegetable, oval, 9 5/8″	140.00

Bowl, fruit, 5 1/8″	30.00
Bowl, soup, coupe, 7 5/8″	40.00
Chocolate Pot	400.00
Chop Plate, 11 1/4″	180.00
Cream Soup and Saucer	85.00
Cream Soup Bowl	75.00
Cup and Saucer, bouillon, 1 7/8″	50.00
Cup and Saucer, flat, 1 7/8″	50.00
Cup and Saucer, oversized, 2″	55.00
Gravy Boat, attached underplate	220.00
Lid, teapot	125.00
Plate, bread and butter, 6 1/4″	25.00
Plate, dinner, 9 3/4″	45.00
Plate, luncheon, 8 5/8″	35.00
Plate, salad, 7 1/2″	30.00
Platter, oval, 11 3/4″	120.00
Platter, oval, 14″	150.00
Platter, oval, 16 1/4″	240.00
Ramekin and Saucer, 3 3/4″	55.00
Ramekin, 3 3/4″	45.00
Saucer, 1 7/8″	15.00
Saucer, demitasse	15.00
Saucer, oversized	20.00
Sugar Bowl, covered	100.00
Tureen, covered	600.00
Vegetable, covered, round	300.00
Vegetable, covered, round, no lid	200.00
Vegetable, oval, 9 1/4″	120.00
Vegetable, oval, 10 1/8″	130.00
Vegetable, round, 8 3/4″	120.00
Vegetable, round, 9 1/4″	130.00

Haviland, Varenne

Bowl, fruit, 5 1/8″	$30.00
Bowl, soup, coupe, 7 1/2″	50.00
Chop Plate, 12 3/4″	200.00
Cream Soup and Saucer	80.00
Cream Soup Saucer	25.00
Creamer	80.00

Haviland, Silver Anniversary, gold trim

Bone Dish, 6″	$40.00
Bowl, cranberry, 5 3/4″	120.00

Cup and Saucer, demitasse	50.00	Platter, oval, 14 1/8″	170.00
Cup and Saucer, flat, 2 1/8″	55.00	Platter, oval, 16 3/8″	230.00
Gravy Boat, attached underplate	200.00	Saucer	20.00
Lid, vegetable	150.00	Saucer, demitasse	15.00
Plate, bread and butter, 6 1/2″	25.00	Sugar Bowl, covered	110.00
Plate, dinner, 9 3/4″	45.00	Sugar Bowl, covered, no lid	70.00
Plate, dinner, 10 3/8″	45.00	Vegetable, covered, round	300.00
Plate, luncheon, 8 3/4″	35.00	Vegetable, oval, 9 3/8″	120.00
Plate, salad	30.00	Vegetable, oval, 9 3/4″	120.00
Platter, oval, 11 5/8″	130.00	Vegetable, round, 10″	160.00

The Herend Porcelain Factory has been in production since 1826. Its name is derived from the small village of Herend, near Budapest, Hungary. Moric Fischer joined the company in 1839 and directed Herend into the field of reproducing old porcelain patterns. His work was highly acclaimed, prompting Herend to begin producing original designs.

At the London World Exhibition in 1851, Queen Victoria ordered a large table service for Windsor Castle. The pattern, later named Queen Victoria, is one of Herend's most famous designs. Many aristocrats followed the Queen's lead, and Herend produced hundreds of different patterns over the next 150 years. Their most popular pattern, Rothschild Bird, was commissioned by Baron de Rothschild in 1850. Herend's first exposure to the American market was a medal-winning entry at the New York Exhibition of Industrial Arts in 1853.

Fischer was elevated to nobility and was titled Moritz Fischer von Farkasbazy in 1866, in honor of his contributions to Hungarian industry. His grandson Jeno took over in 1897 and continued Herend's tradition of successes at international exhibitions.

Upon Jeno's death in 1926, leadership of the factory was passed to Counts Andras and Moric Eszterbazy. The factory was nationalized in 1943.

Lake Balaton, near Budapest, Hungary, is an area evolved from volcanic eruptions. It is surrounded by lush trees and brush and enclosed caves, contributing to much of Hungary's folklore and romantic legends. It is this area and one of its popular legends that inspired Herend's founder, Mor Fischer, in one of his creations.

Legend tells of an early nineteenth-century princess traveling with her entourage along the shores of Lake Balaton. A band of robbers hiding in a cave jumped out, accosted the princess and her companions, and took all of their valuables, including the royal jewels worn by the princess. In their hasty retreat, the robbers dropped a necklace on the ground, where it lay unnoticed. The princess and her group returned to the palace with news of the robbery, and a search party was sent to look for the thieves.

Meanwhile, a bird attracted by the glittering bauble scooped it up and took it to her nest. When the search party arrived at the site of the robbery, one of the members noticed the necklace dangling from a branch alongside the nest. The recovery of the necklace from the tree was considered a good omen, and the jubilant party returned to the palace with the treasure.

This story, passed from generation to generation, was the inspiration for the Rothschild Bird pattern. Fischer incorporated the necklace into the 1850 design of this pattern, one of the most popular Herend patterns to date.

Herend, Rothschild Bird

Ashtray, 5 3/8″	$125.00
Ashtray, medium	75.00
Ashtray, oval, 3 1/2″	35.00
Basket, open weave, 4″	95.00
Basket, open weave, 5″	80.00
Bonbon, covered, 3″	85.00
Bowl, fruit, 11 1/8″	365.00
Bowl, fruit, square	250.00
Bowl, melon, 8 1/2″	235.00
Bowl, soup, flat	70.00
Box, 5″	175.00
Bud Vase, 2 3/4″	55.00
Bud Vase, 5 1/4″	55.00
Candlestick, double light	275.00
Candy Box	265.00
Cheese Dish, covered	245.00
Chop Plate, 12 3/4″	195.00
Chop Plate, handled, 11″	220.00
Cigarette Holder	80.00
Coaster, 3 1/8″	40.00
Coffeepot, covered, mini, no lid	115.00
Cream Soup and Saucer	150.00
Cup, demitasse	70.00
Cup, flat, 2″	85.00

Cup and Saucer, breakfast, 2 1/4″	150.00
Cup and Saucer, chocolate	80.00
Cup and Saucer, demitasse	75.00
Cup and Saucer, flat, 2″	90.00
Cup and Saucer, footed, 2″	90.00
Dish, leaf shape, 9 1/2″	125.00
Eggcup, double, 3 7/8″	60.00
Eggcup, single	40.00
Ginger Jar, covered, 5″, no lid	135.00
Hors d'oeuvre Holder	60.00
Hors d'oeuvre, three section, 9 3/4″	200.00
Ink Stand, no lids	270.00
Lid, tureen	425.00
Match Box Holder	45.00
Nappy, 4 1/4″	60.00
Pepper Shaker	35.00
Plate, bread and butter, 6 1/2″	40.00
Plate, dinner, 10″	70.00
Plate, luncheon, 9″	80.00
Plate, salad	50.00
Platter, oval, 10 1/2″	240.00
Platter, oval, 15″	230.00
Platter, oval, 16 1/2″	345.00
Platter, oval, 18 1/4″	365.00
Ring Holder	55.00
Salt and Pepper Shakers, pair	65.00
Salt Dip, 5 3/4″	55.00
Sauce Boat	125.00
Sauce Boat, covered, individual, no lid	80.00
Saucer	30.00
Saucer, demitasse	25.00
Sugar Bowl, covered, mini, no lid	55.00
Teapot, covered	240.00
Tureen, covered	850.00
Urn, round, footed	210.00
Vase, 4 5/8″	75.00
Vegetable, covered, round	400.00
Vegetable, oval, 8 3/4″	80.00
Vegetable, round, 9 3/4″	130.00

On September 1, 1874, Homer and Shakespeare Laughlin opened The Homer Laughlin China Company in East Liverpool, Ohio. Their aim was to produce ceramics that fired to a stark white, rather than the yellowware pieces produced by the dozen or more area potteries. Their perseverance paid off and in 1876 the company was awarded a medal and certificate for quality whiteware at the Centennial Exhibition in Philadelphia. Shakespeare Laughlin sold his interest in the business in 1877.

In 1886, Homer Laughlin developed genuine American china. It was one of his major ceramic achievements. W. E. Wells entered the business as a bookkeeper in the late 1880s, and when Homer Laughlin left the firm in 1897, Wells, Louis I. Aaron, and Louis's two sons, Marcus and Charles, bought interests in the company.

The Homer Laughlin China Company grew from its original two kilns in 1874 to thirty-two kilns by 1899. When further expansion became necessary, the company moved across the Ohio River to the town of Newell, in West Virginia. The company continued to prosper and expand throughout the 1930s. In 1935, it introduced its most successful and popular dinnerware line—Fiesta.

For most of its years, The Homer Laughlin China Company was the world's largest manufacturer of dinnerware. One-third of all dinnerware sold in the United States was produced at the Homer Laughlin factories.

THE HOMER LAUGHLIN CHINA COMPANY, FIESTA

Frederick Hurton Rhead joined the Homer Laughlin China Company in 1927. His experiments with different shapes and glazes culminated in the creation of Fiesta in 1935. An Art Deco design, it is the most successful and sought-after line of dinnerware produced by Homer Laughlin. The ten colors featured here were all discontinued when Fiesta production ceased in 1972. Fiesta was reintroduced in 1986 with all new colors.

Homer Laughlin, Fiesta-Chartreuse

Cup and Saucer	$45.00
Plate, bread and butter, 6 ½"	10.00
Plate, dinner	50.00
Plate, salad	15.00
Saucer	15.00

Homer Laughlin, Fiesta-Cream

Bowl, fruit, 4 ¾"	$30.00
Bowl, soup, flat, 8 ½"	50.00
Chop Plate, 12 ¼"	50.00
Cream Soup Bowl	50.00
Creamer, ring handle	25.00
Cup and Saucer, footed, 2 ¾"	40.00
Plate, grill, 10 ½"	45.00
Marmalade, covered, no lid	110.00
Plate, bread and butter, 6 ⅜"	7.50
Plate, dinner	35.00
Plate, luncheon, 9 ½"	20.00
Plate, salad, 7 ⅜"	12.50
Salt Shaker	15.00
Sauce Boat	60.00
Saucer	15.00
Saucer, demitasse	25.00
Tumbler, juice, 3 ½"	40.00

Homer Laughlin, Fiesta-Cobalt Blue

Bowl, fruit, 4 ¾"	$35.00
Bowl, fruit, 5 ½"	35.00
Bowl, fruit, 6 ¼"	50.00
Creamer, ring handle, 3"	40.00
Cup and Saucer, footed, 2 ¾"	45.00
Lid, teapot	100.00
Plate, bread and butter, 6 ¼"	15.00
Plate, dinner, 10 ½"	50.00
Plate, luncheon, 9 ½"	30.00
Plate, salad, 7 ½"	17.50
Salt Shaker	20.00
Sauce Boat	85.00

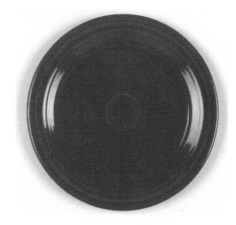

Homer Laughlin, Fiesta-Dark Green

Bowl, soup, flat, 8 ⅜"	$50.00
Creamer, ring handle	35.00
Cup and Saucer	45.00
Plate, bread and butter	15.00

Plate, dinner   50.00
Plate, salad   17.50

Homer Laughlin, Fiesta-Light Green

Bowl, fruit, 4 3/4″	$20.00
Bowl, fruit, 5 1/2″	25.00
Chop Plate, 12 1/4″	50.00
Cup and Saucer, footed, 2 3/4″	35.00
Plate, bread and butter, 6 3/8″	7.50
Plate, dinner, 10 3/8″	35.00
Plate, luncheon, 9 1/2″	20.00
Plate, salad, 7 1/2″	10.00
Platter, oval, 12 5/8″	50.00
Salt Shaker	15.00
Saucer	10.00

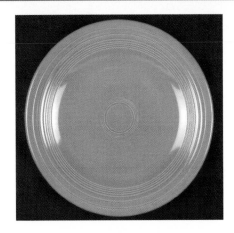

Homer Laughlin, Fiesta-Red

Bowl, fruit, 4 3/4″	$35.00
Bowl, fruit, 5 1/2″	35.00
Creamer, ring handle	35.00
Cup and Saucer, footed, 2 3/4″	40.00
Plate, bread and butter, 6 3/8″	12.50
Plate, dinner	50.00
Plate, luncheon, 9 1/2″	35.00
Plate, salad, 7 1/2″	17.50
Sauce Boat	85.00
Saucer	15.00
Sugar Bowl, covered, no lid	35.00

Homer Laughlin, Fiesta-Medium Green

Cup and Saucer	$60.00
Plate, bread and butter	17.50
Plate, dinner	80.00
Plate, salad	27.50

Homer Laughlin, Fiesta-Rose

Creamer, ring handle	$35.00
Cup and Saucer	50.00
Eggcup, single, 3 1/8″	130.00
Mug, Tom & Jerry, 3″	90.00
Plate, bread and butter, 6 1/2″	10.00
Plate, dinner	50.00
Plate, luncheon, 9 1/2″	25.00
Plate, salad	17.50
Saucer	17.50

Homer Laughlin, Fiesta-Turquoise

Bowl, fruit, 4 3/4″	$25.00
Bowl, fruit, 5 1/2″	25.00
Bowl, soup, flat, 8 3/8″	35.00
Casserole, covered, round, 7 7/8″, no lid	105.00
Chop Plate, 12 1/4″	50.00
Cup and Saucer, footed, 2 3/4″	30.00
Nappy, 8 1/2″	35.00
Plate, bread and butter, 6 1/4″	7.50
Plate, dinner	35.00
Plate, luncheon, 9 1/2″	25.00
Plate, salad, 7 1/2″	12.50
Sauce Boat	50.00
Saucer	10.00

Homer Laughlin, Fiesta-Yellow

Bowl, fruit, 4 3/4″	$20.00
Bowl, fruit, 5 1/2″	25.00
Bowl, fruit, 6 1/4″	30.00
Bowl, soup, flat, 8 3/8″	35.00
Chop Plate, 12 1/8″	45.00
Chop Plate, 14 1/4″	45.00
Cream Soup Bowl	35.00
Creamer, ring handle	25.00
Cup and Saucer, footed, 2 3/4″	30.00
Eggcup, single, 3″	45.00
Marmalade, covered, no lid	135.00
Nappy, 8 1/2″	30.00
Pepper Shaker	10.00
Plate, bread and butter, 6 3/8″	7.50
Plate, dinner	30.00
Plate, luncheon, 9 1/2″	20.00
Plate, salad, 7 1/2″	10.00
Platter, oval, 12 1/2″	45.00
Salt and Pepper Shakers, pair	22.50
Sauce Boat	50.00
Saucer	10.00
Sugar Bowl, covered	35.00
Sugar Bowl, covered, no lid	25.00

Carl Magnus Hutschenreuther established Hutschenreuther AG, a German porcelain decorating factory in Hohenberg, Bavaria, in 1814. Unsatisfied with just decorating, Hutschenreuther yearned to produce his own porcelain wares. After an eight-year struggle with the Bavarian government, which opposed competition to The Royal Manufactory at Nymphenburg, Hutschenreuther finally received the necessary permission in 1822. Hutschenreuther was responsible for bringing porcelain to the common man and was a pioneer of the modern-day German china industry. Upon his death in 1845, his widow Johanna carried on his work with the help of her two grown sons, Christian and Lorenz.

In 1857, Lorenz struck out on his own to establish the first porcelain factory in "Ludwigsmühle" (mill of Ludwig), the origin of today's Selb, or "City of Porcelain." The Lorenz Hutschenreuther and C. M. Hutschenreuther companies were two totally independent businesses.

When Lorenz died in 1886, his sons Viktor and Eugen took over his company. They acquired the Selb factories of Jaeger, Werner & Company in 1906 and the Paul Müller China Factory in 1917. The Bauscher Brothers Porcelain Factory and the Tirschenreuth Porcelain Factory of Weiden were added in 1927. The Konigszelt Porcelain Factory was acquired the following year.

C. M. Hutschenreuther also expanded during these years, acquiring a porcelain factory in Arzberg in 1880 and factories in Selesia, Bohemia, and Saxonia in the early 1900s. These factories were lost when Germany was divided after World War II.

In 1969, the two companies were united. Since 1970, the combined enterprises have been called Hutschenreuther AG.

In early 1971, Hutschenreuther AG acquired a 50 percent interest in the Portuguese factory Sociedade de Porcelanas Limitada in Coimbra. In 1972, Hutschenreuther AG merged with Porcelain Factory Kahla AG of Schonwald. This merger brought Kahla's two crude ceramics factories into the business, along with the well-known trademarks Arzberg and Schonwald.

According to company records, Hutschenreuther AG now comprises fifteen production sites. With a workforce of 6,000, it is the largest porcelain producer on the European continent.

Hutschenreuther, Revere, Sylvia

Bowl, fruit, 5 1/4″	$35.00
Bowl, soup, flat, 8 3/8″	50.00
Butter Dish, covered, round, no lid	180.00
Cake Plate, handled, 12 1/4″	150.00
Coffeepot, covered	250.00
Coffeepot, covered, no lid	190.00
Cream Soup and Saucer	90.00
Cream Soup Saucer	30.00
Creamer, 3 7/8″	80.00
Creamer, 4 7/8″	80.00
Creamer, Sugar, and Tray, covered	200.00
Creamer, mini, 3 3/4″	50.00

Cup, demitasse	50.00
Cup and Saucer, demitasse	55.00
Cup and Saucer, footed, 2 1/4″	60.00
Eggcup, single, 2 1/8″	30.00
Gravy Boat, attached underplate	190.00
Plate, bread and butter, 6 1/4″	25.00
Plate, dinner, 10 1/4″	50.00
Plate, salad, 7 7/8″	35.00
Platter, oval, 12 3/4″	150.00
Platter, oval, 15″	240.00
Relish, 10 1/8″	80.00
Relish, five-part, 12 1/2″	110.00
Saucer	20.00
Sugar Bowl, covered, 3 1/2″	100.00
Sugar Bowl, covered, 3 1/2″, no lid	75.00
Sugar Bowl, covered, mini	70.00
Tray, sandwich, 13″	150.00
Vegetable, covered, round	350.00
Vegetable, oval, 10 1/4″	140.00
Vegetable, round, 10 1/2″	150.00

Hutschenreuther, Richelieu, gold trim

Bowl, soup, flat, 8 1/2″	$40.00
Cream Soup and Saucer	60.00
Cream Soup Saucer	20.00
Creamer, 3 1/2″	55.00
Creamer, 4 1/8″	55.00
Cup and Saucer, demitasse	35.00

Cup and Saucer, flat, 2 1/8″	45.00
Gravy Boat, attached underplate	130.00
Lid, sugar bowl, 3″	35.00
Plate, bread and butter, 6 1/8″	20.00
Plate, dinner, 9 7/8″	40.00
Plate, salad, 7 3/4″	25.00
Platter, oval, 12 5/8″	100.00
Platter, oval, 15 1/4″	140.00
Saucer, demitasse	10.00
Sugar Bowl, covered, 3″	65.00
Sugar Bowl, covered, 3 1/2″	65.00
Vegetable, covered, round	250.00
Vegetable, covered, round, no lid	200.00
Vegetable, oval, 8 7/8″	80.00
Vegetable, oval, 10 1/4″	100.00
Vegetable, round, 9 7/8″	110.00

IMPERIAL CHINA

There is a strong possibility that Imperial China is British in origin. The name appears to be a manufacturer's trade name. Wedgwood & Co., a different company from Wedgwood, is a strong contender based on an examination of the mark listings in Geoffrey Godden's *Encyclopedia of British Pottery and Porcelain Marks*, reprinted by Schiffer Publishing, Ltd.

The backstamp on a piece of Seville pattern Imperial China includes a script signature for "W. Dalton." William B. Dalton, born in London in 1900, was a British studio potter. He probably supplemented his studio income by doing design work. Dalton, the author of several books on pottery, emigrated to the United States in 1941.

Imperial, Seville, gold trim

Bowl, fruit, 5 1/2″	$12.50
Bowl, soup, coupe, 7 1/2″	17.50
Chop Plate, 12″	50.00
Creamer	30.00
Cup and Saucer, footed, 2 1/4″	22.50
Gravy Boat, attached underplate	60.00
Lid, sugar bowl	15.00
Plate, bread and butter, 6 5/8″	5.00
Plate, dinner, 10 3/8″	17.50
Plate, salad	12.50
Platter, oval, 16 3/8″	80.00
Sauce Boat	60.00
Sugar Bowl, covered	30.00
Vegetable, round, 9″	45.00

Imperial, Whitney, platinum trim

Bowl, fruit, 5 1/2″	$10.00
Bowl, soup, coupe, 7 1/2″	15.00
Chop Plate, 12 3/8″	55.00
Creamer	25.00
Cup and Saucer, footed, 2 3/8″	15.00
Gravy Boat, attached underplate	45.00
Lid, coffeepot	35.00
Plate, bread and butter, 6 1/2″	5.00
Plate, dinner, 10 3/8″	15.00
Plate, salad, 7 5/8″	10.00
Platter, oval, 16 3/8″	70.00
Platter, oval, 16 5/8″	70.00
Sauce Boat	45.00
Saucer	5.00
Sugar Bowl, covered	30.00
Vegetable, round, 9 1/8″	40.00
Vinegar	30.00
Vinegar and Oil, stoppers	60.00
Vinegar Stopper	10.00

Johann Haviland, Moss Rose

Bowl, fruit, 5 1/4″	$15.00
Bowl, soup, coupe, 7 3/4″	22.50
Creamer	35.00
Cup and Saucer, footed, 2 5/8″	27.50
Gravy Boat, attached underplate	90.00
Plate, bread and butter, 6 1/4″	10.00
Plate, dinner, 10″	25.00
Plate, salad, 7 3/4″	17.50
Platter, oval, 13″	70.00
Platter, oval, 14 3/4″	80.00
Saucer	10.00
Sugar Bowl, covered	50.00
Vegetable, covered, round, no lid	90.00
Vegetable, oval, 10 3/4″	65.00
Vegetable, round, 8 1/2″	55.00

JOHNSON BROTHERS

Johnson Brothers was established in 1883 when three brothers—Alfred, Frederick, and Henry Johnson—purchased the bankrupt J. W. Pankhurst Company, a tableware manufactory in Hanley, Staffordshire, England. Although it began on a small scale, the company prospered and expanded.

In 1896, another brother, Robert, joined the firm. Robert lived and worked in the United States, expanding the Johnson Brothers' American market. By 1914, Johnson Brothers owned and operated five additional factories scattered throughout Hanley, Tunstall, and Burslem.

Johnson Brothers continued to grow throughout the 1960s, with acquisitions of tableware manufacturing plants in Hamilton, Ontario, Canada, and Croydon, Australia. Two additional local plants were acquired in 1960 and 1965.

Johnson Brothers became part of the Wedgwood Group in 1968.

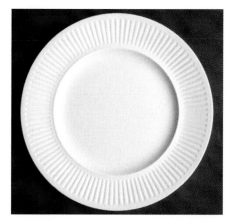

Platter, oval, 13 1/2″	40.00
Salt and Pepper Shakers, pair	32.50
Saucer	5.00
Saucer, demitasse	5.00
Sugar Bowl, covered	30.00
Sugar Bowl, covered, no lid	20.00
Teapot, covered	60.00
Tureen, covered	160.00
Vegetable, covered, oval	85.00
Vegetable, covered, round	85.00
Vegetable, oval, 9 1/8″	30.00
Vegetable, round, 8 3/4″	30.00

Johnson Brothers, Athena, all white

Bowl, cereal, coupe, 6 1/2″	$10.00
Bowl, fruit, 5 1/4″	10.00
Bowl, soup, coupe, 7 3/8″	12.50
Butter Dish, covered, 1/4 lb.	40.00
Chop Plate, 12 3/8″	35.00
Coffeepot, covered	60.00
Creamer	22.50
Cup and Saucer, flat, 2 3/4″	15.00
Gravy Boat and Underplate	50.00
Gravy Boat Underplate	15.00
Lid, coffeepot	30.00
Mug, 3 1/4″	15.00
Pitcher, 4 3/4″	40.00
Plate, bread and butter, 6 3/8″	5.00
Plate, dinner, 10″	15.00
Plate, salad	10.00
Platter, oval, 11 3/4″	32.50

Johnson Brothers, Blue Nordic

Bowl, cereal, coupe, 6 1/8″	$15.00
Bowl, fruit, 5 1/8″	12.50

Bowl, rice, 4 1/4″	30.00
Bowl, soup, flat, 8 5/8″	17.50
Butter Dish, covered, 1/4 lb.	65.00
Coffeepot, covered	90.00
Coffeepot, covered, no lid	60.00
Cream Soup Bowl	25.00
Cream Soup Saucer	10.00
Creamer	35.00
Cup, demitasse	17.50
Cup, flat, 2 5/8″	15.00
Cup and Saucer, flat, 2 5/8″	20.00
Eggcup, single	7.50
Gravy Boat	65.00
Gravy Boat and Underplate	65.00
Lid, butter dish, 1/4 lb.	45.00
Lid, tureen	125.00
Pepper Shaker	17.50
Pitcher, 6″	50.00
Plate, bread and butter, 6 1/4″	7.50
Plate, dinner, 9 3/4″	20.00
Plate, salad, 7 3/4″	15.00
Platter, oval, 12″	45.00
Platter, oval, 13 1/2″	55.00
Platter, oval, 15 3/4″	85.00
Relish, 7 3/4″	22.50
Salt and Pepper Shakers, pair	35.00
Sugar Bowl, covered	40.00
Teapot, covered	90.00
Tray, sandwich, 12 3/4″	55.00
Tureen, covered	250.00
Vegetable, covered, round	100.00
Vegetable, oval, 8 7/8″	40.00
Vegetable, round, 8 1/4″	40.00

Johnson Brothers, Coaching Scenes, blue

Bowl, cereal, coupe, 6″	$15.00
Bowl, fruit, 5 1/8″	12.50
Bowl, soup, flat, 8 5/8″	17.50
Chop Plate, 12″	60.00
Coffeepot, covered	90.00
Cream Soup and Saucer	35.00
Cream Soup Saucer	12.50
Creamer	35.00
Cup, flat, 2 3/4″	15.00
Cup and Saucer, flat, 2 3/4″	20.00
Gravy Boat and Underplate	65.00
Lid, coffeepot	45.00
Lid, teapot	40.00
Lid, tureen	125.00
Pitcher, 5 3/4″	50.00
Plate, bread and butter, 6 1/4″	7.50
Plate, dinner, 9 7/8″	20.00

Plate, luncheon, 8 1/2″	15.00
Plate, salad, 7 7/8″	12.50
Platter, oval, 12″	40.00
Platter, oval, 13 3/4″	60.00
Platter, oval, 14″	70.00
Platter, oval, 15 3/4″	85.00
Saucer	7.50
Sugar Bowl, covered	40.00
Sugar Bowl, covered, mini	25.00
Teapot, covered	85.00
Tureen, covered	250.00
Vegetable, covered, round	100.00
Vegetable, oval, 8 3/4″	35.00
Vegetable, round, 8 1/4″	32.50

Saucer, demitasse	10.00
Sugar Bowl, covered, no lid	35.00
Vegetable, covered, round, no lid	120.00
Vegetable, covered, square, no lid	120.00
Vegetable, oval, 9″	55.00
Vegetable, round, 8 3/8″	50.00

Johnson Brothers, Friendly Village

Bowl, cereal, coupe, 6 1/8″	$7.50
Bowl, cereal, square, 6 1/8″	7.50
Bowl, fruit, 5 1/8″	5.00
Bowl, soup, flat, 8 5/8″	12.50
Butter Dish, covered, 1/4 lb.	50.00
Chop Plate, 12 1/4″	50.00
Coaster, 4 1/8″	5.00
Coffeepot, covered, no lid	45.00
Creamer	25.00
Cup, flat, 2 3/8″	10.00
Cup and Saucer, flat, 2 3/8″	15.00
Cup and Saucer, oversized, 3 1/8″	22.50
Gravy Boat	45.00
Mug, 3 3/4″	12.50
Pitcher, 5 1/2″	40.00
Plate, bread and butter, 6″	5.00
Plate, dessert, 7″	5.00
Plate, dinner, 9 7/8″	12.50
Plate, luncheon, 8 5/8″	10.00
Plate, salad, 7 5/8″	7.50
Plate, salad, square, 7 5/8″	7.50
Platter, oval, 13 1/2″	40.00
Platter, oval, 15 1/8″	55.00
Platter, oval, 20″	160.00
Relish, three-part, 13 7/8″	60.00
Relish, 8″	25.00
Salt and Pepper Shakers, pair	35.00
Spoon Holder	20.00
Teapot, covered	60.00
Tray, serving, two-tiered	35.00

Johnson Brothers, English Chippendale

Bowl, cereal, lug, 5 7/8″	$20.00
Bowl, cereal, lug, 7 1/8″	20.00
Bowl, cereal, flat, 6 1/4″	20.00
Bowl, cereal, square, 6 1/4″	20.00
Bowl, fruit, 5 1/4″	15.00
Bowl, soup, flat, 8″	25.00
Bowl, soup, square, 7″	25.00
Creamer	40.00
Cup and Saucer, flat, 2 1/4″	30.00
Gravy Boat	70.00
Gravy Boat, attached underplate	90.00
Gravy Boat and Underplate	90.00
Lid, teapot	60.00
Lid, tureen	150.00
Plate, bread and butter, 6 3/8″	12.50
Plate, dessert, 7″	15.00
Plate, dinner, 10″	25.00
Plate, luncheon, 8 7/8″	20.00
Plate, salad, square, 7 1/2″	15.00
Platter, oval, 11 1/4″	65.00
Platter, oval, 12″	65.00
Platter, oval, 15 1/2″	100.00
Saucer	10.00

Tureen, covered	200.00
Vegetable, covered, round	75.00
Vegetable, oval, 8 ¾″	30.00
Vegetable, round, 8″	22.50

Johnson Brothers, Fruit Sampler

Bowl, cereal, coupe, 6 ½″	$15.00
Bowl, fruit, 5 ¼″	15.00
Creamer	30.00
Cup and Saucer, flat, 2 ⅝″	22.50
Gravy Boat and Underplate	70.00
Gravy Boat	60.00
Lid, coffeepot	50.00
Plate, bread and butter, 6 ⅜″	7.50
Plate, dinner, 10 ⅛″	20.00
Plate, salad, 8 ⅛″	15.00
Platter, oval, 12 ¼″	50.00
Platter, oval, 14 ⅛″	55.00
Salt and Pepper Shakers, pair	40.00
Saucer	7.50
Sugar Bowl, covered	32.50
Sugar Bowl, covered, no lid	27.50
Teapot, covered	100.00
Vegetable, covered, round	110.00
Vegetable, round, 8 ½″	40.00

Johnson Brothers, Garden Bouquet, shaped rim

Bowl, fruit, 5 ⅛″	$12.50
Bowl, soup, flat, 8″	22.50
Cream Soup Saucer	12.50
Creamer	30.00
Cup and Saucer, flat, 2 ⅜″	25.00
Gravy Boat	70.00
Gravy Boat, attached underplate	80.00
Gravy Boat and Underplate	80.00
Lid, coffeepot	50.00
Plate, bread and butter, 6 ⅜″	7.50
Plate, dessert, 7″	10.00

Plate, dinner, 10″	25.00
Plate, salad, 8″	15.00
Platter, oval, 12 ⅛″	50.00
Platter, oval, 14 ⅛″	60.00
Saucer	10.00
Saucer, demitasse	7.50
Sugar Bowl, covered	40.00
Sugar Bowl, covered, no lid	27.50
Vegetable, covered, round	130.00
Vegetable, covered, round, no lid	90.00
Vegetable, oval, 9 ⅝″	45.00

Johnson Brothers, Hearts & Flowers

Creamer	$30.00
Cup and Saucer, flat, 2 ½″	25.00
Gravy Boat	65.00
Plate, bread and butter, 6 ⅜″	15.00
Plate, dinner, 10″	25.00
Plate, salad	17.50
Platter, oval, 12 ¼″	60.00
Platter, oval, 14″	70.00
Saucer	10.00
Sugar Bowl, covered	40.00

Sugar Bowl, covered, no lid 27.50
Vegetable, covered, round, no lid 120.00
Vegetable, round, 8 3/8" 50.00

Johnson Brothers, Heritage Hall

Bowl, cereal, coupe, 6 1/8" $15.00
Butter Dish, covered, 1/4 lb. 60.00
Butter Dish, covered, 1/4 lb., no lid 30.00
Coffeepot, covered 90.00
Creamer 30.00
Cup, flat, 2 5/8" 20.00
Cup and Saucer, flat, 2 5/8" 25.00
Lid, coffeepot 45.00
Lid, teapot 50.00
Plate, bread and butter, 6 1/4" 10.00
Plate, dessert, 6 7/8" 12.50
Plate, dinner, 9 3/4" 20.00
Plate, salad, 8" 15.00
Platter, oval, 11 7/8" 50.00
Platter, oval, 13 3/4" 65.00
Salt and Pepper Shakers, pair 40.00
Sugar Bowl, covered 40.00
Vegetable, round, 8 3/8" 40.00

Johnson Brothers, His Majesty

Cup, flat, 2 3/8" $17.50
Cup and Saucer, flat, 2 3/8" 22.50
Plate, dinner 20.00
Plate, salad 15.00
Platter, oval, 20 1/4" 160.00

Johnson Brothers, His Majesty.
Photo courtesy of BC Design Incorporated

Johnson Brothers, Indies, blue

Bowl, cereal, coupe, 6" $15.00
Bowl, fruit, 5 1/8" 12.50

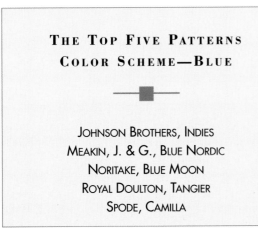

**THE TOP FIVE PATTERNS
COLOR SCHEME—BLUE**

JOHNSON BROTHERS, INDIES
MEAKIN, J. & G., BLUE NORDIC
NORITAKE, BLUE MOON
ROYAL DOULTON, TANGIER
SPODE, CAMILLA

Bowl, soup, coupe, 7 1/4″	17.50
Bowl, soup, flat, 8 5/8″	17.50
Butter Dish, covered, 1/4 lb.	65.00
Chop Plate, 12 1/8″	60.00
Coffeepot, covered	90.00
Cream Soup and Saucer	35.00
Creamer	35.00
Cup and Saucer, flat, 2 3/4″	17.50
Cup and Saucer, oversized, 3 × 4 1/2″	25.00
Eggcup, single, 1 7/8″	15.00
Gravy Boat and Underplate	65.00
Lid, butter dish, 1/4 lb.	40.00
Lid, coffeepot	45.00
Lid, teapot	40.00
Mug, 3 1/4″	17.50
Pitcher, 5 3/4″	50.00
Plate, bread and butter, 6 1/4″	7.50
Plate, dinner, 9 7/8″	20.00
Plate, salad, 7 7/8″	12.50
Plate, salad, square, 7 1/2″	15.00
Platter, oval, 11 7/8″	35.00
Platter, oval, 13 3/4″	60.00
Platter, oval, 15 1/2″	85.00
Salt and Pepper Shakers, pair	45.00
Saucer	7.50
Sugar Bowl, covered	40.00
Teapot, covered	85.00
Tureen, covered	250.00
Vegetable, covered, round	100.00
Vegetable, oval, 8 7/8″	35.00
Vegetable, oval, 9 1/8″	40.00
Vegetable, round, 8 1/4″	30.00

Cup, flat, 2 3/8″	20.00
Cup and Saucer, flat, 2 3/8″	25.00
Gravy Boat	55.00
Gravy Boat and Underplate	70.00
Mug, 3 3/4″	25.00
Plate, dinner, 10 5/8″	20.00
Plate, salad, square, 7 5/8″	15.00
Platter, oval, 20 1/8″	195.00
Relish, 8 1/4″	35.00
Snack Plate and Cup, square, 2 3/8″	40.00
Sugar Bowl, covered	50.00
Vegetable, round, 8 1/4″	45.00

Johnson Brothers, Old Britain Castles, blue

Bowl, cereal, flat, 6 1/8″	$17.50
Bowl, cereal, square, 6 1/4″	17.50
Bowl, fruit, 5 1/8″	15.00
Bowl, soup, flat, 8 3/4″	22.50
Butter Dish, covered, 1/4 lb.	55.00
Coffeepot, covered	100.00
Creamer	35.00
Cup and Saucer, flat, 2 1/4″	25.00
Gravy Boat	70.00
Gravy Boat and Underplate	75.00
Pitcher, 6 3/4″	60.00
Plate, bread and butter, 6 1/4″	12.50
Plate, dinner, 9 7/8″	25.00
Plate, salad, 7 7/8″	15.00
Platter, oval, 11 3/4″	55.00
Platter, oval, 15 1/4″	90.00
Relish, 8″	40.00
Saucer	10.00
Sugar Bowl, covered	45.00
Sugar Bowl, covered, no lid	35.00
Teapot, covered, mini	80.00
Vegetable, covered, round	145.00
Vegetable, covered, round, no lid	120.00
Vegetable, oval, 8 3/4″	40.00
Vegetable, round, 8 3/4″	45.00

Johnson Brothers, Merry Christmas,
shaped rim

Bowl, fruit, flat, 6 3/8″	$15.00
Chop Plate, 12 1/4″	70.00
Coaster, 4 1/8″	10.00
Creamer	40.00

Johnson Brothers, Old Britain Castles, pink

Bowl, cereal, flat, 6 1/8″	$15.00
Bowl, fruit, 5 1/8″	10.00
Bowl, soup, flat, 8 3/4″	17.50
Butter Dish, covered, 1/4 lb.	65.00
Chop Plate, 12″	45.00
Coffeepot, covered	90.00
Cup, flat, 2 1/4″	15.00
Cup and Saucer, flat, 2 1/4″	20.00
Gravy Boat	65.00
Gravy Boat and Underplate	65.00
Lid, coffeepot, mini	30.00
Pepper Shaker	22.50
Pitcher, 6 5/8″	50.00
Plate, bread and butter, 6 1/4″	7.50
Plate, dinner, 10″	17.50
Plate, luncheon, 8 7/8″	15.00
Plate, salad, 8″	10.00
Platter, oval, 11 7/8″	35.00
Platter, oval, 13 3/8″	60.00
Platter, oval, 15 1/4″	85.00
Salt and Pepper Shakers, pair	45.00
Saucer, demitasse	5.00
Teapot, covered	85.00
Tureen, covered	225.00
Vegetable, covered, round	100.00
Vegetable, oval, 8 3/4″	35.00
Vegetable, round, 8 1/2″	30.00

Johnson Brothers, Old English Countryside, brown

Bowl, cereal, square, 6 1/4″	$15.00
Coffeepot, covered, no lid	90.00
Creamer	30.00
Cup and Saucer, flat	25.00
Mug, 3 3/8″	22.50
Plate, bread and butter, 6 1/4″	7.50
Plate, luncheon, 8 7/8″	15.00
Plate, salad, square, 7 3/4″	15.00

Platter, oval, 11 3/8″	40.00
Platter, oval, 12″	45.00
Platter, oval, 13 5/8″	60.00
Saucer	7.50
Sugar Bowl, covered, no lid	27.50
Vegetable, covered, round	120.00
Vegetable, covered, round, no lid	80.00
Vegetable, round, 8 1/2″	50.00

Johnson Brothers, Provincial, floral

Bowl, fruit, 5 3/8″	$17.50
Coffeepot, covered	100.00
Creamer	35.00
Cup and Saucer, flat, 3 1/8″	30.00
Gravy Boat and Underplate	90.00
Plate, bread and butter, 7″	15.00
Plate, dinner	27.50
Plate, salad	20.00
Platter, oval, 11 3/4″	60.00
Platter, oval, 13 3/4″	85.00
Salt and Pepper Shakers, pair	40.00
Salt Shaker	20.00
Saucer	10.00
Sugar Bowl, covered	40.00
Sugar Bowl, covered, no lid	30.00
Vegetable, covered, no lid	105.00

Johnson Brothers, Regency

Johnson Brothers, Rose Chintz, pink

Bowl, cereal, coupe, 5 ½″	$5.00	Bowl, cereal, coupe, 6″	$15.00
Bowl, cereal, coupe, 6 ⅛″	5.00	Bowl, cereal, square, 6 ¼″	15.00
Bowl, cereal, square, 6 ⅛″	5.00	Bowl, fruit, 5 ⅛″	12.50
Bowl, fruit, 5 ¼″	5.00	Bowl, soup, flat, 8 ¾″	17.50
Bowl, soup, flat, 8 ½″	10.00	Butter Dish, covered, ¼ lb.	70.00
Butter Dish, covered, ¼ lb.	35.00	Chop Plate, 12 ⅛″	60.00
Coffeepot, covered	50.00	Coffeepot, covered	100.00
Creamer	15.00	Coffeepot, covered, no lid	80.00
Cup, flat, 2 ¾″	5.00	Cream Soup Saucer	12.50
Cup and Saucer, flat, 2 ¾″	7.50	Cup, oversized, 3×4 ½″	25.00
Gravy Boat	25.00	Cup and Saucer, demitasse	12.50
Gravy Boat and Underplate	35.00	Cup and Saucer, flat, 2 ⅜″	20.00
Lid, coffeepot	22.50	Cup and Saucer, oversized, 3×4 ½″	30.00
Mug, 3 ⅜″	5.00	Eggcup, single, 1 ⅞″	7.50
Pitcher, 6″	22.50	Gravy Boat	50.00
Plate, bread and butter, 6 ⅜″	5.00	Mug, 3 ⅞″	17.50
Plate, dinner, 10 ½″	7.50	Pitcher, 5 ½″	55.00
Plate, luncheon, 8 ⅝″	7.50	Plate, bread and butter, 6 ¼″	10.00
Plate, salad, 7 ⅞″	5.00	Plate, dinner, 9 ¾″	17.50
Plate, salad, square, 7 ⅝″	5.00	Plate, luncheon, 8 ⅝″	15.00
Platter, oval, 11 ¾″	15.00	Plate, salad, 7 ⅞″	12.50
Platter, oval, 13 ⅜″	30.00	Platter, oval, 11 ¾″	35.00
Platter, oval, 15 ⅝″	40.00	Platter, oval, 13 ½″	60.00
Relish, 7 ¾″	12.50	Platter, oval, 15 ¼″	85.00
Salt and Pepper Shakers, pair	25.00	Relish, 7 ⅞″	22.50
Salt Shaker	12.50	Sugar Bowl, covered	45.00
Saucer	2.50	Sugar Bowl, open	35.00
Sugar Bowl, covered	22.50	Teapot, covered	95.00
Teapot, covered	45.00	Tureen, covered	300.00
Teapot, covered, no lid	32.50	Vegetable, covered, round	100.00
Tureen, covered	140.00	Vegetable, covered, round, no lid	80.00
Vegetable, covered, round	45.00	Vegetable, oval, 9 ⅛″	40.00
Vegetable, oval, 9 ⅛″	20.00	Vegetable, round, 8 ¼″	32.50
Vegetable, round, 8 ¼″	15.00		

Johnson Brothers, Sheraton

Bowl, cereal, square, 6 1/4″	$15.00
Bowl, fruit, 5 1/4″	12.50
Bowl, soup, flat, 8″	20.00
Chop Plate, 12 3/4″	70.00
Creamer	25.00
Cup, demitasse	20.00
Cup and Saucer, flat, 2 3/8″	20.00
Gravy Boat	50.00
Lid, vegetable, round	60.00
Plate, bread and butter, 6 3/8″	7.50
Plate, dinner, 10″	22.50
Plate, salad, 7 3/4″	15.00
Plate, salad, square, 7 3/4″	12.50
Platter, oval, 11 7/8″	45.00
Platter, oval, 13 3/4″	60.00
Platter, oval, 15 1/2″	80.00
Relish, 8″	25.00
Saucer	7.50
Sugar Bowl, covered	35.00
Sugar Bowl, covered, no lid	25.00
Sugar Bowl, open, mini	22.50
Vegetable, covered, round	120.00
Vegetable, oval, 8 7/8″	35.00
Vegetable, oval, 9 1/8″	45.00

Johnson Brothers, Strawberry Fair

Bowl, fruit, 5 1/4″	$20.00
Bowl, soup, square, 7″	30.00
Creamer	50.00
Cup and Saucer, flat, 2 3/8″	40.00
Gravy Boat, no underplate	90.00
Lid, coffeepot	100.00
Plate, bread and butter, 6 1/4″	15.00
Plate, dinner	40.00

Plate, salad	25.00
Saucer	12.50
Sugar Bowl, covered, no lid	45.00
Vegetable, covered, round, no lid	160.00
Vegetable, oval, 9″	75.00

Johnson Brothers, Willow Blue

Augratin, 8 7/8″	$35.00
Baker, 10 3/4″	60.00
Bowl, cereal, coupe, 6 1/8″	7.50
Bowl, fruit, 5 1/8″	5.00
Bowl, oatmeal, 5 1/2″	15.00
Bowl, soup, flat, 8 1/8″	10.00
Butter Dish, covered, 1/4 lb.	50.00
Cake Plate and Server	55.00
Chop Plate, 12″	40.00
Coffeepot, covered	70.00
Creamer, 2 7/8″	22.50
Cup and Saucer, flat, 2 5/8″	10.00
Gravy Boat and Underplate	45.00
Lid, coffeepot	32.50
Mug, 3 7/8″	12.50
Pie Server, stainless blade	20.00

Pitcher, 5 ½″	35.00	Salt Shaker	15.00
Plate, bread and butter, 6 ¼″	5.00	Saucer	5.00
Plate, dinner, 10 ¼″	10.00	Sugar Bowl, covered, 2 ½″	30.00
Plate, luncheon, 8 ¾″	10.00	Teapot, covered	60.00
Plate, salad, 7 ⅞″	7.50	Tumbler, 4 ⅛″	7.50
Platter, oval 12″	27.50	Vegetable, covered, round	75.00
Platter, oval, 13 ⅞″	37.50	Vegetable, oval, 9″	22.50
Salt and Pepper Shakers, pair	35.00	Vegetable, round, 8 ¼″	20.00

Johnson Brothers, Willow Blue. *Photo courtesy of BC Design Incorporated.*

In 1889, Walter Scott Lenox and Jonathan Coxon Sr. founded the Ceramic Art Company in Trenton, New Jersey. Lenox acquired sole ownership in 1894, and in 1906 he formed Lenox, Inc.

Lenox gained national recognition in 1917 when President Woodrow Wilson ordered a 1,700-piece dinner set. Presidents Franklin D. Roosevelt and Harry S Truman followed Wilson's lead in future administrations. First Lady Nancy Reagan ordered a 4,732-piece set of gold-embossed bone china from Lenox in 1981. Each raised golden seal in the center of the Reagan service plates took two and one-half to three hours to hand paint, according to Eric Poehner, the Lenox craftsman who did much of the handwork.

During the last two decades, Lenox, Inc. has expanded into many other product lines, acquiring Art Carved, Inc., H. Rosenthal Jewelry Corporation, Imperial Glass Corporation, and many other companies. Today, Lenox, Inc. is a multimillion-dollar enterprise.

Lenox, Adrienne, Coupe Shape, platinum trim

Bowl, soup, coupe, 7 5/8″	$75.00
Coffeepot, covered, no lid	200.00
Creamer	125.00
Cup, flat, 2″	50.00
Cup and Saucer, flat, 2″	60.00
Plate, bread and butter, 6 3/8″	25.00
Plate, dinner, 10 1/2″	55.00
Plate, luncheon, 9″	50.00
Plate, salad, 7 7/8″	35.00
Sugar Bowl, covered	130.00
Vegetable, oval, 9 3/4″	180.00

Lenox, Amethyst, Cosmopolitan Shape, platinum trim

Cream Soup and Saucer	$110.00
Creamer	100.00
Cup and Saucer, demitasse	60.00
Cup and Saucer, footed, 3 1/8″	60.00
Plate, bread and butter, 6 1/2″	25.00
Plate, dinner, 10 3/4″	50.00
Plate, salad, 8 1/4″	35.00
Platter, oval, 16″	220.00
Saucer	20.00
Sugar Bowl, covered	120.00
Vegetable, oval, 9 1/2″	150.00

Lenox, Aristocrat, Dimension Shape, gold trim

Bowl, cereal, coupe, 5 3/8"	$100.00
Bowl, fruit, 5 3/8"	90.00
Creamer	190.00
Cup and Saucer, demitasse	120.00
Cup and Saucer, footed, 3"	120.00
Gravy Boat, attached underplate	370.00
Lid, coffeepot	250.00
Plate, bread and butter, 6 3/8"	45.00
Plate, dinner	90.00
Plate, salad, 8 1/4"	60.00
Platter, oval, 16 1/4"	440.00
Platter, oval, 17 1/4"	530.00
Saucer	40.00
Saucer, demitasse	40.00
Sugar Bowl, covered	220.00
Vegetable, covered, round	700.00
Vegetable, oval, 8 3/4"	220.00
Vegetable, oval, 10 1/4"	300.00

Pepper Shaker	50.00
Pitcher, 7 3/4"	150.00
Plate, bread and butter, 6 3/8"	20.00
Plate, dinner, 10 1/2"	40.00
Plate, salad, 8 3/8"	30.00
Platter, oval, 13 5/8"	180.00
Platter, oval, 16"	220.00
Sugar Bowl, covered	110.00
Vase, 4 5/8"	60.00
Vase, 8"	190.00
Vegetable, oval, 9 5/8"	150.00

Lenox, Ballad, Coupe Shape, center rose

Cup, flat, 2"	$50.00
Cup and Saucer, flat, 2"	55.00
Plate, bread and butter	25.00
Plate, dinner	50.00
Plate, salad	35.00
Sugar Bowl, covered, no lid	90.00

Lenox, Autumn, Presidential Shape, gold trim

Coffeepot, covered	$260.00
Cup, footed, 2 3/4"	45.00
Cup and Saucer, footed, 2 3/4"	60.00

Lenox, Belvidere, Standard Shape, gold trim

Bowl, fruit, 5 1/2"	$50.00
Bowl, soup, flat, 8 3/8"	70.00

Cream Soup and Saucer	100.00
Cream Soup Saucer	35.00
Cup and Saucer, footed, 2 1/8″	60.00
Plate, bread and butter, 6 1/4″	25.00
Plate, dinner, 10 5/8″	45.00
Plate, salad, 8 3/8″	35.00
Saucer	20.00
Sugar Bowl, covered	130.00

Chop Plate, 12 3/4″	230.00
Cream Soup and Saucer	130.00
Cream Soup Bowl	120.00
Cup, oversized, 2 1/2″	70.00
Cup and Saucer, demitasse	85.00
Cup and Saucer, footed, 2 1/8″	70.00
Plate, bread and butter, 6 3/8″	30.00
Plate, dinner, 10 5/8″	55.00
Plate, salad, 8 1/4″	40.00
Platter, oval, 16″	265.00
Sugar Bowl, covered	150.00

Lenox, Blue Breeze

Butter, covered, 1/4 lb.	$70.00
Casserole, open, round, 6 7/8″	85.00
Creamer	30.00
Cup and Saucer, flat, 2 3/4″	20.00
Pepper Shaker	25.00
Plate, bread and butter, 6 1/4″	10.00
Plate, dinner	30.00
Plate, salad	20.00
Roaster, oval, 15 1/4″	95.00
Saucer	5.00
Sugar Bowl, covered	40.00
Sugar Bowl, covered, no lid	25.00

Lenox, Brookdale, Presidential Shape,
platinum trim

Bowl, cereal, coupe, 5 3/4″	$65.00
Bowl, fruit, 5 1/2″	60.00
Coffeepot, covered	350.00
Coffeepot, covered, no lid	260.00
Cream Soup and Saucer	130.00
Cream Soup Bowl	120.00
Creamer	120.00
Cup, demitasse	70.00
Cup, footed, 2 1/8″	60.00
Cup and Saucer, demitasse	80.00
Cup and Saucer, footed, 2 1/8″	70.00
Cup and Saucer, footed, 2 7/8″	70.00
Plate, bread and butter, 6 1/2″	25.00
Plate, dinner, 10 1/2″	55.00
Plate, salad, 8 3/8″	40.00
Platter, oval, 16 1/8″	270.00
Sugar Bowl, covered	140.00

Lenox, Blue Tree, Standard Shape

Bowl, fruit, 5 1/2″	$55.00
Bowl, soup, flat, 8 1/4″	70.00

Lenox, Caribbee, gold trim

Bowl, fruit, 5 1/2"	$60.00
Chop Plate, 12 3/4"	250.00
Coffeepot, covered	300.00
Cream Soup and Saucer	110.00
Creamer	110.00
Cup, demitasse	60.00
Cup and Saucer, demitasse	70.00
Cup and Saucer, footed, 2 1/8"	70.00
Gravy Boat, attached underplate	230.00
Pepper Mill	100.00
Plate, bread and butter, 6 3/8"	30.00
Plate, dinner, 10 5/8"	55.00
Plate, salad, 8 3/8"	40.00
Platter, oval, 13 7/8"	200.00
Vegetable, covered, round	450.00
Vegetable, oval, 9 5/8"	190.00

Lid, coffeepot	175.00
Plate, bread and butter, 6 3/8"	30.00
Plate, dinner, 10 3/4"	65.00
Plate, salad, 8"	50.00
Platter, oval, 13 7/8"	200.00
Platter, oval, 16 1/4"	290.00
Sugar Bowl, covered	140.00
Vegetable, round, 9 1/4"	220.00

Lenox, Chanson, Sculpture Shape, platinum trim

Creamer	$135.00
Cup and Saucer, flat, 2 1/8"	80.00
Gravy Boat, attached underplate	300.00
Plate, bread and butter, 6 3/8"	35.00
Plate, dinner, 10 1/2"	65.00
Plate, luncheon, 9"	60.00
Plate, salad, 7 3/4"	50.00
Platter, oval, 15 3/4"	300.00
Saucer	25.00
Sugar Bowl, covered	150.00
Teapot, covered, no lid	280.00
Vegetable, oval, 9 1/2"	240.00

Lenox, Castle Garden, Dimension Shape,
gold trim

Bowl, fruit, 5 1/4"	$60.00
Bowl, soup, coupe, 7 1/2"	80.00
Cream Soup Bowl	130.00
Creamer	125.00
Cup and Saucer, footed, 3"	80.00

Lenox, Charlestonk Cosmopolitan Shape, platinum trim

Butter Dish, covered, 1/4 lb., no lid	$45.00
Cup, footed, 3 1/4″	25.00
Cup and Saucer, footed, 3 1/4″	30.00
Lid, sugar bowl	30.00
Plate, bread and butter, 6 1/2″	10.00
Plate, dinner, 10 3/4″	20.00
Plate, salad, 8 1/4″	15.00
Vegetable, oval, 9 1/2″	80.00

Lenox, Cinderella, Temple Shape

Bowl, fruit, flat, 6 1/2″	$60.00
Bowl, soup, flat, 8 1/2″	80.00
Chop Plate, 12 3/4″	300.00
Cream Soup Bowl	130.00
Cream Soup Saucer	40.00
Cup, footed, 2 5/8″	70.00
Cup and Saucer, footed, 2 5/8″	75.00
Gravy Boat, attached underplate	240.00
Lid, vegetable, round	235.00
Plate, bread and butter, 6 3/8″	30.00

Plate, dinner, 10 7/8″	60.00
Plate, luncheon, 9 1/4″	55.00
Plate, salad, 8 3/8″	40.00
Platter, oval, 17 1/4″	360.00
Saucer	25.00
Sugar Bowl, covered, no lid	100.00
Vegetable, oval, 9 3/4″	195.00

Lenox, Cretan, Temple Shape, gold trim

Bowl, fruit, flat, 6 3/8″	$40.00
Coffeepot, covered	270.00
Cream Soup and Saucer	100.00
Cream Soup Bowl	90.00
Creamer, 3 3/4″	90.00
Creamer, 4 1/4″	90.00
Cup, demitasse	60.00
Cup, footed, 2 5/8″	45.00
Cup and Saucer, bouillon	60.00
Cup and Saucer, demitasse	65.00
Cup and Saucer, footed, 2 5/8″	50.00
Gravy Boat, attached underplate	190.00
Lid, coffeepot	135.00
Lid, teapot	135.00
Plate, bread and butter, 6 3/8″	20.00
Plate, dinner, 10 7/8″	45.00
Plate, luncheon, 9 1/4″	40.00
Plate, salad, 8 1/2″	30.00
Saucer, 3″	15.00
Sugar Bowl, covered, 3 1/4″	110.00
Sugar Bowl, covered, 3 1/4″, no lid	80.00
Sugar Bowl, covered, 4″	110.00
Sugar Bowl, covered, 4″, no lid	80.00
Vegetable, covered, round	300.00
Vegetable, oval, 9 3/4″	140.00

Lenox, Dewdrops

Baker, rectangular, 15 ¹/₂″	$140.00
Casserole, covered, round, 6 ¹/₄″	90.00
Casserole, open, round, 6 ⁵/₈″	60.00
Creamer	30.00
Cup and Saucer, flat, 2 ³/₄″	20.00
Fondue Pot, 5 ⁷/₈″	100.00
Fondue Pot, Warmer Stand, and	
Burner	140.00
Fondue Warmer Stand	80.00
Lid, coffeepot	50.00
Plate, bread and butter, 6 ³/₈″	10.00
Plate, dinner	30.00
Plate, salad	20.00
Roaster, oval, 15 ¹/₈″	80.00
Salt Shaker and Pepper Mill	80.00
Saucer	5.00
Sugar Bowl, covered	35.00

Lenox, Essex Maroon, Standard Shape

Bowl, fruit, 5 ¹/₂″	$60.00
Cream Soup and Saucer	140.00
Cream Soup Saucer	45.00
Creamer	135.00
Cup, demitasse	80.00

Cup, footed, 2 ¹/₈″	60.00
Cup and Saucer, demitasse	90.00
Cup and Saucer, footed, 2 ¹/₈″	70.00
Gravy Boat, attached underplate	270.00
Lid, sugar bowl	70.00
Plate, bread and butter, 6 ¹/₄″	30.00
Plate, dinner, 10 ⁵/₈″	60.00
Plate, luncheon, 9 ¹/₄″	60.00
Plate, salad, 8 ³/₈″	45.00
Platter, oval, 16 ¹/₂″	300.00
Platter, oval, 17 ¹/₄″	380.00
Platter, oval, 19″	450.00
Sugar Bowl, covered, 3 ¹/₈″	140.00
Vegetable, oval, 9 ³/₄″	210.00

Lenox, Eternal, Dimension Shape, gold trim

Bowl, cereal, coupe, 5 ¹/₂″	$25.00
Bowl, soup, coupe, 7 ¹/₂″	35.00
Cup and Saucer, footed, 3 ¹/₈″	30.00
Lid, coffeepot	60.00
Lid, vegetable, round	85.00
Plate, bread and butter, 6 ¹/₂″	10.00
Plate, dinner, 10 ³/₄″	20.00
Plate, salad	15.00
Saucer	10.00
Saucer, demitasse	15.00
Sugar Bowl, covered	65.00
Vegetable, covered, round	190.00
Vegetable, oval, 10 ¹/₄″	85.00

THE TOP FIVE PATTERNS
PERIOD LOOK—
FORMAL

FRANCISCAN, RENAISSANCE
HUTSCHENREUTHER, RICHELIEU
LENOX, FAIR LADY
OXFORD-LENOX, FONTAINE
WEDGWOOD, FLORENTINE

Lenox, Fancy Free

Bowl, cereal, coupe, 6 1/8″	$25.00
Casserole, covered, round, 6 1/4″	100.00
Casserole, open, round, 6 1/2″	60.00
Coffeepot, covered	100.00
Creamer	30.00
Cup and Saucer, flat, 2 3/4″	20.00
Gravy Boat	70.00
Lid, coffeepot	50.00
Plate, bread and butter, 6 3/8″	10.00
Plate, dinner, 10 3/8″	30.00
Plate, salad, 8″	20.00
Roaster, oval, 15 1/4″	80.00
Saucer	5.00
Sugar Bowl, covered	35.00
Vegetable, oval, 9 1/8″	65.00

Lenox, Fair Lady, Dimension Shape, platinum trim

Creamer	$135.00
Cup and Saucer, footed, 3″	75.00
Gravy Boat, attached underplate	300.00
Lid, sugar bowl	75.00
Plate, bread and butter, 6 3/8″	30.00
Plate, dinner, 10 3/4″	60.00
Plate, salad, 8 1/8″	45.00
Platter, oval, 16 1/4″	330.00
Sugar Bowl, covered	150.00
Vegetable, oval, 10 1/4″	200.00

Lenox, Fire Flower

Baker, rectangular, 13″	$100.00
Baker, rectangular, 15 3/8″	100.00

Bowl, cereal, coupe, 6 1/8″	20.00
Bowl, fruit, 4 3/4″	20.00
Casserole, covered, individual, 4 3/8″	40.00
Casserole, covered, oval, 9 3/4″	150.00
Casserole, covered, round, 6 1/4″	100.00
Casserole, open, oval, 9 5/8″	90.00
Casserole, open, round, 6 7/8″	70.00
Coffeepot, covered	130.00
Creamer	30.00
Cup and Saucer, flat, 2 3/4″	20.00
Fondue Pot	80.00
Fondue Pot, Warmer Stand, and Burner	150.00
Fondue Warmer Stand and Burner	80.00
Fondue Warmer Stand	75.00
Gravy Boat	75.00
Lid, casserole, round	75.00
Pepper Mill	55.00
Plate, bread and butter, 6 1/2″	10.00
Plate, dinner, 10 1/4″	20.00
Plate, salad	15.00
Roaster, oval, 15 1/8″	80.00
Salt Shaker and Pepper Mill	75.00
Saucer	5.00
Sugar Bowl, covered	35.00

Lenox, For the Blue

Baker, rectangular, 13 3/4″	$100.00
Bowl, cereal, 6 1/4″	10.00
Butter Tray	30.00
Casserole, round	90.00
Cup and Saucer	20.00
Lid, casserole, round	65.00
Pepper Shaker	25.00
Pitcher, 7″	100.00
Plate, bread and butter, 6 5/8″	12.50
Plate, dinner	15.00
Plate, salad	10.00
Platter, oval, 14 1/4″	80.00
Salt and Pepper Shakers, pair	50.00
Sauce Boat	50.00
Saucer	5.00
Sugar Bowl, covered	37.50
Vegetable, round, 8 1/2″	55.00
Vegetable, round, 9 3/4″	55.00

Lenox, Flirtation, Dimension Shape, platinum trim

Cream Soup and Saucer	$120.00
Cream Soup Bowl	110.00
Cup, demitasse	60.00
Cup and Saucer, footed, 3″	60.00
Plate, bread and butter, 6 3/8″	25.00
Plate, dinner, 10 5/8″	45.00
Plate, salad	35.00
Saucer	20.00

Lenox, For the Grey

Bowl, cereal, coupe, 6 1/4″	$15.00
Creamer	40.00

Cup and Saucer	20.00	Bowl, soup, flat, 8 1/4″	55.00
Lid, sugar bowl	20.00	Chop Plate, 12 3/4″	170.00
Pepper Shaker	35.00	Cigarette Holder, 4″	40.00
Plate, bread and butter, 6 1/2″	17.50	Cigarette Lighter	50.00
Platter, oval, 14 3/8″	100.00	Coffeepot, covered	270.00
Saucer	5.00	Cream Soup and Saucer	100.00
Sugar Bowl, covered	40.00	Cream Soup Bowl	90.00
		Creamer, 3″	100.00
		Cup, footed, 2 1/8″	55.00
		Cup and Saucer, demitasse, 1 3/4″	60.00
		Cup and Saucer, footed, 2 1/8″	60.00
		Gravy Boat, attached underplate	200.00
		Plate, bread and butter, 6 1/4″	20.00
		Plate, dinner, 10 1/2″	45.00
		Plate, salad, 8 3/8″	30.00
		Platter, oval, 13 1/2″	160.00
		Platter, oval, 16 1/4″	200.00
		Platter, oval, 17 1/2″	230.00
		Salt Shaker	70.00
		Saucer, demitasse	20.00
		Sugar Bowl, covered, 3″	120.00
		Sugar Bowl, covered, 3″, no lid	80.00
		Vegetable, covered, round	350.00
		Vegetable, oval, 9 5/8″	150.00

Lenox, Glories on Grey

Canister, flour, 7″	$70.00
Canister, tea, 4″	40.00
Chop Plate, 12 5/8″	70.00
Creamer	40.00
Cup and Saucer, flat, 2 3/4″	22.50
Mug, 3 3/4″	25.00
Plate, dinner, 10 3/4″	20.00
Plate, salad, 8 3/8″	15.00
Saucer	5.00
Sugar Bowl, covered	40.00

Lenox, Hancock, gold trim

Bowl, soup, flat, 8 3/8″	$45.00
Coffeepot, covered	170.00
Cup, footed, 2 3/4″	35.00
Cup and Saucer, footed, 2 3/4″	40.00
Plate, bread and butter, 6 1/2″	15.00
Plate, dinner, 10 1/2″	30.00
Plate, salad, 8 1/2″	20.00
Sugar Bowl, covered	90.00
Vegetable, oval, 9 3/4″	110.00

Lenox, Golden Wreath, gold trim

Ashtray, 4 3/8″	$30.00
Bowl, fruit, 5 1/2″	50.00

Lenox, Harvest, Standard Shape, gold trim

Ashtray, 4 3/8″	$25.00
Bowl, fruit, 5 5/8″	40.00
Bowl, soup, flat, 8 3/8″	50.00
Bud Vase, 8″	80.00
Chop Plate, 12 5/8″	170.00
Cigarette Box	70.00
Cigarette Holder, 4″ h	40.00
Cigarette Lighter	50.00
Cream Soup and Saucer	70.00
Cream Soup Bowl	65.00
Creamer, 3″	80.00
Cup, oversized, 2 1/2″	50.00
Cup and Saucer, demitasse	50.00
Cup and Saucer, footed, 2 1/8″	50.00
Gravy Boat, attached underplate	180.00
Lid, vegetable	165.00
Pepper Mill	80.00
Plate, bread and butter, 6 1/4″	20.00
Plate, dinner, 10 5/8″	40.00
Plate, luncheon, 9 1/8″	35.00
Plate, salad, 8 3/8″	25.00
Plate, service, 10 1/2″	70.00
Platter, oval, 13 1/2″	160.00
Platter, oval, 17 1/4″	250.00
Salt Shaker and Pepper Mill	130.00
Saucer	15.00
Saucer, demitasse	15.00
Sugar Bowl, covered, 3″	110.00
Sugar Bowl, covered, 3″, no lid	75.00
Teapot, covered, no lid	150.00
Vegetable, covered, round	330.00
Vegetable, oval, 9 5/8″	130.00

Lenox, Hayworth, Cosmopolitan Shape, gold trim

Cup and Saucer, footed, 3 1/8″	$30.00
Plate, bread and butter, 6 1/2″	10.00
Plate, dinner, 10 3/4″	20.00
Plate, salad, 8 1/4″	15.00
Saucer	10.00
Saucer, demitasse	10.00

Lenox, Holiday, Dimension Shape, gold trim

Ashtray, 4 1/4″	$45.00
Basket	60.00
Bowl, fruit, 5 1/4″	40.00
Bowl, fruit, 9 3/8″	75.00
Bowl, pierced, 6″	65.00
Bowl, salad, serving, 9 1/2″	100.00
Bowl, soup, coupe, 7 3/8″	50.00
Bud Vase, 7 3/8″	35.00
Candleholder	50.00
Candleholder, votive	25.00
Candlestick, single light, 4 1/2″	45.00
Candy Dish, 8 1/4″	50.00
Centerpiece, 10 1/8″	85.00
Chop Plate, 12 5/8″	130.00
Coffeepot, covered	190.00
Creamer	85.00

Cup and Saucer, demitasse, 2 3/4″	65.00	Platter, oval, 14″	150.00
Cup and Saucer, footed, 3″	45.00	Platter, oval, 16 3/8″	190.00
Dish, leaf shape, 7″	45.00	Pomander	70.00
Gravy Boat, attached underplate	175.00	Relish, 9 1/8″	50.00
Lid, butter dish, 1/4 lb.	40.00	Relish, 9 3/4″	50.00
Lid, vegetable, round	130.00	Relish, three-part, 8″	45.00
Mint Dish	35.00	Salt and Pepper Shakers, pair, 3 3/4″	65.00
Mug, 3 1/2″	35.00	Sugar Bowl, covered	100.00
Napkin Ring	15.00	Thimble	35.00
Nut Dish, 4 1/4″	35.00	Tray, relish, pierced	50.00
Nut Dish, pierced, 4 1/4″	40.00	Tray, serving, two-tiered	75.00
Ornament	25.00	Tureen, covered, no lid	315.00
Pie Server, stainless blade, 10″	65.00	Vase, 7 1/4″	50.00
Plate, bread and butter, 6 3/8″	15.00	Vase, 7 7/8″	130.00
Plate, dinner, 10 3/4″	30.00	Vase, bulbous, 8″	50.00
Plate, salad, 8″	20.00	Vase, pierced, 8 1/4″	70.00
Plate, service, 11 3/4″	50.00	Vegetable, covered, round	270.00
Plate, serving, round, handled, 10 3/4″	70.00	Vegetable, oval, 10 1/8″	125.00
		Vegetable, round, 9 1/8″	100.00

Lenox, Imperial, Standard Shape

Bowl, fruit, 5 1/2″	$45.00
Bowl, soup, flat, 8 3/8″	60.00
Cigarette Holder	40.00
Cigarette Lighter	50.00
Coffeepot, covered	290.00
Cream Soup and Saucer	100.00
Cream Soup Bowl	90.00
Creamer, 3 1/2″	105.00
Cup and Saucer, demitasse	55.00
Cup and Saucer, footed, 2 1/8″	55.00
Gravy Boat, attached underplate	210.00
Lid, vegetable, round	180.00
Plate, bread and butter, 6 3/8″	25.00
Plate, dinner, 10 1/2″	45.00
Plate, luncheon, 9 1/8″	40.00
Plate, luncheon, square, 8 1/2″	50.00
Plate, salad	35.00
Platter, oval, 13 7/8″	170.00
Platter, oval, 16 1/8″	220.00
Salt Shaker and Pepper Mill	150.00
Saucer, demitasse	20.00
Sugar Bowl, covered, 3″	120.00
Sugar Bowl, covered, 3″, no lid	80.00
Sugar Bowl, covered, 4 1/4″	120.00
Teapot, covered	290.00
Teapot, covered, no lid	210.00
Vegetable, covered, round	360.00
Vegetable, oval, 9 5/8″	160.00

Lenox, Iris on Grey

Cup, flat, 2 3/4″	$20.00
Cup and Saucer, flat, 2 3/4″	25.00
Plate, bread and butter	22.00
Plate, dinner, 10 3/4″	35.00
Plate, salad	22.00

Lenox, Kingsley, Standard Shape, platinum trim

Ashtray, 8 1/8″	$40.00
Bowl, fruit, 5 5/8″	55.00
Bowl, soup, flat, 8 3/8″	80.00
Bud Vase, 7 7/8″	100.00
Chop Plate, 12 7/8″	270.00
Coffeepot, covered	350.00
Cream Soup and Saucer	130.00
Cream Soup Bowl	120.00
Creamer	120.00
Cup and Saucer, demitasse	90.00
Cup and Saucer, footed, 2″	70.00
Gravy Boat, attached underplate	230.00
Plate, bread and butter, 6 3/8″	25.00
Plate, dinner, 10 5/8″	50.00
Plate, salad, 8 3/8″	40.00
Platter, oval, 13 3/4″	200.00
Platter, oval, 16 1/8″	290.00

Platter, oval, 17 $^3/_8''$	350.00
Saucer	25.00
Saucer, demitasse	30.00
Sugar Bowl, covered	140.00
Sugar Bowl, covered, no lid	100.00
Vegetable, covered, round	470.00
Vegetable, oval, 9 $^5/_8''$	190.00

Lenox, Laurent, Sculpture Shape, gold trim

Bowl, fruit, 5 $^5/_8''$	$50.00
Chop Plate, 13''	160.00
Cream Soup and Saucer	110.00
Creamer	90.00
Cup and Saucer, demitasse	70.00
Cup and Saucer, flat, 2 $^1/_8''$	60.00
Gravy Boat, attached underplate	200.00
Lid, coffeepot	150.00
Plate, bread and butter, 6 $^3/_8''$	20.00
Plate, dinner	50.00
Plate, salad, 7 $^7/_8''$	30.00
Platter, oval, 13 $^7/_8''$	170.00
Platter, oval, 15 $^3/_4''$	200.00
Platter, oval, 17 $^5/_8''$	280.00
Saucer, demitasse	25.00
Sugar Bowl, covered	110.00
Vegetable, oval, 9 $^5/_8''$	150.00

Lenox, Lace Point, Dimension Shape, platinum trim

Coffeepot, covered	$350.00
Cream Soup and Saucer	130.00
Cream Soup Bowl	120.00
Creamer	130.00
Cup and Saucer, demitasse	85.00
Cup and Saucer, footed, 3''	70.00
Lid, sugar bowl	75.00
Plate, bread and butter, 6 $^3/_8''$	30.00
Plate, dinner, 10 $^5/_8''$	55.00
Plate, salad, 8 $^1/_4''$	40.00
Platter, oval, 14''	215.00
Platter, oval, 16 $^1/_4''$	265.00
Saucer	25.00
Sugar Bowl, covered	150.00
Vegetable, oval, 8 $^3/_4''$	175.00
Vegetable, oval, 10 $^1/_4''$	230.00

Lenox, Lenox Rose, Standard Shape, gold trim

Ashtray, 3 $^7/_8''$	$20.00
Bowl, cereal, coupe, 6 $^1/_8''$	50.00
Bowl, fruit, 5 $^1/_2''$	40.00
Bowl, soup, flat, 8 $^3/_8''$	50.00

Bud Vase, 6 1/4″	80.00
Bud Vase, 7 3/4″	80.00
Cigarette Box	85.00
Cream Soup and Saucer	100.00
Cream Soup Bowl	90.00
Creamer, 3 1/2″	90.00
Cup, flat, 2 1/4″	50.00
Cup, footed, 2 1/8″	50.00
Cup and Saucer, bouillon, 4″ w	55.00
Cup and Saucer, demitasse, flat	70.00
Cup and Saucer, flat, 2 1/4″	55.00
Cup and Saucer, footed, 2 1/8″	55.00
Cup and Saucer, oversized, 2 1/2″	60.00
Dish, shell shape, 7 3/4″	70.00
Gravy Boat, attached underplate	190.00
Plate, bread and butter, 6 3/8″	20.00
Plate, dinner, 10 5/8″	45.00
Plate, luncheon, 9 1/8″	40.00
Plate, salad, 8 1/4″	30.00
Plate, sandwich, 9″	130.00
Platter, oval, 13 3/8″	180.00
Platter, oval, 15 5/8″	200.00
Platter, oval, 16 3/8″	210.00
Powder Box	120.00
Ramekin and Saucer	60.00
Salt and Pepper Shakers, pair	90.00
Saucer, demitasse	25.00
Saucer, oversized, 2 1/2″	20.00
Sugar Bowl, covered, 3 1/2″	100.00
Sugar Bowl, open	95.00
Teapot, covered	300.00
Vegetable, covered, round	350.00
Vegetable, oval, 9 5/8″	140.00

Casserole, open, round, 6 7/8″	70.00
Coffeepot, covered	100.00
Creamer	35.00
Cup and Saucer, flat, 2 3/4″	20.00
Gravy Boat	75.00
Gravy Boat, attached underplate	75.00
Lid, coffeepot	50.00
Pepper Shaker	20.00
Plate, bread and butter, 6 1/4″	10.00
Plate, dinner, 10 1/4″	25.00
Plate, salad, 8 1/8″	20.00
Roaster, oval, 15 1/8″	80.00
Saucer	5.00
Sugar Bowl, covered	35.00

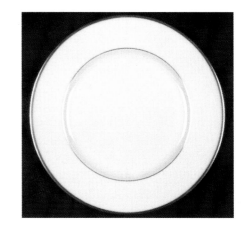

Lenox, Mansfield, Presidential Shape, gold trim

Cream Soup and Saucer	$70.00
Cream Soup Saucer	25.00
Creamer	50.00
Cup, demitasse	35.00
Cup, footed, 2 1/8″	30.00
Cup, footed, 2 3/4″	30.00
Cup and Saucer, footed, 2 1/8″	30.00
Lid, coffeepot	70.00
Plate, bread and butter, 6 1/4″	12.50
Plate, dinner	25.00
Plate, salad, 8 3/8″	17.50
Sugar Bowl, covered	65.00
Teapot, covered, no lid	100.00
Vegetable, covered, round	200.00
Vegetable, oval, 9 3/4″	90.00

Lenox, Magic Garden

Baker, rectangular, 15 1/8″	$110.00
Bowl, cereal, coupe, 6 1/4″	20.00
Bowl, fruit, 4 3/4″	25.00
Casserole, covered, round, 6 1/4″	100.00

Lenox, Melissa, Sculpture Shape, platinum trim

Cup and Saucer, flat, 2 $^1/_8$″	$80.00
Plate, bread and butter, 6 $^1/_4$″	35.00
Plate, dinner	65.00
Plate, salad, 7 $^7/_8$″	50.00
Saucer	25.00

Lenox, Memoir, Dimension Shape, platinum trim

Cream Soup and Saucer	$130.00
Cup and Saucer, demitasse	90.00
Cup and Saucer, footed, 3″	70.00
Plate, bread and butter, 6 $^3/_8$″	25.00
Plate, dinner, 10 $^3/_4$″	55.00
Plate, salad, 8 $^1/_4$″	40.00
Platter, oval, 14″	230.00
Saucer	25.00
Sugar Bowl, covered	130.00
Vegetable, oval, 10 $^1/_8$″	200.00

Lenox, Merriment Temperware

Bowl, cereal, coupe, 6 $^1/_8$″	$25.00
Casserole, covered, round, 6 $^1/_4$″	100.00
Casserole, open, round, 6 $^7/_8$″	60.00

Creamer	25.00
Cup and Saucer, flat, 2 $^3/_4$″	20.00
Lid, casserole, oval, 10″	85.00
Plate, bread and butter, 6 $^3/_8$″	15.00
Plate, dinner	30.00
Plate, salad, 8″	20.00
Roaster, oval, 15 $^1/_4$″	80.00
Saucer	5.00
Sugar Bowl, covered	35.00
Sugar Bowl, covered, no lid	30.00

Lenox, Ming

Baked Apple Dish	$90.00
Bonbon, covered, 6 $^1/_2$″, no lid	175.00
Bowl, cereal, coupe, 6″	50.00
Bowl, cereal, flat, 7 $^1/_4$″	50.00
Bowl, fruit, 5 $^1/_2$″	40.00
Bowl, fruit, flat, 6 $^1/_4$″	40.00
Bowl, soup, coupe, 7 $^1/_2$″	55.00
Bowl, soup, flat, 8 $^5/_8$″	55.00
Butter Dish, covered, round, no lid	100.00
Butter Tub	120.00
Cake Plate, handled, 10 $^7/_8$″	100.00
Cake Plate, square, handled, 10 $^3/_8$″	100.00

Chop Plate, 12 5/8″ 160.00
Compote, 2 3/4″ 100.00
Cream Soup and Saucer, flat 90.00
Cream Soup Bowl, flat 80.00
Cream Soup Saucer, flat 30.00
Creamer, 2 3/8″ 90.00
Cup, bouillon, footed, 2 1/8″ 40.00
Cup and Saucer, bouillon, flat 45.00
Cup and Saucer, bouillon,
    footed, 2 1/8″ 45.00
Cup and Saucer, chocolate, 3 1/4″ 65.00
Cup and Saucer, demitasse 60.00
Cup and Saucer, flat, 2 1/8″ 55.00
Cup and Saucer, footed, 2 1/8″ 55.00
Cup and Saucer, oversized, 2 1/2″ 60.00
Eggcup, double, 3 3/4″ 45.00
Eggcup, single, 3 1/2″ 35.00
Eggcup, mini, 2 1/2″ 25.00
Gravy Boat, attached underplate 190.00
Gravy Boat, no underplate 160.00
Jam, covered, no lid 80.00
Lid, coffeepot 150.00
Lid, sugar bowl, 3 3/4″ 55.00
Mayonnaise and Underplate,
    no ladle, 5 1/8″ 80.00
Mayonnaise Underplate, 5 1/8″ 35.00
Muffin Dish, covered, no lid 160.00
Oyster Cocktail Sauce Cup, 2 7/8″ 40.00
Plate, bread and butter, 5 3/4″ 20.00
Plate, bread and butter, 6 1/4″ 20.00
Plate, dessert, 7 3/8″ 25.00
Plate, dinner 50.00
Plate, luncheon, 9″ 40.00
Plate, salad, 8 3/8″ 30.00
Plate, sandwich, 9″ 100.00
Platter, oval, 11″ 120.00
Platter, oval, 13 3/8″ 150.00
Ramekin Saucer 20.00
Relish, 8 1/4″ 50.00
Salt Shaker, 3 1/2″ 45.00
Sauce Boat 200.00
Saucer 20.00
Saucer, demitasse 20.00
Snack Plate and Cup, 7 3/8″ 60.00
Snack Plate and Cup, 8 1/4″ 60.00
Sugar Bowl, covered, 2″ 110.00
Sugar Bowl, covered, 3 3/4″ 110.00
Sugar Bowl, covered, 4 1/4″ 110.00
Syrup, 4 3/4″ 110.00
Teapot, covered, 3″ 260.00
Teapot, covered, 3″, no lid 190.00
Teapot, covered, mini 175.00
Teapot, covered, 4 1/2″, no lid 190.00
Teapot, covered, 4 7/8″, no lid 190.00
Vegetable, covered, oval 370.00

Vegetable, covered, round 370.00
Vegetable, covered, round, no lid 280.00
Vegetable, oval, 9 1/2″ 140.00

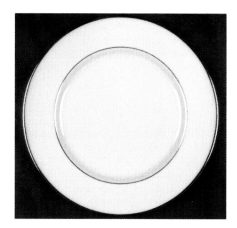

**Lenox, Montclair, Presidential Shape,
platinum trim**

Creamer $50.00
Cup, demitasse 35.00
Cup, footed, 2 3/4″ 30.00
Cup and Saucer, demitasse 40.00
Cup and Saucer, footed, 2 1/8″ 32.50
Plate, bread and butter, 6 3/8″ 12.50
Plate, dinner, 10 5/8″ 25.00
Plate, salad 17.50
Saucer 10.00
Sugar Bowl, covered 65.00

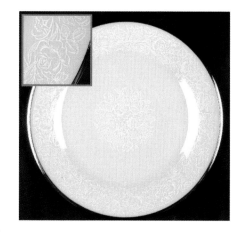

**Lenox, Moonspun, Dimension Shape,
platinum trim**

Bowl, cereal, coupe, 5 3/8″ $65.00
Bowl, fruit, 5 3/8″ 55.00
Bowl, soup, coupe, 7 5/8″ 70.00

Chop Plate, 12 3/4″	230.00
Coffeepot, covered	300.00
Cream Soup Bowl	120.00
Creamer	120.00
Cup and Saucer, demitasse	85.00
Cup and Saucer, footed, 3″	70.00
Gravy Boat, attached underplate	250.00
Plate, bread and butter, 6 3/8″	25.00
Plate, dinner, 10 3/4″	50.00
Plate, luncheon, 9 1/2″	50.00
Plate, salad, 8 1/8″	40.00
Platter, oval, 13 7/8″	230.00
Platter, oval, 16 3/8″	270.00
Platter, oval, 17 3/8″	330.00
Saucer	25.00
Sugar Bowl, covered	130.00
Vegetable, oval, 8 3/4″	140.00
Vegetable, oval, 10 1/4″	190.00
Vegetable, round, 9 3/8″	200.00

Lenox, Musette, Sculpture Shape, platinum trim

Creamer	$135.00
Cup and Saucer, demitasse	100.00
Cup and Saucer, flat, 2 1/8″	80.00
Gravy Boat, attached underplate	300.00
Plate, bread and butter	35.00
Plate, dinner	65.00
Plate, salad	50.00
Saucer	25.00
Sugar Bowl, covered	150.00

Lenox, Morning Blossom, Dimension Shape, gold trim

Coffeepot, covered	$350.00
Creamer	135.00
Cup, footed, 3 1/8″	70.00
Cup and Saucer, demitasse	100.00
Cup and Saucer, footed, 3 1/8″	80.00
Gravy Boat, attached underplate	300.00
Plate, bread and butter	35.00
Plate, dinner	65.00
Plate, salad	50.00
Platter, oval, 16 3/8″	300.00
Sugar Bowl, covered	150.00
Vegetable, covered, round	515.00
Vegetable, oval, 10 1/8″	250.00

Lenox, Noblesse, Presidential Shape, gold trim

Cup and Saucer, footed, 2 1/4″	$80.00
Lid, coffeepot	180.00
Plate, bread and butter, 6 3/8″	30.00
Plate, dinner	60.00
Plate, salad	45.00
Saucer	25.00
Sugar Bowl, covered	145.00

Lenox, Olympia, Coupe Shape, platinum trim

Ashtray, 4 3/8″	$15.00
Bowl, fruit, 5 1/2″	50.00
Chop Plate, 12 7/8″	150.00
Cigarette Holder	35.00
Cigarette Lighter	40.00
Cream Soup and Saucer	110.00
Cream Soup Bowl	100.00
Creamer	100.00
Cup and Saucer, demitasse	60.00
Cup and Saucer, flat, 2″	50.00
Lid, teapot	150.00
Plate, bread and butter, 6 3/8″	20.00
Plate, dinner, 10 3/8″	45.00
Plate, salad, 8″	30.00
Platter, oval, 13 7/8″	150.00
Platter, oval, 15 1/2″	200.00
Salt Shaker and Pepper Mill	140.00
Salt Shaker	45.00
Saucer, demitasse	20.00
Sugar Bowl, covered	110.00
Vegetable, covered, round	370.00
Vegetable, oval, 9 5/8″	130.00
Vegetable, round, 9 1/8″	135.00

Plate, salad, 7 7/8″	35.00
Platter, oval, 16 1/8″	260.00
Saucer	20.00
Sugar Bowl, covered	130.00
Vegetable, oval, 9 1/2″	170.00

Lenox, Pavlova, Temple Shape

Bowl, fruit, flat, 6 3/8″	$55.00
Bowl, soup, flat, 8 1/2″	70.00
Coffeepot, covered	320.00
Cream Soup and Saucer	100.00
Cream Soup Bowl	90.00
Creamer, 4 1/4″	120.00
Cup, demitasse	70.00
Cup and Saucer, demitasse	75.00
Cup and Saucer, footed, 2 1/2″	70.00
Plate, bread and butter, 6 1/4″	25.00
Plate, dinner, 10 3/4″	50.00
Plate, luncheon, 9 1/8″	50.00
Plate, salad, 8 1/2″	40.00
Platter, oval, 13 1/2″	200.00
Saucer	25.00
Vegetable, oval, 9 1/2″	190.00

Lenox, Orleans, Sculpture Shape, gold leaves and trim

Bowl, fruit, 5 5/8″	$50.00
Coffeepot, covered	300.00
Creamer	110.00
Cup and Saucer, demitasse	80.00
Cup and Saucer, flat, 2 1/8″	65.00
Gravy Boat, attached underplate	200.00
Plate, bread and butter, 6 3/8″	25.00
Plate, dinner, 10 3/8″	50.00
Plate, luncheon, 9″	45.00

Lenox, Pine, Standard Shape, flat rim, gold trim

Bowl, fruit, 5 1/2″	$40.00
Bowl, soup, flat, 8 1/2″	55.00
Chop Plate, 12 3/4″	160.00
Cream Soup and Saucer	100.00
Cream Soup Bowl	90.00
Creamer, 3 5/8″	90.00
Cup, demitasse	55.00
Cup and Saucer, demitasse	60.00
Cup and Saucer, footed, 2 1/8″	50.00
Gravy Boat, attached underplate	190.00
Lid, sugar bowl, 3 1/8″	50.00
Lid, teapot	135.00
Plate, bread and butter, 6 3/8″	20.00
Plate, dinner, 10 5/8″	40.00
Plate, salad, 8 3/8″	30.00
Platter, oval, 13 5/8″	160.00
Platter, oval, 16 1/4″	220.00
Platter, oval, 17 3/8″	260.00
Sugar Bowl, covered, 3 1/8″	100.00
Sugar Bowl, covered, 3 5/8″	100.00
Sugar Bowl, covered, 3 5/8″, no lid	70.00
Vegetable, oval, 9 5/8″	140.00

Lenox, Plum Blossoms, Standard Shape, platinum trim

Creamer	$130.00
Cup and Saucer, footed, 2 1/8″	70.00
Plate, bread and butter	30.00
Plate, dinner, 10 5/8″	60.00
Plate, salad	45.00
Sugar Bowl, covered	140.00
Sugar Bowl, covered, no lid	100.00

Lenox, Poppies on Blue

Baker, rectangular, 13 3/4″	$75.00
Bowl, cereal, coupe, 6 1/4″	12.50
Bowl, fruit, 5 1/4″	17.50
Bowl, salad, serving, 10 1/2″	55.00
Candlestick, single light, 4 3/4″	35.00
Canister, coffee, 4 1/2″	50.00
Canister, flour, 7″	75.00
Canister, sugar, 6″	55.00
Canister, tea, 4″	35.00
Casserole, covered, round, 8 × 2″ h	155.00
Chop Plate, 12 1/2″	95.00
Creamer	45.00
Cup, flat, 2 3/4″	15.00
Cup and Saucer, flat, 2 3/4″	20.00

Desk Clock	75.00
Kettle	60.00
Knife, cheese, stainless blade	30.00
Mug, 3 3/4″	25.00
Napkin Ring	10.00
Picture Frame, 3 × 5″	50.00
Pie Plate, 10 1/4″	45.00
Pie Server, stainless blade	35.00
Pitcher, 6 1/2″	120.00
Plate, bread and butter	15.00
Plate, dinner, 10 3/4″	20.00
Plate, salad, 8 1/2″	15.00
Plate, serving, round, handled, 10 5/8″	40.00
Platter, oval, 14 1/2″	95.00
Ramekin	15.00
Relish, three-part, 10 1/4″	75.00
Sauce Boat	60.00
Saucer	7.50
Soufflé	35.00
Spoon Holder	25.00
Tray, serving, two-tiered	40.00
Trivet, 7 1/2″	40.00
Utensil Holder, 8 1/4″	65.00
Vegetable, round, 8 5/8″	65.00
Vegetable, round, 9 3/4″	75.00

Creamer	100.00
Cup and Saucer, demitasse	70.00
Cup and Saucer, flat, 2 1/8″	60.00
Lid, coffeepot	150.00
Lid, sugar bowl	55.00
Lid, vegetable	200.00
Pepper Mill	90.00
Plate, bread and butter, 6 3/8″	22.50
Plate, dinner, 10 1/2″	45.00
Plate, luncheon, 9″	45.00
Plate, salad, 7 7/8″	30.00
Platter, oval, 13 3/4″	190.00
Platter, oval, 16 1/8″	230.00
Platter, oval, 17 1/2″	300.00
Salt Shaker and Pepper Mill	135.00
Saucer	20.00
Sugar Bowl, covered	110.00
Vegetable, covered, round	400.00
Vegetable, oval, 8 1/2″	130.00
Vegetable, oval, 9 3/4″	150.00

Lenox, Promise, Standard Shape, platinum trim

Creamer	$100.00
Cup, footed, 2 1/8″	55.00
Cup and Saucer, footed, 2 1/8″	60.00
Gravy Boat, attached underplate	240.00
Plate, bread and butter, 6 3/8″	25.00
Plate, dinner, 10 1/2″	45.00
Plate, salad, 8 1/4″	30.00
Sugar Bowl, covered	120.00

Lenox, Princess, Coupe Shape, platinum trim

Ashtray, 6 1/4″	$22.50
Bowl, fruit, 5 5/8″	50.00
Bowl, soup, coupe, 7 1/2″	70.00
Bud Vase, 8″	70.00
Chop Plate, 12 3/4″	190.00
Cigarette Holder	40.00
Cigarette Lighter	50.00
Coffeepot, covered	300.00
Cream Soup and Saucer	100.00
Cream Soup Bowl	90.00

Lenox, Quakertown, temperware

Baker, rectangular, 15 3/8″	$130.00
Casserole, covered, round, 6 3/8″	100.00
Casserole, open, round, 6 3/8″	60.00
Creamer	30.00
Cup and Saucer, flat, 2 3/4″	17.50
Gravy Boat	70.00
Lid, casserole, individual, 5″	22.50
Pepper Shaker	22.50
Plate, bread and butter, 6 3/8″	10.00
Plate, dinner, 10 3/8″	32.50
Plate, salad, 8″	20.00
Roaster, oval, 15 1/8″	80.00
Saucer	5.00
Sugar Bowl, covered	35.00
Sugar Bowl, covered, no lid	30.00

Lenox, Repertoire, Dimension Shape,
platinum trim

Bowl, soup, coupe, 7 1/2″	$70.00
Cup, demitasse	70.00
Cup and Saucer, footed, 3″	60.00

Lid, coffeepot	150.00
Lid, sugar bowl	60.00
Plate, bread and butter, 6 3/8″	25.00
Plate, dinner, 10 3/4″	50.00
Plate, salad, 8 1/4″	35.00
Sugar Bowl, covered	120.00
Vegetable, oval, 8 3/4″	130.00
Vegetable, oval, 10 1/8″	180.00

Lenox, Rhodora, Standard Shape, gold trim

Ashtray, 6 1/4″	$35.00
Bowl, fruit, 5 1/2″	60.00
Bowl, soup, flat, 8 3/8″	80.00
Bud Vase, 8″	100.00
Chop Plate, 12 5/8″	280.00
Cigarette Box	130.00
Cream Soup and Saucer	130.00
Cream Soup Bowl	120.00
Creamer, 3 1/8″	120.00
Cup, demitasse, 2 1/4″	70.00
Cup, footed, 2 1/8″	60.00
Cup and Saucer, demitasse, 2 1/4″	80.00
Cup and Saucer, footed, 2 1/8″	70.00
Gravy Boat, attached underplate	250.00
Lid, coffeepot	165.00
Lid, sugar bowl, 3 5/8″	70.00
Plate, bread and butter, 6 1/4″	30.00
Plate, dinner, 10 5/8″	55.00
Plate, luncheon, 9 1/8″	55.00
Plate, salad, 8 1/4″	40.00
Sugar Bowl, covered, 3 1/8″	140.00
Sugar Bowl, covered, 3 1/8″, no lid	100.00
Vase, 9 1/4″	180.00
Vegetable, oval, 9 5/8″	195.00

Lenox, Rosedale, Sculpture Shape, platinum trim

Creamer	$110.00
Cup and Saucer, flat, 2 1/4″	60.00
Lid, sugar bowl	65.00
Plate, bread and butter, 6 1/4″	25.00
Plate, dinner	50.00
Plate, salad, 7 7/8″	35.00
Saucer	20.00

Lenox, Roselyn, Coupe Shape, gold trim

Ashtray, 6 1/4″	$30.00
Bowl, fruit, 5 1/2″	50.00
Bud Vase, 8″	70.00
Chop Plate, 12 3/4″	200.00
Cigarette Box	90.00
Cigarette Holder	40.00
Cigarette Lighter	55.00
Cream Soup and Saucer	125.00
Cream Soup Bowl	120.00
Creamer	100.00
Cup, demitasse	65.00
Cup and Saucer, demitasse	70.00
Cup and Saucer, flat, 2″	60.00
Lid, teapot	150.00
Nut Dish, 4″	35.00

Pepper Mill	100.00
Plate, bread and butter, 6 1/4″	25.00
Plate, dinner, 10 3/8″	50.00
Plate, salad, 7 3/4″	35.00
Platter, oval, 17 1/2″	300.00
Sugar Bowl, covered	120.00
Sugar Bowl, covered, no lid	80.00
Vegetable, oval, 9 3/4″	170.00

Lenox, Rutledge, Temple Shape, gold inner ring

Bowl, fruit, flat, 6 1/2″	$50.00
Bowl, soup, flat, 8 5/8″	60.00
Cream Soup and Saucer	100.00
Creamer, 3 3/4″	100.00
Cup, demitasse, double	65.00
Cup, demitasse, single	65.00
Cup and Saucer, demitasse, double	70.00
Cup and Saucer, footed, 2 5/8″	60.00
Gravy Boat, attached underplate	200.00
Lid, coffeepot	170.00
Lid, vegetable, round	170.00
Plate, bread and butter, 6 3/8″	20.00
Plate, dinner	40.00
Plate, salad, 8 1/2″	30.00
Platter, oval, 15 3/4″	210.00
Platter, oval, 17″	280.00
Saucer	20.00
Sugar Bowl, covered, 3 1/2″	110.00
Sugar Bowl, covered, 3 1/2″, no lid	75.00
Vegetable, covered, round	350.00
Vegetable, oval, 9 3/4″	150.00

Lenox, Silhouette, temperware

Casserole, open, round, 6 5/8"	$70.00
Creamer	25.00
Cup and Saucer, flat, 2 3/4"	17.50
Lid, casserole, round, 6 5/8"	50.00
Plate, bread and butter, 6 3/8"	10.00
Plate, dinner, 10 1/4"	30.00
Plate, salad	20.00
Roaster, oval, 15 1/8"	80.00
Salt and Pepper Shakers, pair	45.00
Saucer	5.00
Sugar Bowl, covered	35.00

Lenox, Solitaire, Dimension Shape, platinum trim

Ashtray, 4 1/4"	$12.50
Bowl, fruit, 5 1/4"	25.00
Candlestick, single light, 4"	25.00
Chop Plate, 12 3/4"	90.00
Cream Soup and Saucer	80.00
Cream Soup Saucer	25.00
Creamer	50.00
Cup, footed, 3"	25.00
Cup and Saucer, footed, 3"	30.00
Lid, sugar bowl	27.50
Lid, vegetable, round	85.00
Plate, bread and butter, 6 3/8"	10.00
Plate, dinner, 10 3/4"	20.00
Plate, salad, 8 1/8"	15.00
Platter, oval, 14"	100.00
Saucer	10.00
Sugar Bowl, covered	65.00

Lenox, Snow Lily, Dimension Shape, platinum trim

Cream Soup Bowl	$130.00
Creamer	120.00
Cup and Saucer, footed, 3"	75.00
Plate, bread and butter, 6 1/2"	30.00
Plate, dinner, 10 3/4"	55.00
Plate, salad, 8 1/4"	40.00
Platter, oval, 16 3/8"	290.00
Sugar Bowl, covered	140.00
Vegetable, covered, round	440.00
Vegetable, oval, 10 1/4"	210.00

Lenox, Springdale, Presidential Shape, green leaves, platinum trim

Bowl, fruit, 5 1/2"	$55.00
Cup, footed, 2 1/8"	55.00
Cup and Saucer, demitasse	70.00

Cup and Saucer, footed, 2 1/8″	60.00
Plate, bread and butter, 6 3/8″	25.00
Plate, dinner, 10 5/8″	45.00
Plate, salad, 8 3/8″	35.00
Platter, serving, oval, 16″	250.00
Saucer, demitasse	25.00
Sugar Bowl, covered	120.00
Sugar Bowl, covered, no lid	90.00
Vegetable, oval, 9 3/4″	160.00

Vegetable, oval, 9 5/8″	150.00
Vegetable, round, 9″	180.00

Lenox, Temple Blossom, Temple Shape, gold trim

Bowl, fruit, flat, 6 1/2″	$55.00
Bowl, soup, flat, 8 1/2″	75.00
Chop Plate, 12 3/4″	230.00
Cream Soup and Saucer	130.00
Creamer	110.00
Cup and Saucer, demitasse	80.00
Cup and Saucer, footed, 2 1/2″	70.00
Plate, bread and butter, 6 3/8″	25.00
Plate, dinner, 10 7/8″	50.00
Plate, salad, 8 1/2″	40.00
Platter, oval, 13 1/2″	190.00
Platter, oval, 15 7/8″	240.00
Saucer	22.50
Sugar Bowl, covered	130.00
Vegetable, covered, round	400.00
Vegetable, oval, 9 3/4″	175.00

Lenox, Starlight, Coupe Shape, gold trim

Bowl, cereal, coupe, 5 1/4″	$55.00
Bowl, fruit, 5 1/2″	45.00
Bowl, soup, coupe, 7 1/2″	60.00
Chop Plate, 12 3/4″	160.00
Cigarette Holder	40.00
Cigarette Lighter	50.00
Coffeepot, covered	250.00
Cream Soup and Saucer	100.00
Cream Soup Bowl	90.00
Creamer	100.00
Cup, flat, 2 1/8″	55.00
Cup and Saucer, demitasse	60.00
Cup and Saucer, flat, 2 1/8″	60.00
Gravy Boat, attached underplate	200.00
Lid, coffeepot	125.00
Lid, teapot	150.00
Plate, bread and butter, 6 1/4″	20.00
Plate, dinner, 10 1/2″	40.00
Plate, luncheon, 9″	40.00
Plate, salad, 7 7/8″	30.00
Platter, oval, 13 3/4″	150.00
Platter, oval, 16″	200.00
Platter, oval, 17 1/4″	270.00
Sugar Bowl, covered	110.00
Sugar Bowl, covered, no lid	75.00
Teapot, covered	290.00
Teapot, covered, no lid	200.00
Vegetable, covered, round	350.00

Lenox, Tuscany, Dimension Shape, gold trim

Bowl, fruit, 5 1/2″	$80.00
Bowl, soup, coupe, 7 5/8″	110.00

Chop Plate, 12 3/4″	260.00
Coffeepot, covered	460.00
Cream Soup and Saucer	190.00
Cream Soup Bowl	180.00
Creamer	180.00
Cup and Saucer, demitasse	120.00
Cup and Saucer, footed, 3″	100.00
Lid, coffeepot	230.00
Lid, sugar bowl	100.00
Plate, bread and butter, 6 3/8″	40.00
Plate, dessert, 7 1/4″	50.00
Plate, dinner	80.00
Plate, salad, 8 1/8″	60.00
Platter, oval, 14 1/8″	350.00
Platter, oval, 16 3/8″	400.00
Platter, oval, 17 1/4″	500.00
Saucer, demitasse	40.00
Sugar Bowl, covered	200.00
Vegetable, oval, 8 5/8″	200.00
Vegetable, oval, 10 1/4″	300.00
Vegetable, round, 9 1/2″	250.00

Saucer	25.00
Sugar Bowl, covered, 3 1/8″	130.00
Sugar Bowl, covered, 3 1/8″, no lid	85.00
Teapot, covered	300.00
Teapot, covered, no lid	190.00
Vegetable, oval, 8 1/2″	135.00
Vegetable, oval, 9 3/4″	190.00
Vegetable, round, 9 1/2″	170.00

Lenox, Venture, Innovation Shape, platinum trim

Bowl, fruit, 5 5/8″	$50.00
Creamer	100.00
Cup, flat, 2 7/8″	50.00
Cup and Saucer, flat, 2 7/8″	55.00
Lid, coffeepot	150.00
Plate, bread and butter, 6 3/8″	20.00
Plate, dinner, 10 3/8″	45.00
Plate, salad, 8″	35.00
Sugar Bowl, covered	110.00

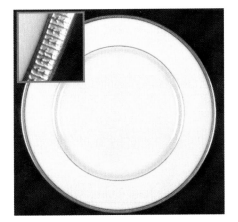

Lenox, Tuxedo, Presidential Shape, gold trim

Bowl, fruit, 5 5/8″	$55.00
Bowl, soup, flat, 8 3/8″	70.00
Coffeepot, covered	300.00
Creamer, 3 1/8″	110.00
Cup, demitasse	70.00
Cup and Saucer, demitasse	80.00
Cup and Saucer, footed, 2 1/8″	80.00
Gravy Boat, attached underplate	230.00
Lid, coffeepot	140.00
Lid, teapot	140.00
Plate, bread and butter, 6 3/8″	25.00
Plate, dinner, 10 1/2″	55.00
Plate, salad, 8 1/2″	40.00
Platter, oval, 13 5/8″	230.00
Platter, oval, 16 1/4″	280.00

Lenox, Versailles, Dimension Shape, gold trim

Creamer	$125.00
Cup and Saucer, demitasse	80.00
Cup and Saucer, footed, 3″	70.00

Gravy Boat, attached underplate	270.00
Lid, sugar bowl	70.00
Lid, vegetable	235.00
Plate, bread and butter, 6 3/8″	30.00
Plate, dinner	60.00
Plate, salad, 8 1/8″	40.00
Platter, oval, 16 3/8″	280.00
Saucer	25.00
Saucer, demitasse	25.00
Sugar Bowl, covered	140.00
Vegetable, oval, 10 1/8″	210.00

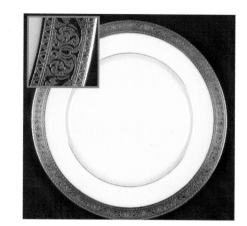

Cup and Saucer, demitasse, flat	100.00
Cup and Saucer, demitasse, footed	100.00
Cup and Saucer, footed, 2″	110.00
Gravy Boat, attached underplate	350.00
Lid, sugar bowl	130.00
Plate, bread and butter, 6 3/8″	35.00
Plate, dinner, 10 5/8″	75.00
Plate, salad, 8 1/2″	55.00
Platter, oval, 13 1/2″	330.00
Platter, oval, 16 1/8″	400.00
Platter, oval, 17″	480.00
Sugar Bowl, covered	200.00
Vegetable, oval, 9 1/2″	250.00

Lenox, Weatherly, Sculpture Shape, platinum trim

Chop Plate, 13″	$200.00
Cream Soup Bowl	120.00
Cup and Saucer, flat, 2 1/4″	60.00
Lid, teapot	150.00
Plate, bread and butter, 6 1/4″	30.00
Plate, dinner	55.00
Plate, salad, 7 7/8″	40.00
Saucer	20.00
Saucer, demitasse	30.00
Sugar Bowl, covered	130.00
Vegetable, oval, 9 1/2″	175.00

Lenox, Westwind, Coupe Shape

Lenox, Westchester, Presidential Shape, gold trim

Bowl, cereal, coupe, 5 7/8″	$90.00
Bowl, fruit, 5 1/2″	80.00
Bowl, soup, flat, 8 3/8″	100.00
Chop Plate, 12 3/4″	270.00
Creamer	170.00
Cup, bouillon	80.00
Cup, demitasse, flat	90.00
Cup, footed, 2″	90.00

Bowl, cereal, coupe, 5 1/4″	$50.00
Bowl, fruit, 5 1/2″	40.00
Bowl, soup, coupe, 7 1/2″	60.00
Chop Plate, 12 7/8″	160.00
Cream Soup and Saucer	100.00
Creamer	90.00
Cup and Saucer, demitasse	70.00
Cup and Saucer, flat, 2 1/8″	55.00
Gravy Boat, attached underplate	190.00
Lid, vegetable, round	175.00

Pepper Mill	100.00	Salt Shaker	85.00
Plate, bread and butter, 6 1/4″	20.00	Saucer	15.00
Plate, dinner, 10 3/8″	40.00	Sugar Bowl, covered, 3″	100.00
Plate, salad, 7 7/8″	30.00	Sugar Bowl, covered, 3″, no lid	70.00
Platter, oval, 13 3/4″	150.00	Teapot, covered	270.00
Platter, oval, 15 7/8″	200.00	Vegetable, covered, round	300.00
Saucer	17.50	Vegetable, oval, 8 1/2″	100.00
Saucer, demitasse	25.00	Vegetable, oval, 9 5/8″	120.00
Sugar Bowl, covered	110.00		
Teapot, covered	300.00		
Vegetable, covered, round	350.00		
Vegetable, oval, 9 3/4″	140.00		

Lenox, Windsong, Dimension Shape, platinum trim

Lenox, Wheat, Coupe Shape, gold trim

Ashtray, 4 3/8″	$17.50
Ashtray, 5 1/2″	17.50
Ashtray, 8″	40.00
Bowl, cereal, coupe, 5 1/4″	45.00
Bowl, fruit, 5 1/2″	40.00
Bowl, soup, coupe, 7 3/8″	55.00
Bud Vase, 8″	70.00
Chop Plate, 12 3/4″	150.00
Cigarette Box	70.00
Cigarette Holder	35.00
Cigarette Lighter	45.00
Coffeepot, covered	270.00
Cream Soup and Saucer	90.00
Creamer, 2 7/8″	80.00
Cup, demitasse, 1 5/8″	45.00
Cup and Saucer, demitasse, 1 5/8″	50.00
Cup and Saucer, flat, 2 1/8″	50.00
Gravy Boat, attached underplate	180.00
Hors d'oeuvre Dish, 5 7/8″	30.00
Pepper Mill	80.00
Plate, bread and butter, 6 1/4″	17.50
Plate, dinner, 10 3/8″	40.00
Plate, salad, 7 7/8″	25.00
Platter, oval, 13 5/8″	160.00
Platter, oval, 15 3/4″	190.00
Platter, oval, 17 1/2″	230.00

Bowl, soup, coupe, 7 3/8″	$80.00
Creamer	125.00
Cup and Saucer, demitasse	80.00
Cup and Saucer, footed, 3″	75.00
Plate, bread and butter, 6 3/8″	30.00
Plate, dessert, 7 1/4″	35.00
Plate, dinner, 10 3/4″	55.00
Plate, luncheon, 9 3/8″	60.00
Plate, salad, 8 1/8″	40.00
Platter, oval, 13 3/4″	240.00
Platter, oval, 14 1/8″	240.00
Platter, oval, 16 3/8″	290.00

Saucer	25.00
Saucer, demitasse	25.00
Vegetable, oval, 8 3/4″	150.00
Vegetable, oval, 10 1/4″	210.00

Lenox, Wyndcrest, Coupe Shape, platinum trim

Bowl, soup, coupe, 7 3/8″	$55.00		
Cigarette Holder	40.00	Plate, salad, 7 7/8″	25.00
Cigarette Lighter	50.00	Platter, oval, 16″	200.00
Creamer	90.00	Platter, oval, 16 1/4″	200.00
Cup and Saucer, demitasse	70.00	Salt Shaker and Pepper Mill	115.00
Cup and Saucer, flat, 2″	50.00	Saucer	15.00
Gravy Boat, attached underplate	180.00	Saucer, demitasse	25.00
Plate, bread and butter, 6 3/8″	17.50	Sugar Bowl, covered	100.00
Plate, dinner, 10 3/8″	40.00	Vegetable, covered, round	350.00
Plate, luncheon, 9″	35.00	Vegetable, oval, 9 5/8″	130.00

LONGCHAMP

The Longchamp Earthenware and Tile Works was founded in 1867 near Dijon, France. Longchamp produced dinnerware almost exclusively for the U.S. market and is well known for its patterns depicting people and scenery from the French countryside. Longchamp's tableware was produced until 1990.

Longchamp, Tulip

Bowl, salad, serving, 10 1/2″	$150.00
Candlestick, single light, 7 3/4″	35.00
Chop Plate, 11 5/8″	100.00
Chop Plate, 12 3/8″	110.00
Coffeepot, covered	130.00
Comport, 6 5/8″	100.00

Cream Soup Saucer	22.50
Creamer	50.00
Cup, snack set	45.00
Cup and Saucer, flat, 2 1/4″	30.00
Cup and Saucer, oversized	35.00
Gravy Boat	100.00
Jug, 6 3/8″	80.00
Lid, tureen	160.00
Plate, bread and butter	20.00
Plate, dinner	50.00
Plate, salad	32.50
Platter, oval, 13 3/4″	100.00
Platter, oval, 16 5/8″	130.00
Salt and Pepper Shakers, pair	60.00
Saucer	10.00
Snack Plate and Cup	50.00
Sugar Bowl, covered	60.00
Sugar Bowl, covered, no lid	35.00
Teapot, covered	150.00
Tureen, covered	350.00
Vegetable, 9 5/8″	90.00
Vegetable, covered, round	200.00

Miles Mason began his business career as an importer of china wares, matching pieces for incomplete sets. Mason's Ironstone was founded in 1795 when Mason joined into a partnership with earthenware manufacturer George Wolfe of Lane Delph in Fenton, Staffordshire, England, and Thomas Wolfe and John Lucock of the Islington China Manufactory of Liverpool to produce Chinese-style porcelain tableware. The partnership was dissolved in 1804.

From 1800 to 1813, Miles Mason produced blue-and-white transferware at the Victoria Works and the Minerva Works, two factories in Lane Delph. The Minerva Works was expanded to incorporate the Bagnell Factory and was renamed Fenton Stone Works. Miles Mason retired in 1813, turning over the management of the company to his sons Charles and George.

In 1813, the company patented its ironstone formula and manufacturing technique. Ironstone was produced at Fenton from 1813 to 1848.

George withdrew from the company in 1829. Charles remained until 1848, when economic difficulties caused him to sell the family business to Francis Morley. Morley and his partner Taylor Ashworth acquired the Mason designs and molds.

Francis Morley retired in 1862 and Ashworth's father purchased the business for Taylor and his brother, George Leach Ashworth. The new company was named George L. Ashworth & Brothers.

Financial trouble in 1883 forced the sale of the business to John Hackett Goddard and his son John Shaw Goddard. Ashworth & Brothers continued to sell Mason's-type ware in Oriental-style patterns for the next 100 years. In 1968, the company was renamed Mason's Ironstone China, Ltd. Today it is part of the Wedgwood Group.

Mason's, Vista Brown

Ashtray, 3 1/2″	$15.00
Bowl, cereal, coupe, 6 1/4″	20.00
Cake Plate, square, handled, 11″	70.00
Creamer, 4″	40.00
Cup and Saucer, flat, 2 1/4″	32.50
Cup and Saucer, oversized, 2 5/8″	35.00
Gravy Boat, attached underplate	100.00
Plate, bread and butter, 5 7/8″	12.50
Plate, dinner	32.50
Plate, salad	20.00
Platter, oval, 13 5/8″	80.00
Sugar Bowl, covered, 3 1/4″	50.00
Vegetable, oval, 8 3/4″	50.00
Vegetable, round, 8 3/4″	60.00

J. & G. MEAKIN

James Meakin established a pottery at Lane End in 1845 and moved it to Hanley, Staffordshire, in 1848. Upon his retirement in 1852, his sons James and George continued the company, trading as J. & G. Meakin.

The Meakins built the Eagle Pottery in 1859 and acquired the Eastwood Pottery at Joiners Square in 1887. They produced both earthenware and graniteware, decorated in the style of French porcelain for the American market. Meakin also produced Staffordshire and flow blue decorated pieces.

In 1970, J. & G. Meakin joined the Wedgwood Group.

J. & G. Meakin, Blue Nordic, shaped rim

Bowl, fruit, 5 3/8″	$15.00
Coffeepot, covered	100.00
Coffeepot, covered, no lid	80.00
Creamer	30.00
Cup and Saucer, flat, 2 7/8″	20.00
Gravy Boat, no underplate	65.00
Pitcher, 5 1/2″	80.00
Pitcher, 6 3/4″	80.00
Plate, bread and butter	10.00
Plate, dessert, 7″	10.00
Plate, dessert, square, 7″	10.00
Plate, dinner	22.50
Plate, salad	12.50
Platter, oval, 12 1/8″	50.00
Saucer	7.50
Sugar Bowl, covered	40.00
Sugar Bowl, covered, no lid	30.00
Vegetable, covered, round	110.00
Vegetable, covered, round, no lid	90.00

T. C. Prouty and his son Willis founded Metlox Pottery in Manhattan Beach, California, in 1927 to manufacture ceramic letters and tiles. The name "Metlox" combines the two words "Metal" and "Oxides."

Following T. C. Prouty's death in 1931 and the decline of the sign business due to the Depression, Willis adapted the plant to manufacture dinnerware. California Pottery, finished in brightly colored glazes, was the first line of dishes produced by Metlox. Next came Poppytrail, a table and kitchenware line introduced in 1934 and manufactured until 1942. Dinnerware production was halted during World War II, when the factory was converted for war production, but it was quickly resumed after the war.

In 1946, Evan K. Shaw purchased the company from Willis Prouty. In 1958, Metlox purchased the trade name and dinnerware molds of Vernon Kilns and developed its Vernon Ware branch. Although Evan Shaw died in 1980, his family continued to manage Metlox until it closed in 1989.

Metlox, Antique Grape, Poppytrail, white

Bowl, cereal, coupe, 7 3/8″	$20.00
Bowl, fruit, 6 1/4″	15.00
Bowl, salad, serving, 12 1/4″	80.00
Butter Dish, covered, 1/4 lb.	60.00
Candy Box, covered, no lid	35.00
Casserole, covered, round, 6 3/4″	100.00
Casserole, covered, round, 6 3/4″, no lid	50.00
Chop Plate, 12 1/4″	60.00
Coffeepot, covered	80.00
Compote, 5″	80.00
Creamer	25.00

Cup, flat, 3″	15.00
Cup and Saucer, flat, 3″	17.50
Gravy Boat, attached underplate	40.00
Lid, canister, flour, 8 1/4″	55.00
Lid, canister, sugar, 7 1/4″	45.00
Lid, coffeepot	40.00
Lid, sugar bowl	20.00
Pitcher, 4 1/2″	40.00
Pitcher, 5 1/4″	70.00
Pitcher, 8 1/4″	100.00
Plate, bread and butter, 6 3/8″	12.50
Plate, dinner	25.00
Plate, salad, 7 5/8″	15.00
Platter, oval, 9 1/2″	40.00
Platter, oval, 12 1/2″	45.00
Platter, oval, 14 3/8″	50.00
Relish, two-part, 9″	50.00
Salt and Pepper Shakers, pair	30.00
Sauce Boat	45.00
Saucer	5.00
Sugar Bowl, covered	40.00
Tumbler, water, 5″	40.00
Vegetable, covered, round, 6″	80.00
Vegetable, oval, 10 1/4″	50.00
Vegetable, round, 8 1/2″	40.00
Vegetable, round, 9 1/2″	40.00
Vegetable, round, divided, 8 1/2″	45.00
Vegetable, round, divided, 9 1/2″	45.00

Metlox, California Ivy, Poppytrail

Butter Dish, covered, 1/4 lb.	$45.00
Chop Plate, 13 1/4"	55.00
Creamer	17.50
Cup and Saucer, flat, 2 1/2"	15.00
Gravy Boat and Underplate	50.00
Gravy Boat, no underplate	40.00
Lid, butter dish, 1/4 lb.	35.00
Pitcher, 9 1/4"	85.00
Plate, bread and butter	5.00
Plate, dinner, 10 3/8"	20.00
Plate, salad	15.00
Platter, oval, 13 3/8"	45.00
Saucer	5.00
Vegetable, covered, round	90.00
Vegetable, covered, round, no lid	70.00
Vegetable, oval, divided, 11 1/4"	45.00
Vegetable, round, 9 1/8"	40.00

THE TOP FIVE PATTERNS
PERIOD LOOK—
COUNTRY MOTIF

———◼———

ARABIA OF FINLAND, ANEMONE
JOHNSON BROTHERS, HEARTS AND FLOWERS
METLOX POTTERY, CALIFORNIA PROVINCIAL
PFALTZGRAFF, AMERICA
PFALTZGRAFF, GOURMET

Canister, flour, 7 3/4"	140.00
Canister, sugar, 6 1/4"	120.00
Canister, tea, 5"	90.00
Chop Plate, 12"	60.00
Creamer	25.00
Cup and Saucer, flat, 2 3/8"	22.50
Grandmug, 5"	40.00
Gravy Boat	70.00
Hen on Nest, 5 5/8"	140.00
Lid, canister, sugar	40.00
Lid, coffeepot	50.00
Lid, cookie jar	70.00
Lid, sugar bowl	22.50
Mustard, no lid	32.50
Plate, bread and butter, 6 3/8"	12.50
Plate, dinner, 10"	25.00
Plate, luncheon, 9"	25.00
Plate, salad, 7 1/2"	17.50
Platter, oval, 11 1/4"	55.00
Platter, oval, 13 5/8"	60.00
Salt and Pepper Shakers, pair	35.00
Saucer	7.50
Soup Server, open, individual, 6 1/8"	25.00
Sugar Bowl, covered	45.00
Sugar Bowl, covered, no lid	30.00
Tray, bread, 9 3/4"	65.00
Tumbler, water, 5 1/4"	60.00
Vegetable, covered, round	100.00
Vegetable, rectangular, divided, 8 5/8"	55.00
Vegetable, round, 9 1/8"	45.00
Vegetable, round, 10"	50.00

Metlox, California Provincial, Poppytrail

Bowl, cereal, flat, 7 1/4"	$25.00
Bowl, fruit, flat, 6"	17.50
Bowl, soup, flat, 8 1/2"	25.00
Butter Dish, covered, 1/4 lb.	90.00

Vegetable, oval, 11 1/8″	45.00
Vegetable, round, 8″	35.00
Vegetable, round, 9 1/8″	35.00
Vegetable, round, divided, 8 1/8″	50.00
Vegetable, round, divided, 9″	50.00

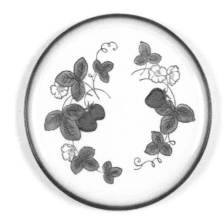

Metlox, California Strawberry, Poppytrail

Bowl, cereal, coupe, 5 3/4″	$12.50
Bowl, cereal, lug, 7″	15.00
Bowl, fruit, 5 1/2″	12.50
Bowl, salad, serving, 11 1/4″	50.00
Bowl, soup, coupe, 6 7/8″	15.00
Butter Dish, covered, 1/4 lb.	40.00
Canister, coffee, 6″	40.00
Canister, coffee, 6″, no lid	20.00
Canister, flour, 8″	80.00
Canister, flour, 8″, no lid	40.00
Canister, sugar, 7 1/4″	50.00
Canister, tea, 5 1/4″	40.00
Canister, tea, 5 1/4″, no lid	15.00
Chop Plate, 13 1/4″	50.00
Coffeepot, covered	70.00
Coffeepot, covered, no lid	50.00
Creamer	25.00
Cup and Saucer, flat, 2 3/4″	20.00
Fork, salad, serving, wooden prongs	20.00
Gravy Boat, attached underplate	50.00
Lid, casserole, 4 7/8″	40.00
Mug, 3 3/8″	22.50
Pepper Shaker	12.50
Pitcher, 4 1/2″	35.00
Pitcher, 5 1/4″	40.00
Pitcher, 8″	60.00
Plate, bread and butter, 6 1/2″	10.00
Plate, dinner, 10 3/8″	20.00
Plate, salad	15.00
Platter, oval, 9 3/4″	37.50
Platter, oval, 13 1/8″	40.00
Salt and Pepper Shakers, pair	25.00
Sauce Boat	50.00
Saucer	5.00
Sugar Bowl, covered	30.00
Teapot, covered, round, no lid	50.00
Tumbler, water, 5″	17.50
Vegetable, covered, round	70.00
Vegetable, covered, round, no lid	60.00

Metlox, Della Robbia, Vernonware, shaped rim

Bowl, cereal, flat, 7 1/4″	$20.00
Bowl, fruit, flat, 6 1/2″	15.00
Bowl, soup, flat, 8 1/2″	22.50
Butter Dish, covered, 1/4 lb.	80.00
Casserole, covered, round, 6″	165.00
Coffeepot, covered	80.00
Creamer	27.50
Cup and Saucer, flat, 3 1/4″	20.00
Gravy Boat, attached underplate	60.00
Lid, butter dish, 1/4 lb.	55.00
Lid, coffeepot	40.00
Lid, teapot	50.00
Mug, 3 3/4″	25.00
Plate, bread and butter, 6 1/2″	10.00
Plate, dinner	22.50
Plate, salad, 7 5/8″	15.00
Platter, oval, 9 3/4″	40.00
Platter, oval, 11 1/8″	50.00
Platter, oval, 14 1/2″	50.00
Salt and Pepper Shakers, pair	27.50
Saucer	5.00
Sugar Bowl, covered	37.50
Teapot, covered	100.00
Vegetable, oval, 12 1/4″	50.00
Vegetable, oval, divided, 12 1/4″	50.00
Vegetable, round, 10 5/8″	45.00
Vegetable, round, divided, 9 1/2″	50.00

Metlox, Homestead Provincial, Poppytrail

Ashtray, 4 5/8″	$17.50
Bowl, fruit, flat, 6″	15.00
Bowl, salad, serving, 11 3/8″	75.00
Bowl, soup, flat, 8 1/2″	22.50
Canister, coffee, 5 5/8″	60.00
Canister, flour	110.00
Canister, sugar, 6 3/8″	75.00
Chop Plate, 12″	50.00
Coffeepot, covered	80.00
Creamer	27.50
Cup and Saucer, flat, 2 1/8″	20.00
Gravy Boat	60.00
Hen on Nest, 5 5/8″	135.00
Jam	80.00
Jam, no lid	60.00
Lid, canister, flour	35.00
Lid, coffeepot	40.00
Lid, teapot	50.00
Pepper Shaker	15.00
Pitcher, 6 5/8″	70.00
Plate, bread and butter, 6 1/2″	10.00
Plate, dinner, 10″	22.50
Plate, salad, 7 1/2″	15.00
Platter, oval, 11 1/4″	50.00
Platter, oval, 13 1/2″	50.00
Salt and Pepper Shakers, pair	30.00
Salt Shaker, mill set	35.00
Saucer	5.00
Soup Server, open, individual, 6 1/4″	22.50
Sugar Bowl, covered	40.00
Sugar Bowl, covered, no lid	27.50
Vegetable, covered, round	100.00
Vegetable, rectangular, divided, 8 5/8″	50.00
Vegetable, round, 8 1/4″	40.00
Vegetable, round, 10″	45.00

Metlox, Red Rooster, Poppytrail

Bowl, fruit, flat, 6″	$10.00
Bowl, soup, flat, 8 1/2″	15.00
Carafe, no lid	60.00
Chop Plate, 12″	45.00
Coffeepot, covered	120.00
Creamer	20.00
Creamer, red	20.00
Cup, flat, 2 1/4″	15.00
Cup and Saucer, flat, 2 1/4″	17.50
Gravy Boat	50.00
Lid, carafe	60.00
Lid, teapot	60.00
Lid, teapot, cream	60.00
Plate, bread and butter, 6 3/8″	10.00
Plate, dinner, 10″	20.00
Plate, salad	12.50
Platter, oval, 11 1/4″	40.00
Platter, oval, 13 1/2″	45.00
Salt and Pepper Shakers, pair, red	27.50
Saucer	5.00
Sugar Bowl, covered	30.00
Tray, bread, 9 3/4″	50.00
Vegetable, covered, round	100.00
Vegetable, covered, round, no lid	70.00
Vegetable, rectangular, divided, 8 3/4″	60.00
Vegetable, round, 9″	40.00
Vegetable, round, 10″	40.00

Metlox, Sculptured Daisy, Poppytrail

Metlox, Sculptured Grape, Poppytrail

Ashtray, 6 ¹/₂″	$30.00
Baker, oval, 11 ¹/₈″	55.00
Bowl, cereal, coupe, 7 ¹/₈″	15.00
Bowl, fruit, flat, 6 ¹/₈″	12.50
Bowl, salad, serving, 12 ¹/₄″	65.00
Bowl, soup, flat, 8 ¹/₂″	17.50
Butter Dish, covered, ¹/₄ lb., no lid	30.00
Canister, sugar, no lid	45.00
Casserole, covered, round, 6 ⁵/₈″	100.00
Chop Plate, 12 ¹/₄″	65.00
Coffeepot, covered	60.00
Creamer	20.00
Cup and Saucer, flat, 3″	17.50
Gravy Boat	40.00
Gravy Boat, attached underplate	40.00
Lid, casserole, round, 6 ⁵/₈″	50.00
Lid, coffeepot	35.00
Lid, teapot	35.00
Lid, vegetable, round	35.00
Mug, 3 ¹/₂″	20.00
Pitcher, 5 ³/₄″	40.00
Pitcher, 7″	50.00
Pitcher, 8 ³/₄″	60.00
Plate, bread and butter, 6 ¹/₄″	7.50
Plate, dinner, 10 ⁵/₈″	20.00
Plate, salad, 7 ⁵/₈″	12.50
Platter, oval, 9 ³/₄″	30.00
Platter, oval, 11 ¹/₈″	40.00
Platter, oval, 14 ³/₈″	50.00
Salt and Pepper Shakers, pair	25.00
Salt Shaker	12.50
Saucer	5.00
Sugar Bowl, covered	30.00
Sugar Bowl, covered, no lid	22.50
Teapot, covered, no lid	55.00
Vegetable, covered, round, 6 ³/₈″	70.00
Vegetable, round, 7 ⁷/₈″	35.00
Vegetable, round, 9 ¹/₈″	40.00
Vegetable, round, divided, 9 ¹/₈″	40.00

Bowl, cereal, coupe, 7 ¹/₄″	$20.00
Butter Dish, covered, ¹/₄ lb.	60.00
Canister, tea, 5″, no lid	45.00
Casserole, covered, round, 6 ³/₄″	100.00
Casserole, covered, round, 6 ³/₄″, no lid	50.00
Coffeepot, covered	80.00
Compote, 5″	80.00
Creamer	25.00
Cup and Saucer, flat, 3″	17.50
Gravy Boat, attached underplate	40.00
Lid, butter dish	20.00
Lid, sugar bowl	20.00
Lid, teapot	55.00
Plate, bread and butter	12.50
Plate, dinner	25.00
Plate, salad, 7 ¹/₂″	15.00
Platter, oval, 9 ¹/₂″	40.00
Platter, oval, 12 ³/₈″	45.00
Platter, oval, 14 ¹/₄″	50.00
Salt and Pepper Shakers, pair	30.00
Saucer	5.00
Sugar Bowl, covered	40.00
Vegetable, covered, round, 6″	80.00
Vegetable, covered, round, 6″, no lid	60.00
Vegetable, oval, 10 ¹/₈″	50.00
Vegetable, round, 9 ¹/₂″	40.00
Vegetable, round, divided, 9 ¹/₂″	45.00

MIKASA

Mikasa, Inc. is a designer, developer, and marketer of tabletop products. Mikasa owns no manufacturing facilities, but over the past thirty years has developed relationships with more than 150 manufacturers in twenty-two countries. The company's range of products includes casual and formal dinnerware, crystal stemware and serving pieces, stainless steel flatware, and gifts and decorative accessories. The name "Mikasa" means "The Company."

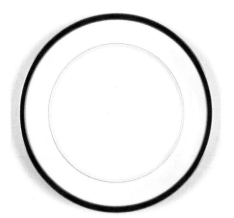

Mikasa, Black Tie, gold trim

Bowl, fruit, 6 ¼"	$22.50
Chop Plate, 12 ⅜"	120.00
Creamer	70.00
Cup and Saucer, footed, 3 ¼"	50.00
Lid, sugar bowl	50.00
Lid, vegetable, oval	165.00
Plate, bread and butter, 7 ⅛"	20.00
Plate, dinner, 10 ¾"	45.00
Plate, salad, 8 ⅜"	25.00
Saucer	15.00
Sugar Bowl, covered	100.00
Vegetable, round, 9 ¼"	100.00

Mikasa, Blue Daisies

Bowl, soup, flat, 8 ½"	$15.00
Chop Plate, 12 ½"	40.00
Creamer	20.00
Cup and Saucer, flat, 3 ½"	17.50
Plate, bread and butter	10.00
Plate, dinner	22.50
Plate, salad, 8"	10.00
Saucer	5.00
Sugar Bowl, covered	30.00
Vegetable, round, 9 ¾"	35.00

Creamer, 4 1/2″	25.00
Cup and Saucer, flat, 3 3/8″	20.00
Lid, casserole, oval, 8 1/4″	60.00
Plate, dinner	22.50
Plate, salad	15.00
Saucer	7.50
Sugar Bowl, covered	30.00
Vegetable, round, 9 3/4″	40.00

Mikasa, Buckskin, potters art

Bowl, cereal, coupe, 6 3/4″	$15.00
Bowl, fruit, 4 3/4″	15.00
Butter Dish, covered, 1/4 lb.	50.00
Butter Dish, covered, 1/4 lb., no lid	25.00
Casserole, covered, round, 7 3/4″	100.00
Chop Plate, 12 3/8″	40.00
Creamer	25.00
Cup, cappuccino, 3 7/8″	20.00
Cup and Saucer, flat, 2 3/8″	17.50
Gravy Boat and Underplate	60.00
Plate, dinner, 10 3/4″	20.00
Plate, salad, 8″	12.50
Platter, oval, 15 1/4″	140.00
Salt and Pepper Shakers, pair	30.00
Salt Shaker	15.00
Snack Plate and Cup	25.00
Sugar Bowl, covered	40.00
Vegetable, round, 9″	40.00
Warmer Stand	55.00

Mikasa, Capistrano, #F2010

Bowl, soup, coupe, 8 3/8″	$15.00
Chop Plate, 12 1/2″	55.00
Coffeepot, covered	100.00

Mikasa, Charisma, gray

Bowl, fruit, flat, 5 5/8″	$12.50
Bowl, soup, flat, 8 1/4″	15.00
Chop Plate, 12 1/4″	50.00
Coffeepot, covered	130.00
Coffeepot, covered, no lid	105.00
Creamer	25.00
Cup and Saucer, footed, 3 1/4″	20.00
Lid, sugar bowl	20.00
Plate, bread and butter, 6 1/4″	10.00
Plate, dinner, 10 5/8″	20.00
Plate, salad, 7 5/8″	12.50
Saucer	7.50
Sugar Bowl, covered	40.00
Vegetable, round, 9 1/4″	45.00

Mikasa, Country Cabin

Bean Pot, covered, 5 3/4″	$120.00
Bowl, cereal, coupe, 6 3/4″	15.00
Bowl, fruit, 4 5/8″	15.00
Butter Dish, covered, 1/4 lb.	45.00
Casserole, covered, round, 8″	130.00
Chop Plate, 12 1/4″	50.00
Creamer	30.00
Cup and Saucer, flat, 2 1/2″	15.00
Gravy Boat and Underplate	70.00
Gravy Boat, no underplate	50.00
Gravy Boat Underplate	25.00
Lid, bean pot	60.00
Lid, teapot	60.00
Napkin Ring	12.50
Plate, bread and butter	10.00
Plate, dinner, 10 3/4″	25.00
Plate, salad, 8 1/8″	15.00
Platter, oval, 15 1/8″	100.00
Salt and Pepper Shakers, pair	30.00
Sugar Bowl, covered	45.00
Teapot, covered	120.00
Vegetable, round, 9″	50.00
Warmer Stand	70.00

Canister, tea, 3 1/8″, no lid	22.50
Cup and Saucer, flat, 3 1/2″	17.50
Plate, bread and butter	7.50
Plate, dinner, 10 3/4″	22.50
Plate, salad, 8″	12.50
Tureen, covered	150.00

Mikasa, Dresden Rose, Fine China, platinum trim

Bowl, fruit, flat, 5 1/2″	$15.00
Bowl, soup, flat, 8 3/8″	15.00
Chop Plate, 12 1/4″	50.00
Creamer	30.00
Cup and Saucer, footed, 3″	20.00
Plate, bread and butter	12.50
Plate, dinner	25.00
Plate, salad, 7 1/2″	10.00
Saucer	5.00
Sugar Bowl, covered	50.00
Vegetable, round, 9 1/4″	50.00

Mikasa, Day Dreams

Bowl, soup, flat, 8 1/2″	$12.50
Candlestick, 7 1/8″	25.00
Candlestick, single light, 7″	15.00
Canister, coffee, 3 3/4″	40.00
Canister, coffee, 3 3/4″, no lid	30.00
Canister, flour, 6 3/8″	65.00
Canister, sugar, 4 7/8″	50.00
Canister, sugar, 4 7/8″, no lid	40.00
Canister, tea, 3 1/8″	30.00

Mikasa, Fire Song, potters art

Bean Pot, covered	$120.00
Bowl, cereal, coupe, 6 3/4″	17.50
Butter Dish, covered, 1/4 lb.	40.00
Casserole, covered, round, 8″	130.00
Chop Plate, 12 1/2″	50.00
Creamer	30.00
Cup, flat, 2 1/2″	15.00
Cup and Saucer, flat, 2 1/2″	17.50
Gravy Boat and Underplate	60.00
Gravy Boat Underplate	20.00
Lid, sugar bowl	22.50
Lid, teapot	50.00
Pepper Shaker	15.00
Plate, dinner, 10 7/8″	25.00
Plate, salad, 8 1/8″	15.00
Platter, oval, 15 1/4″	120.00
Salt and Pepper Shakers, pair	30.00
Sugar Bowl, covered	45.00
Teapot, covered	100.00
Vegetable, round, 9″	40.00

Butter Dish, covered, 1/4 lb.	40.00
Butter Dish, covered, 1/4 lb., no lid	30.00
Candlestick, 7 1/8″	35.00
Casserole, covered, individual, 4 1/2″	30.00
Casserole, covered, oval, 8 1/4″	100.00
Chop Plate, 12 1/2″	45.00
Coffeepot, covered	100.00
Coffeepot, covered, no lid	65.00
Creamer	20.00
Cup and Saucer, flat, 3 1/2″	17.50
Dish, leaf shape, 10 1/2″	20.00
Dish, leaf shape, 15 1/4″	20.00
Dish, shell shape, 5 5/8″	20.00
Goblet, 5 3/4″	15.00
Gravy Boat and Underplate	60.00
Gravy Boat, no underplate	45.00
Lid, casserole, individual, 4 1/2″	15.00
Lid, casserole, round, 8 1/4″	50.00
Lid, tureen	95.00
Mug, 4 1/8″	15.00
Pitcher, 8″	40.00
Plate, bread and butter	12.50
Plate, dinner	22.50
Plate, salad, 8″	10.00
Platter, oval, 14 1/2″	90.00
Quiche Dish, 10 1/4″	35.00
Salt and Pepper Shakers, pair	30.00
Saucer	5.00
Soufflé, 7 1/8″	50.00
Sugar Bowl, covered	30.00
Sugar Bowl, covered, no lid	20.00
Tureen, covered	190.00
Vegetable, round, 9 3/4″	30.00
Wine, 4 3/4″	15.00

Mikasa, Garden Club, no decal

Baker, rectangular, 15″	$100.00
Bowl, soup, flat, 8 3/8″	15.00

Mikasa, Just Flowers

Bowl, fruit, 5″	$12.50
Box, covered, round, 4 5/8″	55.00
Box, covered, round, 5 1/8″, no lid	40.00

Bud Vase, 8 1/8"	50.00
Butter Tray, 9"	35.00
Butter Tray, 9 1/4"	35.00
Candleholder, 3"	45.00
Candlestick, single light, 5 3/4"	45.00
Coaster, 5"	12.50
Coffeepot, covered, 8"	200.00
Coffeepot, covered, mini, 6 1/2"	100.00
Cream Soup and Saucer	50.00
Creamer	45.00
Creamer, mini, 3 1/8"	25.00
Cup, demitasse, 2 1/2"	17.50
Cup and Saucer, demitasse, 2 1/2"	25.00
Cup and Saucer, flat, 2 7/8"	25.00
Egg Box, covered, 4 5/8"	50.00
Gravy Boat and Underplate	110.00
Gravy Boat Underplate	35.00
Lid, coffeepot	100.00
Lid, teapot, 5 7/8"	100.00
Lid, vegetable	110.00
Plate, bread and butter, 6 5/8"	12.50
Plate, dinner, 10 5/8"	25.00
Plate, luncheon, 9 1/8"	25.00
Plate, salad, 7 5/8"	17.50
Platter, oval, 13"	130.00
Platter, oval, 14 7/8"	130.00
Platter, oval, 16 7/8"	180.00
Salt and Pepper Shakers, pair	40.00
Saucer	7.50
Sugar Bowl, covered	60.00
Sugar Bowl, covered, mini	40.00
Sugar Bowl, covered, no lid	40.00
Teapot, covered, mini, 2 7/8"	125.00
Vegetable, covered, round	210.00
Vegetable, round, 9 1/4"	80.00

Chop Plate, 12 5/8"	50.00
Coffeepot, covered	200.00
Coffeepot, covered, no lid	150.00
Creamer	40.00
Cup and Saucer, flat, 3 1/8"	25.00
Gravy Boat and Underplate	110.00
Plate, bread and butter, 6 1/2"	15.00
Plate, dinner	32.50
Plate, salad, 8 1/4"	17.50
Saucer	7.50
Sugar Bowl, covered	60.00
Sugar Bowl, covered, no lid	45.00
Vegetable, round, 10 3/8"	70.00

Mikasa, Mount Holyoke

Bowl, fruit, 5 5/8"	$20.00
Bowl, soup, coupe, 7 3/4"	30.00
Coffeepot, covered	230.00
Cream Soup and Saucer	80.00
Creamer	50.00
Cup, footed, 3"	35.00
Cup and Saucer, demitasse	30.00
Cup and Saucer, footed, 3"	40.00
Gravy Boat, attached underplate	120.00
Plate, bread and butter, 6 1/2"	15.00
Plate, dinner	35.00
Plate, salad, 7 1/2"	20.00
Platter, oval, 12 3/4"	80.00
Platter, oval, 14 3/4"	150.00
Salt Shaker	25.00
Sugar Bowl, covered	70.00
Sugar Bowl, covered, no lid	55.00

Mikasa, Margaux, Fine Ivory

Bowl, cereal, flat, 6 5/8"	$30.00
Bowl, soup, flat, 9 3/8"	30.00

Mikasa, Renaissance, white

Bowl, soup, flat, 9 3/8″	$20.00
Chop Plate, 12 1/2″	75.00
Coffeepot, covered	200.00
Creamer	40.00
Cup and Saucer, flat, 3 1/8″	27.50
Lid, tureen	125.00
Plate, bread and butter	15.00
Plate, dinner	30.00
Plate, salad	17.50
Platter, oval, 14 7/8″	120.00
Saucer	10.00
Sugar Bowl, covered	50.00
Tureen, covered	250.00
Vegetable, round, 10 1/2″	70.00

Mikasa, Silk Flowers, Continental

Augratin, 10 1/4″	$30.00
Augratin, 12″	30.00
Baker, rectangular, 12 5/8″	60.00
Bowl, fruit, 4 5/8″	10.00
Bowl, soup, flat, 8 3/8″	12.50
Butter Dish, covered, 1/4 lb.	40.00
Cake Plate, 12 1/4″	30.00

Canister, coffee, 5 1/4″	40.00
Canister, flour, 6 1/2″	70.00
Canister, sugar, 6″	60.00
Canister, sugar, 6″, no lid	45.00
Canister, tea, 4 1/2″	35.00
Casserole, covered, oval, 8″	80.00
Casserole, covered, round, 6 1/4″	100.00
Cheese and Cracker	70.00
Cheese Dish, 10 1/2″	65.00
Chip and Dip, 4 7/8″, no plate	65.00
Chop Plate, 12 1/4″	40.00
Chop Plate, 14 3/8″	40.00
Cream Soup and Saucer	27.50
Cream Soup Bowl	25.00
Creamer	22.50
Cup, flat, 3″	15.00
Cup, footed, 3 1/8″	15.00
Cup, oversized	20.00
Cup and Saucer, demitasse	15.00
Cup and Saucer, flat, 3″	20.00
Cup and Saucer, footed, 3 1/8″	20.00
Gift Box, covered, 7 3/4″	80.00
Gravy Boat and Underplate	55.00
Mug, 4 3/4″	12.50
Pie Server	17.50
Plate, bread and butter	7.50
Plate, dinner, 10 3/8″	17.50
Plate, salad, 8 1/4″	10.00
Platter, serving, oval, 14 3/4″	80.00
Quiche Dish, 9 7/8″	40.00
Ramekin, 4″	12.50
Salt and Pepper Shakers, pair	30.00
Saucer	5.00

Soufflé, 7 3/8″	40.00
Soufflé, individual, 4″	10.00
Sugar Bowl, covered	35.00
Sugar Bowl, covered, no lid	25.00
Tureen, covered	120.00
Vase, covered, 12 1/4″	90.00
Vase, covered, 13 1/2″	120.00
Vegetable, round, 8 1/2″	40.00

Mikasa, Strawberry Festival

Bowl, soup, flat, 8 1/2″	$15.00
Casserole, covered, oval, 8 3/8″	100.00
Chop Plate, 12 3/8″	50.00
Coffeepot, covered	90.00
Creamer	22.50
Cup and Saucer, flat, 3 1/2″	17.50
Gravy Boat and Underplate	60.00
Plate, bread and butter	12.50
Plate, dinner, 10 7/8″	22.50
Plate, salad, 8″	12.50
Platter, oval, 14 3/4″	90.00
Saucer	5.00
Sugar Bowl, covered	30.00
Sugar Bowl, covered, no lid	22.50
Vegetable, round, 9 3/4″	35.00

Mikasa, Sketch Book, fire

Augratin, individual, 8 3/8″	$22.50
Baker, covered, oval, 7 3/4″	165.00
Baker, oval, 12 1/4″	90.00
Baker, round, 10 7/8″	150.00
Bowl, soup, flat, 9″	20.00
Canister, coffee	60.00
Canister, flour, 5 7/8″, no lid	80.00
Canister, tea	45.00
Casserole, covered, individual, 5 1/4″	60.00
Casserole, covered, oval, 8″	160.00
Casserole, covered, round, 6 1/4″	120.00
Casserole, covered, round, 7 1/2″	150.00
Casserole, covered, round, 8 3/4″	180.00
Casserole, covered, round, 9 1/2″	200.00
Casserole, covered, round, 10 1/2″	230.00
Chop Plate, 12 3/8″	60.00
Creamer	40.00
Cup and Saucer, flat, 2 5/8″	27.50
Kettle	80.00
Lid, casserole, round, 9″	100.00
Plate, bread and butter	15.00
Plate, dinner	27.50
Plate, salad	15.00
Ramekin, 4″	22.50
Saucer	10.00
Skillet, covered, 10″	155.00
Soufflé, 7 1/2″	70.00
Sugar Bowl, covered	60.00
Vegetable, round, 9″	55.00

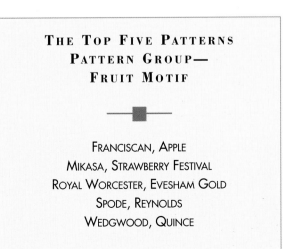

THE TOP FIVE PATTERNS
PATTERN GROUP—
FRUIT MOTIF

FRANCISCAN, APPLE
MIKASA, STRAWBERRY FESTIVAL
ROYAL WORCESTER, EVESHAM GOLD
SPODE, REYNOLDS
WEDGWOOD, QUINCE

Mikasa, Tango, #EJ702, Rondo

Baker, rectangular, 12 ³/₄″	$150.00
Bowl, fruit, 4 ⁵/₈″	15.00
Bowl, soup, coupe, 7 ⁵/₈″	22.50
Cake Plate, 12 ¹/₄″	55.00
Cake Plate and Server	90.00
Casserole, covered, round, 8 ³/₄″	185.00
Cheese and Cracker	90.00
Chop Plate, 12 ⁵/₈″	50.00
Coffeepot, covered	200.00
Creamer	40.00
Cup, flat, 3″	25.00
Cup and Saucer, breakfast, 2 ⁵/₈″	40.00
Cup and Saucer, demitasse	30.00
Cup and Saucer, flat, 3″	30.00
Lid, casserole, oval, 8 ⁷/₈″	80.00
Lid, casserole, round, 8 ⁷/₈″	95.00
Lid, sugar bowl	30.00
Lid, teapot	100.00
Lid, tureen	85.00
Mug, 4 ¹/₄″	30.00
Pie Server, solid piece	35.00
Plate, bread and butter	15.00
Plate, dinner, 10 ⁷/₈″	30.00
Plate, luncheon, 9 ⁷/₈″	22.50
Plate, salad, 8 ¹/₈″	17.50
Quiche Dish, 9″	100.00

Salt and Pepper Shakers, pair	30.00
Saucer	10.00
Snack Plate and Cup	40.00
Soufflé, 7 ¹/₂″	100.00
Sugar Bowl, covered	60.00
Teapot, covered	200.00

Mikasa, Whole Wheat, #E8000 DX10

Bowl, soup, flat, 8 ¹/₂″	$15.00
Butter Dish, covered, ¹/₄ lb.	40.00
Casserole, covered, oval, 8 ¹/₄″	100.00
Chop Plate, 12 ¹/₂″	50.00
Coffeepot, covered, no lid	70.00
Creamer	22.50
Cup and Saucer	17.50
Goblet, 5 ⁵/₈″	15.00
Plate, bread and butter	12.50
Plate, dinner, 10 ⁷/₈″	20.00
Plate, salad, 8″	12.50
Saucer	5.00
Sugar Bowl, covered, no lid	20.00
Wine, 4 ⁵/₈″	15.00

In 1793, Thomas Minton, William Pownall, and Joseph Poulson formed a partnership and built a pottery factory in Stoke-on-Trent in Staffordshire, England. They began producing blue-printed earthenwares in 1796. Cream-colored earthenware and bone china were introduced in 1798. By 1810, Minton was producing a wide range of styles and wares.

Minton's sons, Thomas and Herbert, entered into a partnership with their father in 1817. Thomas left soon after and a new partnership comprised of Thomas Minton and his son Herbert was formed in 1823.

Thomas Minton died in 1836, leaving Herbert in control. Rapid expansion over the previous decade led Herbert to form a partnership with John Boyle, an experienced local potter, in 1836. Minton & Boyle operated until its dissolution in 1842. Herbert's nephews, Daintry Hollins and Colin Minton Campbell joined him in 1842 and 1849, respectively.

Herbert Minton achieved international renown with Minton's entries in the Great Exhibition of 1851. Queen Victoria made her first Minton purchase in 1840, which lead to Minton receiving commissions from many of the royal and aristocratic houses of Europe and from wealthy families in America, India, and Australia.

Following Herbert Minton's death in 1858, Colin Minton Campbell succeeded his uncle. In 1883, the modern company was formed and named Mintons Limited. After Campbell's death in 1885, Minton continued to be the leading English pottery producer of the nineteenth century.

In 1968, Minton became a member of the Royal Doulton Tableware Group. Minton still produces bone china tableware and some ornamental pieces today.

Minton, Ancestral

Cake Plate, square, handled, 9 7/8"	$150.00	Cream Soup Saucer	32.50
Chop Plate, 12 1/2"	240.00	Creamer	90.00
Coffeepot, covered	370.00	Cup, demitasse, flat	55.00
Cream Soup and Saucer	100.00	Cup, flat	65.00
		Cup and Saucer, demitasse, flat	60.00
		Cup and Saucer, demitasse, footed	60.00
		Cup and Saucer, flat	70.00
		Eggcup, single, 1 5/8"	50.00
		Gravy Boat, attached underplate	260.00
		Gravy Boat and Underplate, flat	260.00
		Gravy Boat and Underplate, footed	260.00
		Gravy Boat Underplate, footed	85.00
		Lid, coffeepot	185.00
		Lid, sugar bowl	75.00
		Lid, sugar bowl, mini	50.00
		Lid, teapot	185.00
		Lid, vegetable	235.00
		Plate, bread and butter, 6 1/8"	30.00
		Plate, dinner	70.00
		Plate, luncheon, 9"	65.00

Plate, salad, 7 7/8″	45.00
Platter, oval, 10 3/8″	170.00
Platter, oval, 15 1/8″	320.00
Platter, oval, 18″	450.00
Salt and Pepper Shakers, pair	80.00
Saucer	22.50
Sugar Bowl, covered	150.00
Sugar Bowl, covered, mini	100.00
Sugar Bowl, open	90.00
Teapot, covered	370.00
Vegetable, covered, oval	470.00
Vegetable, oval	180.00

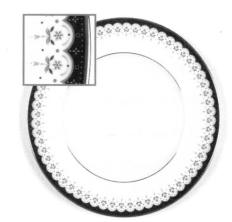

Plate, dinner, 10 5/8″	105.00
Plate, luncheon, 9″	130.00
Plate, salad, 8″	70.00
Platter, oval, 13 1/2″	370.00
Platter, oval, 16 3/8″	540.00
Sugar Bowl, covered	280.00

Minton, Bellemeade, platinum trim

Cup and Saucer	$32.50
Lid, sugar bowl	40.00
Lid, teapot	85.00
Plate, bread and butter	12.50
Plate, dinner	32.50
Plate, luncheon, 9″	40.00
Plate, salad	25.00
Saucer, demitasse	10.00
Sugar Bowl, covered	80.00
Sugar Bowl, covered, mini	60.00

Minton, Grasmere, gold trim

Minton, Consort, gold trim

Coffeepot, covered	$550.00
Creamer	180.00
Cup, demitasse	65.00
Cup, footed, 3″	70.00
Cup and Saucer, demitasse	100.00
Cup and Saucer, footed, 3″	110.00
Gravy Boat Underplate	180.00
Plate, bread and butter, 6 5/8″	50.00

Bowl, fruit, 5 1/4″	$30.00
Bowl, soup, flat, 8 1/4″	55.00
Coffeepot, covered	230.00
Coffeepot, covered, no lid	160.00
Cream Soup and Saucer	85.00
Creamer	80.00
Cup, demitasse	40.00
Cup, footed, 3″	45.00
Cup and Saucer, demitasse	45.00
Cup and Saucer, footed, 3″	50.00
Gravy Boat, no underplate	120.00
Lid, sugar bowl	60.00
Lid, teapot	115.00
Plate, bread and butter, 6 1/2″	20.00
Plate, dinner, 10 5/8″	45.00
Plate, salad, 8″	30.00
Platter, oval, 13 5/8″	170.00

Sugar Bowl, covered	120.00
Teapot, covered	230.00
Vegetable, oval, 10 3/4″	120.00

Plate, dinner, 10 5/8″	70.00
Plate, salad, 7 7/8″	50.00
Plate, salad, crescent, 8 1/2″	70.00
Sugar Bowl, covered	165.00
Teapot, covered	375.00

Minton, Henley, #1793, gold trim

Cup and Saucer, footed, 3″	$75.00
Plate, bread and butter, 6 1/2″	40.00
Plate, dinner, 10 3/4″	80.00
Plate, salad, 8″	50.00
Cream Soup Saucer	40.00
Cup and Saucer, demitasse	80.00
Saucer, demitasse	25.00
Vegetable, covered, oval	550.00

Minton, Penrose, platinum trim

Cup and Saucer, footed, 3″	$45.00
Lid, sugar bowl	50.00
Lid, teapot	125.00
Lid, vegetable, oval, 7″	165.00
Plate, bread and butter	25.00
Plate, dinner, 10 5/8″	45.00
Plate, salad, 8″	30.00
Saucer	15.00
Saucer, demitasse	15.00
Sugar Bowl, covered	95.00

Minton, Marlow Gold, #H5017, gold trim

Chop Plate, 12 5/8″	$240.00
Cream Soup and Saucer	120.00
Creamer	95.00
Cup and Saucer, demitasse	75.00
Cup and Saucer, flat, 2 1/4″	75.00
Gravy Boat, attached underplate	265.00
Lid, sugar bowl	85.00
Plate, bread and butter, 6 1/4″	35.00

Minton, Stanwood, gold trim

Cup, footed, 3″	$60.00
Cup and Saucer, footed, 3″	65.00
Plate, bread and butter, 6 5/8″	25.00
Plate, dinner, 10 3/4″	65.00
Plate, salad, 8″	45.00

THE ART OF FINE DINING—
A LOOK BACK

Fine dining is a practiced formal art. Strict rules of etiquette apply. In the 1920s and 1930s, formal dining was the norm, even in small towns and rural America. Not so in the 1990s, in spite of Miss Manners's best efforts.

How formal was the art of fine dining? Consider these tips on table manners, found in Ellye Howell Glover's *"Dame Curtsey's" Book of Etiquette, Eighth Edition*, published in 1922 by A. C. McClurg & Co.:

"There is but one way to judge people by a casual glance, and that is by their knowledge of etiquette, or, as one of more gifted tongue than the writer puts it, 'by the several politenesses of the time.' The little niceties of social usage should not be things apart from the every-day life, but be so moulded into the very existence that they are not realized, but are as natural as the air breathed without effort.

"There should be no such thing as 'company manners.' From earliest childhood one should be taught to sit erect at [the] table; not to reach forward to catch a mouthful of food; not to eat fast; to have the seat at just the right distance from the table; not to put one's elbows on the table during the progress of a meal; not to toy with napkin-ring, fork, or spoon, but keep the hands quietly in the lap when not occupied in eating. . . .

"When a meal is finished in a *café* or hotel, the napkin is never folded but laid as it was used on the table beside the plate. The same rule applies when at a repast in the home of a friend, if it is for one occasion only. . . .

"To eat slowly and deliberately is not only an evidence of good manners, but shows a knowledge of hygiene. Only the unlettered bolt their food, scrape the dish for the last mouthful, and make a noise while eating. . . .

"Finger bowls are always necessary with a fruit course; the bowl is half-filled with water and placed upon a doily-covered plate. Unless a second plate is provided, the doily is removed with the bowl and placed to one side, and the fruit put on the plate. . . .

"A morsel that proves too hot, or spoiled, may be quietly removed with the napkin and consigned to the side of the plate without comment. . . .

"Bread and butter plates are universally used at luncheons, breakfasts, and suppers, also at informal family dinners, with a small silver butter spreader. On this plate all breads, muffins, and rolls must be laid. At a formal dinner the roll in the napkin is taken out and laid on the cloth, at the right of the plate. . . .

"At formal dinners, or luncheon, a guest is never asked to have a second portion and should never ask for it,—but all is different at a dinner *'en famille'*; the hostess considers a second helping complimentary. . . . Never, when a meal is finished, push back the last plate used and brush the crumbs up into little heaps but leave everything exactly in place with the napkin beside the plate; if called unexpectedly from the table or a sudden illness seizes one, the request 'Please excuse me,' must always be made of the hostess."

Nikko Ceramics, Inc. of Japan has been producing fine dinnerware since 1908 and supplying the American dinnerware market since 1968. Nikko distributes its china through department and other stores offering fine tableware. The company originally supplied ironstone dinnerware, but over the last ten years it has expanded its product line to include both fine and bone china.

NIKKO CERAMICS, CHRISTMASTIME AND HAPPY HOLIDAYS

Nikko Ceramics has produced the popular Happy Holidays and Christmastime patterns for many years. Every year, accessory pieces as well as giftware items are added to each line so collectors of either pattern may add to their assortments.

Nikko, Christmastime

Bell	20.00
Bowl, 6 5/8″	7.50
Bowl, fruit, flat, 5 7/8″	7.50
Bowl, salad, serving, 9 3/4″	35.00
Bowl, soup, flat, 8 1/4″	10.00
Box, 4″	10.00
Box, 5″	17.50
Bud Vase, 6″	15.00
Butter Dish, covered, 1/4 lb.	30.00
Cake Plate, footed, 11″	35.00
Candlestick, single light	15.00
Candy Dish, 11 3/4″	25.00
Casserole, covered, round, 7 1/4″	75.00
Cheese and Cracker	27.50
Cheese and Cracker Board, 9 1/4″	17.50
Cheese Dish	17.50
Coaster, 4 5/8″	5.00
Coffeepot, covered	55.00

Baker, oval, 13 3/8″	$35.00
Basket	25.00

Compote, 6″	15.00
Cookie Jar	40.00
Creamer	17.50
Cup and Saucer, demitasse	12.50
Cup and Saucer, footed, 3 5/8″	12.50
Dish, heart shape, 5 3/4″	25.00
Dish, tree, 6 3/4″	7.50
Lamp, candle	10.00
Lasagna, 11 3/4″	40.00
Lid, tureen	50.00
Mug, 4 1/4″	10.00
Napkin Holder	22.50
Napkin Ring	5.00
Nut Dish, 6″	7.50
Pepper Shaker, 2 7/8″	10.00
Pie Plate, 10 1/2″	22.50
Pitcher, 6 1/4″	25.00
Plate, bread and butter, 6 5/8″	7.50
Plate, dinner, 10 7/8″	12.50
Plate, salad, 8 1/4″	10.00
Plate, serving, round, handled, 11″	25.00
Platter, oval, 13 1/4″	35.00
Platter, oval, 16″	45.00
Platter, oval, 20 3/8″	90.00
Potpourri	15.00
Quiche Dish, 9 1/2″	20.00
Ramekin, 3 1/2″	5.00
Relish, three-part, 8 5/8″	35.00
Salt and Pepper Shakers, pair, 2 7/8″	20.00
Saucer	5.00
Snack Plate and Cup	12.50
Soufflé, 7 7/8″	25.00
Sugar Bowl, covered	27.50
Teapot, covered	45.00
Tray, hors d'oeuvre	45.00
Tray, mint, 8 7/8″	15.00
Tray, serving, three-tiered	45.00
Tray, serving, two-tiered	35.00
Tureen and Ladle, covered	90.00

Nikko, Happy Holidays

Basket	$25.00
Bell	20.00
Bowl, fruit, 5 1/2″	5.00
Bowl, salad, serving, 8 1/2″	35.00
Bowl, soup, flat, 9 1/4″	10.00
Box, 4″	10.00
Box, 5″	17.50
Bud Vase, 5 1/4″	15.00
Butter Dish, covered, 1/4 lb.	30.00
Cake Plate, footed, 11″	35.00
Cake Plate and Server	40.00
Candlestick, single light, 4″	15.00
Candy Dish, 11 3/4″	25.00

Casserole, covered, round, 8 3/4″	70.00
Cheese and Cracker	27.50
Cheese and Cracker Board, 9 1/4″	17.50
Coaster, 4 3/4″	5.00
Coffeepot, covered	55.00
Compote, 6″	15.00
Creamer	17.50
Cup and Saucer, demitasse	12.50
Cup and Saucer, footed, 3 3/8″	12.50
Dish, tree, 6 3/4″	7.50
Gravy Boat and Underplate	45.00
Lamp, candle	10.00
Mug, 4 1/8″	10.00
Napkin Holder	22.50
Napkin Ring	5.00
Pie Server, 10″	15.00
Pitcher, 6 1/8″	27.50
Plate, bread and butter, 7″	7.50
Plate, dinner, 10 3/4″	12.50
Plate, round, torte, 12 3/8″	25.00
Plate, salad, 7 3/4″	10.00
Plate, serving, round, handled, 10 3/4″	25.00
Platter, oval, 14 1/4″	35.00
Platter, oval, 19 7/8″	100.00
Potpourri	15.00
Ramekin, 3 1/2″	5.00
Relish, 9 1/4″	15.00
Relish, three-part, 8 5/8″	35.00
Salt and Pepper Shakers, pair	22.50
Snack Cup	12.50
Snack Plate and Cup	12.50
Sugar Bowl, covered	27.50
Sugar Bowl, covered, no lid	20.00
Tray, hors d'oeuvre	45.00
Tray, mint, 8 7/8″	15.00
Tray, serving, two-tiered	35.00
Tureen and Ladle, covered	90.00
Vegetable, covered, round	55.00
Vegetable, round, 9 1/2″	22.50
Vegetable, round, 11 1/4″	27.50

NORITAKE

Ichizaemon Morimura, one of the founders of Noritake, established Morimura-kumi, a Japanese exporting company located in Tokyo in 1867. An import shop also was founded in New York to sell traditional Japanese goods.

A few years later, after attending the World's Fair in Paris, Morimura was inspired to open a factory to produce porcelain in Japan. He founded Nippon Toki Kaisha Ltd., the forerunner of Noritake, in Nagoya, Japan, in 1904. In 1914, Morimura produced the first white porcelain dinner plate in Japan. Dinner sets, which were produced for export around the world, became the company's main product line, and in 1932 the company produced the first bone china in Japan.

The factory was heavily damaged during World War II, and production was greatly reduced. The company sold its china under the "Rose China" mark between 1946 and 1948. Although the quality of this china did not match that of earlier Noritake china, high quality was once again secured by 1948, and Noritake Company Inc. was established for selling tableware in the United States. Over the next thirty years, companies were created in Australia, Canada, the United Kingdom, Sri Lanka, Guam, the Philippines, and Ireland for the manufacture and distribution of Noritake products. The company's name was changed to Noritake Company Limited in 1981.

Noritake, Adagio, #7237,
Victorian II Shape, ivory

Bowl, fruit, 5 1/2″	$15.00
Bowl, soup, coupe, 7 1/2″	25.00
Creamer	35.00
Cup and Saucer, footed, 3 1/8″	25.00
Gravy Boat, attached underplate	70.00
Plate, bread and butter, 6 3/8″	10.00
Plate, dinner, 10 5/8″	30.00
Plate, salad, 8 3/8″	15.00
Platter, oval, 11 1/2″	65.00
Platter, oval, 13 3/4″	85.00

Platter, oval, 16 1/4″	120.00
Salt and Pepper Shakers, pair	40.00
Salt Shaker	20.00
Saucer	7.50
Sugar Bowl, covered	40.00
Sugar Bowl, covered, no lid	30.00
Vegetable, round, 10″	75.00

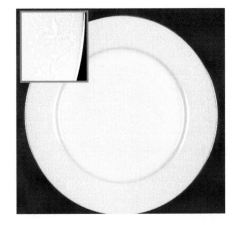

Noritake, Affection, #7192, Victorian II Shape

Bell	$35.00
Bowl, fruit, 5 5/8″	15.00

Bowl, soup, coupe, 7 ½″	25.00
Candlestick, single light	45.00
Creamer	35.00
Cup and Saucer, footed, 3 ⅛″	27.50
Napkin Ring	15.00
Plate, bread and butter, 6 ⅜″	12.50
Plate, dinner, 10 ½″	30.00
Plate, round, handled	30.00
Plate, salad, 8 ⅜″	15.00
Platter, oval, 11 ⅝″	65.00
Platter, oval, 13 ¾″	80.00
Platter, oval, 16 ¼″	120.00
Salt and Pepper Shakers, pair	40.00
Saucer	10.00
Sugar Bowl, covered	40.00
Sugar Bowl, covered, no lid	30.00
Vegetable, oval, 10 ⅛″	55.00

Noritake, Anticipation, #2963,
NOI I Shape, platinum trim

Bowl, fruit, flat, 5 ½″	$15.00
Bowl, soup, flat, 9″	25.00
Coffeepot, covered	140.00
Cream Soup and Saucer	45.00
Creamer	40.00
Cup and Saucer, footed, 3 ¼″	25.00
Gravy Boat and Underplate	80.00
Plate, bread and butter, 6 ¼″	12.50
Plate, dinner, 10 ⅝″	25.00
Plate, salad, 8 ¼″	15.00
Platter, oval, 13 ⅝″	110.00
Platter, oval, 15 ⅝″	140.00
Relish, 9 ¼″	25.00
Salt and Pepper Shakers, pair	50.00
Saucer	10.00
Sugar Bowl, covered	50.00
Teapot, covered	140.00
Vegetable, covered, round	150.00
Vegetable, oval, 10 ⅛″	60.00
Vegetable, round, 8 ⅞″	80.00

Noritake, Amenity, #7228, Victorian II Shape

Creamer	$40.00
Cup, footed, 3″	30.00
Cup and Saucer, footed, 3″	35.00
Gravy Boat, attached underplate	90.00
Plate, bread and butter, 6 ⅜″	15.00
Plate, dinner, 10 ⅝″	35.00
Plate, salad, 8 ⅜″	20.00
Platter, oval, 13 ⅝″	100.00
Saucer	10.00
Sugar Bowl, covered	50.00
Sugar Bowl, covered, no lid	40.00
Vegetable, oval, 10 ⅛″	70.00

Noritake, Asian Song, #7151, Victorian II Shape

Bowl, fruit, 5 ⅝″	$20.00
Bowl, soup, coupe, 7 ½″	30.00

Creamer	35.00
Cup and Saucer, footed, 3″	30.00
Gravy Boat, attached underplate	80.00
Plate, bread and butter, 6 3/8″	10.00
Plate, dinner	30.00
Plate, salad, 8 3/8″	17.50
Platter, oval, 11 5/8″	80.00
Platter, oval, 13 3/4″	90.00
Saucer	10.00
Sugar Bowl, covered	50.00
Sugar Bowl, covered, no lid	35.00
Vegetable, oval, 10 1/8″	65.00

Noritake, Azalea

Bowl, cranberry, 5 1/4″	$70.00
Bowl, fruit, 5 1/4″	15.00
Bowl, soup, coupe, 7 1/2″	30.00
Butter Dish, covered, round	120.00
Butter Tub	45.00
Cake Plate, handled, 9 3/4″	55.00
Candy Jar, covered	750.00
Celery, 12 1/2″	45.00
Compote, 2 3/4″	120.00
Condiment, four-piece	100.00
Condiment Tray	45.00
Cream Soup Bowl, flat	165.00
Creamer	30.00
Creamer, berry	85.00
Creamer, gold finial	70.00
Cup and Saucer, bouillon	35.00
Cup and Saucer, flat, 2 1/4″	25.00
Eggcup, single, 3 1/8″	55.00
Gravy Boat, attached underplate	60.00
Lemon Dish	30.00
Lid, sugar, gold finial	45.00

Mayonnaise, Underplate, and Ladle	550.00
Mustard, covered, no lid, no spoon	45.00
Mustard, covered, no spoon	60.00
Olive Dish, 7 1/8″	80.00
Plate, bread and butter, 6 1/2″	12.50
Plate, dinner, 10″	40.00
Plate, grill, 10 1/2″	220.00
Plate, luncheon, 8 1/2″	25.00
Plate, salad, 7 5/8″	20.00
Platter, oval, 10 1/4″	250.00
Platter, oval, 11 3/4	60.00
Platter, oval, 13 5/8″	90.00
Platter, oval, 16 1/4″	500.00
Relish, 8 1/4″	25.00
Relish, twin, loop	360.00
Relish, two-part	55.00
Salt and Pepper Shakers, pair, bulbous	40.00
Salt Shaker, bell shape	20.00
Salt Shaker, individual	15.00
Saucer	10.00
Snack Plate and Cup, 1 3/4″	50.00
Sugar Bowl, covered	40.00
Sugar Bowl, covered, gold finial	90.00
Sugar Bowl, berry	80.00
Sugar Bowl, open, mini	60.00
Syrup	100.00
Tea Tile, 5 3/4″	50.00
Teapot, covered	140.00
Teapot, covered, gold finial	530.00
Toothpick Holder	120.00
Tray, celery, closed handle, 10″	360.00
Vegetable, covered, round	140.00
Vegetable, covered, round, gold finial	500.00
Vegetable, covered, round, no lid	90.00
Vegetable, oval, 9 1/2″	60.00
Vegetable, oval, 10 1/2″	65.00
Vegetable, round, 10″	60.00
Vinegar	240.00
Whipped Cream, Underplate, and Ladle	45.00
Whipped Cream and Underplate, no ladle	30.00
Whipped Cream, no underplate, no ladle	30.00
Whipped Cream Ladle	20.00
Whipped Cream Underplate	15.00

Noritake, Barrymore, #9737, Sheer Ivory Bone Shape

Bud Vase, 8 5/8″	$30.00
Cake Plate, handled, 11 7/8″	85.00
Canapé, 10 5/8″	75.00
Coffeepot, covered	155.00
Coffeepot, covered, no lid	120.00
Creamer	40.00
Cup and Saucer, footed, 3″	27.50
Dish, shell shape, 7 3/4″	60.00
Pepper Shaker	22.50
Pie Server, stainless blade	45.00
Plate, bread and butter, 6 1/2″	12.50
Plate, dinner, 10 5/8″	25.00
Plate, salad, 8 1/4″	17.50
Platter, oval, 14 1/4″	100.00
Platter, oval, 16 1/4″	130.00
Relish, 7 7/8″	27.50
Salt and Pepper Shakers, pair	45.00
Sugar Bowl, covered	60.00

Cream Soup and Saucer	12.50
Creamer	25.00
Cup and Saucer, flat, 1 7/8″	20.00
Gravy Boat, attached underplate	50.00
Plate, bread and butter, 6 1/4″	7.50
Plate, dinner, 10 1/2″	22.50
Plate, salad, 8 1/4″	15.00
Platter, oval, 12 1/8″	50.00
Platter, oval, 13 7/8″	65.00
Platter, oval, 16 1/4″	75.00
Saucer	7.50
Saucer, demitasse	5.00
Sugar Bowl, covered	35.00
Sugar Bowl, covered, no lid	22.50
Sugar Bowl, open	30.00
Vegetable, covered, round	100.00
Vegetable, covered, round, no lid	70.00
Vegetable, oval, 10 5/8″	45.00
Vegetable, round, 10 1/2″	50.00

Noritake, Belmont, #5609, platinum trim

Bowl, fruit, 5 3/4″	$12.50
Bowl, fruit, flat, 5 5/8″	12.50

Noritake, Blossom Time, #7150, Victorian II Shape, platinum trim

Bowl, fruit, 5 5/8″	$17.50
Bowl, soup, coupe, 7 1/2″	30.00
Creamer	40.00
Cup and Saucer, footed, 3 1/8″	27.50
Gravy Boat, attached underplate	80.00
Plate, bread and butter, 6 3/8″	10.00
Plate, dinner, 10 5/8″	27.50
Plate, salad, 8 3/8″	17.50
Platter, oval, 13 5/8″	90.00
Platter, oval, 16 1/4″	110.00
Saucer	10.00
Sugar Bowl, covered	50.00
Sugar Bowl, covered, no lid	35.00

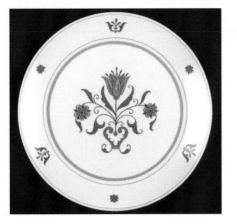

Noritake, Blue Haven, #9004

Bowl, fruit, 5 5/8″	$15.00
Butter Dish, covered, 1/4 lb.	50.00
Creamer	25.00
Cup and Saucer, flat, 3″	20.00
Fondue Pot, 5″	165.00
Gravy Boat	55.00
Handle, metal, detachable	15.00
Lid, sauce pan, 7 1/2″	45.00
Lid, skillet, 8 1/4″	50.00
Lid, skillet, 9″	50.00
Plate, bread and butter, 6 3/8″	10.00
Plate, dinner, 10 1/2″	27.50
Plate, salad, 8 1/4″	17.50
Platter, oval, 13 5/8″	60.00
Platter, oval, 15 1/2″	75.00
Salt and Pepper Shakers, pair	35.00
Salt Shaker	17.50
Sauce Pan, covered, 7 3/8″	100.00
Saucer	5.00
Skillet, covered, 8 1/4″	100.00
Sugar Bowl, covered	35.00
Teapot, covered	85.00
Vegetable, oval, 9 3/4″	45.00
Vegetable, round, 8 1/2″	45.00

Noritake, Blue Hill, #2482, Commander Shape,
platinum trim

Bell	$25.00
Bowl, fruit, 5 1/2″	10.00
Bowl, soup, coupe, 7 1/2″	15.00
Butter Dish, covered, 1/4 lb.	50.00
Candlestick, single light	30.00
Coffeepot, covered	90.00
Creamer	25.00
Cup, footed, 3″	15.00
Cup and Saucer, demitasse	17.50
Cup and Saucer, footed, 3″	22.50
Gravy Boat, attached underplate	50.00
Lid, butter dish, 1/4 lb.	25.00
Lid, coffeepot	45.00
Napkin Ring	10.00
Pepper Shaker	15.00
Plate, bread and butter, 6 1/4″	10.00
Plate, dinner, 10 5/8″	22.50
Plate, salad, 8 1/4″	10.00
Plate, round, handled	30.00
Platter, oval, 12″	40.00
Platter, oval, 14 1/8″	75.00
Platter, oval, 16 1/8″	90.00
Salt and Pepper Shakers, pair	30.00
Saucer	7.50
Sugar Bowl, covered	40.00
Sugar Bowl, covered, no lid	27.50
Teapot, covered	90.00
Teapot, covered, no lid	70.00
Vegetable, covered, round	100.00
Vegetable, oval, 9 3/4″	45.00
Vegetable, round, 8 1/4″	40.00
Vegetable, round, 9″	45.00

Noritake, Blue Moon, #9022

Creamer	$25.00
Cup and Saucer, flat, 3″	20.00
Gravy Boat	50.00
Percolator, covered, 9″	85.00
Percolator, covered, 9″, no lid	70.00
Plate, bread and butter, 6 1/4″	10.00
Plate, dinner, 10 3/8″	25.00
Plate, salad, 8 3/8″	15.00
Platter, oval, 13 1/2″	50.00
Sauce Pan, covered, 8 1/4″	110.00
Saucer	7.50
Sugar Bowl, covered	30.00
Sugar Bowl, covered, no lid	25.00
Vegetable, oval, 9 7/8″	40.00

Noritake, Bluebell, #5558, platinum trim

Ashtray, 5″	$10.00
Bowl, fruit, 5 1/2″	12.50
Bowl, soup, coupe, 7 1/2″	17.50
Coffeepot, covered, mini	60.00
Coffeepot, covered, mini, no lid	40.00
Creamer, 2 3/8″	30.00
Creamer, 4 1/4″	30.00

Cup and Saucer, demitasse	20.00
Cup and Saucer, flat, 1 7/8″	25.00
Gravy Boat, attached underplate	60.00
Plate, bread and butter, 6 1/4″	7.50
Plate, dinner, 10 3/8″	25.00
Plate, salad, 8″	12.50
Platter, oval, 12 1/8″	50.00
Platter, oval, 16 1/4″	90.00
Salt and Pepper Shakers, pair	40.00
Saucer	5.00
Saucer, demitasse	5.00
Snack Plate and Cup	30.00
Sugar Bowl, covered, 2 3/8″	35.00
Teapot, covered	100.00
Vegetable, oval, 10 5/8″	50.00
Vegetable, round, 8 3/4″	50.00

Noritake, Bluedawn, #622 4715

Bowl, cereal, lugged, 6″	$20.00
Bowl, fruit, 5 1/4″	12.50
Bowl, fruit, flat, 5 5/8″	12.50
Bowl, soup, coupe, 7 1/2″	20.00
Bowl, soup, flat, 8 1/4″	20.00
Cream Soup and Saucer	40.00
Cream Soup Bowl	35.00
Creamer	35.00
Cup and Saucer, footed, 2 1/4″	35.00
Gravy Boat, attached underplate	60.00
Lid, vegetable	50.00
Plate, bread and butter, 6 3/8″	10.00
Plate, dinner, 10″	25.00
Plate, luncheon, 8 3/4″	20.00
Plate, salad, 7 5/8″	15.00
Platter, oval, 11 5/8″	55.00
Platter, oval, 13 7/8″	70.00
Platter, oval, 16 1/4″	90.00
Saucer	10.00
Sugar Bowl, covered	40.00

Sugar Bowl, covered, no lid   25.00
Vegetable, covered, round   100.00
Vegetable, covered, round, no lid   70.00

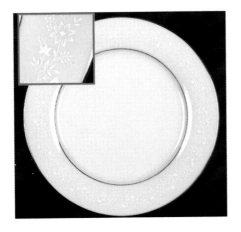

Noritake, Buckingham, #6438, LaSalle Shape, platinum trim

Bowl, fruit, 5 ¹/₂″ $15.00
Bowl, soup, coupe, 7 ¹/₂″   27.50
Creamer   30.00
Cup and Saucer, footed, 2 ¹/₄″   25.00
Gravy Boat, attached underplate   70.00
Lid, butter dish, ¹/₄ lb.   50.00
Lid, coffeepot   70.00
Lid, teapot   70.00
Plate, bread and butter, 6 ³/₈″   10.00
Plate, dinner   30.00
Plate, salad, 8 ¹/₄″   15.00
Platter, oval, 11 ⁵/₈″   65.00
Platter, oval, 13 ⁵/₈″   80.00
Salt and Pepper Shakers, pair   50.00
Saucer   7.50
Sugar Bowl, covered   40.00
Vegetable, covered, round   150.00
Vegetable, oval, 10″   55.00
Vegetable, round, 8 ³/₈″   55.00

Noritake, Buenavista, #9728, Sheer Ivory Bone Shape, platinum trim

Bowl, soup, flat, 8 ¹/₄″ $40.00
Creamer, 3 ⁵/₈″   45.00
Cup, footed, 3″   30.00
Cup and Saucer, footed, 3″   35.00
Gravy Boat Underplate   30.00
Lid, teapot   75.00

Lid, vegetable   85.00
Plate, bread and butter, 6 ¹/₂″   12.50
Plate, dinner, 10 ⁵/₈″   35.00
Plate, salad, 8 ¹/₄″   20.00
Platter, oval, 12 ¹/₄″   100.00
Platter, oval, 14 ³/₈″   120.00
Sugar Bowl, covered   65.00
Vegetable, oval, 10 ¹/₂″   80.00

Noritake, Canton, #5027, gold trim

Bowl, fruit, 5 ⁵/₈″ $10.00
Bowl, soup, coupe, 7 ¹/₂″   15.00
Creamer   30.00
Cup and Saucer, flat, 2″   22.50
Gravy Boat, attached underplate   50.00
Plate, bread and butter, 6 ¹/₄″   10.00
Plate, dinner, 10 ³/₈″   20.00
Plate, salad, 7 ⁷/₈″   12.50
Platter, oval, 12 ¹/₄″   50.00
Platter, oval, 16 ¹/₄″   70.00
Saucer   7.50
Saucer, demitasse   5.00
Sugar Bowl, covered   35.00
Sugar Bowl, covered, no lid   22.50
Vegetable, covered, round   100.00
Vegetable, covered, round, no lid   60.00

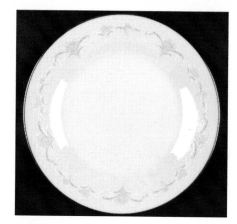

Noritake, Carolyn, #2693, Commander Shape, platinum trim

Bell	$25.00
Bowl, fruit, 5 5/8"	10.00
Bowl, soup, coupe, 7 1/2"	15.00
Butter Dish, covered, 1/4 lb.	50.00
Coffeepot, covered	90.00
Creamer	25.00
Cup and Saucer, demitasse	17.50
Cup and Saucer, footed, 3"	22.50
Gravy Boat, attached underplate	50.00
Napkin Ring	10.00
Plate, bread and butter, 6 3/8"	10.00
Plate, dinner, 10 1/2"	22.50
Plate, salad, 8 1/4"	12.50
Platter, oval, 11 1/2"	40.00
Platter, oval, 13 5/8"	75.00
Platter, oval, 16 1/4"	90.00
Salt and Pepper Shakers, pair	30.00
Saucer	7.50
Sugar Bowl, covered	40.00
Sugar Bowl, covered, no lid	27.50
Teapot, covered	90.00
Vegetable, covered, round	100.00
Vegetable, oval, 9 5/8"	45.00
Vegetable, round, 8 1/4"	40.00
Vegetable, round, 9"	45.00

Cup and Saucer, demitasse	20.00
Cup and Saucer, flat, 2 3/4"	20.00
Gravy Boat, attached underplate	50.00
Lid, sugar bowl	17.50
Plate, bread and butter, 6 1/2"	7.50
Plate, dinner, 10 1/2"	25.00
Plate, salad, 8 1/4"	12.50
Platter, oval, 12"	45.00
Saucer	7.50
Snack Plate	20.00
Snack Plate and Cup	25.00
Sugar Bowl, covered, 2 3/8"	35.00
Sugar Bowl, covered, 3"	35.00
Sugar Bowl, covered, 3", no lid	25.00
Sugar Bowl, covered, mini, no lid	15.00
Teapot, covered	80.00
Vegetable, oval, 9 5/8"	45.00

Noritake, Casablanca, #6842, platinum trim

Ash Tray, 5"	$5.00
Bowl, fruit, 5 1/2"	10.00
Bowl, soup, coupe, 7 3/8"	15.00
Coffeepot, covered, mini, no lid	45.00
Creamer, 3 1/2"	25.00
Creamer, 4"	25.00
Cup, demitasse	15.00

Noritake, Cervantes, #7261, Remembrance II Shape

Cup and Saucer, footed, 3 1/8"	$25.00
Lid, vegetable, round	60.00
Plate, bread and butter, 6 1/2"	10.00
Plate, dinner, 10 1/2"	25.00

Plate, salad, 8 1/4″   15.00
Saucer   7.50
Sugar Bowl, covered   35.00

Noritake, Chatham, #5502

Bowl, cereal, lug, 6 7/8″	$15.00
Bowl, fruit, 5 1/2″	10.00
Bowl, soup, coupe, 7 3/8″	17.50
Cream Soup and Saucer	40.00
Cream Soup Bowl	35.00
Creamer	25.00
Cup, flat, 1 7/8″	20.00
Cup and Saucer, demitasse	20.00
Cup and Saucer, flat, 1 7/8″	22.50
Lid, butter dish, 1/4 lb.	35.00
Plate, bread and butter, 6 1/2″	7.50
Plate, dinner, 10 5/8″	25.00
Plate, salad, 8 1/4″	12.50
Platter, oval, 12 3/8″	50.00
Platter, oval, 14 1/4″	60.00
Sugar Bowl, covered	30.00
Sugar Bowl, covered, no lid	20.00
Teapot, covered, 3 1/8″	100.00
Vegetable, covered, round	100.00
Vegetable, oval, 9 3/4″	40.00

Noritake, Colburn, #6107, LaSalle Shape,
platinum trim

Bowl, cereal, lug, 6 5/8″	$22.50
Bowl, fruit, 5 5/8″	17.50
Creamer	35.00
Cup, footed, 2 1/4″	25.00
Cup and Saucer, footed, 2 1/4″	27.50
Plate, bread and butter, 6 3/8″	12.50
Plate, dinner, 10 1/2″	30.00
Plate, salad, 8 3/8″	15.00
Platter, oval, 11 1/2″	70.00
Platter, oval, 13 5/8″	80.00
Platter, oval, 16 1/4″	120.00
Salt and Pepper Shakers, pair	45.00
Salt Shaker	22.50
Saucer	10.00
Sugar Bowl, covered	45.00
Vegetable, oval, 10″	65.00
Vegetable, round, 8 1/4″	60.00
Vegetable, round, 10″	70.00

Noritake, Colony, #5932, platinum trim

Bowl, cereal, lug, 6 3/4″	$15.00
Bowl, fruit, 5 1/2″	12.50

Bowl, soup, coupe, 7 1/4"	20.00
Butter Dish, covered, 1/4 lb.	45.00
Coffeepot, covered	90.00
Creamer	25.00
Creamer, mini	20.00
Cup, demitasse	15.00
Cup, flat, 1 7/8"	17.50
Cup and Saucer, demitasse	17.50
Cup and Saucer, flat, 1 7/8"	20.00
Cup and Saucer, footed, 2 3/8"	20.00
Gravy Boat, attached underplate	55.00
Lid, butter dish, 1/4 lb.	30.00
Pepper Shaker	20.00
Plate, bread and butter, 6 3/8"	10.00
Plate, dinner, 10 1/2"	25.00
Plate, salad, 8 1/4"	15.00
Platter, oval, 12 3/8"	50.00
Platter, oval, 14 1/4"	60.00
Platter, oval, 16 3/8"	90.00
Relish, 9"	30.00
Salt and Pepper Shakers, pair	40.00
Saucer	7.50
Sugar Bowl, covered	35.00
Sugar Bowl, covered, mini, no lid	15.00
Vegetable, covered, round	110.00
Vegetable, oval, 10 1/8"	45.00
Vegetable, round, 8 3/4"	45.00

Platter, oval, 11 3/4"	50.00
Platter, oval, 13 5/8"	60.00
Platter, oval, 14"	70.00
Platter, oval, 16 1/8"	100.00
Relish, 9"	30.00
Saucer	7.50
Sugar Bowl, covered	40.00
Sugar Bowl, covered, no lid	27.50
Teapot, covered	110.00
Vegetable, covered, round	120.00
Vegetable, oval, 10 1/2"	50.00

Noritake, Crestmont, platinum trim

Bowl, cereal, lug, 6 3/4"	$15.00
Bowl, fruit, 5 5/8"	10.00
Butter Dish, covered, 1/4 lb.	50.00
Cream Soup Bowl	30.00
Creamer	25.00
Cup, footed, 2 1/4"	17.50
Cup and Saucer, demitasse	25.00
Cup and Saucer, footed, 2 1/4"	22.50
Gravy Boat, attached underplate	50.00
Plate, bread and butter, 6 1/4"	7.50
Plate, dinner, 10 1/2"	20.00
Plate, salad, 8 3/8"	12.50
Platter, oval, 11 3/4"	50.00
Platter, oval, 13 3/4"	55.00
Platter, oval, 16 1/4"	80.00
Salt and Pepper Shakers, pair	40.00
Sugar Bowl, covered	35.00
Vegetable, covered, round	120.00
Vegetable, oval, 10 1/2"	40.00
Vegetable, oval, divided, 10 1/8"	60.00
Vegetable, round, 10 1/2"	50.00

Noritake, Crest, platinum trim

Bowl, fruit, 5 5/8"	$12.50
Bowl, soup, coupe, 7 1/2"	22.50
Creamer	30.00
Cup and Saucer, flat, 2 1/8"	25.00
Cup and Saucer, footed, 2 1/8"	25.00
Gravy Boat, attached underplate	60.00
Lid, vegetable, round	60.00
Plate, bread and butter, 6 1/4"	10.00
Plate, dinner, 10 1/2"	25.00
Plate, salad, 7 1/2"	12.50

Noritake, Cumberland, #2225, Commander
Shape, platinum trim

Bowl, cereal, lug, 6 1/2"	$15.00
Bowl, fruit, 5 1/2"	10.00
Bowl, soup, coupe, 7 1/2"	15.00
Butter Dish, covered, 1/4 lb.	50.00
Creamer	22.50
Cup, footed, 3"	17.50
Cup and Saucer, footed, 3"	20.00
Gravy Boat, attached underplate	45.00
Plate, bread and butter, 6 1/2"	7.50
Plate, dinner, 10 1/2"	20.00
Plate, salad, 8 3/8"	10.00
Platter, oval, 11 3/4"	45.00
Platter, oval, 13 5/8"	65.00
Salt Shaker	15.00
Saucer	5.00
Sugar Bowl, covered	35.00
Sugar Bowl, covered, no lid	20.00
Vegetable, oval, 9 1/2"	45.00

Noritake, Duetto, Coupe Shape, gold trim

Bowl, fruit, 5 1/2"	$10.00
Bowl, soup, coupe, 7 1/2"	15.00

Creamer	27.50
Cup, flat, 2 3/4"	17.50
Cup and Saucer, flat, 2 3/4"	20.00
Gravy Boat, attached underplate	60.00
Plate, bread and butter, 6 1/2"	10.00
Plate, dinner, 10 1/2"	25.00
Plate, salad, 8 1/4"	12.50
Platter, oval, 12 1/8"	50.00
Platter, oval, 15 7/8"	70.00
Platter, oval, 16"	100.00
Saucer	7.50
Sugar Bowl, covered	35.00
Sugar Bowl, covered, no lid	25.00
Vegetable, round, 8 7/8"	50.00

Noritake, Edgewood, shaped rim, platinum trim

Bowl, fruit, 5 5/8"	$15.00
Cream Soup Bowl	40.00
Creamer	35.00
Cup and Saucer, footed, 2 1/4"	27.50
Lid, butter dish, 1/4 lb.	50.00
Lid, coffeepot	65.00
Lid, teapot	65.00
Plate, bread and butter, 6 1/4"	10.00
Plate, dinner, 10 1/2"	30.00
Plate, salad, 8 1/4"	15.00
Platter, oval, 11 3/4"	70.00
Platter, oval, 13 3/4"	80.00
Salt and Pepper Shakers, pair	45.00
Saucer	10.00
Sugar Bowl, covered	50.00
Vegetable, oval, 10"	55.00

Noritake, Envoy, #6325, LaSalle Shape,
platinum trim

Coffeepot, covered	$100.00
Creamer	25.00
Cup, demitasse	15.00
Cup, footed, 2 1/4″	20.00
Cup and Saucer, demitasse	17.50
Cup and Saucer, footed, 2 1/4″	22.50
Gravy Boat, attached underplate	50.00
Lid, teapot	50.00
Plate, bread and butter, 6 3/8″	7.50
Plate, dinner, 10 1/2″	25.00
Plate, salad, 8 1/4″	12.50
Platter, oval, 13 5/8″	55.00
Salt and Pepper Shakers, pair	40.00
Saucer	7.50
Saucer, demitasse	5.00
Sugar Bowl, covered	30.00
Sugar Bowl, covered, no lid	20.00
Vegetable, covered, round	110.00
Vegetable, oval, 10″	50.00
Vegetable, round, 10″	50.00

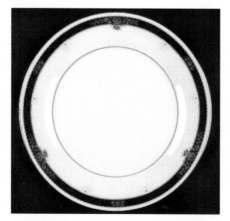

Noritake, Etienne, #7260, Remembrance II Shape

Bowl, fruit, 5 3/4″	$15.00
Bowl, soup, coupe, 7 3/4″	25.00

Coffeepot, covered	130.00
Creamer	40.00
Cup, demitasse	22.50
Cup, footed, 3″	25.00
Cup and Saucer, footed, 3″	32.50
Gravy Boat and Underplate	70.00
Gravy Boat Underplate	22.50
Lid, sugar bowl	27.50
Napkin Ring	12.50
Plate, bread and butter, 6 3/8″	10.00
Plate, dinner, 10 1/2″	30.00
Plate, salad, 8 1/4″	15.00
Platter, oval, 12 1/8″	60.00
Platter, oval, 14″	100.00
Platter, oval, 16″	130.00
Salt and Pepper Shakers, pair	45.00
Saucer	10.00
Sugar Bowl, covered	60.00
Teapot, covered	130.00
Vegetable, oval, 10″	70.00
Vegetable, round, 9 1/2″	70.00

Noritake, Fairmont, #6102

Bowl, fruit, 5 1/2″	$17.50
Celery, 12″	45.00
Creamer	35.00
Cup, footed, 2 1/4″	25.00
Cup and Saucer, footed, 2 1/4″	27.50
Gravy Boat, attached underplate	75.00
Lid, vegetable, round	75.00
Plate, bread and butter, 6 1/4″	10.00
Plate, dinner	30.00
Plate, salad, 8 1/4″	15.00
Platter, oval, 11 1/2″	70.00
Platter, oval, 13 3/4″	80.00
Platter, oval, 16 1/8″	130.00
Salt Shaker	22.50
Sugar Bowl, covered	50.00
Vegetable, oval, 10″	65.00

Noritake, Fjord, #B951, Primastone Shape

Bowl, cereal, flat, 6 ¹/₂″	$35.00
Butter Dish, covered, ¹/₄ lb.	75.00
Butter Dish, covered, ¹/₄ lb., no lid	40.00
Creamer	35.00
Cup and Saucer, flat, 3 ¹/₈″	27.50
Gravy Boat	95.00
Lid, casserole, round, 6 ¹/₄″	55.00
Mug, 3 ⁵/₈″	40.00
Plate, bread and butter, 6 ¹/₄″	15.00
Plate, dinner	40.00
Plate, salad	22.50
Platter, oval, 14 ¹/₄″	80.00
Salt and Pepper Shakers, pair	50.00
Salt Shaker	25.00
Saucer	10.00
Sugar Bowl, covered	40.00
Sugar Bowl, covered, no lid	30.00
Vegetable, round, 8 ³/₄″	75.00

Noritake, Fremont, #6127, platinum trim

Bowl, fruit, 5 ¹/₂″	$12.50
Coffeepot, covered	100.00

Creamer	30.00
Cup, flat, 2 ³/₈″	17.50
Cup and Saucer, flat, 2 ³/₈″	20.00
Gravy Boat, attached underplate	50.00
Lid, butter dish, ¹/₄ lb.	25.00
Plate, bread and butter, 6 ³/₈″	10.00
Plate, dinner, 10 ⁵/₈″	25.00
Plate, salad, 8 ¹/₄″	15.00
Platter, oval, 11 ¹/₂″	50.00
Platter, oval, 13 ¹/₄″	60.00
Platter, oval, 15 ¹/₄″	70.00
Saucer	7.50
Sugar Bowl, covered	35.00
Vegetable, oval, 9 ⁷/₈″	40.00
Vegetable, round, 8 ⁷/₈″	45.00

Noritake, Gallery, #7246, Remembrance II Shape

Bell	$45.00
Butter Tray	30.00
Creamer	35.00
Cup and Saucer	30.00
Cup and Saucer, demitasse	30.00
Gravy Boat and Underplate	90.00
Napkin Ring	15.00
Pepper Shaker	25.00
Plate, bread and butter, 6 ³/₈″	12.50
Plate, dinner, 10 ⁵/₈″	32.50
Plate, salad, 8 ¹/₄″	17.50
Platter, oval, 12″	80.00
Platter, oval, 14″	100.00
Saucer	10.00
Sugar Bowl, covered	50.00
Sugar Bowl, covered, no lid	40.00

Noritake, Glenwood, platinum trim

Bowl, cereal, lug, 6 ¾"	$22.50
Bowl, fruit, flat, 5 ¾"	15.00
Bowl, soup, flat, 7 ¾"	25.00
Cream Soup and Saucer	40.00
Cream Soup Saucer	12.50
Creamer	35.00
Cup and Saucer, flat, 1 ⅞"	30.00
Cup and Saucer, footed, 2 ¼"	30.00
Gravy Boat, attached underplate	70.00
Lid, vegetable, round	65.00
Plate, bread and butter, 6 ¼"	10.00
Plate, dinner, 10 ½"	25.00
Plate, salad, 8 ⅜"	15.00
Platter, oval, 11 ⅝"	60.00
Platter, oval, 13 ⅝"	70.00
Platter, oval, 16 ¼"	110.00
Saucer, flat	10.00
Sugar Bowl, covered	45.00
Sugar Bowl, covered, mini, no lid	20.00
Sugar Bowl, covered, no lid	30.00
Vegetable, covered, round	130.00
Vegetable, oval, 10 ½"	60.00
Vegetable, oval, divided, 10 ¼"	80.00
Vegetable, round, 10 ½"	65.00

Noritake, Goldkin, #4985 5675

Bowl, fruit, 5 ⅝"	$12.50
Bowl, fruit, flat, 5 ¾"	12.50
Bowl, soup, coupe, 7 ½"	25.00
Bowl, soup, flat, 8 ⅛"	25.00
Cream Soup and Saucer	45.00
Cream Soup Bowl	40.00
Creamer, 2 ⅝"	40.00
Creamer, 3 ¾"	40.00
Cup and Saucer, footed, 2 ⅛"	32.50
Gravy Boat, attached underplate	70.00
Plate, bread and butter, 6 ⅜"	10.00
Plate, dinner, 10 ⅜"	30.00
Plate, salad, 8 ¼"	15.00
Platter, oval, 11 ⅞"	70.00
Platter, oval, 16 ⅜"	110.00
Saucer, 2 ⅛" cup	10.00
Sugar Bowl, covered, 2 ¼"	50.00
Sugar Bowl, covered, 3 ⅛"	50.00
Vegetable, covered, round	140.00
Vegetable, covered, round, no lid	100.00
Vegetable, oval, 10 ½"	70.00

►

Noritake, Heather, #7548, platinum trim

Bowl, fruit, 5 ½"	$17.50
Coffeepot, covered, no lid	80.00
Creamer	35.00
Cup and Saucer, footed, 2 ½"	27.50
Gravy Boat, attached underplate	70.00
Plate, bread and butter, 6 ⅜"	10.00
Plate, dinner, 10 ⅝"	30.00
Plate, salad, 8 ⅜"	15.00
Platter, oval, 13 ⅝"	80.00
Saucer	10.00
Sugar Bowl, covered	40.00
Sugar Bowl, covered, no lid	27.50
Vegetable, oval, 10 ⅛"	60.00

Noritake, Holly, #2228, Commander Shape

Ashtray, 3 3/4″	$15.00
Bowl, cereal, lug, 6 1/2″	40.00
Butter Pat, 3 7/8″	15.00
Coffeepot, covered	160.00
Creamer	45.00
Cup, footed, 3″	35.00
Cup and Saucer, footed, 3″	40.00
Lid, coffeepot	80.00
Mug, 3 5/8″	40.00
Napkin Ring	20.00
Plate, bread and butter, 6 1/2″	17.50
Plate, dinner	40.00
Plate, salad, 8 3/8″	25.00
Platter, oval, 11 5/8″	95.00
Platter, oval, 13 5/8″	120.00
Sugar Bowl, covered	60.00
Sugar Bowl, covered, no lid	45.00
Tray, serving, three-tiered	100.00
Vegetable, covered, round	230.00

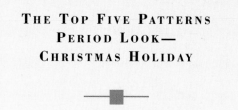

Noritake, Homage, #7236, Victorian II Shape

Bowl, fruit, 5 5/8″	$17.50
Bowl, soup, coupe, 7 3/8″	30.00

**THE TOP FIVE PATTERNS
PERIOD LOOK—
CHRISTMAS HOLIDAY**

BLOCK CHINA CO., POINSETTIA
JOHNSON BROTHERS, MERRY CHRISTMAS
NIKKO CERAMICS INC., CHRISTMASTIME
NORITAKE, HOLLY
SPODE, CHRISTMAS TREE

Coffeepot, covered, no lid	100.00
Creamer	35.00
Cup and Saucer, footed, 3″	27.50
Plate, bread and butter, 6 1/2″	10.00
Plate, dinner, 10 5/8″	30.00
Plate, salad, 8 3/8″	15.00
Platter, oval, 11 3/4″	70.00
Platter, oval, 13 5/8″	90.00
Saucer	10.00
Sugar Bowl, covered	45.00

Noritake, Homecoming, #9002

Bowl, cereal, coupe, 6 1/2″	$17.50
Bowl, fruit, 5 5/8″	15.00
Creamer	25.00
Cup and Saucer, flat, 3″	17.50
Fondue Warmer Stand	50.00
Fondue Warmer Stand and Burner	55.00
Gravy Boat	50.00
Gravy Boat, attached underplate	50.00
Lid, sauce pan, 8 1/2″	55.00
Lid, skillet, 9 1/2″	55.00

Lid, teapot	45.00
Pepper Shaker	15.00
Plate, bread and butter, 6 1/4"	10.00
Plate, dinner, 10 1/2"	25.00
Plate, salad, 8 3/8"	15.00
Platter, oval, 13 5/8"	35.00
Platter, oval, 15 1/2"	60.00
Salt and Pepper Shakers, pair	30.00
Sauce pan, covered, 8 1/2"	90.00
Saucer	5.00
Skillet, covered, 9 1/2"	80.00
Sugar Bowl, covered	30.00
Vegetable, oval, 9 3/4"	35.00

Noritake, Kilkee Keltcraft, #9109, Coupe Shape

Bowl, cereal, coupe, 7"	$15.00
Bowl, fruit, 6"	15.00
Casserole, covered, round, 6 1/8"	100.00
Chop Plate, 12 5/8"	50.00
Creamer	20.00
Cup, flat, 3"	12.50
Cup and Saucer, 3"	15.00
Gravy Boat	50.00
Lid, vegetable	50.00
Pepper Shaker	17.50
Plate, bread and butter	12.50
Plate, dinner, 10 1/2"	22.50
Plate, salad, 7 5/8"	15.00
Salt and Pepper Shakers, pair	35.00
Saucer	5.00
Sugar Bowl, covered	25.00
Sugar Bowl, covered, no lid	20.00
Vegetable, round, 9 5/8"	40.00

Noritake, Inverness, #6716, platinum trim

Bowl, cereal, lug, 6 5/8"	$15.00
Bowl, fruit, 5 1/2"	15.00
Bowl, soup, coupe, 7 1/2"	25.00
Coffeepot, covered	120.00
Creamer	30.00
Cup, flat, 2 3/4"	22.50
Cup and Saucer, flat, 2 3/4"	25.00
Gravy Boat, attached underplate	60.00
Plate, bread and butter, 6 1/2"	10.00
Plate, dinner, 10 1/2"	25.00
Plate, salad, 8 1/4"	12.50
Platter, oval, 12"	55.00
Platter, oval, 13 7/8"	75.00
Platter, oval, 14"	75.00
Salt and Pepper Shakers, pair	35.00
Saucer	7.50
Sugar Bowl, covered	40.00
Sugar Bowl, covered, no lid	27.50
Vegetable, covered, round	130.00
Vegetable, oval, 9 1/2"	50.00
Vegetable, oval, divided, 10 1/4"	70.00
Vegetable, round, 9"	55.00

Noritake, Laureate, #5651, platinum trim

Bowl, fruit, 5 1/2"	$15.00
Coffeepot, covered, mini	70.00
Coffeepot, covered, mini, no lid	45.00

Cream Soup Bowl	32.50
Creamer	30.00
Cup and Saucer, flat, 1 7/8"	27.50
Gravy Boat, attached underplate	60.00
Plate, bread and butter, 6 3/8"	10.00
Plate, dinner	27.50
Plate, salad, 8 3/8"	12.50
Platter, oval, 12 3/8"	55.00
Platter, oval, 14 3/8"	75.00
Platter, oval, 16 1/4"	100.00
Saucer	7.50
Saucer, demitasse	7.50
Sugar Bowl, covered	40.00
Sugar Bowl, covered, no lid	25.00
Teapot, covered, 4 1/2"	130.00
Vegetable, covered, round	120.00
Vegetable, oval, 10"	50.00

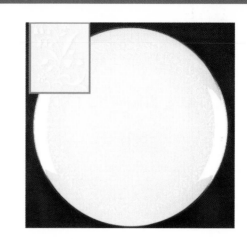

Noritake, Lorelei, #7541, platinum trim

Bowl, cereal, coupe, 6 1/4"	$17.50
Bowl, fruit, 4 3/4"	15.00
Creamer	30.00
Cup and Saucer, flat, 2 3/4"	25.00
Gravy Boat, attached underplate	60.00
Plate, bread and butter, 6 1/2"	10.00
Plate, dinner	30.00
Plate, salad, 8 3/8"	15.00
Platter, oval, 12 1/2"	60.00
Platter, oval, 15"	85.00
Saucer	7.50
Sugar Bowl, covered	40.00
Vegetable, oval, 9 3/4"	50.00

Noritake, Limerick, #3063, NOI I Shape,
platinum trim

Bowl, fruit, flat, 5 1/2"	$20.00
Cream Soup Bowl	40.00
Creamer	40.00
Cup and Saucer, demitasse	25.00
Cup and Saucer, footed, 3 1/4"	30.00
Lid, sugar bowl	25.00
Plate, bread and butter, 6 3/8"	12.50
Plate, dinner, 10 1/2"	27.50
Plate, salad, 8 1/4"	17.50
Platter, oval, 13 1/2"	100.00
Saucer	10.00
Saucer, demitasse	7.50
Sugar Bowl, covered	50.00

Noritake, Magnificence, #9736,
Sheer Ivory Bone Shape

Bowl, fruit, flat, 6 1/8"	$17.50
Bowl, individual, 4 1/2"	50.00
Bowl, soup, flat, 8 3/8"	30.00
Cake Plate, handled, 12"	85.00

Canapé Plate	70.00
Coffeepot, covered	200.00
Cream Soup and Saucer	60.00
Cream Soup Bowl	50.00
Creamer	50.00
Cup and Saucer, footed, 3″	50.00
Dish, shell shape, 7 3/4″	60.00
Gravy Boat and Underplate	90.00
Lid, coffeepot	100.00
Pie Server, stainless blade, 10 1/4″	40.00
Plate, bread and butter, 6 1/2″	17.50
Plate, dinner, 10 1/2″	35.00
Plate, salad, 8 1/4″	22.50
Platter, oval, 12 1/8″	80.00
Platter, oval, 14 3/8″	135.00
Platter, oval, 16 1/4″	165.00
Relish, 7 7/8″	35.00
Salt and Pepper Shakers, pair	55.00
Saucer	15.00
Sugar Bowl, covered	75.00
Sugar Bowl, covered, no lid	55.00
Teapot, covered	170.00
Vegetable, covered, oval	220.00
Vegetable, oval, 10 1/2″	90.00
Vegetable, round, 9 1/2″	90.00

Platter, oval, 12 1/4″	50.00
Platter, oval, 14 1/4″	70.00
Platter, oval, 16 1/4″	90.00
Snack Plate and Cup	25.00
Sugar Bowl, covered, 2″	40.00
Sugar Bowl, covered, 2″, no lid	27.50
Sugar Bowl, open	35.00
Teapot, covered	120.00
Vegetable, covered, no lid	75.00
Vegetable, oval, 10 1/8″	50.00
Vegetable, round, 8 7/8″	50.00

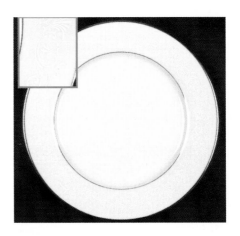

Noritake, Marseille, #7550, platinum trim

Bowl, fruit, 5 5/8″	$15.00
Bowl, soup, coupe, 7 1/2″	25.00
Creamer	30.00
Cup and Saucer, footed, 2 1/2″	27.50
Gravy Boat, attached underplate	70.00
Plate, bread and butter, 6 3/8″	10.00
Plate, dinner	27.50
Plate, salad, 8 1/4″	12.50
Platter, oval, 13 3/4″	60.00
Salt and Pepper Shakers, pair	45.00
Saucer	10.00
Sugar Bowl, covered	40.00
Sugar Bowl, covered, no lid	30.00
Vegetable, covered, round	140.00
Vegetable, oval, 10″	60.00

Noritake, Margot, #7541, platinum trim

Bowl, fruit, 5 1/2″	$12.50
Bowl, soup, coupe, 7 1/4″	22.50
Cream Soup and Saucer	40.00
Cream Soup Saucer	12.50
Creamer, 2″	30.00
Cup and Saucer, demitasse	17.50
Cup and Saucer, flat, 1 7/8″	25.00
Lid, coffeepot, mini	40.00
Lid, teapot	60.00
Plate, bread and butter, 6 3/8″	10.00
Plate, dinner	25.00
Plate, salad, 8 1/4″	12.50

Noritake, Marywood, #2181, Commander Shape,
platinum trim

Bowl, fruit, 5 5/8″	$12.50
Creamer	25.00
Cup and Saucer, footed, 2 1/4″	20.00
Gravy Boat, attached underplate	50.00
Lid, coffeepot	55.00
Plate, bread and butter, 6 3/8″	7.50
Plate, dinner, 10 1/2″	22.50
Plate, salad, 8 1/4″	12.50
Platter, oval, 11 7/8″	50.00
Platter, oval, 13 3/4″	60.00
Platter, oval, 16 1/4″	80.00
Saucer	7.50
Snack Plate and Cup	25.00
Sugar Bowl, covered	30.00
Sugar Bowl, covered, no lid	20.00
Vegetable, covered, round, no lid	50.00
Vegetable, oval, 10 1/2″	45.00
Vegetable, round, 10 1/2″	50.00

Cup and Saucer, footed, 2 1/4″	20.00
Gravy Boat, attached underplate	50.00
Lid, coffeepot	55.00
Plate, bread and butter, 6 3/8″	7.50
Plate, dinner, 10 1/2″	22.50
Plate, salad, 8 1/4″	12.50
Platter, oval, 11 7/8″	50.00
Platter, oval, 13 3/4″	60.00
Platter, oval, 16 1/4″	80.00
Saucer	7.50
Snack Plate and Cup	25.00
Sugar Bowl, covered	30.00
Sugar Bowl, covered, no lid	20.00
Vegetable, covered, round, no lid	50.00
Vegetable, oval, 10 1/2″	45.00
Vegetable, round, 10 1/2″	50.00

Noritake, Mayfair, #6109, platinum trim

Bowl, cereal, lug, 6 5/8″	$17.50
Bowl, fruit, 5 1/2″	12.50
Butter Dish, covered, 1/4 lb.	60.00
Creamer	30.00
Creamer, mini	25.00
Cup, flat, 2 3/8″	20.00
Cup and Saucer, flat, 2 3/8″	25.00
Gravy Boat, attached underplate	60.00
Plate, bread and butter, 6 3/8″	10.00
Plate, dinner	25.00
Plate, salad, 8 1/4″	12.50
Platter, oval, 13 3/8″	70.00
Saucer	7.50
Saucer, demitasse	7.50
Sugar Bowl, covered	40.00
Sugar Bowl, covered, mini	27.50
Vegetable, oval, 10″	50.00

Noritake, Mavis, #5543, platinum trim

Bowl, fruit, 5 5/8″	$12.50
Creamer	25.00

Noritake, Melissa, #3080, Commander Shape,
platinum trim

Creamer	$35.00
Cup, footed, 3″	25.00
Cup and Saucer, demitasse	20.00
Cup and Saucer, footed, 3″	27.50
Plate, bread and butter, 6 3/8″	10.00
Plate, dinner, 10 1/2″	25.00
Plate, salad, 8 1/4″	15.00
Platter, oval, 11 3/4″	60.00
Platter, oval, 13 5/8″	80.00
Platter, oval, 16″	110.00
Saucer	10.00
Sugar Bowl, covered	40.00
Sugar Bowl, covered, no lid	30.00
Vegetable, oval, 9 1/2″	50.00

Noritake, Milford, #2227, Commander Shape,
platinum trim

Creamer	$35.00
Cup and Saucer, footed, 3″	27.50
Gravy Boat, attached underplate	65.00
Plate, bread and butter, 6 3/8″	10.00
Plate, dinner, 10 1/2″	25.00

Plate, salad, 8 1/4″	15.00
Platter, oval, 11 1/2″	60.00
Platter, oval, 13 5/8″	80.00
Saucer	10.00
Sugar Bowl, covered	45.00
Sugar Bowl, covered, no lid	30.00
Vegetable, 9 5/8″	50.00

Noritake, Mirano, #6878

Bowl, fruit, 5 1/2″	$15.00
Coffeepot, covered	130.00
Coffeepot, covered, no lid	90.00
Cream Soup and Saucer	40.00
Creamer	35.00
Cup and Saucer, flat, 2 3/4″	27.50
Plate, bread and butter, 6 3/8″	10.00
Plate, dinner	27.50
Plate, salad, 8 1/4″	12.50
Platter, oval, 12″	60.00
Platter, oval, 14″	70.00
Saucer	10.00
Sugar Bowl, covered	45.00
Sugar Bowl, covered, mini, no lid	25.00
Sugar Bowl, covered, no lid	35.00
Vegetable, covered, round	130.00
Vegetable, covered, round, no lid	90.00
Vegetable, oval, 9 5/8″	50.00

Noritake, Monteleone, #7569, platinum trim

Bowl, soup, coupe, 7 ¹/₂″	$25.00
Creamer	30.00
Cup and Saucer, footed, 2 ¹/₂″	25.00
Lid, coffeepot	60.00
Lid, teapot	60.00
Plate, bread and butter, 6 ³/₈″	10.00
Plate, dinner, 10 ¹/₂″	25.00
Plate, salad, 8 ¹/₄″	12.50
Platter, oval, 13 ³/₄″	70.00
Salt and Pepper Shakers, pair	45.00
Saucer	7.50
Saucer, demitasse	7.50
Sugar Bowl, covered	40.00
Sugar Bowl, covered, no lid	27.50
Vegetable, covered, round	140.00
Vegetable, oval, 10 ¹/₈″	55.00

Creamer, 4 ¹/₂″	40.00
Cup and Saucer, demitasse	25.00
Cup and Saucer, footed, 3 ¹/₄″	30.00
Plate, bread and butter, 6 ³/₈″	15.00
Plate, dinner, 10 ¹/₂″	30.00
Plate, salad, 8 ¹/₄″	22.50
Platter, oval, 13 ¹/₂″	110.00
Platter, oval, 15 ⁵/₈″	140.00
Relish, 9 ¹/₄″	25.00
Salt and Pepper Shakers, pair	50.00
Saucer	10.00
Sugar Bowl, covered	50.00
Sugar Bowl, covered, no lid	35.00
Teapot, covered	140.00
Vegetable, covered, round	160.00
Vegetable, oval, 10 ¹/₈″	80.00
Vegetable, round, 9″	80.00

Noritake, Norma, #7016, platinum trim

Bowl, soup, coupe, 7 ¹/₂″	$30.00
Creamer	35.00
Cup and Saucer, footed, 2 ¹/₂″	27.50
Gravy Boat, attached underplate	80.00
Lid, coffeepot	65.00
Plate, bread and butter, 6 ¹/₂″	10.00
Plate, dinner	30.00
Plate, salad, 8 ³/₈″	15.00
Platter, oval, 11 ⁵/₈″	70.00
Platter, oval, 13 ³/₄″	90.00
Saucer	10.00
Sugar Bowl, covered	50.00
Vegetable, oval, 10 ¹/₈″	65.00

Noritake, Morning Jewel, #2767, NOI I Shape, gold trim

Bowl, fruit, flat, 5 ¹/₂″	$25.00
Bowl, soup, flat, 8 ⁷/₈″	30.00
Coffeepot, covered	140.00

Noritake, Outlook, #B305 W10, Versatone I

Augratin, individual, 6″	$45.00
Coffeepot, covered	100.00
Creamer	30.00
Cup and Saucer, footed, 2 7/8″	20.00
Gravy Boat, attached underplate	60.00
Lid, coffeepot	50.00
Lid, sugar bowl	17.50
Plate, bread and butter	12.50
Plate, dinner, 10 1/2″	25.00
Plate, salad, 8 3/8″	15.00
Platter, oval, 13″	60.00
Salt and Pepper Shakers, pair	40.00
Saucer	7.50
Sugar Bowl, covered	35.00
Vegetable, oval, 10 1/2″	55.00

Noritake, Painted Desert, #8603, Concept I
Stoneware

Baker, round, 9 1/2″	$75.00
Chop Plate, 12″	60.00
Coffeepot, covered	70.00
Creamer	20.00
Gravy Boat	45.00

Lamp, hurricane, bottom only	15.00
Mug, 3 3/4″	15.00
Plate, dinner	22.50
Plate, salad	15.00
Quiche Dish, 9 1/2″	30.00
Soufflé, 7 3/4″	35.00
Sugar Bowl, open	25.00
Vegetable, round, 7 3/4″	30.00

Noritake, Paradise, #8223, Victorian IV
Shape, green

Creamer	$35.00
Cup and Saucer, footed, 3 1/8″	27.50
Plate, bread and butter, 6 3/8″	10.00
Plate, dinner	27.50
Plate, salad, 8 3/8″	15.00
Platter, oval, 13 7/8″	90.00
Saucer	10.00
Sugar Bowl, covered	50.00
Sugar Bowl, covered, no lid	35.00

Noritake, Pasadena, #6311, platinum trim

Bowl, fruit, 5 1/2″	$15.00
Bowl, soup, coupe, 7 1/2″	20.00

Coffeepot, covered	100.00
Creamer	30.00
Cup, flat, 2 3/8″	20.00
Cup and Saucer, flat, 2 3/8″	22.50
Gravy Boat, attached underplate	60.00
Lid, vegetable, round	65.00
Plate, bread and butter, 6 3/8″	10.00
Plate, dinner, 10 5/8″	25.00
Plate, salad, 8 3/8″	15.00
Platter, oval, 13 3/8″	65.00
Salt and Pepper Shakers, pair	40.00
Saucer	7.50
Sugar Bowl, covered	35.00
Sugar Bowl, covered, no lid	30.00
Vegetable, covered, round	130.00
Vegetable, oval, 9 7/8″	45.00
Vegetable, oval, 10 1/8″	50.00
Vegetable, oval, divided, 10 1/4″	65.00
Vegetable, round, 8 3/4″	45.00

Saucer	10.00
Sugar Bowl, covered	40.00
Vegetable, covered, round	150.00
Vegetable, oval, 10 1/8″	65.00

Noritake, Pleasure, #8344, Primastone Shape

Creamer	$30.00
Cup, flat, 3 1/4″	20.00
Cup and Saucer, flat, 3 1/4″	25.00
Plate, bread and butter	15.00
Plate, dinner	27.50
Plate, salad	15.00
Platter, oval, 14 1/4″	70.00
Ramekin	25.00
Saucer	7.50
Sugar Bowl, covered	40.00
Sugar Bowl, covered, no lid	30.00

Noritake, Patience, #2964, NOI I Shape

Bowl, soup, flat, 9″	$25.00
Coffeepot, covered	140.00
Cream Soup and Saucer	45.00
Cream Soup Saucer	15.00
Creamer	35.00
Cup, footed, 3 1/4″	25.00
Cup and Saucer, demitasse	20.00
Cup and Saucer, footed, 3 1/4″	27.50
Gravy Boat and Underplate	70.00
Gravy Boat Underplate	22.50
Jam	40.00
Plate, bread and butter, 6 1/2″	10.00
Plate, dinner, 10 5/8″	27.50
Plate, luncheon, 9″	25.00
Plate, salad, 8 1/4″	15.00
Platter, oval, 13 1/2″	85.00
Platter, oval, 15 1/4″	100.00

Noritake, Polonaise, #2045, Commander Shape, gold trim

Bowl, cereal, lug, 6 1/2″	$35.00
Bowl, fruit, 5 1/2″	22.50

Bowl, soup, coupe, 7 1/2"	40.00
Creamer	50.00
Cup and Saucer, footed, 3"	40.00
Gravy Boat, attached underplate	110.00
Plate, bread and butter, 6 1/2"	12.50
Plate, dinner, 10 5/8"	40.00
Plate, salad, 8 1/4"	22.50
Platter, oval, 11 5/8"	90.00
Platter, oval, 13 3/4"	120.00
Platter, oval, 16 1/8"	160.00
Saucer	12.50
Sugar Bowl, covered	70.00
Vegetable, covered, round	200.00
Vegetable, oval, 9 5/8"	70.00

Noritake, Princeton, #6911, Commander Shape, platinum trim

Bowl, fruit, 5 1/2"	$12.50
Bowl, soup, coupe, 7 1/2"	20.00
Butter Dish, covered, 1/4 lb.	55.00
Creamer	25.00
Cup and Saucer, demitasse	20.00
Cup and Saucer, footed, 3"	20.00
Gravy Boat, attached underplate	60.00
Pepper Shaker	20.00
Plate, bread and butter, 6 3/8"	7.50
Plate, dinner, 10 5/8"	25.00
Plate, salad, 8 1/4"	12.50
Platter, oval, 11 1/2"	50.00
Platter, oval, 13 5/8"	60.00
Saucer	7.50
Sugar Bowl, covered	35.00
Vegetable, oval, 9 3/4"	50.00
Vegetable, round, 8 1/4"	50.00

Noritake, Prelude, #7570

Creamer	$30.00
Cup and Saucer, footed, 2 1/2"	25.00
Lid, coffeepot	65.00
Lid, sugar bowl	20.00
Lid, teapot	65.00
Plate, bread and butter, 6 3/8"	10.00
Plate, dinner	27.50
Plate, salad, 8 3/8"	15.00
Platter, oval, 13 3/4"	70.00
Saucer	7.50
Saucer, demitasse	7.50
Sugar Bowl, covered	40.00
Sugar Bowl, covered, no lid	30.00
Vegetable, oval, 10 1/8"	60.00
Vegetable, round, 10"	70.00

Noritake, Randolph, #9721, Sheer Ivory Bone Shape, platinum trim

Creamer	$45.00
Cup and Saucer, footed, 3"	40.00

Lid, coffeepot	100.00
Plate, bread and butter, 6 1/2″	15.00
Plate, dinner, 10 5/8″	35.00
Plate, salad, 8 1/4″	25.00
Platter, oval, 12 1/4″	80.00
Salt Shaker	30.00
Saucer	15.00
Sugar Bowl, covered	65.00
Sugar Bowl, covered, no lid	45.00
Vegetable, covered, oval	230.00

Vegetable, covered, round	110.00
Vegetable, oval, 9 5/8″	55.00
Vegetable, round, 8 1/4″	45.00
Vegetable, round, 9″	55.00

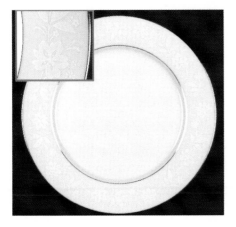

Noritake, Reina, #6450Q

Noritake, Ranier, #6909, Commander Shape, platinum trim

Bell	$40.00
Bowl, cereal, lug, 6 1/2″	15.00
Bowl, fruit, 5 1/2″	12.50
Bowl, soup, coupe, 7 3/8″	20.00
Butter Dish, covered, 1/4 lb.	60.00
Candlestick, single light, 4 1/2″	35.00
Coffeepot, covered	110.00
Creamer	35.00
Cup and Saucer, demitasse	22.50
Cup and Saucer, footed, 3″	25.00
Lid, butter dish, 1/4 lb.	45.00
Lid, sugar bowl	25.00
Napkin Ring	10.00
Pepper Shaker	17.50
Plate, bread and butter, 6 3/8″	10.00
Plate, dinner, 10 1/2″	25.00
Plate, salad, 8 1/4″	15.00
Platter, oval, 11 5/8″	50.00
Platter, oval, 13 5/8″	90.00
Platter, oval, 16 1/8″	100.00
Salt and Pepper Shakers, pair	35.00
Saucer	10.00
Sugar Bowl, covered	50.00
Sugar Bowl, covered, no lid	40.00
Teapot, covered	110.00

Ashtray, 5″	$5.00
Bowl, fruit, 5 1/2″	10.00
Bowl, soup, coupe, 7 3/8″	15.00
Coffeepot, covered, mini	60.00
Creamer, 3 5/8″	25.00
Creamer, 4″	25.00
Creamer, mini	20.00
Cup, demitasse	12.50
Cup and Saucer, demitasse	15.00
Cup and Saucer, flat, 2 3/4″	22.50
Gravy Boat, attached underplate	60.00
Plate, bread and butter, 6 1/2″	7.50
Plate, dinner	25.00
Plate, salad, 8 1/4″	12.50
Platter, oval, 12″	50.00
Platter, oval, 14 1/8″	70.00
Salt Shaker	20.00
Saucer	7.50
Snack Plate and Cup	25.00
Sugar Bowl, covered, 2 3/8″	30.00
Sugar Bowl, covered, 3″	30.00
Sugar Bowl, covered, mini	25.00
Teapot, covered	80.00
Vegetable, oval, 9 1/2″	50.00
Vegetable, round, 8 3/4″	50.00

Noritake, Reverie, #7191, Victorian II Shape

Creamer	$25.00
Cup and Saucer, footed, 3 1/8″	20.00
Gravy Boat, attached underplate	50.00
Lid, sugar bowl	15.00
Plate, bread and butter, 6 3/8″	10.00
Plate, dinner, 10 5/8″	22.50
Plate, salad, 8 3/8″	15.00
Platter, oval, 11 3/4″	50.00
Platter, oval, 13 3/4″	55.00
Platter, oval, 16 1/4″	100.00
Saucer	7.50
Sugar Bowl, covered	35.00
Vegetable, covered, round	130.00
Vegetable, oval, 10 1/8″	45.00
Vegetable, round, 10″	60.00

Noritake, Ridgewood, #5201

Bowl, fruit, 5 1/2″	$12.50
Bowl, soup, coupe, 7 1/2″	20.00
Creamer	30.00
Cup, footed, 2 1/8″	25.00
Cup and Saucer, footed, 2 1/8″	27.50
Gravy Boat, attached underplate	60.00
Lid, vegetable, round	55.00

Plate, bread and butter, 6 1/4″	10.00
Plate, dinner, 10 1/2″	22.50
Plate, salad, 7 1/2″	12.50
Platter, oval, 11 3/4″	60.00
Platter, oval, 13 3/4″	70.00
Saucer	10.00
Sugar Bowl, covered	40.00
Sugar Bowl, covered, no lid	30.00
Vegetable, covered, round	110.00
Vegetable, oval, 10 5/8″	50.00

Noritake, Rosay, #6216

Bowl, cereal, lug, 6 3/4″	$17.50
Bowl, fruit, 5 1/2″	15.00
Bowl, soup, coupe, 7 3/8″	25.00
Butter Dish, covered, 1/4 lb.	65.00
Coffeepot, covered, mini, no lid	60.00
Coffeepot, covered, no lid	100.00
Creamer	30.00
Cup, flat, 2 3/8″	20.00
Cup and Saucer, flat, 2 3/8″	25.00
Gravy Boat, attached underplate	65.00
Plate, bread and butter, 6 3/8″	10.00
Plate, dinner, 10 1/2″	27.50
Plate, salad, 8 1/4″	15.00
Platter, oval, 11 3/8″	60.00
Platter, oval, 13 3/8″	70.00
Salt and Pepper Shakers, pair	40.00
Saucer	7.50
Saucer, demitasse	7.50
Snack Plate	15.00
Sugar Bowl, covered	40.00
Sugar Bowl, covered, no lid	30.00
Teapot, covered	120.00
Vegetable, covered, round	130.00
Vegetable, oval, 9 7/8″	50.00
Vegetable, round, 8 7/8″	50.00

Noritake, Rosemarie, #6044

Bowl, fruit, 5 ¹/₂″	$10.00
Bowl, soup, coupe, 7 ¹/₂″	15.00
Creamer, 2 ¹/₈″	25.00
Cup and Saucer, demitasse	17.50
Cup and Saucer, flat, 1 ⁷/₈″	20.00
Gravy Boat, attached underplate	50.00
Lid, teapot	50.00
Plate, bread and butter, 6 ¹/₄″	7.50
Plate, dinner	25.00
Plate, salad, 8 ¹/₄″	12.50
Platter, oval, 12 ³/₈″	50.00
Saucer	7.50
Snack Plate	12.50
Snack Plate and Cup	25.00
Sugar Bowl, covered, 2″	35.00
Sugar Bowl, covered, 2″, no lid	25.00
Teapot, covered	100.00
Vegetable, oval, 10″	45.00
Vegetable, round, 8 ⁷/₈″	45.00

Noritake, Rothschild, platinum trim

Bowl, 4 ³/₈″	$50.00
Bud Vase, 6 ⁷/₈″	50.00

Chop Plate, 11 ³/₈″	90.00
Creamer	35.00
Cup and Saucer, flat, 3″	27.50
Pie Server, stainless blade	45.00
Plate, bread and butter, 7″	10.00
Plate, dinner, 10 ⁵/₈″	22.50
Plate, salad, 8 ¹/₄″	15.00
Saucer	10.00
Sugar Bowl, covered	50.00
Vase, 4 ⁵/₈″	50.00

Noritake, Royal Orchard

Augratin, 9 ³/₄″	$70.00
Bowl, fruit, 5 ³/₄″	15.00
Bud Vase, 5″	25.00
Cheese and Cracker Board, 8 ⁵/₈″	35.00
Creamer	40.00
Cup and Saucer, flat, 3″	30.00
Gravy Boat, attached underplate	65.00
Mug, 3 ⁵/₈″	22.50
Plate, bread and butter, 6 ³/₄″	10.00
Plate, dinner, 10 ⁵/₈″	25.00
Plate, salad, 8 ¹/₂″	15.00
Platter, oval, 14 ³/₄″	100.00
Quiche Dish, 10 ¹/₈″	60.00
Relish, 8 ¹/₄″	22.50
Roaster, oval, 14 ⁵/₈″	110.00
Salt and Pepper Shakers, pair	45.00
Saucer	10.00
Soufflé, 8 ¹/₄″	70.00
Sugar Bowl, covered	55.00
Vegetable, covered, round	140.00
Vegetable, oval, 9 ⁷/₈″	60.00
Vegetable, round, 8 ³/₄″	60.00

Plate, dinner, 10 1/2″	25.00
Plate, salad, 8 1/4″	15.00
Platter, oval, 11 5/8″	60.00
Platter, oval, 13 3/4″	80.00
Platter, oval, 16 1/8″	105.00
Salt and Pepper Shakers, pair	35.00
Salt Shaker	17.50
Saucer	10.00
Sugar Bowl, covered	40.00
Teapot, covered	110.00
Vegetable, covered, round	130.00
Vegetable, oval, 9 5/8″	55.00
Vegetable, round, 9″	50.00

Noritake, Running Free, #B968, Primastone Shape

Bowl, cereal, flat, 6 1/2″	$35.00
Creamer	60.00
Cup, flat, 3 1/8″	40.00
Cup and Saucer, flat, 3 1/8″	45.00
Plate, bread and butter	15.00
Plate, dinner	37.50
Plate, salad	22.50
Sugar Bowl, covered	70.00

Noritake, Savannah, #2031, Commander Shape, shaped rim, platinum trim

Bowl, cereal, lug, 6 1/2″	$15.00
Bowl, fruit, 5 1/2″	15.00
Bowl, soup, coupe, 7 1/2″	20.00
Butter Dish, covered, 1/4 lb.	60.00
Coffeepot, covered	105.00
Creamer	35.00
Cup and Saucer, footed, 3″	30.00
Gravy Boat, attached underplate	60.00
Lid, sugar bowl	20.00
Plate, bread and butter, 6 3/8″	10.00

Noritake, Shenandoah, #9729, Sheer Ivory Bone Shape, platinum trim

Bowl, 4 1/2″	$40.00
Bowl, fruit, flat, 6″	15.00
Box, oblong, 5 1/4″	25.00
Cake Plate, handled, 11 3/4″	85.00
Creamer	40.00
Cup, footed, 3″	25.00
Cup and Saucer, footed, 3″	27.50
Dish, shell shape, 7 3/4″	60.00
Lid, teapot	70.00
Pie Server, stainless blade	45.00
Plate, bread and butter, 6 1/2″	12.50
Plate, dinner, 10 1/2″	25.00
Plate, salad, 8 1/4″	17.50
Platter, oval, 14 3/8″	100.00
Salt and Pepper Shakers, pair	45.00
Saucer	10.00
Sugar Bowl, covered	60.00
Vegetable, oval, 10 3/8″	70.00

Noritake, Somerset, #5317

Bowl, fruit, 5 ½″	$12.50
Bowl, soup, coupe, 7 ½″	22.50
Creamer	30.00
Cup and Saucer, footed, 2 ¼″	25.00
Gravy Boat, attached underplate	60.00
Plate, bread and butter, 6 ¼″	10.00
Plate, dinner, 10 ½″	25.00
Plate, salad, 7 ½″	12.50
Platter, oval, 11 ¾″	50.00
Platter, oval, 13 ¾″	60.00
Platter, oval, 16 ¼″	100.00
Saucer	7.50
Sugar Bowl, covered	40.00
Vegetable, covered, round	110.00
Vegetable, covered, round, no lid	90.00
Vegetable, oval, 10 ⅝″	50.00

Noritake, Spell Binder, #9733, Sheer
Ivory Bone Shape

Bowl, fruit, flat, 6 ⅛″	$25.00
Butter Tray, 7 ⅞″	30.00
Cake Plate, handled, 12″	90.00
Creamer	45.00
Cup, footed, 3″	35.00
Cup and Saucer, footed, 3″	35.00

Pepper Shaker	30.00
Pie Server, stainless blade	30.00
Plate, bread and butter, 6 ½″	15.00
Plate, dinner, 10 ⅝″	35.00
Plate, salad, 8 ¼″	22.50
Salt and Pepper Shakers, pair	60.00
Sugar Bowl, covered	60.00

Noritake, Temptation, #2752, Remembrance I
Shape, platinum trim

Creamer	$40.00
Cup and Saucer, footed, 3 ¼″	30.00
Gravy Boat Underplate	30.00
Lid, coffeepot	75.00
Plate, bread and butter, 6 ¼″	10.00
Plate, dinner	32.50
Plate, salad, 8 ¼″	15.00
Platter, oval, 14″	100.00
Saucer	10.00
Sugar Bowl, covered	50.00
Vegetable, oval, 10″	70.00

Noritake, Trudy, #7087, platinum trim

Bowl, fruit, 5 ⅝″	$17.50
Bowl, soup, coupe, 7 ½″	27.50

Creamer	35.00
Cup, footed, 3 1/8"	20.00
Cup and Saucer, footed, 3 1/8"	25.00
Gravy Boat, attached underplate	70.00
Plate, bread and butter, 6 3/8"	10.00
Plate, dinner, 10 1/2"	27.50
Plate, salad, 8 3/8"	15.00
Platter, oval, 11 3/4"	70.00
Platter, oval, 13 3/4"	85.00
Platter, oval, 16 1/4"	120.00
Saucer	7.50
Sugar Bowl, covered	40.00
Sugar Bowl, covered, no lid	30.00
Vegetable, oval, 10 1/8"	65.00

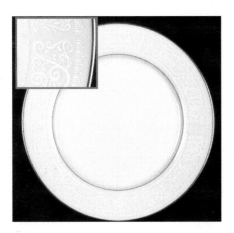

Noritake, Tulane, #7562, Victorian II Shape

Creamer	$ 40.00
Cup and Saucer, footed, 2 1/2"	30.00
Lid, coffeepot	70.00
Plate, bread and butter, 6 3/8"	12.50
Plate, dinner	32.50
Plate, salad	15.00
Saucer	10.00
Sugar Bowl, covered	50.00
Sugar Bowl, covered, no lid	35.00
Vegetable, oval, 10"	70.00

Noritake, Up-Sa-Daisy, #9001

Bowl, cereal, coupe, 6 1/2"	$17.50
Bowl, fruit, 5 5/8"	10.00
Bowl, soup, coupe, 7 1/2"	17.50
Butter Dish, covered, 1/4 lb.	37.50
Coffeepot, covered	80.00
Creamer	25.00
Cup and Saucer, flat, 3"	17.50
Gravy Boat	50.00
Lid, sauce pan, 8 1/4"	45.00
Lid, teapot	40.00
Percolator	80.00
Plate, bread and butter, 6 3/8"	10.00
Plate, dinner, 10 1/2"	25.00
Plate, salad, 8 1/4"	12.50
Platter, oval, 13 5/8"	50.00
Salt and Pepper Shakers, pair	30.00
Salt Shaker	15.00
Sauce Pan, covered, 7 1/2"	80.00
Sauce Pan, covered, 8 1/4"	90.00
Sauce Pan, covered, no lid	60.00
Saucer	5.00
Skillet, covered, 9"	80.00
Skillet, covered, 10"	90.00
Sugar Bowl, covered	30.00
Sugar Bowl, covered, no lid	25.00
Teapot, covered	80.00
Vegetable, oval, 9 7/8"	35.00
Vegetable, round, 8 1/2"	35.00

Noritake, Veranda, #3015, Remembrance II Shape

Creamer	$30.00
Cup and Saucer, footed, 3″	25.00
Plate, bread and butter, 6 3/8″	10.00
Plate, dinner, 10 1/2″	25.00
Plate, salad, 8 1/4″	15.00
Platter, oval, 12″	60.00
Platter, oval, 14″	75.00
Saucer	7.50
Sugar Bowl, covered	35.00

Noritake, Violette, #3054

Bowl, fruit, flat, 5 5/8″	$12.50
Bowl, soup, flat, 8 1/4″	20.00
Bowl, soup, flat, 9″	25.00
Cream Soup Saucer	12.50
Creamer, 3 3/4″	32.50
Cup and Saucer	32.50
Gravy Boat, attached underplate	60.00
Lid, vegetable, round	60.00
Plate, bread and butter, 6 3/8″	10.00
Plate, dinner, 10 1/2″	27.50
Plate, salad, 7 5/8″	15.00
Platter, oval, 11 7/8″	55.00

Platter, oval, 13 3/4″	70.00
Platter, oval, 16 3/8″	90.00
Sugar Bowl, covered	40.00
Sugar Bowl, covered, no lid	30.00
Vegetable, covered, round	120.00
Vegetable, oval, 10 1/2″	55.00

Noritake, White and Gold, #175, LaSalle Shape, gold trim

Cup and Saucer	$30.00
Plate, bread and butter, 6 1/2″	10.00
Plate, dinner, 10 ″	25.00
Plate, salad, 8″	15.00

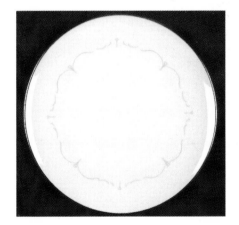

Noritake, Whitebrook, #6441, platinum trim

Bowl, cereal, lug, 6 7/8″	$17.50
Bowl, fruit, 5 1/2″	15.00
Butter Dish, covered, 1/4 lb.	60.00
Creamer	30.00
Cup and Saucer, flat, 2 3/8″	25.00
Plate, bread and butter, 6 3/8″	10.00
Plate, dinner	27.50
Plate, salad, 8 1/4″	12.50

Platter, oval, 11 3/8″	60.00
Platter, oval, 13 3/8″	70.00
Saucer	7.50
Sugar Bowl, covered	40.00
Sugar Bowl, covered, no lid	30.00
Teapot, covered	110.00
Teapot, covered, no lid	80.00
Vegetable, covered, round	120.00
Vegetable, oval, 9 7/8″	45.00

Noritake, Whitehall, #6115

Butter Dish, covered, 1/4 lb.	$70.00
Creamer	30.00
Cup, demitasse	20.00
Cup and Saucer, demitasse	25.00
Cup and Saucer, footed, 2 1/4″	25.00
Lid, teapot	65.00
Lid, vegetable, round	65.00

Plate, bread and butter, 6 3/8″	10.00
Plate, dinner	27.50
Plate, salad, 8 1/4″	15.00
Platter, oval, 11 5/8″	60.00
Platter, oval, 13 7/8″	70.00
Sugar Bowl, covered	40.00

Oxford Bone China was introduced to the American market by Lenox, Inc. in 1962. It is widely known for its pure white color, translucency, delicate appearance, and remarkable strength.

Cup and Saucer, footed, 2 3/4"	80.00
Plate, bread and butter, 6 3/8"	35.00
Plate, dinner, 10 3/4"	70.00
Plate, salad, 8 1/8"	50.00

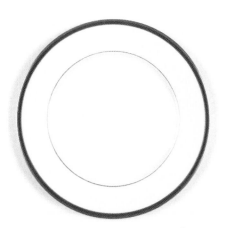

Oxford-Lenox, Annapolis Blue

Bowl, cereal, coupe, 5 3/4"	$70.00
Bowl, fruit, 5 5/8"	60.00
Creamer	120.00
Cup and Saucer, footed, 2 3/4"	80.00
Plate, bread and butter	35.00
Plate, dinner	70.00
Plate, salad	50.00
Platter, oval, 16 1/8"	290.00
Sugar Bowl, covered	140.00
Sugar Bowl, covered, no lid	95.00

Oxford-Lenox, Filigree, shaped rim, platinum trim

Bowl, fruit, 5 3/4"	$60.00
Creamer	120.00
Cup and Saucer, footed, 2 3/4"	70.00
Lid, sugar bowl	65.00
Plate, bread and butter, 6 1/2"	30.00
Plate, dinner, 10 3/4"	60.00
Plate, salad, 8 1/8"	45.00
Platter, oval, 13 5/8"	240.00
Platter, oval, 16 1/8"	315.00
Saucer	25.00
Saucer, demitasse	35.00
Sugar Bowl, covered	130.00
Vegetable, oval, 8 3/4"	170.00
Vegetable, oval, 10 1/4"	230.00

Oxford-Lenox, Bryn Mawr, shaped rim, platinum trim

Cup, footed, 2 3/4"	$75.00

Oxford-Lenox, Fontaine, shaped rim, gold trim

Bowl, cereal, coupe, 5 5/8″	$85.00
Bowl, soup, coupe, 7 3/4″	90.00
Creamer	150.00
Cup and Saucer, footed, 2 3/4″	80.00
Plate, bread and butter, 6 1/2″	35.00
Plate, dessert, 7 3/8″	55.00
Plate, dinner, 10 3/4″	70.00
Plate, salad, 8 1/4″	50.00
Saucer	25.00
Sugar Bowl, covered	145.00
Vegetable, oval, 10 1/4″	250.00

Plate, luncheon, 9 3/8″	45.00
Plate, salad, 8 1/8″	35.00
Saucer	22.50

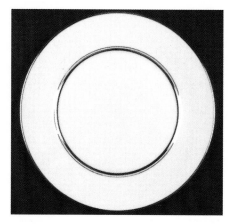

Oxford-Lenox, Lexington, shaped rim, platinum trim

Creamer	$105.00
Cup and Saucer, 2 3/4″	60.00
Plate, bread and butter	25.00
Plate, dessert	45.00
Plate, dinner	50.00
Plate, salad	40.00
Platter, oval, 15 7/8″	230.00
Sugar Bowl, covered	125.00
Sugar Bowl, covered, no lid	100.00

Oxford-Lenox, Holyoke, shaped rim, platinum trim

Bowl, cereal, coupe, 5 3/4″	$55.00
Bowl, soup, coupe, 7 3/4″	70.00
Cream Soup and Saucer	130.00
Cream Soup Saucer	40.00
Cup and Saucer, footed, 2 3/4″	60.00
Plate, bread and butter, 6 1/2″	25.00
Plate, dinner	50.00

Oxford-Lenox, Spring, shaped rim, platinum trim

Creamer	$120.00
Cup and Saucer, demitasse	80.00
Cup and Saucer, footed, 2 3/4″	65.00
Gravy Boat, attached underplate	250.00
Plate, bread and butter, 6 3/8″	25.00

Plate, dessert, 7 3/8″	45.00	Platter, oval, 15 7/8″	300.00
Plate, dinner, 10 3/4″	50.00	Platter, oval, 16″	300.00
Plate, salad, 8 1/4″	40.00		

Oxford-Lenox, Twilight Dell, platinum trim

Bowl, fruit, 5 3/4″	$60.00
Bowl, soup, coupe, 7 3/4″	75.00
Cup, footed, 2 3/4″	60.00
Cup and Saucer, footed, 2 3/4″	65.00
Lid, sugar bowl	65.00
Plate, bread and butter, 6 1/2″	30.00
Plate, dinner, 10 3/4″	50.00
Plate, salad, 8 1/4″	40.00

Oxford-Lenox, White Echo, shaped rim, platinum trim

Bowl, cereal, coupe, 5 3/4″	$60.00
Bowl, fruit, 5 3/4″	55.00
Bowl, soup, coupe, 7 3/4″	75.00
Cream Soup and Saucer	130.00
Cup and Saucer, footed, 2 3/4″	60.00
Plate, bread and butter	25.00
Plate, dinner, 10 3/4″	50.00
Plate, salad, 8 1/4″	35.00
Saucer	20.00

The Pfaltzgraff name originated in the Pfalz area of the German Rhineland, where Pfaltzgraff's trademark castle bearing the family name still stands. By 1811, George Pfaltzgraff, a German immigrant potter, began producing salt-glazed stoneware in York, Pennsylvania.

The Pfaltzgraff Company's earlier products were storage crocks and jugs for preserving food for use in winter. When demand for stoneware diminished, production was changed to animal and poultry feeders and red clay flower pots. The 1940s and 1950s saw production lines again change, with a shift to household products and giftwares and the company's first dinnerware line.

In 1964, the company name was changed from The Pfaltzgraff Pottery Company to The Pfaltzgraff Company. Over the next fifteen years, Pfaltzgraff expanded with construction of a new manufacturing plant and distribution center at Thomasville, North Carolina, the purchase of the Stangl Pottery of Trenton, New Jersey, and the acquisition of factories in Dover, Aspers, and Bendersville, Pennsylvania, and retail stores in York County, Pennsylvania, Flemington, New Jersey, and Fairfax, Virginia.

Pfaltzgraff, America, American

Augratin, 11 3/4"	$50.00
Baker, rectangular, 14 1/8"	100.00
Bell, 1988	35.00
Bell, 1989	35.00
Bowl, cereal, coupe, 5 5/8"	17.50
Bowl, soup, flat, 8 3/4"	22.50
Candlestick, single light, 3 5/8"	17.50
Canister, coffee, 5 3/4"	50.00
Canister, flour, 7 1/4"	90.00
Canister, sugar, 6 1/2"	65.00
Canister, sugar, 6 1/2", no lid	55.00
Canister, tea, 5"	40.00
Carafe, covered, no lid	55.00
Casserole, covered, round, 6 3/4"	100.00
Casserole, covered, round, 5 1/4", no lid	75.00
Creamer	30.00
Cup and Saucer, flat, 2 1/2"	15.00
Custard Cup, 2 3/4"	12.50
Gravy Boat, no underplate	55.00
Jam, covered, no lid	35.00
Lid, box, heart shape	20.00
Lid, butter tub	30.00
Lid, salt box	80.00
Lid, teapot	40.00
Mixing Bowl, 7"	45.00
Pepper Shaker	15.00
Pie Plate, 9 5/8"	60.00
Plate, bread and butter	15.00
Plate, dinner	25.00
Plate, salad, 7 1/4"	17.50
Plate, service, 12 1/4"	35.00
Platter, oval, 14 1/8"	65.00
Potpourri, no base	15.00
Salt and Pepper Shakers, pair	30.00
Saucer	5.00
Sherbet, 3"	15.00
Soap Dish, 5"	22.50
Spice Shaker, 6 1/2"	30.00

Sugar Bowl, covered	40.00
Toothpick Holder	22.50
Tray, bread, 12 1/2"	50.00
Vegetable, round, 8 5/8"	45.00

Pfaltzgraff, Christmas Heirloom

Bell	$45.00
Candlestick, single light, 5"	25.00
Creamer	35.00
Cup, flat, 3 1/4"	25.00
Cup and Saucer, flat, 3 1/4"	30.00
Custard Cup, 2 3/4"	22.50
Mug, 4 7/8"	22.50
Plate, dinner	30.00
Plate, salad	20.00
Potpourri, 4 1/4"	40.00
Potpourri and Stand	20.00
Relish, 8 1/4"	35.00
Salt and Pepper Shakers, pair	40.00
Sugar Bowl, covered	50.00

Pfaltzgraff, Gourmet, brown

Ashtray, 9 1/4"	$15.00
Ashtray, 12 3/8"	15.00
Augratin, 9 3/4"	35.00

Augratin, individual, 7″	12.50	Gravy Boat and Underplate	50.00
Baker, oval, 7 3/4″	45.00	Gravy Boat, no underplate	40.00
Baker, oval, 10″	45.00	Jam	30.00
Baker, rectangular, 13 7/8″	75.00	Lazy Susan	85.00
Baker, square, 10 1/4″	75.00	Lazy Susan Side Dish	12.50
Bean Pot, covered, 2 1/2 qt.	85.00	Lid, canister, coffee	17.50
Bean Pot, covered, 2 1/2 qt., no lid	55.00	Lid, casserole, 1 qt.	40.00
Bean Pot, covered, 3 1/2 qt.	85.00	Lid, casserole, round, 2 qt.	40.00
Beverage Server and Stand	175.00	Lid, casserole, round, 5 1/2″	40.00
Boiled Corn Holder	10.00	Lid, casserole, round, 7 1/8″	40.00
Bowl, cereal, coupe, 5 5/8″	10.00	Mixing Bowl, 5 7/8″	22.50
Bowl, fruit, 4 5/8″	10.00	Mixing Bowl, 7 3/4″	32.50
Bowl, salad, serving, 10 1/4″	45.00	Mixing Bowl, 10″	45.00
Butter Dish, covered, 1/4 lb.	35.00	Mug, 3 1/2″	12.50
Butter Dish, covered, 1/4 lb., no lid	25.00	Oil Cruet	30.00
Canister, coffee, 5 3/4″	35.00	Pepper Shaker, 4″	12.50
Canister, coffee, wood top, 4 1/2″	30.00	Pie Plate, 9 5/8″	45.00
Canister, flour, 7 1/4″	65.00	Pitcher, 4 3/4″	40.00
Canister, flour, 7 1/4″, no lid	50.00	Pitcher, 6 1/2″	40.00
Canister, sugar, 6 1/2″	40.00	Pitcher, 7 1/2″	40.00
Canister, sugar, 6 1/2″, no lid	20.00	Pitcher and Bowl, 9 1/2″	170.00
Canister, tea, 5″	25.00	Plate, bread and butter	5.00
Casserole, covered, 12 oz., no lid	60.00	Plate, deviled egg	45.00
Casserole, covered, 1 1/2 qt., no lid	60.00	Plate, dinner	22.50
Casserole, covered, 2 qt., no lid	60.00	Plate, grill, 10 7/8″	17.50
Casserole, covered, individual, 3 3/8″	30.00	Plate, luncheon, 8 3/4″	15.00
Casserole, covered, individual, 3 7/8″, no lid	20.00	Plate, salad, 6 7/8″	15.00
Casserole, covered, individual, 4 3/8″	30.00	Relish and Stand, three-part	20.00
Casserole, covered, round, 12 oz.	85.00	Relish, three-part	20.00
Casserole, covered, round, 1 qt.	85.00	Relish, three-part, 9″	20.00
Casserole, covered, round, 1 1/2 qt.	85.00	Relish, three-part, 15 3/8″	20.00
Casserole, covered, round, 2 qt.	85.00	Salt and Pepper Shakers, pair, 4″	25.00
Casserole, covered, round, 3 qt.	85.00	Salt Shaker, 4 1/2″	12.50
Chip and Dip	55.00	Soufflé, 6 3/4″	35.00
Coffeepot, covered	60.00	Soufflé, 8 1/4″	35.00
Condiment Set, four-piece	60.00	Soufflé, individual, 4 5/8″	30.00
Condiment Set, three-piece	60.00	Sugar Bowl, covered	30.00
Condiment Set, two-piece	60.00	Sugar Bowl, covered, no lid	20.00
Cookie Jar, covered, no lid	40.00	Sugar Bowl, open	30.00
Creamer, 2 1/4″	22.50	Teapot, covered	60.00
Cup, flat, 2 1/4″	17.50	Tray, 14 5/8″	65.00
Cup and Saucer, flat, 2 1/4″	20.00	Tray, bread, 12 3/8″	55.00
Custard Cup	10.00	Tureen, covered, 2 1/2 qt., no lid	105.00
Flower Pot	30.00	Tureen, covered, 5 qt.	150.00
Gravy Boat	50.00	Tureen, covered, 5 qt., no lid	105.00
		Vegetable, oval, divided, 12 3/8″	50.00

Pfaltzgraff, Heirloom, gray and white

Baker, oval, 12 $^3/_8$″	$27.50
Bowl, batter, 5 $^3/_4$″	55.00
Bowl, batter, mini	35.00
Bowl, heart shape	27.50
Box, covered, heart shape	20.00
Butter Dish, covered, $^1/_4$ lb.	25.00
Butter Dish, covered, $^1/_4$ lb., no lid	10.00
Candlestick, single light, 5″	15.00
Canister, coffee, 6 $^1/_2$″	30.00
Canister, coffee, 6 $^1/_2$″, no lid	20.00
Canister, flour, 7 $^1/_4$″	50.00
Canister, tea, 6″, no lid	15.00

Casserole, covered, round, 6 $^1/_2$″	50.00
Clock, quartz	30.00
Coffeepot, covered	55.00
Cookie Jar	60.00
Creamer	15.00
Cup and Saucer, flat, 3 $^1/_8$″	15.00
Ginger Jar, covered	25.00
Ginger Jar, covered, no lid	20.00
Grandmug, 5″	17.50
Jello Mold, 7 $^1/_4$″	30.00
Lamp, hurricane	25.00
Lid, canister, sugar	20.00
Lid, sugar bowl	7.50
Mixing Bowl, 8 $^1/_4$″	30.00
Mug, 5″	12.50
Napkin Holder	25.00
Pepper Shaker	12.50
Plate, dinner	12.50
Plate, salad	7.50
Potpourri	30.00
Salt and Pepper Shakers, pair	25.00
Saucer	5.00
Soap Dish, oval	15.00
Sugar Bowl, covered	20.00
Tray, bread, 12 $^1/_4$″	40.00
Trivet, 9 $^1/_4$″	22.50
Tureen, covered, no lid	90.00
Tureen Underplate	40.00
Vegetable, round, 8 $^5/_8$″	30.00

Measuring Cup, 5 1/8″	10.00	Soufflé, 6 3/4″	22.50
Milk Bottle, 8″	20.00	Soup Server, open, individual, 5″	7.50
Mixing Bowl, 6″	10.00	Spoon Holder	12.50
Mixing Bowl, 8″	12.50	Sugar Bowl, covered	15.00
Mixing Bowl, 10″	22.50	Sugar Bowl, covered, no lid	10.00
Oil Cruet	22.50	Sugar Bowl, open	15.00
Pepper Shaker, 4″	7.50	Sweetener Crock, covered	20.00
Pitcher, 4 7/8″	27.50	Sweetener Holder	12.50
Pitcher and Bowl	120.00	Tankard, 5 1/2″	12.50
Pitcher and Bowl, mini	50.00	Tea Bag Holder	10.00
Plate, dinner, 10 3/8″	7.50	Tea Tile, 7 5/8″	10.00
Plate, grill, 10″	10.00	Teapot, covered	45.00
Plate, salad, 6 7/8″	5.00	Teapot, covered, mini	27.50
Platter, oval, 12″	15.00	Teapot, covered, mini, no lid	20.00
Platter, oval, 14″	20.00	Toothpick Holder	10.00
Quiche Dish, 9″	20.00	Tray, bread, 12 1/2″	20.00
Relish, 7 1/2″	12.50	Utensil Holder, 6 1/2″	15.00
Relish, 9″	12.50	Vegetable, round, 7 1/2″	12.50
Relish and Metal Tray, four-part, 17″	55.00	Vegetable, round, 8 1/4″	17.50
Salt and Pepper Shakers, pair, 4″	15.00	Vegetable, round, 8 5/8″	17.50
Salt Box, covered	50.00	Vinegar and Oil, stoppers	45.00
Saucer	2.50	Wine and Cheese Set, four pieces	30.00

POPE-GOSSER CHINA COMPANY

I. Bentley Pope and Charles F. Gosser founded the Pope-Gosser China Company in Coshocton, Ohio, in 1902. The company, located just outside the East Liverpool District, began producing fine china in 1903. Within a few years, Pope-Gosser had received national recognition, winning awards at both the 1904 Louisiana Purchase Exposition in St. Louis and the Jamestown Exposition.

Upon the deaths of I. Bentley Pope and Charles F. Gosser in 1918, a controlling interest in the company was inherited by Mrs. Fannie Burns. She installed her son-in-law, George Mitchell, as president of the company. He remained in that position until 1929.

In 1928, influenced by depressed economic conditions, the Pope-Gosser China Company merged with other Ohio potteries to form the American Chinaware Corporation. The various potteries were to maintain their own identities, but administrative work was to be done by the new board of directors. The operation was unsuccessful, and in 1931 the corporation filed for bankruptcy.

The Pope-Gosser plant was idle until 1933, when William I. Pope, son of I. Bentley Pope and plant superintendent from 1903 to 1918, acquired the company. With the help of Frank P. Judge, an experienced pottery executive, the firm was reorganized and china production was resumed. The company remained in operation until 1958.

Pope Gosser China Company, Rose Point

Bowl, cereal, lug, 7 ¼″	$15.00
Bowl, fruit, flat, 5 ⅞″	10.00
Cream Soup Saucer	10.00
Creamer	22.50
Cup, demitasse	15.00
Cup and Saucer, flat, 2 ¼″	20.00
Cup and Saucer, footed, 2 ¼″	20.00
Lid, sugar bowl	15.00
Plate, bread and butter, 6 ¼″	5.00
Plate, dinner	20.00
Plate, salad	10.00
Saucer	5.00
Vegetable, oval, 10 ⅜″	30.00

PORTMEIRION

In 1960, Susan Williams-Ellis and her husband Euan Cooper-Willis purchased A. E. Gray Ltd., a small pottery decorating business in Stoke-on-Trent. For years, Gray's had been producing Susan's designs exclusively for her souvenir shops in Portmeirion and London. In 1961, they acquired Kirkhams Ltd., a pottery factory at Stoke-on-Trent. They modernized the factory and moved their Gray's Pottery employees to the new premises. They renamed the company The Portmeirion Potteries Ltd. in 1962.

The company experienced enormous growth in the next thirty-five years, despite recessions in the 1970s and l980s and a devastating fire in 1977.

Since 1960, Susan Williams-Ellis has been responsible for nearly every design produced by Portmeirion Potteries. In the past few years, while retaining overall supervision, she has been relinquishing the responsibility for much of Portmeirion's designing to her daughters Angharad Menna and Anwyl and others in the design department.

PORTMEIRION, BOTANIC GARDEN

By the early 1970s, Portmeirion's Susan Williams-Ellis had had the idea for a multimotif floral design in the back of her mind for quite a few years, but its creation came about almost by accident. While visiting an antiquarian bookseller in 1970, the clerk showed her a brightly hand-colored "herbal" book from 1817, *The Universal—or—Botanical, Medical and Agricultural Dictionary* by Thomas Green, which was illustrated with a large selection of plants and flowers. This inspired Williams-Ellis to create Botanic Garden. Illustrations from Green's book, along with floral illustrations by William Clarke, became the basis for the new design.

Botanic Garden began its life as a coffee set. Each piece was given a different flower motif, so when the whole table was laid, it would give the impression of a Botanic Garden. Butterflies, moths, and other insects were added to each motif to improve the fit on the pottery shapes and to add more variety. A small triple leaf, repeated and laid end to end, became the Botanic Garden border.

Botanic Garden was immediately popular. The original launch included twenty-eight different plant motifs with a range of some thirty-five different items. As fashions changed, Portmeirion introduced new flowers to replace the older motifs when they began to lose their appeal. To date, forty-six flowers have been featured. Since its introduction, the line has continued to grow and has recently spread into novelty teapots, hinged boxes, textiles, trays, saucepans, and glassware. The collection now includes over 160 pieces.

Portmeirion, Botanic Garden, white

Baker, oval, 11 1/4″	$65.00
Baker, oval, 14 1/4″	75.00
Baker, oval, 15 5/8″	95.00
Baker, oval, 19 3/8″	100.00
Baker, rectangular, 12 1/2″	75.00
Bud Vase, 6 3/4″	35.00
Canister, coffee, 4 1/2″	50.00
Canister, flour, 8″	95.00
Canister, sugar, 7″	60.00
Canister, tea, 5 1/2″	35.00
Casserole, covered, round, 6 1/4″	100.00
Casserole, covered, round, 8 5/8″	135.00
Cheese Dish	130.00
Clock, desk	70.00
Coffeepot, covered, 7 5/8″	85.00
Creamer	30.00
Cup, 3 1/2″	35.00
Cup, flat, 2 5/8″	25.00
Cup and Saucer, 3 1/2″	40.00
Cup and Saucer, flat, 2 5/8″	22.50
Cup and Saucer, oversized, 3 3/4″	40.00
Eggcup, single, 2 1/2″	10.00
Flan, blue, 11″	50.00
Gravy Boat	40.00
Kettle	90.00
Lid, teapot	40.00
Pie Plate, 10 3/4″	40.00
Pitcher, 7″	55.00
Planter, 3 3/8″	30.00
Planter, 4 1/8″	40.00
Plate, bread and butter, 7 1/4″	15.00
Plate, dinner, 10 3/8″	22.50
Plate, salad, 8 1/2″	20.00
Platter, oval, 10 3/4″	45.00
Quiche Dish, 9 1/2″	35.00
Quiche Dish, 10 5/8″	44.00
Quiche Dish, 12 3/8″	50.00
Ramekin, 3 1/4″	7.50
Salt Shaker	15.00
Spice Jar, covered, 3″	25.00
Sugar Shaker, 6 3/4″	40.00
Teapot, covered, 4″	80.00
Tureen Ladle	65.00
Vase, 6 5/8″	70.00
Vase, 8 1/4″	80.00
Vase, 11 1/4″	65.00

ROSENTHAL

Philip Rosenthal established the Rosenthal factory in Selb, Bavaria, in 1879. The company flourished, providing figurals and tableware of high-quality workmanship that were simplistic in design. From 1897 to 1936, Rosenthal acquired factories in Kronach, Marktredwitz, Selb, Waldenburg, Sophienthal, and Waldershof.

Following World War II, many of Rosenthal's factories were either lost or outdated. Philip Rosenthal II took control of the company, formed Rosenthal Porcelain AG, and began to rebuild. His goal was to produce moderate-priced dinnerware for the American market. New designers were hired, and under Philip's supervision, Rosenthal again became a success in the tableware market.

Rosenthal, Classic Rose

Platter, oval, 13″	130.00
Platter, oval, 15 3/8″	150.00
Saucer	15.00
Sugar Bowl, covered, 3″	80.00
Sugar Bowl, covered, 3″, no lid	55.00
Sugar Bowl, open	60.00
Tray, sandwich, 14 1/8″	120.00
Vegetable, covered, round, 7 1/2″	200.00
Vegetable, covered, round, 9 1/8″	200.00
Vegetable, round, 7 1/2″	80.00
Vegetable, round, 9 1/8″	110.00

Bowl, fruit, 5″	$30.00
Coffeepot, covered, 8″	160.00
Coffeepot, covered, no lid	140.00
Cream Soup and Saucer	70.00
Cream Soup and Saucer, handled	70.00
Cream Soup Saucer	22.50
Creamer, 3 5/8″	60.00
Creamer, 4 1/4″	60.00
Cup and Saucer, demitasse	40.00
Cup and Saucer, footed, 2 3/8″	50.00
Gravy Boat, attached underplate	160.00
Gravy Boat and Underplate	160.00
Pitcher, 7 3/4″	110.00
Plate, bread and butter, 6″	17.50
Plate, dinner, 10 1/2″	45.00
Plate, luncheon, 8 1/2″	35.00
Plate, salad, 7 5/8″	25.00
Platter, oval, 11″	105.00

Rosenthal, Maria

Bowl, fruit, 5 3/4″	$15.00
Bowl, soup, flat, 8 1/2″	20.00
Butter Dish, covered, round	90.00

Butter Pat, 3 1/2″	10.00	Mustard, covered, no lid	27.50
Cake Plate, handled, 11 3/4″	40.00	Plate, bread and butter	10.00
Candlestick, single light, 2 1/4″	25.00	Plate, dinner, 10 3/4″	25.00
Cheese and Cracker Board, 8 3/4″	40.00	Plate, salad, 7 3/4″	15.00
Coffeepot, covered, 7 3/4″	100.00	Platter, oval, 13″	70.00
Coffeepot, covered, mini, 6 1/8″	70.00	Platter, oval, 15″	110.00
Coffeepot, covered, mini, 6 1/8″, no lid	50.00	Platter, oval, 15 1/4″	110.00
Cream Soup and Saucer	40.00	Relish, 10″	25.00
Cream Soup Bowl	35.00	Sauce Boat	80.00
Creamer, 4″	27.50	Saucer, 2 5/8″ cup	10.00
Creamer, mini	22.50	Saucer, demitasse, 2″ cup	7.50
Cup and Saucer, bouillon	27.50	Sugar Bowl, covered, 3 3/8″	50.00
Cup and Saucer, demitasse, 2″	25.00	Sugar Bowl, covered, mini	30.00
Cup and Saucer, footed, 2 5/8″	27.50	Teapot, covered, 5″	100.00
Eggcup, single, 2 3/4″	12.50	Tray, sandwich, 14 1/4″	70.00
Fondue Warmer Stand	90.00	Tureen, covered	250.00
Gravy Boat, attached underplate	80.00	Vegetable, covered, octagonal, handled	130.00
Gravy Boat, individual, no underplate	20.00	Vegetable, covered, round	130.00
Lid, coffeepot	50.00	Vegetable, octagonal, 8″	60.00
Lid, sugar bowl	25.00	Vegetable, octagonal, 9 1/4″	70.00
Lid, tureen	125.00	Vegetable, octagonal, 10″	80.00
Lid, vegetable, octagonal	65.00	Vegetable, round, 9 3/8″	60.00
Marmalade	50.00	Vegetable, round, 10 1/4″	70.00
Mug, 5″	20.00	Vegetable, round, divided, 10 3/4″	90.00

Rosenthal, Moss Rose

Bowl, fruit, 5 1/4″	$30.00
Bowl, soup, flat, 8 1/2″	40.00
Coffeepot, covered	230.00
Cream Soup and Saucer	80.00
Cream Soup Saucer	25.00
Creamer, 4 3/8″	70.00
Cup and Saucer, footed, 2 5/8″	65.00
Gravy Boat, attached underplate	170.00
Lid, teapot	135.00
Plate, bread and butter, 6 1/4″	20.00
Plate, dinner	55.00
Plate, salad, 7 7/8″	27.50
Platter, oval, 12 7/8″	130.00
Platter, oval, 13″	130.00
Platter, oval, 14 7/8″	150.00
Platter, oval, 19 1/8″	300.00
Relish, 9 3/4″	60.00
Saucer, 2 5/8″	22.50
Saucer, demitasse, 2 1/8″ cup	15.00
Sugar Bowl, covered, 3 1/4″	90.00
Vegetable, covered, round	250.00
Vegetable, round, 10″	135.00
Vegetable, round, 11 1/4″	150.00

ROSINA CHINA COMPANY

The Rosina China Company Ltd., Queen's Pottery, was founded in Longton, Staffordshire, England, in 1887. Queen's China was a brand name of porcelain produced by Queen's Pottery.

Rosina China, Yuletide, Bone China

Bowl, cereal, coupe, 6 1/2″	$25.00
Bowl, footed, 6″	27.50
Box, covered, round	40.00
Bud Vase, 3 3/8″	30.00
Bud Vase, 4 1/2″	30.00
Bud Vase, 7 1/8″	30.00
Cachepot, 5 1/2″	70.00
Cachepot, 6 1/4″	90.00
Cake Plate, handled, 10″	35.00
Cheese and Cracker Board, 10 3/4″	70.00
Coaster, 4″	10.00
Coffeepot, covered	110.00
Coffeepot, covered, no lid	85.00

Compote	65.00
Cream Soup and Saucer	50.00
Creamer	25.00
Creamer, mini, 3 1/4″	25.00
Cup, flat, 2 1/2″	22.50
Cup and Saucer, demitasse	25.00
Cup and Saucer, flat, 2 1/2″	25.00
Dish, leaf shape, 5 1/2″	20.00
Dish, sweet meat, 4 3/4″	15.00
Jar, covered, 4 1/2″	70.00
Jar, covered, 6 1/8″	70.00
Lid, teapot	60.00
Pill Box	25.00
Plate, bread and butter	15.00
Plate, dinner, 10 1/2″	35.00
Plate, salad, 8 1/4″	25.00
Platter, oval, 13 1/2″	90.00
Salt and Pepper Shakers, pair	50.00
Saucer	7.50
Saucer, demitasse	7.50
Sugar Bowl, covered	32.50
Sugar Bowl, open	30.00
Sugar Bowl, open, mini	25.00
Teapot, covered, mini	85.00
Tray, oblong, 7 7/8″	30.00
Tray, serving, two-tiered	65.00
Tureen, covered	475.00
Vase, 6 1/4″	75.00
Vegetable, covered, round	180.00
Vegetable, oval, 9 1/4″	100.00

Attempts to determine precisely who Rossetti is have proven unsuccessful to date. Numerous "Spring Violets" pieces are marked "Rossetti / Chicago U. S. A. / Made in Occupied Japan." This strongly suggests that Rossetti was a late 1940s or early 1950s ceramic importer.

Gene Florence's *The Collector's Encyclopedia of Occupied Japan Collectibles, Third Series,* published by Collector Books, contains the following about a "Spring Violets" set that he encountered: "Not all pieces in the dinnerware set were marked 'OJ.' What was unusual was that there were several odd items in the set such as butter pats and ashtrays. I had never seen those pieces in any other 'OJ' dinnerware patterns."

THE TOP FIVE PATTERNS
PATTERN GROUP—
FLORAL MOTIF, CASUAL

— ■ —

FRANCISCAN, FLORAL
INTERNATIONAL CHINA CO., TERRACE BLOSSOMS
MIKASA, SILK FLOWERS
ROSSETTI, SPRING VIOLETS
VILLEROY & BOCH, INDIAN SUMMER

Rossetti, Spring Violets

Ashtray, 3 1/4″	$15.00
Ashtray, 4″	15.00
Chop Plate, 12 1/4″	110.00
Compote, 2 7/8″	75.00
Creamer	60.00
Cup, demitasse, 2 1/4″	30.00
Cup, footed, 2 7/8″	37.50
Cup and Saucer, demitasse, 2 1/4″	35.00
Cup and Saucer, footed, 2 7/8″	40.00
Gravy Boat, attached underplate	130.00
Lid, sugar bowl	40.00
Lid, teapot	100.00
Plate, bread and butter	17.50
Plate, dinner	40.00
Plate, salad	25.00
Platter, oval, 12 1/8″	110.00
Platter, oval, 14 1/8″	120.00
Saucer	15.00
Saucer, demitasse, 2 3/8″ cup	10.00
Sugar Bowl, covered	80.00
Sugar Bowl, covered, no lid	55.00
Teapot, covered, mini, no lid	95.00
Vegetable, covered, round	230.00
Vegetable, oval, 11 1/8″	100.00
Vegetable, round, 9 1/8″	100.00

ROYAL ALBERT

Royal Albert Bone China was manufactured by Thomas C. Wild & Sons, Ltd., of Longton, Staffordshire, England. The company, founded in 1894, produced tea, coffee, and table services in the Royal Albert line. Today, Royal Albert is produced by Royal Doulton Tableware, Inc.

Royal Albert, Christmas Magic

Bowl, footed, 3 1/4″	$75.00
Bowl, salad, serving, 9 1/2″	120.00
Candlestick, single light, 2″	60.00
Cup and Saucer	45.00
Mug, 4″	35.00
Plate, dinner	50.00
Plate, salad	30.00
Platter, oval, 13 1/2″	150.00
Saucer	15.00
Trinket Box, covered	60.00

Royal Albert, Old Country Roses

Ashtray, 4 7/8″	$30.00
Bell	40.00
Bonbon, 4 5/8″	35.00
Bonbon, 6″	35.00
Bowl, cereal, coupe, 6 1/4″	27.50
Bowl, fruit, 5 3/8″	17.50
Bowl, fruit, 10 1/8″	200.00
Bowl, soup, flat, 8″	32.50
Bud Vase, 3 1/4″	35.00
Cake Plate, handled, 10 3/8″	40.00
Candlestick, single light	45.00
Cheese Knife, stainless blade, 7 3/4″	35.00
Clock, plate, 10 3/8″	80.00
Coaster, 4 3/4″	15.00
Cream Soup and Saucer	55.00
Cream Soup Bowl	40.00
Creamer	40.00
Cup and Saucer, demitasse	35.00

Cup and Saucer, footed, 2 3/4″	22.50	Platter, oval, 15 1/4″	150.00
Dish, mint, 8 1/4″	25.00	Platter, oval, 16 1/2″	160.00
Dish, shell shape, 5″	35.00	Quiche Dish, 9 3/4″	55.00
Ginger Jar, covered	40.00	Ramekin, 4 3/8″	20.00
Gravy Boat and Underplate	100.00	Saucer	7.50
Gravy Boat, no underplate	80.00	Saucer, demitasse	12.50
Gravy Boat Underplate	35.00	Soufflé, 7″	50.00
Jam Spoon, 6 1/2″	35.00	Soufflé, 8 3/4″	65.00
Lid, coffeepot	40.00	Sugar Bowl, covered	70.00
Lid, coffeepot, mini	40.00	Sugar Bowl, open	40.00
Lid, vegetable, round	110.00	Teapot, covered, 4 3/4″	65.00
Marmalade	55.00	Tray, 7″	30.00
Pepper Shaker	17.50	Tray, oblong, 6 1/2″	30.00
Plate, anniversary, 8 1/2″	40.00	Tray, sandwich, 11 3/4″	45.00
Plate, bread and butter, 6 1/4″	12.50	Tray, serving, two-tiered	50.00
Plate, dinner, 10 3/8″	32.50	Tureen, covered, 5 3/4″ x 9″	490.00
Plate, round, handled	45.00	Vase, covered, 9″	85.00
Plate, salad, 8 1/8″	15.00	Vegetable, covered, round	250.00
Platter, oval, 13″	90.00	Vegetable, round, 9 3/8″	120.00

The Royal China Company began operations in the remodeled factory that originally housed the Oliver China Company and later the E. H. Sebring Company. The building had been abandoned since the collapse of The American Chinaware Corporation conglomerate, but by 1939 the remodeled factory was producing again.

Royal China acquired the French-Saxon China Company in Sebring, Ohio, in 1964 as a wholly owned subsidiary. In 1969, Royal China was purchased by the Jeanette Company. Jeanette operated the company until February 1970, when a fire destroyed the old E. H. Sebring building. Jeanette quickly resumed production in the nearby French-Saxon building.

In 1976, the Coca-Cola Bottling Company of New York bought the Jeanette Corporation and its subsidiaries. Coca-Cola operated Royal until 1981, when it was sold to J. Corporation of Boston. In 1984, Royal was sold to Nordic Capitol of New York City.

The Royal name was kept and used on new lines through all of these changes. Operations ceased in 1986.

ROYAL CHINA COMPANY, CURRIER & IVES

The Currier & Ives pattern, first produced in late 1949 or early 1950, was probably the most popular pattern produced by the Royal China Company. It was originally manufactured in four colors—blue, pink, green, and brown.

The pattern was inspired by popular Currier & Ives prints and combined central print patterns with a unique scrolled border, designed by Royal China's Art Director, Gordon Parker.

In 1970, following Royal China's takeover by the Jeanette Company, the pattern was discontinued in favor of more modern designs. Although Jeanette soon realized its mistake and reintroduced Currier & Ives by Royal China in the mid 1970s, the original colors and quality were never duplicated.

Early marks on this pattern were date-coded. According to Curt Fahnert, director of dinnerware design development at Royal China until 1986, the old dating codes were lost when a fire destroyed the Royal China Company plant in 1970.

**Royal Doulton, Glen Audlyn, Bone China,
light blue**

Coffeepot, covered	$300.00
Cream Soup and Saucer	90.00
Cream Soup Saucer	30.00
Creamer	70.00
Cup, demitasse	55.00
Cup and Saucer, demitasse	60.00
Cup and Saucer, footed, 2 5/8″	55.00
Lid, teapot	150.00
Plate, bread and butter, 6 5/8″	25.00
Plate, dinner, 10 5/8″	55.00

Plate, salad, 8 1/8″	40.00
Platter, oval, 13 1/2″	190.00
Saucer	17.50
Sugar Bowl, covered	120.00
Sugar Bowl, covered, no lid	90.00
Vegetable, covered, round	390.00
Vegetable, oval, 10 5/8″	140.00

Royal Doulton, Grantham

Ashtray, 3 5/8″	$20.00
Bowl, cereal, coupe, 6″	30.00

Bowl, fruit, 5 5/8″	20.00
Bowl, soup, flat, 8 5/8″	30.00
Cake Plate, handled, 10″	80.00
Chop Plate, 12 5/8″	100.00
Coaster, 4″	15.00
Coffeepot, covered	200.00
Cream Soup and Saucer	50.00
Cream Soup Saucer	15.00
Creamer	45.00
Cup and Saucer, demitasse	30.00
Cup and Saucer, flat, 2 3/8″	40.00
Eggcup, single, 3 1/2″	25.00
Gravy Boat and Underplate	110.00
Gravy Boat Underplate	35.00
Lid, vegetable, round	90.00
Plate, bread and butter, 6 1/2″	15.00
Plate, dinner, 9 1/2″	30.00
Plate, dinner, 10 3/8″	30.00
Plate, luncheon, 8 5/8″	22.50
Plate, salad, square, 7 3/4″	25.00
Platter, oval, 11 1/4″	80.00
Platter, oval, 13 3/8″	100.00
Platter, oval, 15 1/2″	130.00
Relish, 8″	40.00
Saucer	12.50
Saucer, demitasse	10.00
Sugar Bowl, covered	70.00
Sugar Bowl, open, mini	30.00
Teapot, covered	200.00
Vegetable, covered, round	200.00
Vegetable, oval, 8 1/2″	60.00
Vegetable, oval, 9 1/2″	70.00
Vegetable, oval, 10 3/8″	80.00
Vegetable, round, 8 1/4″	70.00
Vegetable, round, 9 1/4″	80.00

Coffeepot, covered	200.00
Coffeepot, covered, no lid	160.00
Creamer	50.00
Cup and Saucer, demitasse	40.00
Cup and Saucer, flat, 2 3/4″	40.00
Cup and Saucer, footed, 2 3/4″	40.00
Gravy Boat Underplate	50.00
Gravy Boat, no underplate	120.00
Lid, casserole, oval, 8 1/4″	90.00
Lid, casserole, round, 6″	80.00
Plate, bread and butter, 6 1/2″	20.00
Plate, dinner	45.00
Plate, salad, 8″	30.00
Platter, oval, 13 1/4″	120.00
Ramekin, 2″	30.00
Saucer	12.50
Saucer, demitasse	12.50
Sugar Bowl, covered	80.00
Sugar Bowl, open, mini	35.00
Vegetable, covered, oval	200.00

Royal Doulton, Old Colony, Fine China

Bowl, soup, flat, 8″	$40.00
Bowl, soup, flat, 9 1/8″	40.00
Coffeepot, covered	190.00
Cream Soup and Saucer	65.00
Cream Soup Saucer	22.50
Creamer	40.00
Cup and Saucer, demitasse	35.00
Cup and Saucer, footed, 2 3/4″	40.00
Eggcup, single, 2″	25.00
Gravy Boat, attached underplate	150.00
Gravy Boat and Underplate	150.00
Lid, teapot	95.00
Lid, vegetable, round	120.00
Lid, vegetable, 8 1/8″	120.00
Pitcher, 5 5/8″	100.00
Plate, bread and butter, 6 5/8″	15.00
Plate, dinner, 10 5/8″	35.00
Plate, salad, 8 1/8″	25.00

Royal Doulton, Miramont, Stirling Rim, Fine China

Casserole, covered, round, 6 1/4″, no lid	$125.00
Casserole, individual, 4 3/8″	60.00

Platter, oval, 13 $1/4''$	120.00
Platter, oval, 15 $7/8''$	170.00
Platter, oval, 16$''$	170.00
Saucer	12.50
Saucer, demitasse	12.50
Sugar Bowl, covered	80.00
Sugar Bowl, covered, no lid	55.00
Sugar Bowl, open	40.00
Teapot, covered	190.00
Teapot, mini, no lid	90.00
Vegetable, covered, oval	240.00
Vegetable, covered, round	240.00
Vegetable, oval, 9 $3/8''$	80.00

Vegetable, covered, round	230.00
Vegetable, oval, 9 $1/2''$	75.00
Vegetable, round, 9 $1/8''$	80.00

Royal Doulton, Provencal, Fine China

Bowl, cereal, coupe, 7$''$	$35.00
Bowl, fruit, 5 $3/8''$	25.00
Bowl, soup, flat, 8$''$	40.00
Cake Plate, handled, 10 $3/4''$	80.00
Casserole, covered, oval, 8$''$	180.00
Casserole, covered, round, 6 $3/8''$	160.00
Casserole, covered, round, 7 $3/8''$	180.00
Casserole, covered, round, 7 $3/8''$, no lid	145.00
Casserole, individual, 4 $3/8''$	70.00
Coffeepot, covered	160.00
Cream Soup and Saucer	50.00
Creamer	45.00
Cup and Saucer, demitasse	40.00
Cup and Saucer, footed, 2 $3/4''$	30.00
Gray Boat, attached underplate	130.00
Gravy Boat and Underplate	130.00
Gravy Boat Underplate	45.00
Lid, sugar bowl, mini	40.00
Lid, teapot	80.00
Lid, vegetable, round	100.00
Plate, bread and butter, 6 $1/2''$	15.00
Plate, dinner, 10 $3/4''$	40.00
Plate, luncheon, 9 $1/4''$	35.00
Plate, salad, 8$''$	25.00
Platter, oval, 13 $1/4''$	100.00
Platter, oval, 16$''$	150.00
Ramekin, 3 $3/8''$	25.00
Saucer	10.00
Saucer, demitasse	12.50
Soufflé, 6 $5/8''$	65.00
Sugar Bowl, covered	80.00

Royal Doulton, Old Leeds Spray, no trim

Bowl, cereal, coupe, 6$''$	$35.00
Bowl, fruit, 5 $5/8''$	20.00
Bowl, soup, flat, 8 $1/2''$	35.00
Cream Soup and Saucer	60.00
Cream Soup Saucer	20.00
Cup, oversized, flat, 2 $3/4''$	40.00
Cup and Saucer, bouillon	40.00
Cup and Saucer, demitasse	30.00
Cup and Saucer, flat, 2 $3/8''$	40.00
Cup and Saucer, footed, 2 $3/8''$	40.00
Gravy Boat, attached underplate	120.00
Gravy Boat, no underplate	95.00
Lid, coffeepot	90.00
Lid, sugar bowl	40.00
Plate, bread and butter, 6 $1/2''$	15.00
Plate, dinner	35.00
Plate, luncheon, 8 $5/8''$	30.00
Plate, salad, 7 $1/4''$	22.50
Platter, oval, 11$''$	90.00
Platter, oval, 13 $1/4''$	110.00
Platter, oval, 15 $3/8''$	150.00
Saucer	15.00
Saucer, demitasse	10.00

DOS AND DON'TS FOR A SUCCESSFUL DINNER PARTY

A successful dinner party is one everyone enjoys. Your guests should be comfortable. You should be relaxed and cheerful. While knowing the proper way to serve your guests is important, the real key to success is advance planning. By taking care of as many details as possible before your guests arrive, you will enjoy their good company and conversation.

Follow these dos and don'ts to help ensure the success of your dinner.

- **DO** make your guests feel at home.
- **DO** polish your china, flatware, and stemware until it sparkles.
- **DO** set an interesting table. Create a centerpiece that does not obstruct your guests' views of one other. If candles are used, keep the flames above eye level when your guests are seated.
- **DO** have all of the serving bowls and platters you need ready in the kitchen. You will not have time to search for them at the last minute.
- **DO** serve the guest on your right first, and continue serving to the right.
- **DO** serve food from the left; however, you may remove from the left or right, whichever is more convenient, as long as you are consistent.
- **DO** serve water, wine, and other drinks from the right.

And most importantly,
- **DO** smile when something is spilled or broken. It will ease your guests' discomfort.

- **DON'T** invite more guests than your home and number of dinnerware place settings can accommodate.
- **DON'T** invite guests who are incompatible in personality or interests.
- **DON'T** allow the pre-dinner period to last for more than thirty minutes. Keep hors d'oeuvres and drinks light. What's the use of serving a delicious meal if your guests can't enjoy what they are eating?
- **DON'T** crowd your guests. Allow at least 20" for each place setting.
- **DON'T** experiment with new recipes for your dinner party. Tried-and-true dishes will be the most successful.
- **DON'T** lift the glasses from the table when filling them.
- **DON'T** leave the place in front of your guest bare. Always exchange one plate for another until dessert time.

One note for guests:
- **DON'T** inspect the bottom of your dinnerware to see who made it. There is no discreet way to do this.

Sugar Bowl, covered, no lid	60.00
Teapot, covered	160.00
Tureen, covered	330.00
Vegetable, covered, round	200.00
Vegetable, oval, 9 ¹/₂″	100.00

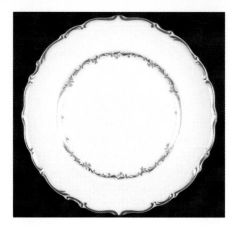

Royal Doulton, Richeileau, Bone China, gold design

Creamer	$75.00
Cup, footed, 2 ⁵/₈″	50.00
Cup and Saucer, footed, 2 ⁵/₈″	55.00
Lid, teapot	165.00
Plate, bread and butter, 6 ¹/₂″	25.00
Plate, dinner, 10 ⁵/₈″	55.00
Plate, salad, 8″	35.00

Royal Doulton, Real Old Willow, Majestic

Bowl, cereal, coupe, 6 ¹/₄″	$45.00
Bowl, fruit, 5 ¹/₄″	35.00
Bowl, soup, flat, 8 ³/₄″	40.00
Cake Plate, 11″	70.00
Cream Soup and Saucer	80.00
Creamer	70.00
Cup, demitasse	35.00
Cup and Saucer, demitasse	40.00
Cup and Saucer, flat, 2 ⁵/₈″	40.00
Gravy Boat and Underplate	180.00
Lid, coffeepot	90.00
Mug, 3 ¹/₂″	35.00
Plate, bread and butter, 7″	20.00
Plate, dinner, 10 ¹/₂″	35.00
Plate, luncheon, 10″	45.00
Plate, salad, 8 ¹/₂″	25.00
Platter, oval, 13 ³/₈″	160.00
Platter, oval, 16 ¹/₄″	200.00
Sugar Bowl, covered	140.00
Sugar Bowl, covered, no lid	80.00
Tureen, covered, no lid	270.00
Vegetable, oval, 10 ³/₈″	120.00

Royal Doulton, Rondo, Bone China, gold design

Coffeepot, covered	$250.00
Coffeepot, covered, mini, no lid	140.00
Creamer	70.00
Cup and Saucer, demitasse, 1 ⁷/₈″	45.00
Cup and Saucer, footed, 2 ¹/₂″	50.00
Gravy Boat Underplate	65.00
Lid, teapot	125.00
Plate, bread and butter, 6 ⁵/₈″	25.00
Plate, dinner, 10 ⁵/₈″	50.00
Plate, salad, 8 ¹/₈″	35.00
Platter, oval, 13″	160.00
Platter, oval, 13 ⁵/₈″	160.00
Saucer	15.00

Sugar Bowl, covered	100.00
Sugar Bowl, covered, no lid	70.00
Teapot, covered	250.00
Vegetable, oval, 10 5/8″	120.00

Royal Doulton, Sarabande, Bone China, platinum trim

Cup and Saucer, demitasse	$30.00
Cup and Saucer, footed, 3″	30.00
Lid, sugar bowl	40.00
Plate, bread and butter, 6 5/8″	15.00
Plate, dinner, 10 5/8″	25.00
Plate, luncheon, 9″	30.00
Plate, salad, 8″	17.50
Platter, oval, 16 3/8″	140.00
Salt Shaker	17.50
Sugar Bowl, covered	85.00
Vegetable, covered, round	215.00
Vegetable, oval, 10 7/8″	90.00

Royal Doulton, Sovereign, Classic Shape, Bone China, gold design

Coffeepot, covered	$370.00
Coffeepot, covered, no lid	260.00

Cream Soup and Saucer	120.00
Creamer	90.00
Cup, demitasse, 2 5/8″	60.00
Cup and Saucer, demitasse, 2″	70.00
Cup and Saucer, footed, 2 1/2″	70.00
Gravy Boat, attached underplate	260.00
Gravy Boat and Underplate	260.00
Gravy Boat, no underplate	200.00
Lid, sugar bowl	80.00
Plate, bread and butter, 6 5/8″	30.00
Plate, dinner, 10 5/8″	75.00
Plate, salad, 8″	50.00
Platter, oval, 13 3/4″	230.00
Platter, oval, 16 1/8″	330.00
Saucer	25.00
Sugar Bowl, covered	165.00
Sugar Bowl, open	90.00
Teapot, covered	370.00
Vegetable, covered, oval	460.00

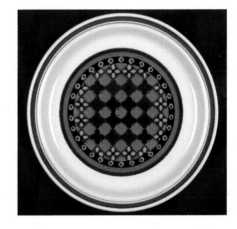

Royal Doulton, Tangier, Lambethware

Casserole, covered, round, 6″	$160.00
Casserole, covered, round, 6 3/4″, no lid	125.00
Casserole, covered, round, 7 1/8″, no lid	135.00
Coffeepot, covered	200.00
Creamer	40.00
Cup and Saucer, flat, 2 7/8″	30.00
Eggcup, single, 1 7/8″	17.50
Gravy Boat	120.00
Lid, coffeepot	100.00
Lid, teapot	100.00
Plate, bread and butter	20.00
Plate, dinner	40.00
Plate, salad	30.00
Platter, oval, 13 1/4″	100.00
Roaster, oval, 10 3/8″	110.00
Saucer	10.00
Sugar Bowl, covered	60.00

Sugar Bowl, covered, no lid	40.00
Vegetable, oval, 10 ¾″	100.00

Royal Doulton, Tapestry, Fine China

Casserole, covered, round, 7″	$150.00
Coffeepot, covered	150.00
Creamer	40.00
Cup and Saucer, flat, 3″	30.00
Gravy Boat and Underplate	130.00
Plate, bread and butter, 6 ½″	15.00
Plate, dinner	35.00
Plate, salad, 8″	20.00
Platter, oval, 13 ⅛″	100.00
Platter, oval, 15 ⅞″	150.00
Saucer	10.00
Sugar Bowl, covered	60.00
Sugar Bowl, covered, no lid	30.00
Teapot, covered, no lid	130.00

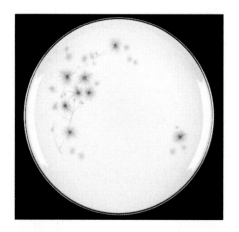

Royal Doulton, Thistledown, Bone China

Coffeepot, covered	$210.00
Creamer	50.00

Cup and Saucer, demitasse	40.00
Cup and Saucer, flat, 2 ⅛″	40.00
Gravy Boat and Underplate	160.00
Lid, sugar bowl	40.00
Plate, bread and butter, 6 ¼″	17.50
Plate, dinner	40.00
Plate, salad, 8 ⅜″	25.00
Platter, oval, 13 ⅛″	145.00
Platter, oval, 16 ¼″	200.00
Saucer	15.00
Saucer, demitasse	15.00
Sugar Bowl, covered	80.00
Sugar Bowl, open	50.00
Vegetable, covered, round	270.00

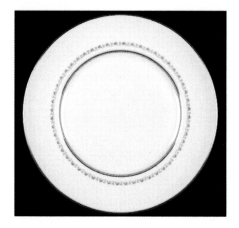

Royal Doulton, Tiara, Bone China

Cream Soup Bowl	$80.00
Creamer, 4 ⅛″	75.00
Creamer, 5 ⅛″	75.00
Cup and Saucer, demitasse, 2″	60.00
Cup and Saucer, footed, 2 ⅝″	55.00
Gravy Boat and Underplate	200.00
Lid, coffeepot	150.00
Lid, vegetable, oval	185.00
Plate, bread and butter, 6 ⅛″	25.00
Plate, dinner, 10 ⅝″	55.00
Plate, salad, 8″	35.00
Platter, oval, 13 ⅝″	190.00
Platter, oval, 15 ¼″	240.00
Platter, oval, 16″	270.00
Sugar Bowl, covered	120.00
Sugar Bowl, covered, no lid	90.00
Vegetable, covered, oval	375.00
Vegetable, covered, round, no lid	260.00
Vegetable, oval, 10 ⅝″	140.00

In 1885, brothers Sidney
tery in Stoke-on-Trent. De
successful that it soon em
company became Grim
China.

Grimwades introduc
by Queen Mary and Ki
Grimwades' work, is be
dinnerware.

Royal Doulton, Ting, Lambethware, brown

Bowl, cereal, coupe, 6 1/2″	$35.00
Bowl, fruit, flat, 6″	20.00
Casserole, covered, oval, 8″	120.00
Casserole, individual, 4 3/4″	60.00
Coffeepot, covered	200.00
Creamer	40.00
Cup and Saucer, flat, 2 7/8″	30.00
Eggcup, single, 1 7/8″	17.50
Gravy Boat	120.00
Pitcher, 6″	100.00
Plate, bread and butter	20.00
Plate, dinner, 10 3/8″	40.00
Plate, salad, 8 5/8″	30.00
Platter, oval, 13 1/4″	100.00
Saucer	10.00
Soufflé, 5 1/2″	50.00
Sugar Bowl, covered	60.00
Sugar Bowl, covered, no lid	40.00
Teapot, covered, no lid	140.00
Vegetable, oval, 10 3/4″	100.00

Grimwades' Summertir
pany's most popular po
sold and still turn up r
plied to clocks, sick fe
graphed in the center.
Variations also exist in

Royal Doulton, Tonkin, Sheraton Rim, Fine China

Bowl, cereal, coupe, 6 7/8″	$45.00
Bowl, cranberry, 4 5/8″	90.00

Bowl, fruit, 5 3/8″	35.00
Bowl, salad, serving, 10 3/8″	170.00
Bowl, soup, flat, 8″	45.00
Bowl, soup, flat, 9 1/8″	45.00
Cake Plate, handled, 10 5/8″	90.00
Chop Plate, 13 3/8″	150.00
Coffeepot, covered	230.00
Cream Soup and Saucer	70.00
Creamer, 5 1/8″	60.00
Cup and Saucer, demitasse	45.00
Cup and Saucer, flat, 2 7/8″	50.00
Eggcup, single, 2″	30.00
Gravy Boat and Underplate	170.00
Gravy Boat, no underplate	140.00
Lid, coffeepot	115.00
Lid, teapot	115.00
Lid, vegetable, round	150.00
Pickle Dish, 8 3/8″	70.00
Plate, bread and butter, 6 1/2″	25.00
Plate, dinner	45.00
Plate, salad, 8″	35.00
Platter, oval, 13 1/4″	155.00
Sugar Bowl, covered	90.00
Sugar Bowl, covered, mini	60.00
Teapot, covered	230.00
Tureen, covered	350.00
Vegetable, covered, round	300.00

Royal Doulton, White Nile, Fine China

Bowl, cereal, coupe, 6 1/4″	$40.00
Bowl, cranberry, 4 5/8″	70.00
Bowl, soup, flat, 8″	45.00
Cake Plate, handled, 10 3/4″	80.00
Casserole, covered, round, 7 1/8″	200.00
Coffeepot, covered	170.00
Cream Soup and Saucer	60.00
Cup, flat, 2 7/8″	40.00
Cup and Saucer, demitasse	35.00
Cup and Saucer, flat, 2 7/8″	40.00
Gravy Boat and Underplate	130.00

Lid, coffeepot
Lid, teapot
Pickle Dish, 8 ¼"
Plate, bread and butter
Plate, dinner, 10 ½"
Plate, salad, 8"
Platter, oval, 13 ⅜"
Platter, oval, 16 ½"

Royal Winton, Summertime

Bowl, cereal, 6 ½"	$75.00
Cake Plate, open handles	165.00
Creamer, Sugar, and Tray, open, mini	230.00
Cup and Saucer	100.00
Jam Pot	100.00
Jug, 5"	450.00
Lid, teapot	200.00
Mint Boat and Underplate	215.00
Nut Dish, 5 ⅜"	100.00

Plate, bread and butter, 6 ¼"	55.00
Plate, dinner	150.00
Plate, salad	85.00
Relish, five-section	475.00
Sugar Bowl, covered, no lid	130.00
Syrup	350.00
Tray, Salt and Pepper Shakers, pair	175.00
Trivet, round	175.00
Vegetable, 8"	150.00
Vegetable, 9"	175.00

**THE TOP FOUR PATTERNS
PATTERN GROUP—
CHINTZ**

JOHNSON BROTHERS, ROSE CHINTZ
ROYAL WINTON, SUMMERTIME
SPODE, ROSEBUD CHINTZ
STAFFORDSHIRE, CALICO

ROYAL WORCESTER

The Worcester Porcelain Company, led by Dr. John Wall and William Davis, acquired the Bristol Pottery of Benjamin Lund in 1751. Operations were moved to Worcester, and the production of utilitarian wares, especially tea and dessert sets, was begun. Transfer printing was used extensively, beginning in 1755. Following William Davis's death in 1783, a series of partnerships was established over the next fifty-five years, including associations with Thomas Flight, Martin Barr, and Martin's son. The company received a royal warrant from George III in 1789.

In 1840, the company merged with the Chamberlain Factory of Diglis and was renamed Chamberlain and Company. Over the next twelve years quality declined, and in 1852 Kerr & Binns acquired the factory. Quality was reestablished over the following ten years, and in 1862 R. W. Binns formed the Worcester Royal Porcelain Company Ltd., the firm whose products carried the "Royal Worcester" mark.

During the 1860s, Limoges-style enameled porcelains, figurines, dessert services, vases, and ornamental pieces were produced. Porcelains in the Japanese style, many designed by John Hadley, were introduced in the 1870s. In 1889, Worcester Royal Porcelain Company acquired a factory owned by Thomas Grainger, and by 1905 it acquired a factory originally established by James Hadley in 1896.

During the 1920s and 1930s, the company produced high-quality bone china with colorful floral borders or blue-and-white transfer prints. World War II restrictions curtailed the company's production, but it was resumed after the war. Figurines produced by Worcester in the 1940s and 1950s, especially those created by Doris Linder and Dorothy Doughty, are still very popular.

In the 1960s, Worcester produced tea, dinner, and oven-to-table wares in both new and traditional patterns. Demand continued to increase, and in 1970 a new factory opened. Today, much of Royal Worcester's porcelain is still hand-decorated.

Royal Worcester, Astley, gold trim, smooth

Bowl, fruit, 5 1/2"	$25.00
Bowl, salad, individual	40.00
Casserole, covered, oval, 8 5/8", no lid	100.00
Casserole, covered, oval, 9"	150.00
Casserole, covered, round, 5 3/8"	100.00
Casserole, covered, round, 6 1/4"	120.00
Casserole, covered, round, 7"	130.00
Coffeepot, covered	145.00
Cup and Saucer, flat, 2 1/2"	40.00
Cup and Saucer, oversized, 2 3/4"	45.00
Egg Coddler, 2 1/2"	15.00

Eggcup, single, 2″	17.50
Lid, casserole, round, 8″	70.00
Oil Cruet, no stopper	50.00
Plate, bread and butter	15.00
Plate, dinner	40.00
Plate, salad	25.00
Pot de Creme, covered	50.00
Pot de Creme, no lid	35.00
Quiche Dish, 7 7/8″	55.00
Saucer	12.50
Saucer, oversized	15.00
Sugar Bowl, covered	70.00
Vinegar, no stopper	70.00
Vinegar and Oil, stoppers	150.00

Royal Worcester, Evesham Gold, gold trim

Baker, oval, 9 5/8″	$50.00
Baker, oval, 10 1/2″	45.00
Baker, oval, 11 1/2″	50.00
Baker, rectangular, 11 1/2″	70.00
Baker, rectangular, 14 1/2″	70.00
Baker, square, 10 1/2″	70.00
Bowl, cereal, coupe, 6 3/4″	20.00
Bowl, fruit, 5 5/8″	15.00
Bowl, salad, individual, 5 3/8″	25.00
Bowl, soup, coupe, 8 1/4″	25.00
Butter Dish, covered, 1/4 lb.	45.00
Canister, flour, 7 1/8″	85.00
Casserole, covered, oval, 8 3/4″	80.00
Casserole, covered, oval, 9 5/8″	80.00
Casserole, covered, round, 5 1/4″	65.00
Casserole, covered, round, 6 1/8″	65.00

Casserole, covered, round, 6 1/8″, no lid	50.00
Casserole, covered, round, 7 3/4″	75.00
Casserole, covered, round, 8″	80.00
Coffeepot, covered	75.00
Cream Soup and Saucer	45.00
Creamer, 3 3/4″	30.00
Cup and Saucer, breakfast, 2 3/4″	30.00
Cup and Saucer, demitasse, 2 3/8″	20.00
Cup and Saucer, flat, 2 1/2″	20.00
Dish, shell shape, 4 7/8″	30.00
Entree Dish, 7 3/8″	17.50
Fish Dish, 13 1/2″	40.00
Flan, 9 5/8″	45.00
Flan, 10 3/4″	45.00
Gravy Boat, individual, no underplate	25.00
Jam	30.00
Jug, 5″	45.00
Lid, canister, flour	30.00
Lid, casserole, covered, round, 6 1/2″	35.00
Mug, 3 3/4″	15.00
Oil Cruet, no stopper	25.00
Pie Plate, serving, 10 3/8″	40.00
Pitcher, 7 1/8″	60.00
Plate, bread and butter, 6 1/2″	7.50
Plate, collector, 10 1/4″	25.00
Plate, dinner	17.50
Plate, luncheon, 9 1/8″	15.00
Plate, salad, 8 1/4″	10.00
Platter, oval, 12 7/8″	65.00
Platter, oval, 15″	85.00
Pot de Creme, covered	40.00
Pot de Creme, no lid	35.00
Quiche Dish, 7 3/4″	40.00
Quiche Dish, 9″	45.00
Quiche Dish, 10 1/4″	50.00
Ramekin, 3 1/4″	10.00
Relish, three-part, 9 1/4″	50.00
Salt and Pepper Shakers, pair, 4 3/4″	40.00
Soufflé, 5 5/8″	30.00
Soufflé, 6 1/8″	40.00
Soufflé, 7 3/8″	40.00
Sugar Bowl, covered	35.00
Teapot, covered, 4 1/4″	75.00
Tray, two-tiered	55.00
Vegetable, covered, round	65.00
Vegetable, round, 8″	35.00
Vinegar	30.00

Royal Worcester, Holly Ribbons, red

Bowl, cereal, coupe, 6 ⅝″ $40.00

Bowl, fruit, 5 ½″	30.00
Bowl, soup, flat, 9 ¼″	45.00
Chop Plate, 12 ⅝″	100.00
Coffeepot, covered	205.00
Cup and Saucer, demitasse	50.00
Cup and Saucer, flat, 2 ½″	50.00
Gravy Boat and Underplate	185.00
Lid, coffeepot	100.00
Plate, bread and butter, 6 ¼″	20.00
Plate, dinner, 10 ¾″	40.00
Plate, salad, 8″	30.00
Platter, oval, 13 ⅜″	160.00
Platter, oval, 15 ½″	190.00
Sugar Bowl, covered	110.00
Teapot, covered	205.00
Tureen, covered	480.00
Vegetable, covered, round	275.00

SALEM CHINA COMPANY

Biddam Smith, John McNichol, and Dan Cronin, formerly with Standard Pottery in East Liverpool, Ohio, founded the Salem China Company in Salem, Ohio, in 1898. Due to financial problems, it was sold to F. A. Sebring in 1918. Under the management of Frank McKee and Sebring's son, Frank Jr., the company became very successful, producing fine dinnerware, much of which was trimmed with 22K gold.

Viktor Schrenckengost created many of Salem's shapes and designs during the 1930s and 1940s. Salem China Company continued to manufacture dinnerware until 1967. In 1968, Salem became a sales and distribution business.

Salem China, English Village

Bowl, fruit, 5 1/4″	$12.50
Creamer	25.00
Cup and Saucer, flat, 2 7/8″	20.00
Plate, bread and butter	7.50
Plate, dinner, 9 7/8″	20.00
Plate, salad	15.00
Platter, oval, 12 1/4″	40.00

Saucer	5.00
Sugar Bowl, covered	35.00
Sugar Bowl, covered, no lid	22.50
Vegetable, covered, round	110.00
Vegetable, round, 8 1/2″	35.00

THE TOP FIVE PATTERNS
PATTERN GROUP—
SCENIC

—■—

JOHNSON BROTHERS, FRIENDLY VILLAGE
JOHNSON BROTHERS, OLD BRITAIN CASTLES
ROYAL CHINA CO., CURRIER & IVES
SALEM CHINA CO., ENGLISH VILLAGE
STAFFORDSHIRE, LIBERTY BLUE

SANGO COMPANY

The Sango Company is a dinnerware supplier based in Japan. Its American division, Sango U. S. A., was one of the first companies to sell dinnerware beyond department stores' china departments. Sango supplies porcelain, stoneware, and semi-porcelain dinnerware. The dinnerware is manufactured in various Asian countries, although not in Japan.

Sango is in the process of expanding its product line. Toward this end, the company has computerized its design process, has added full-time and freelance designers, and plans to add glassware to its product line to become a more complete tabletop resource.

Sango, Versailles

Bowl, fruit, flat, 5 1/2″	$15.00
Bowl, soup, flat, 8 1/2″	20.00
Creamer	35.00
Cup and Saucer, footed, 3″	25.00
Gravy Boat, attached underplate	90.00
Plate, bread and butter, 6 5/8″	10.00
Plate, dinner, 10 5/8″	27.50
Plate, salad, 7 3/4″	15.00
Platter, oval, 12 1/8″	60.00
Platter, oval, 14 1/4″	70.00
Platter, oval, 16 1/8″	100.00
Sugar Bowl, covered	40.00
Vegetable, oval, 9 1/8″	55.00
Vegetable, round, 9 1/8″	60.00

SCHUMANN BAVARIA

Heinrich Schumann founded the Carl Schumann Porcelain Factory in Arzberg, Bavaria, Germany, in 1881. Bavaria was an important porcelain production center, similar to the Staffordshire District of England. The company produced a wide variety of tableware and accessories.

Schumann Bavaria, Empress Dresden Flowers

Ashtray, 3″	$35.00
Ashtray, 3 1/4″	35.00
Ashtray, 4 1/8″	35.00
Bowl, cereal, coupe, 6″	55.00
Bowl, fruit, 5 1/4″	40.00
Bowl, soup, coupe, 7 7/8″	65.00
Cigarette Box	105.00
Cigarette Holder	80.00
Coaster, 4 1/4″	35.00
Coffeepot, covered, 7″	300.00

Coffeepot, covered, 7″, no lid	250.00
Coffeepot, covered, mini, no lid	150.00
Compote, 3 5/8″	150.00
Compote, 4 7/8″	150.00
Cream Soup and Saucer	150.00
Cream Soup Bowl	120.00
Creamer	105.00
Creamer, mini	70.00
Cup and Saucer, bouillon	75.00
Cup and Saucer, demitasse	70.00
Cup and Saucer, flat	75.00
Cup and Saucer, footed	75.00
Eggcup, double, 3 7/8″	60.00
Gravy Boat, attached underplate	250.00
Lid, butter dish, round	150.00
Lid, teapot	150.00
Lid, tureen	400.00
Plate, bread and butter, 6 1/4″	35.00
Plate, dessert, 7″	40.00
Plate, dinner	75.00
Plate, salad, 7 3/4″	50.00
Platter, oval, 12 1/4″	200.00
Saucer	25.00
Saucer, demitasse	25.00
Sugar Bowl, covered	135.00
Sugar Bowl, covered, mini	90.00
Vegetable, covered, round	500.00

Josiah Spode founded the Spode Factory in Stoke-on-Trent in 1770. Spode had been the manager of the works owned by Turner and Banks, and upon Turner's death, Spode took over the factory. By 1776, he was producing earthenware in his own name. Spode died in 1797, leaving a successful business to his son, Josiah Spode. Josiah Spode III succeeded his father and grandfather until his death in 1829.

William Taylor Copeland, a partner of Josiah III, bought the firm in 1833. He entered into a partnership with colleague Thomas Garrett, and the firm was known as Copeland & Garrett until 1847.

Although the company's name was changed from Spode, the high standard and quality of its products did not change. The Spode Factory has held royal warrants since 1806.

The Copeland family sold the firm to the Carborundum Company Ltd. in 1966. To commemorate the company's 200th anniversary in 1970, the name was changed back to Spode in honor of its founder. In 1976, Spode joined with the Worcester Royal Porcelain Company to form Royal Worcester Spode.

Spode, Billingsley Rose, Jewel Embossed Shape (newer)

Bowl, cereal, coupe, 6 3/8″	$40.00
Bowl, fruit, 5 1/4″	25.00
Bowl, rice, 4 1/2″	35.00
Bowl, soup, flat, 7 3/4″	55.00
Bowl, soup, flat, 9″	55.00
Cream Soup Saucer	25.00
Creamer	50.00
Cup, demitasse	35.00
Cup and Saucer, demitasse	40.00
Cup and Saucer, flat, 2 1/2″	45.00
Gravy Boat, attached underplate	150.00
Lid, coffeepot	100.00
Lid, sugar bowl	40.00

Lid, tureen	200.00
Lid, vegetable	150.00
Plate, bread and butter, 6 1/4″	20.00
Plate, dinner	50.00
Plate, salad, 7 7/8″	30.00
Platter, oval, 13 1/8″	140.00
Platter, oval, 15 1/4″	180.00
Sugar Bowl, covered	80.00

Spode, Billingsley Rose, Jewel Embossed Shape (older)

Bowl, fruit, 5 1/4″	$30.00
Bowl, soup, flat, 7 7/8″	50.00
Chop Plate, 13 3/8″	150.00
Cream Soup and Saucer	75.00

Cream Soup Bowl	70.00
Cup and Saucer, demitasse	45.00
Cup and Saucer, flat, 2 1/4″	50.00
Lid, vegetable, round	150.00
Plate, bread and butter, 6 1/4″	20.00
Plate, dinner, 10 5/8″	45.00
Plate, salad, 7 7/8″	30.00
Platter, oval, 13 3/8″	140.00
Platter, oval, 17 1/4″	250.00
Saucer	15.00
Saucer, oversized	20.00

Spode, Buttercup, Chelsea Wicker Shape (newer)

Bowl, cereal, coupe, 6 1/4″	$25.00
Butter Dish, covered, square	80.00
Cake Plate, handled, square, 11 5/8″	65.00
Chop Plate, 13″	90.00
Cup and Saucer, demitasse	25.00
Cup and Saucer, flat, 2 1/8″	30.00
Eggcup, single, 2 1/2″	20.00
Gravy Boat and Underplate	110.00
Jam	50.00
Lid, jam	25.00
Lid, teapot	60.00
Mug, 3 1/2″	20.00
Pickle Dish, 8 5/8″	60.00
Plate, bread and butter, 6 1/2″	12.50
Plate, dinner, 10 1/2″	25.00
Plate, salad, 7 7/8″	20.00
Platter, oval, 12 3/4″	80.00
Platter, oval, 15″	130.00
Saucer	10.00
Sugar Bowl, covered, 2 3/4″	60.00
Tray, sandwich, 13 1/2″	70.00
Vegetable, covered, round	180.00
Vegetable, covered, no lid	120.00
Vegetable, oval, 10 1/2″	60.00
Vegetable, square, 8″	80.00
Vegetable, square, 9 1/4″	90.00

Spode, Bridal Rose, Savoy Shape, Bone China

Compote, 5 1/4″	$280.00
Cream Soup Saucer	45.00
Creamer	90.00
Cup and Saucer, flat, 2 1/4″	90.00
Cup and Saucer, oversized, 2 3/8″	100.00
Lid, sugar bowl, 2 3/4″	70.00
Plate, bread and butter, 6 1/4″	40.00
Plate, dinner, 10 1/2″	85.00
Plate, luncheon, 8 5/8″	70.00
Plate, salad, 7 7/8″	55.00
Platter, oval, 11 1/4″	120.00
Platter, oval, 15 1/4″	290.00
Saucer	30.00
Sugar Bowl, covered, 3 ″	140.00

Spode, Buttercup, Chelsea Wicker Shape (older)

Coffeepot, covered, no lid	$140.00
Cream Soup and Saucer	60.00
Cup, bouillon	35.00
Cup, flat, 2 1/8″	35.00
Cup and Saucer, demitasse	40.00
Cup and Saucer, flat, 2 1/8″	40.00
Gravy Boat, attached underplate	150.00
Lid, coffeepot	85.00
Lid, teapot	85.00
Lid, teapot, mini	60.00
Lid, tureen, 7 3/4″	300.00
Lid, vegetable	125.00
Plate, bread and butter, 6 1/2″	20.00
Plate, dinner, 10 1/2″	45.00
Plate, luncheon, 9″	35.00
Plate, salad, 7 3/4″	30.00
Platter, oval, 12 3/4″	100.00
Platter, oval, 14 7/8″	150.00
Platter, oval, 19″	300.00
Saucer, demitasse	15.00
Sugar Bowl, covered, 2 3/4″	70.00
Sugar Bowl, covered, mini	45.00
Sugar Bowl, open	45.00
Vegetable, covered, oval	250.00
Vegetable, oval, 10″	90.00

Spode, Camilla, Camilla Shape

Creamer, 3 1/2″	$75.00
Cup and Saucer, bouillon	60.00
Cup and Saucer, flat, 2″	65.00
Gravy Boat, attached underplate	200.00
Plate, bread and butter, 6 1/4″	25.00
Plate, dinner	70.00
Plate, salad	45.00
Saucer	20.00
Saucer, oversized	25.00
Vegetable, oval, 8 1/8″	105.00
Vegetable, oval, 9 1/8″	110.00

Spode, Chelsea Gardens, Chelsea Shape, Bone China

Cream Soup Saucer	$40.00
Creamer	75.00
Creamer, mini	50.00
Cup and Saucer, demitasse, 2 1/8″	65.00
Cup and Saucer, footed, 2 1/2″	70.00
Gravy Boat, attached underplate	300.00
Gravy Boat, no underplate	200.00
Lid, coffeepot	115.00
Lid, coffeepot, mini	80.00

Lid, sugar bowl	55.00	Candy Dish, 9 1/4″	50.00
Lid, sugar bowl, mini	35.00	Canister, 7 3/4″	40.00
Plate, bread and butter, 6 1/4″	30.00	Canister, coffee, 4 5/8″	35.00
Plate, dessert, 7″	40.00	Canister, sugar, 6 1/8″	40.00
Plate, dinner	75.00	Canister, sugar, 6 1/8″, no lid	30.00
Plate, luncheon, 9 1/8″	70.00	Casserole, covered, round, 5 5/8″	60.00
Plate, salad, 8″	50.00	Casserole, covered, round, 6 3/8″	70.00
Saucer	25.00	Casserole, covered, round, 8″	70.00
Saucer, demitasse	20.00	Cheese Dish, covered, 6 1/4″	100.00
Saucer, oversized	30.00	Cheese Knife, stainless blade	15.00
Sugar Bowl, covered	110.00	Cheese Spreader, individual	5.00
Vegetable, oval, 9 3/4″	150.00	Cheese Spreader, serving	20.00
		Child Set, three pieces	30.00
		Child's Mug	15.00
		Chop Plate, 12 1/4″	60.00
		Coaster, 4″	5.00
		Coffeepot, covered	100.00
		Creamer	20.00
		Cup, flat, 2 1/2″	10.00
		Cup and Saucer, demitasse, 2 1/4″	20.00
		Cup and Saucer, flat, 2 1/2″	15.00
		Cup and Saucer, jumbo, 5 1/2″	40.00

Spode, Christmas Tree, Regimental Shape,
green band

Ashtray, 4 1/2″	$15.00	Dish, heart shape, 4 1/4″	10.00
Baker, oval, 12 5/8″	40.00	Fish Dish, oval, 14 5/8″	40.00
Baker, rectangular, 10 1/4″	25.00	Gravy Boat and Underplate	80.00
Baker, square, 11″	40.00	Jug, 4 5/8″	30.00
Bowl, cereal, coupe, 6 1/4″	10.00	Lid, cheese dish, 8″	40.00
Bowl, fruit, 5 1/8″	10.00	Lid, sauce boat	50.00
Bowl, pasta, individual, 8 3/4″	15.00	Lid, tureen	160.00
Bowl, round, fluted, 6 3/4″	20.00	Marmalade	20.00
Bowl, round, fluted, 8 1/2″	25.00	Mint Dish, 9″	20.00
Bowl, round, fluted, 10″	35.00	Mug, 3 1/4″	10.00
Bowl, salad, serving, 9 1/2″	80.00	Ornament, 1985	10.00
Bowl, soup, flat, 9 1/8″	10.00	Ornament, 1992	10.00
Box, covered, round	20.00	Ornament, round	20.00
Bud Vase, 7 5/8″	30.00	Pastry Server, stainless blade, 9 7/8″	15.00
Buffet Dish, square, 11″	40.00	Pickle Dish, 8 3/4″	30.00
Cachepot, 5 1/2″	55.00	Pitcher, 8″	70.00
Cachepot, 6 1/2″	65.00	Plate, bread and butter, 6 1/2″	10.00
Cake Knife, stainless blade, 12″	15.00	Plate, cookie, 10 5/8″	15.00
Cake Plate, handled, 12 3/4″	45.00	Plate, dinner, 10 3/4″	10.00
Cake Plate, square, handled, 11 1/2″	45.00	Plate, salad, 7 3/4″	10.00
Canapé Knife, individual, pair	25.00	Plate, serving, round, handled	20.00
Candleholder	30.00	Platter, oval, 16 1/4″	120.00
Candleholder, votive, 2 1/8″	10.00	Pomander	40.00
Candlestick, 5 1/2″	35.00	Potpourri, 5 1/2″	15.00
		Punch Bowl, 14 3/4″	260.00
		Quiche Dish, 9″	40.00
		Ramekin, 3 1/4″	10.00
		Relish, three-part, 9 5/8″	50.00
		Salt and Pepper Shakers, pair	25.00
		Salt and Pepper Shakers, pair, oversized, 6 1/8″	25.00
		Sauce Boat Underplate	50.00
		Sole Dish, oval, handled, 14″	35.00

Sole Dish, oval, 16 ³/₄″	40.00
Soufflé, 2 ³/₄″	35.00
Soufflé, 3 ³/₄″	40.00
Soufflé, 7″	30.00
Sweetener Holder, 1 ³/₄″	10.00
Teapot, covered, no lid	70.00
Tidbit	20.00
Tray, handled	35.00
Tray, hors d'oeuvre, 11 ³/₄″	70.00
Tray, sandwich, 13 ¹/₂″	50.00
Tray, triangular, 10 ³/₈″	55.00
Tray, two-tiered	35.00
Tree Dish, one part, 7 ⁵/₈″	20.00
Tree Dish, 9 ¹/₄″	30.00
Tunis Dish, 5″	15.00
Tunis Dish, 8 ⁵/₈″	50.00
Tureen, covered	320.00
Vase, 5 ¹/₂″	30.00
Vase, 7 ¹/₂″	55.00
Vase, 10″	70.00
Vegetable, covered, round	130.00
Vegetable, rectangular, 11 ¹/₂″	80.00

Plate, luncheon, square, 8 ³/₄″	45.00
Plate, salad, 7 ⁷/₈″	25.00
Platter, jubilee, 11″	105.00
Platter, oval, 14 ³/₄″	150.00
Platter, oval, 15″	160.00
Saucer, 2 ¹/₈″	15.00
Saucer, demitasse	15.00
Saucer, oversized	20.00
Sugar Bowl, covered	80.00
Sugar Bowl, covered, mini	60.00
Sugar Bowl, covered, no lid	60.00
Sugar Bowl, open	55.00
Vegetable, oval, 10 ¹/₄″	100.00
Vegetable, square, 8″	130.00
Vegetable, square, 9″	150.00

Spode, Fairy Dell, Charlotte Shape, 2 8093

Bowl, cranberry, 5″	$80.00
Bowl, fruit, 5 ³/₈″	30.00
Bowl, soup, flat, 8″	50.00
Cake Plate, square, handled, 11″	120.00
Cream Soup and Saucer	70.00
Cream Soup Saucer	25.00
Creamer, 3 ¹/₂″	60.00
Cup and Saucer, bouillon	45.00
Cup and Saucer, demitasse	40.00
Cup and Saucer, flat, 2 ¹/₈″	50.00
Gravy Boat	150.00
Gravy Boat, attached underplate	170.00
Lid, coffeepot	100.00
Lid, sugar bowl	40.00
Plate, bread and butter	20.00
Plate, dessert, 7 ¹/₄″	25.00
Plate, dinner, 10 ¹/₂″	40.00
Plate, luncheon, 9″	35.00
Plate, luncheon, square, 9″	35.00
Plate, salad, 8″	25.00
Platter, oval, 13 ¹/₈″	140.00
Platter, oval, 15″	180.00
Platter, oval, 16 ⁷/₈″	220.00

Spode, Cowslip, Chelsea Wicker Shape, S713

Bowl, cranberry, 5 ⁵/₈″	$60.00
Bowl, fruit, 5 ¹/₄″	30.00
Bowl, soup, flat, 7 ³/₄″	50.00
Chop Plate, 12 ⁷/₈″	120.00
Cream Soup and Saucer	70.00
Cream Soup Saucer	25.00
Creamer, mini	40.00
Cup and Saucer, demitasse	45.00
Cup and Saucer, flat, 2 ¹/₈″	45.00
Lid, butter dish, round	85.00
Lid, coffeepot, mini, 1″	75.00
Lid, sugar bowl, mini	30.00
Plate, bread and butter, 6 ¹/₂″	20.00
Plate, dinner, 10 ¹/₂″	40.00
Plate, luncheon, 8 ⁷/₈″	30.00

Saucer, demitasse	12.50
Sugar Bowl, covered	80.00
Sugar Bowl, open	60.00
Tureen and Underplate, covered	720.00
Vegetable, oval, 8 7/8″	100.00
Vegetable, oval, 9 7/8″	110.00
Vegetable, oval, 10 7/8″	120.00
Vegetable, square, 9 1/2″	160.00

THE TOP FIVE PATTERNS PERIOD LOOK— ORIENTAL MOTIF

---■---

ADAMS, WM. & SONS, MING JADE
CHURCHILL CHINA, BLUE WILLOW
LENOX, PLUM BLOSSOMS
SPODE, FITZHUGH
WEDGWOOD, KUTANI CRANE

Spode, Fitzhugh, Lowestoft Shape

Cream Soup and Saucer	$120.00
Creamer, 4 1/4″	75.00
Cup, demitasse, 2 1/8″	60.00
Cup, footed, 2 5/8″	65.00
Cup and Saucer, demitasse, 2 1/8″	65.00
Cup and Saucer, footed, 2 5/8″	70.00
Cup and Saucer, oversized	90.00
Gravy Boat, attached underplate	250.00
Gravy Boat and Underplate	250.00
Lid, gravy boat	115.00
Lid, vegetable	200.00
Plate, bread and butter	32.50
Plate, dinner	75.00
Plate, salad	50.00
Saucer, oversized	30.00
Sugar Bowl, covered, 3 1/4″	110.00
Sugar Bowl, covered, no lid	90.00
Sugar Bowl, open	75.00
Tea Caddy, covered, no lid	100.00

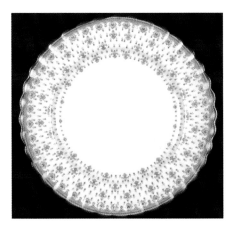

Spode, Fleur de Lis, Chelsea Shape

Bowl, fruit, 5 1/8″	$55.00
Bowl, soup, flat, 8″	85.00
Creamer, 3 1/4″	100.00
Cup and Saucer, demitasse	70.00
Cup and Saucer, footed, 2 5/8″	90.00
Gravy Boat, attached underplate	300.00
Gravy Boat Underplate	100.00
Lid, coffeepot	125.00
Lid, teapot	125.00
Plate, bread and butter, 6 3/8″	40.00
Plate, dinner, 10 1/2″	90.00
Plate, luncheon, 9 1/8″	70.00
Plate, salad, 8″	60.00
Platter, oval, 14 5/8″	230.00
Saucer	30.00
Sugar Bowl, covered	170.00
Vegetable, oval, 9 3/4″	150.00

Spode, Florence, Charlotte Shape

Bowl, soup, flat, 8″	$50.00
Cream Soup and Saucer	80.00
Cream Soup Saucer	25.00
Creamer, 3″	60.00
Cup and Saucer, bouillon	50.00
Cup and Saucer, flat, 2 1/8″	50.00
Lid, coffeepot	100.00
Plate, bread and butter, 6 1/4″	20.00
Plate, dinner	45.00
Plate, luncheon, 9″	35.00
Plate, salad, 8″	30.00
Platter, oval, 13 1/8″	150.00
Saucer	15.00
Sugar Bowl, covered, 2 3/4″	90.00

Spode, Geisha, Blanche de Chine Shape

Bowl, fruit, 5″	$60.00
Bowl, soup, flat, 9 1/8″	105.00
Chop Plate, 12 1/2″	200.00
Cream Soup and Saucer	160.00
Cream Soup Saucer	55.00
Creamer	100.00
Cup and Saucer, demitasse	90.00

Cup and Saucer, flat, 2 3/4″	90.00
Cup and Saucer, footed, 2 5/8″	90.00
Lid, teapot	150.00
Lid, vegetable, round	200.00
Plate, bread and butter, 6 1/4″	40.00
Plate, dinner, 10 3/4″	90.00
Plate, luncheon, 9 1/8″	95.00
Plate, salad, 8″	65.00
Platter, oval, 13″	200.00
Platter, oval, 14 3/4″	270.00
Platter, oval, 15″	300.00
Platter, oval, 16 3/4″	340.00
Saucer	30.00
Saucer, demitasse	30.00
Sugar Bowl, covered, 3 1/4″	200.00
Sugar Bowl, open	100.00
Vegetable, covered, round	600.00
Vegetable, oval, 10 3/8″	200.00

Spode, Gloucester, Lowestoft Shape

Creamer, 3 3/8″	$75.00
Cup, footed, 2 1/4″	65.00
Cup and Saucer, footed, 2 1/4″	70.00
Plate, bread and butter	32.50
Plate, dinner	75.00
Plate, salad	50.00
Tureen, covered, no lid	640.00

Spode, Indian Tree, Chelsea Shape

Bowl, cereal, coupe, 6 1/4″	$35.00
Bowl, fruit, 5 3/8″	25.00
Butter Pat, 3 1/2″	17.50
Chop Plate, 13 1/4″	130.00
Coffeepot, covered, no lid	140.00
Creamer	40.00
Cup, flat, 2 1/8″	37.50
Cup and Saucer, flat, 2 1/2″	40.00
Gravy Boat, no underplate	130.00
Lid, coffeepot, mini	75.00
Lid, sugar bowl	35.00
Lid, teapot	75.00
Mug, 3 1/4″	35.00
Plate, bread and butter, 6 1/2″	15.00
Plate, dinner	45.00
Plate, salad	27.50
Platter, oval, 12 5/8″	110.00
Platter, oval, 14 3/4″	140.00
Platter, oval, 15″	160.00
Sugar Bowl, covered	70.00
Sugar Bowl, open	60.00
Syrup, covered, no lid	80.00
Teapot, covered	150.00
Vegetable, oval, 10 1/4″	95.00

Spode, Irene, Chelsea Shape, Bone China, Y6470

Cream Soup and Saucer	$180.00
Creamer	110.00
Cup, footed, 2 1/8″	80.00
Cup and Saucer, demitasse	90.00
Cup and Saucer, footed, 2 1/8″	90.00
Gravy Boat, no underplate	250.00
Lid, sugar bowl, mini	65.00
Plate, bread and butter, 6 3/8″	40.00
Plate, dinner, 10 3/4″	95.00
Plate, luncheon, 9 1/4″	90.00
Plate, salad, 8 1/8″	65.00
Saucer, demitasse	30.00
Sugar Bowl, covered	180.00
Vegetable, oval, 9 3/4″	170.00

Spode, Jewel Embossed Imperial, plain white

Bowl, cereal, coupe, 6 1/4″	$40.00
Bowl, fruit, 5 1/4″	25.00
Bowl, rice, 4 1/2″	40.00
Bowl, soup, flat, 9 1/8″	45.00
Cake Plate, square, handled, 11 3/8″	90.00
Cream Soup and Saucer	55.00
Cream Soup Bowl	50.00

Creamer	40.00
Cup, demitasse	30.00
Cup and Saucer, demitasse	35.00
Cup and Saucer, flat, 2 1/2″	40.00
Gravy Boat, attached underplate	145.00
Plate, bread and butter, 6 1/8″	15.00
Plate, dinner, 10 5/8″	45.00
Plate, salad, 7 7/8″	25.00
Platter, oval, 13 1/8″	125.00
Platter, oval, 15 1/4″	170.00
Saucer	15.00
Sugar Bowl, covered, 3 1/2″	75.00
Sugar Bowl, covered, 3 1/2″, no lid	55.00
Tureen, covered	500.00
Vegetable, covered, no lid	200.00
Vegetable, oval, 10 1/8″	100.00
Vegetable, square, 9 3/4″	100.00

Spode, Mayflower, Gadroon Shape, floral

Bowl, soup, flat, 7 3/4″	$75.00
Cream Soup and Saucer	115.00
Cream Soup Bowl	100.00
Cream Soup Saucer	40.00
Cup and Saucer, flat, 2 1/4″	70.00
Plate, bread and butter, 6 1/2″	25.00
Plate, dinner	70.00
Plate, luncheon, 9 1/2″	55.00
Plate, salad, 7 3/4″	45.00
Platter, oval, 15″	200.00
Saucer	25.00
Sugar Bowl, covered, no lid	80.00
Tureen, covered, no lid	365.00
Vegetable, square, 9 1/8″	150.00

**Spode, Maritime Rose, Flower Embossed Shape,
Bone China**

Bowl, soup, flat, 7 3/8″	$90.00
Cream Soup Saucer	45.00
Creamer, mini	60.00
Cup and Saucer, demitasse, 2 1/4″	75.00
Cup and Saucer, footed, 2 1/2″	85.00
Gravy Boat, attached underplate	300.00
Lid, coffeepot	115.00
Lid, sugar bowl	95.00
Lid, teapot	115.00
Plate, bread and butter, 6 1/4″	35.00
Plate, dessert, 7 1/4″	50.00
Plate, dinner, 10 3/4″	85.00
Plate, luncheon, 8 3/4″	70.00
Plate, salad, 8 1/8″	55.00
Saucer	25.00
Saucer, demitasse, 2 3/8″	25.00
Sugar Bowl, covered, 3″	190.00

Spode, Reynolds, Marlborough Shape, S2188

Bowl, cereal, coupe, 6 1/4″	$45.00
Bowl, fruit, 5 1/4″	30.00
Butter Pat, 3″	15.00
Coffeepot, covered	230.00
Cream Soup and Saucer	95.00
Cream Soup Saucer	30.00
Creamer, 3 5/8″	65.00

Cup and Saucer, demitasse	50.00
Cup and Saucer, flat, 2 ³/₄″	60.00
Gravy Boat, attached underplate	210.00
Gravy Boat Underplate	70.00
Lid, coffeepot	115.00
Lid, gravy boat	80.00
Lid, muffin dish	125.00
Lid, teapot	115.00
Plate, bread and butter, 6 ³/₄″	25.00
Plate, dinner	55.00
Plate, luncheon, 8 ³/₄″	45.00
Plate, salad, 7 ³/₄″	35.00
Saucer, 2 ³/₄″	20.00
Saucer, oversized	20.00
Sugar Bowl, covered, 3 ⁵/₈″	95.00
Sugar Bowl, covered, 3 ⁵/₈″, no lid	65.00
Sugar Bowl, open, 2 ¹/₄″	65.00
Vegetable, covered, round	350.00
Vegetable, oval, 9 ¹/₂″	120.00
Vegetable, square, 9 ³/₈″	150.00

Plate, dinner, 10 ¹/₂″	40.00
Plate, luncheon, 8 ⁷/₈″	30.00
Plate, salad, 7 ⁷/₈″	27.50
Platter, oval, 13″	140.00
Saucer, oversized	17.50
Sugar Bowl, covered	90.00
Sugar Bowl, open	60.00
Vegetable, oval, 9″	110.00
Vegetable, oval, 11 ¹/₈″	130.00
Vegetable, square, 7 ⁷/₈″	115.00

Spode, Rose Briar, Chelsea Wicker Shape, 2 7896

Bowl, fruit, 5 ¹/₄″	$25.00
Bowl, soup, coupe, 7 ¹/₂″	45.00
Bowl, soup, flat, 7 ³/₄″	45.00
Chop Plate, 13″	130.00
Cream Soup and Saucer	60.00
Creamer, 3 ¹/₄″	45.00
Creamer, mini, 2 ³/₄″	30.00
Cup and Saucer, demitasse	35.00
Cup and Saucer, flat, 2 ³/₄″	40.00
Cup and Saucer, oversized	50.00
Gravy Boat, attached underplate	150.00
Lid, butter dish, ¹/₄ lb.	90.00
Lid, teapot	95.00
Lid, vegetable	120.00
Plate, bread and butter, 5 ¹/₂″	20.00
Plate, bread and butter, 6 ⁵/₈″	20.00
Plate, dinner, 10 ³/₈″	35.00
Plate, luncheon, 9″	30.00
Plate, salad, 7 ⁷/₈″	25.00
Platter, oval, 14 ³/₄″	150.00
Saucer, oversized	15.00
Sugar Bowl, covered, mini, 2 ¹/₄″	50.00
Vegetable, oval, 9 ¹/₈″	85.00
Vegetable, oval, 10 ¹/₄″	90.00
Vegetable, square, 8″	100.00

Spode, Rosalie, Chelsea Wicker Shape

Bowl, cranberry	$90.00
Bowl, fruit, 5 ³/₈″	30.00
Bowl, soup, flat, 7 ³/₄″	50.00
Butter Pat, 3 ³/₈″	15.00
Chop Plate, 12 ⁷/₈″	170.00
Cream Soup and Saucer	70.00
Cream Soup Bowl	60.00
Creamer	60.00
Cup, demitasse	40.00
Cup, flat, 2 ¹/₈″	45.00
Cup and Saucer, bouillon	50.00
Cup and Saucer, demitasse	45.00
Cup and Saucer, flat, 2 ¹/₈″	50.00
Lid, sugar bowl	45.00
Lid, sugar bowl, mini	30.00
Lid, teapot	100.00
Plate, bread and butter, 6 ⁵/₈″	20.00

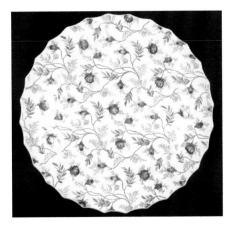

Spode, Rosebud Chintz, Charlotte Shape, 2 8401

Bowl, soup, flat, 9"	$55.00
Cream Soup Saucer	30.00
Cup and Saucer, flat, 2 1/8"	50.00
Plate, bread and butter, 6 1/4"	20.00
Plate, dinner, 10 1/2"	45.00
Plate, luncheon, 9"	40.00
Plate, salad, 8"	30.00
Platter, oval, 11"	120.00
Platter, oval, 12 3/4"	140.00
Platter, oval, 13"	145.00
Platter, oval, 14 1/2"	175.00
Saucer	17.50
Sugar Bowl, covered	90.00
Vegetable, oval, 9"	120.00
Vegetable, oval, 10 3/4"	130.00

Cream Soup Saucer	20.00
Creamer, mini	35.00
Cup, bouillon	35.00
Cup, demitasse	35.00
Cup and Saucer, demitasse	40.00
Cup and Saucer, flat, 2 1/4"	40.00
Cup and Saucer, oversized, 2 1/2"	55.00
Eggcup, double, 3 3/4"	45.00
Lid, butter dish, square	100.00
Lid, coffeepot, mini	70.00
Mug, 4 1/4"	40.00
Plate, bread and butter, 5 3/8"	20.00
Plate, dinner, 10 5/8"	45.00
Plate, salad, 7 3/4"	25.00
Sauce Boat Underplate	70.00
Saucer	15.00
Saucer, oversized, 6 1/2"	17.50
Sugar Bowl, covered, 3"	75.00
Sugar Bowl, covered, 3", no lid	50.00

Spode, Trade Winds, Lowestoft Shape

Ashtray, 4 1/2"	$35.00
Cream Soup Saucer	32.50
Cup, footed, 2 1/8"	50.00
Cup and Saucer, demitasse	50.00
Cup and Saucer, footed, 2 1/8"	55.00
Gravy Boat and Underplate, covered	260.00
Gravy Boat and Underplate	230.00
Gravy Boat, no underplate	155.00
Plate, bread and butter	25.00
Plate, dinner	55.00
Plate, salad	40.00
Sugar Bowl, covered, 3 1/4"	95.00
Sugar Bowl, covered, 3 1/4", no lid	80.00
Sugar Bowl, covered, mini, no lid	55.00
Tureen, covered, no lid	480.00

Spode, Tower, Gadroon Shape

Bowl, cereal, coupe, 6 3/8"	$35.00
Bowl, cranberry, 5"	85.00
Bowl, fruit, 5 1/2"	25.00
Bowl, soup, flat, 7 3/4"	50.00
Cream Soup and Saucer	65.00
Cream Soup Bowl	60.00

Spode, Wicker Dale, Chelsea Wicker Shape, 2 4088

Bowl, fruit, 5 1/4″	$30.00
Cream Soup and Saucer	80.00
Cream Soup Bowl	70.00
Creamer, 3 1/4″	65.00
Creamer, mini, 2 5/8″	45.00
Cup, demitasse	45.00
Cup, flat, 2 1/8″	45.00
Cup, oversized, 2 1/4″	60.00
Cup and Saucer, bouillon	50.00
Cup and Saucer, demitasse	50.00
Cup and Saucer, flat, 2 1/8″	50.00
Cup and Saucer, oversized, 2 1/4″	65.00
Gravy Boat, attached underplate	200.00
Lid, coffeepot	110.00
Lid, syrup	50.00
Lid, teapot	110.00
Plate, bread and butter, 6 5/8″	20.00
Plate, dinner	45.00
Plate, luncheon, 9″	40.00
Plate, salad, 7 3/4″	30.00
Platter, oval, 11 1/8″	130.00
Sugar Bowl, covered	90.00
Sugar Bowl, covered, mini, no lid	45.00
Teapot, mini, no lid	120.00
Vegetable, covered, no lid	210.00
Vegetable, oval, 9 3/8″	115.00
Vegetable, oval, 10 3/8″	120.00
Vegetable, square, 9 1/4″	140.00

Spode, Wicker Lane, Chelsea Wicker Shape

Bowl, fruit, 5 3/8″	$25.00
Bowl, soup, flat, 7 3/4″	45.00
Cake Plate, square, 9 1/2″	110.00
Chop Plate, 13″	120.00
Coffeepot, mini, no lid	95.00
Cream Soup and Saucer	60.00
Cream Soup Saucer	20.00
Creamer, mini	30.00
Cup, bouillon	35.00
Cup, demitasse	30.00
Cup, flat	40.00
Cup and Saucer, bouillon	40.00
Cup and Saucer, demitasse	35.00
Cup and Saucer, flat	45.00
Gravy Boat, attached underplate	170.00
Gravy Boat	150.00
Lid, coffeepot	100.00
Lid, teapot, mini	70.00
Plate, bread and butter, 6″	17.50
Plate, dinner, 10 1/2″	40.00
Plate, luncheon, 9″	25.00
Plate, salad, 7 3/4″	25.00
Platter, jubilee, 11″	90.00
Platter, oval, 11″	100.00
Platter, oval, 12 3/4″	110.00
Platter, oval, 13″	120.00
Relish, 8 1/2″	60.00
Saucer, demitasse	12.50
Sugar Bowl, covered, 2 5/8″	70.00
Sugar Bowl, covered, mini	50.00
Sugar Bowl, open	50.00
Vegetable, covered, oval	240.00
Vegetable, covered, round	240.00
Vegetable, oval, 9 7/8″	85.00
Vegetable, oval, 10 1/2″	90.00
Vegetable, square, 7 1/2″	90.00
Vegetable, square, 8″	100.00

STAFFORDSHIRE

Many small potteries were firmly established in the north Staffordshire area of England by the early 1700s. Staffordshire was the hub of the English pottery industry, with eighty working potteries by 1786, and more than 175 by the year 1800. The pottery district includes the towns of Burslem, Cobridge, Etruria, Fenton, Foley, Hanley, Lalane Delph, Lane End, Longport, Shelton, Stoke, and Tunstall. Among the area's many famous potters were Adams, Davenport, Spode, Stevenson, Wedgwood, and Wood.

Transfer-printed pottery depicting American historical events, cities, buildings, and landscapes was popular from 1810 to 1820. Its popularity enabled the Staffordshire potters to gain dominance in the American market. Dark blue pieces were popular in the 1820s, with the preference shifting to lighter shades of blue and pink, black, brown, and green during the 1830s and 1840s.

The United States has been importing Staffordshire District dinnerware since the 1800s. Today, the term *Staffordshire* has become synonymous with transfer-printed decoration.

Staffordshire, Calico

Bowl, cereal, coupe, 6 ³⁄₈″	$15.00
Bowl, fruit, 4 ³⁄₄″	15.00
Bowl, oatmeal, 5″	15.00
Bowl, soup, flat, 7 ¹⁄₂″	15.00
Candlestick, 6 ¹⁄₄″	32.50
Canister, tea, 4″	30.00
Coffeepot, covered	80.00
Creamer, 4″	25.00
Creamer, cow	30.00
Cup and Saucer, flat, 2 ⁵⁄₈″	20.00

Gravy Boat and Underplate	70.00
Gravy Boat, no underplate	50.00
Jar, covered, 5 ³⁄₄″	50.00
Jar, covered, 7 ³⁄₄″	70.00
Lotion Dispenser	17.50
Pepper Shaker, 3 ¹⁄₂″	20.00
Pitcher and Bowl	70.00
Pitcher, 5 ³⁄₈″	35.00
Pitcher, 6 ¹⁄₂″	65.00
Plate, bread and butter, 6″	10.00
Plate, dinner, 10 ¹⁄₂″	22.50
Plate, salad, 7 ¹⁄₂″	15.00
Platter, oval, 11 ¹⁄₄″	50.00
Platter, oval, 13 ³⁄₈″	70.00
Platter, oval, 15 ³⁄₄″	90.00
Rolling Pin	60.00
Soap Dish, 5 ¹⁄₂″	12.50
Sugar Bowl, covered	50.00
Tea Tile, 6″	25.00
Teapot, covered, mini	45.00
Teapot, covered, mini, no lid	30.00
Tray, bread, 10″	30.00
Tumbler, water, 3 ³⁄₄″	10.00
Tureen and Ladle, covered	300.00
Tureen Ladle	40.00
Utensil Holder, 5 ⁵⁄₈″	35.00
Vegetable, covered, square	130.00

STAFFORDSHIRE, LIBERTY BLUE

In 1973, the Grand Union Company, a retail supermarket chain based in New Jersey, commissioned Liberty Blue dinnerware to be offered as a premium in grocery stores throughout the eastern United States. Ironically, though intended to celebrate America's independence, the dinnerware was produced in Staffordshire, England, the home of hundreds of potteries from the early 1700s to the present. The dinnerware, introduced in 1975, was produced of ironstone and portrayed patriotic scenes in blue on a white background.

Liberty Blue dinnerware combined several elements of the traditional Staffordshire, while remaining unique. The blue color is reminiscent of that used during the late eighteenth and early nineteenth centuries. The Wild Rose border was reproduced from a design dating back to 1784. Original engravings featured events from the Revolutionary period, including Paul Revere's Ride, Washington's Farewell to the Continental Army, and the Boston Tea Party. Others displayed historic buildings, such as Monticello, the Governor's House at Williamsburg, and Independence Hall.

Liberty Blue dinnerware is easy to identify. Most of the dishes contain the words "Liberty Blue" on the underside and all are marked "Made in England." The back of each dish also identifies the scene it portrays.

Staffordshire, Liberty Blue

Bowl, fruit, 5″	$10.00
Cup and Saucer, flat, 2 5/8″	15.00
Lid, teapot	60.00
Plate, bread and butter, 6″	5.00
Plate, dinner, 9 7/8″	15.00
Plate, salad	17.50
Platter, oval, 11 7/8″	60.00
Saucer	5.00
Sugar Bowl, covered	35.00

In 1841, W. H. Farrar established a small pottery in Syracuse, New York. In 1858, he moved the plant a short distance to the site of today's Syracuse China Fayette Plant. Within a few years, the Empire Pottery Company was organized to take over the Farrar Pottery. The new enterprise was unsuccessful, and in 1871 the Onondaga Pottery Company assumed control.

In 1880, under the supervision of James Pass, the Onondaga Pottery Company built a new manufacturing plant adjacent to the original structures. Finally, in 1891, the manufacture of Syracuse China was begun. Business increased during the 1890s, and in 1897 all other products were discontinued in favor of Syracuse China and hotelware.

In 1921, the Court Plant was established on the northeast side of Syracuse. Over the years, the plant was expanded and modernized. The present-day structure encompasses over sixteen acres and is given over entirely to the production of Syracuse China for commercial use.

A third plant was established in 1959, with the acquisition of a controlling interest in Vandesca, Ltd., of Joliette, Quebec, Canada. This plant is now known as Vandesca-Syracuse Limited, and it supplies a portion of the Canadian market.

Today's Fayette Plant, located on approximately the same site as the original Fayette Plant, specializes in the production of Syracuse China for household use.

In 1966, the Onondaga Pottery Company name was changed to Syracuse China Corporation. In 1971, as the company marked its 100th anniversary, management changed and a new Syracuse China Corporation was formed. One year later, Syracuse China Corporation acquired the Will & Baumer Candle Company, a family business established in Syracuse in 1855. The Country Ware Corporation was formed in 1975 as a wholly owned subsidiary to design, manufacture, and market cast metal tableware and accessories. In 1978, Syracuse China Corporation merged with Canadian Pacific Investments, Ltd. (CPI) as a wholly owned subsidiary of CPI, retaining its corporate identity as well as the management team that had been so successful. Today, the company is known as Syracuse China Company, a unit of Libbey Inc.

Introduced in 1941, Bracelet combines richness with economy of design, retaining the influence of classic ornamentation in a pattern of geometric treatment. The wide encrusted gold rim balances traditional decorative interest against the simplicity of a slender tracery of plain gold. The Bracelet pattern is well-suited either for modern or period backgrounds. Bracelet was discontinued in 1970.

Syracuse China, Bracelet, Virginia Shape,
old ivory

Bowl, fruit, 5″	$30.00
Bowl, soup, flat, 8 ⅞″	35.00
Coffeepot, covered, no lid	140.00
Cream Soup and Saucer	70.00

Cream Soup Saucer	22.50
Creamer	70.00
Cup and Saucer, bouillon	50.00
Cup and Saucer, demitasse	40.00
Cup and Saucer, footed, 2 ⅜″	50.00
Gravy Boat, attached underplate	150.00
Gravy Boat and Underplate	150.00
Gravy Boat Underplate	50.00
Plate, bread and butter, 6 ¼″	15.00
Plate, dinner, 9 ¾″	40.00
Plate, luncheon, 9″	30.00
Plate, salad, 8″	25.00
Platter, oval, 12 ¼″	110.00
Platter, oval, 14″	130.00
Platter, oval, 16″	200.00
Saucer	15.00
Sugar Bowl, covered	70.00
Vegetable, covered, round	250.00
Vegetable, covered, round, no lid	150.00
Vegetable, oval, 10 ¼″	100.00
Vegetable, round, 9″	110.00

SYRACUSE CHINA COMPANY, BRIARCLIFF

Introduced in 1938, the Briarcliff pattern, designed by Pascal L'Anglais, consists of delicately colored floral sprays surrounding a dainty floral wreath. Briarcliff harmonizes well with many types of furniture. The pattern was discontinued in 1969.

Syracuse China, Briarcliff, Federal Shape

Bowl, fruit, 5 ⅛″	$25.00
Bowl, soup, flat, 8″	32.50

Cream Soup and Saucer	50.00
Cream Soup Saucer	15.00
Creamer	50.00
Cup, demitasse	35.00
Cup and Saucer, demitasse	40.00
Cup and Saucer, footed, 2 ¼″	50.00
Gravy Boat, attached underplate	130.00
Lid, coffeepot	95.00
Lid, vegetable, round	90.00
Plate, bread and butter, 6 ½″	15.00
Plate, dinner 10″	35.00
Plate, luncheon, 9″	25.00
Plate, salad, 8″	25.00
Platter, oval, 12″	90.00
Platter, oval, 14″	100.00
Platter, oval, 16 ⅜″	140.00
Relish, 8 ⅞″	45.00
Saucer	15.00
Sugar Bowl, covered	60.00

Sugar Bowl, covered, no lid	40.00	Vegetable, oval, 10 ⅝″	80.00
Vegetable, covered, round	190.00	Vegetable, round, 8 ¾″	70.00
Vegetable, oval, 9 ⅜″	70.00	Vegetable, round, 9″	80.00

SYRACUSE CHINA COMPANY, CELESTE

Celeste, designed by Dick Garvin, was introduced in 1954 and discontinued in 1969.

Syracuse China, Celeste, Carolina Shape, blue leaves

Creamer	$50.00
Cup and Saucer, footed, 2″	40.00
Plate, bread and butter, 6 ¼″	15.00
Plate, dinner, 10 ¼″	35.00
Plate, salad, 8″	20.00
Platter, oval, 12″	90.00
Platter, oval, 14 ⅛″	110.00
Saucer	15.00
Sugar Bowl, covered	60.00

SYRACUSE CHINA COMPANY, CORALBEL

Coralbel, introduced in 1937, was hailed as an "extremely smart modern pattern distinguished by its unique line treatment and its simple conventionalized floral spray." Coralbel's green and platinum lines on an ivory body accent the colorful flowers and leaves of the pattern. Coralbel was discontinued in 1970.

Syracuse China, Coralbel, Virginia Shape, old ivory

Bowl, cereal, flat, 6 3/8"	$25.00
Bowl, cranberry, 5"	50.00
Bowl, fruit, 5"	25.00
Bowl, soup, coupe, 7 5/8"	30.00
Bowl, soup, flat, 8 7/8"	30.00
Cake plate, handled, 10 7/8"	80.00
Chop Plate, 12 1/2"	100.00

Coffeepot, covered	160.00
Cream Soup and Saucer	50.00
Cream Soup Bowl	45.00
Creamer, 2 3/4"	40.00
Cup and Saucer, bouillon	45.00
Cup and Saucer, demitasse	30.00
Cup and Saucer, footed, 2 3/8"	45.00
Gray Boat, attached underplate	100.00
Gravy Boat and Underplate	100.00
Gravy Boat Underplate	35.00
Lid, vegetable, round	95.00
Plate, bread and butter, 6 1/4"	15.00
Plate, dessert, 7 1/8"	17.50
Plate, dinner, 10 1/4"	32.50
Plate, salad, 8"	22.50
Platter, oval, 12 1/4"	90.00
Platter, oval, 14"	100.00
Platter, oval, 16 1/8"	150.00
Saucer	15.00
Sugar Bowl, covered, 2 3/4"	50.00
Teapot, covered	160.00
Teapot, covered, no lid	100.00
Vegetable, covered, round	190.00
Vegetable, oval, 10"	80.00
Vegetable, round, 9"	90.00

SYRACUSE CHINA COMPANY, MEADOW BREEZE AND MINUET

The Meadow Breeze and Minuet patterns, designed by Dick Garvin, were introduced in 1955 and discontinued in 1970.

Syracuse China, Meadow Breeze, Carolina Shape

Cup and Saucer, footed, 2"	$45.00
Plate, bread and butter, 6 1/4"	15.00
Plate, dinner, 10 3/4"	35.00
Plate, salad, 8"	22.50
Platter, oval, 12"	120.00
Platter, oval, 14 1/8"	150.00
Saucer	15.00
Sugar Bowl, covered	70.00
Teapot, covered, no lid	120.00

Syracuse China, Minuet, Carolina Shape

Bowl, soup, coupe, 7 5/8″	$50.00
Cream Soup Bowl	70.00
Creamer	60.00
Cup and Saucer, footed, 2 1/8″	55.00
Gravy Boat, attached underplate	180.00
Lid, teapot	115.00
Plate, bread and butter, 6 1/4″	20.00
Plate, dinner, 10 5/8″	45.00
Plate, salad, 8 1/8″	25.00
Platter, oval, 14 1/8″	140.00
Platter, oval, 16″	190.00
Saucer	17.50
Sugar Bowl, covered	80.00
Sugar Bowl, covered, no lid	55.00

SYRACUSE CHINA COMPANY, SHERWOOD

Robinhood's Sherwood Forest inspired designer Ed Otis to create the Sherwood pattern in 1940. The formal pattern consists of a berry and leaf border in two-tone blue coloring dotted with yellow. Sherwood was discontinued in 1970.

Syracuse China, Sherwood, Virginia Shape, blue laurel

Bowl, fruit, 5″	$25.00
Bowl, soup, flat, 8 3/4″	30.00

Cream Soup and Saucer	60.00
Creamer	50.00
Cup and Saucer, bouillon	45.00
Cup and Saucer, demitasse	35.00
Cup and Saucer, footed, 2 3/8″	50.00
Gravy Boat, attached underplate	130.00
Lid, vegetable, round	95.00
Plate, bread and butter, 6 1/4″	17.50
Plate, dinner, 9 3/4″	35.00
Plate, luncheon, 9″	30.00
Plate, salad, 8″	25.00
Platter, oval, 12 1/8″	90.00
Platter, oval, 14 1/8″	100.00
Saucer	15.00
Sugar Bowl, covered	60.00
Sugar Bowl, covered, no lid	40.00
Vegetable, covered, round	190.00
Vegetable, oval, 10 3/8″	90.00
Vegetable, round, 9″	90.00

Introduced in 1938, Stansbury is an old Haviland design. The delicate trailing flowers are reminiscent of the atmosphere of a woodland in spring. The pattern evokes a feeling of airiness and freedom, and the arrangement of soft pinks, light greens, and grays are restful to the eye. Stansbury was discontinued in 1969.

Syracuse China, Stansbury, Federal Shape

Bowl, cereal, coupe, 5 × 2"	$30.00	Cream Soup and Saucer	60.00
Bowl, fruit, 5 ¹/₈"	25.00	Creamer	50.00
Bowl, soup, flat, 8"	32.50	Cup and Saucer, footed, 2 ¹/₄"	45.00
		Gravy Boat, attached underplate	130.00
		Lid, vegetable, round	90.00
		Plate, bread and butter, 6 ¹/₂"	15.00
		Plate, dessert, 7 ¹/₄"	17.50
		Plate, dinner, 10 ³/₈"	35.00
		Plate, salad, 8"	22.50
		Platter, oval, 12 ¹/₈"	90.00
		Platter, oval, 14 ¹/₈"	100.00
		Platter, oval, 16 ³/₈"	140.00
		Saucer	15.00
		Saucer, demitasse	12.50
		Sugar Bowl, covered	60.00
		Sugar Bowl, covered, no lid	40.00
		Vegetable, covered, round	190.00
		Vegetable, oval, 9 ¹/₄"	80.00
		Vegetable, oval, 10 ⁵/₈"	90.00
		Vegetable, round, 9"	90.00

Suzanne, designed by Pascal L'Anglais and introduced in 1938, is comprised of dainty pink, blue, and yellow floral sprays. The pattern was discontinued in 1970.

Syracuse China, Suzanne, Federal Shape

Bowl, fruit, 5″	$25.00
Bowl, soup, flat	32.50

Cream Soup and Saucer	55.00
Cream Soup Saucer	17.50
Cup, demitasse	32.50
Cup and Saucer, footed, 2 1/4″	45.00
Gravy Boat, attached underplate	130.00
Lid, vegetable, round, handled	95.00
Plate, bread and butter, 6 1/2″	15.00
Plate, dinner, 10″	35.00
Plate, salad, 8″	22.50
Platter, oval, 12 1/8″	90.00
Platter, oval, 14 1/8″	100.00
Platter, oval, 16 1/4″	140.00
Saucer	15.00
Sugar Bowl, covered	60.00
Sugar Bowl, covered, no lid	40.00
Vegetable, covered, round	190.00
Vegetable, oval, 9 3/8″	80.00
Vegetable, oval, 10 5/8″	90.00

SYRACUSE CHINA COMPANY, SWEETHEART

The Sweetheart pattern was introduced in 1960 and discontinued in 1970.

Syracuse China, Sweetheart

Creamer	$70.00
Cup and Saucer, footed, 2 7/8″	60.00
Plate, bread and butter, 6 1/2″	22.50
Plate, dinner, 10 1/2″	50.00
Plate, salad, 8 1/4″	30.00
Saucer	20.00
Sugar Bowl, covered	90.00
Sugar Bowl, covered, no lid	65.00
Vegetable, oval, 10″	130.00

SYRACUSE CHINA COMPANY, VICTORIA

Victoria, designed by John Wigley and introduced in 1939, is reminiscent of the Victorian era with its lifelike center rose and buds, old ivory background, and fluted shape. Victoria was discontinued in 1970.

Syracuse China, Victoria, Federal Shape

Bowl, fruit, 5″	$25.00
Bowl, oatmeal, 5 1/8″	30.00
Bowl, soup, flat, 8″	32.50

Cream Soup and Saucer	60.00
Cream Soup Saucer	20.00
Creamer	55.00
Cup and Saucer, footed, 2 1/4″	45.00
Gravy Boat, attached underplate	140.00
Lid, coffeepot	100.00
Lid, vegetable, round	115.00
Plate, bread and butter, 6 1/2″	15.00
Plate, dessert, 7 1/4″	20.00
Plate, dinner, 10″	35.00
Plate, salad, 8″	22.50
Platter, oval, 12 1/8″	90.00
Platter, oval, 14 1/8″	100.00
Platter, oval, 16 1/4″	140.00
Saucer	15.00
Saucer, demitasse	12.50
Sugar Bowl, covered	70.00
Sugar Bowl, covered, no lid	50.00
Vegetable, covered, round	190.00
Vegetable, oval, 10 5/8″	90.00

SYRACUSE CHINA COMPANY, WAYSIDE

Wayside, created by designers Garvin and Petta in 1962, was discontinued in 1970.

Syracuse China, Wayside, Carefree Line

Butter Dish, covered, 1/4 lb.	$65.00
Butter Dish, covered, 1/4 lb., no lid	45.00
Creamer	40.00
Cup and Saucer, flat, 2 1/4″	27.50
Gravy Boat, attached underplate	100.00
Lid, coffeepot	55.00
Plate, bread and butter, 6 3/8″	15.00
Plate, dinner, 10 1/8″	32.50
Plate, salad, 8″	20.00
Platter, oval, 11 3/8″	65.00
Platter, oval, 12 1/2″	75.00
Sugar Bowl, covered	50.00
Sugar Bowl, covered, no lid	35.00
Vegetable, oval, divided, 9 7/8″	95.00
Vegetable, round, 8″	60.00

The Wedding Ring pattern was introduced in 1960 and discontinued in 1970.

Syracuse China, Wedding Ring

Creamer	$70.00
Cup and Saucer, footed, 2 3/4″	55.00
Plate, bread and butter, 6 1/2″	20.00
Plate, dinner	45.00
Plate, salad, 8 3/8″	25.00
Platter, oval, 14 1/8″	145.00
Sugar Bowl, covered	80.00
Sugar Bowl, covered, no lid	60.00

VILLEROY & BOCH

Pierre Joseph Boch founded a pottery near Luxembourg, Germany, in 1767. His son, Jean-François Boch, founded a dinnerware factory at the Abbey of Mettlach, Germany, in 1809. The two factories merged with the Nicholas Villeroy plant in Wallerfongen, Saar, in 1836 to form the Villeroy and Boch Company.

Jean-François introduced Europe's first coal-fired kiln and perfected a water-power-driven potter's wheel. Stonewares, first produced in 1840, were the most famous of the Villeroy and Boch products. Also produced were steins, punch bowls, beakers, wall plaques, beverage sets, drinking cups, hanging baskets, and vases. Terra-cotta for architectural use was added in 1850, mosaic tiles in 1852, and cream-colored earthenwares for domestic use were introduced in 1853. A new factory was built at Dresden in 1853. Artists at Mettlach manufactured plates and vases decorated in the Delft and faience styles, beginning around 1890. Art Nouveau decorations appeared circa 1900.

Due to unfavorable economic conditions and a lack of skilled workers during World War I, business declined. A major fire destroyed all molds, formulas, and factory records in 1921. The factory continued to produce tiles, dinnerwares, and plumbing fixtures, but almost fifty years passed before the production of plaques and steins was resumed.

Villeroy & Boch, Acapulco

Ashtray, 3 1/8″	$20.00
Augratin, 8″	170.00
Butter Tray, 8″	105.00
Casserole, covered, round, 6 3/4″	240.00
Casserole, covered, round, 6 3/4″, no lid	190.00
Casserole, covered, round, 7 5/8″	250.00
Casserole, open, 7 1/8″	130.00
Chop Plate, 12 1/8″	150.00
Coffeepot, covered	175.00
Coffeepot, covered, mini	115.00

Cream Soup and Saucer	70.00
Cream Soup Bowl	50.00
Creamer	65.00
Creamer, mini	45.00
Cup, demitasse	35.00
Cup, flat, 2 1/4″	35.00
Cup, oversized, 2 3/4″	45.00
Cup and Saucer, demitasse	40.00
Cup and Saucer, flat, 2 1/4″	40.00
Cup and Saucer, oversized, 2 3/4″	50.00
Eggcup, single, 1 3/8″	22.50
Gravy Boat, attached underplate	170.00
Lid, casserole, round, 7 3/4″	125.00
Lid, coffeepot, mini	65.00
Lid, tureen	225.00
Pepper Shaker	35.00
Pitcher, 5 1/2″	130.00
Platter, oval, 11 1/2″	130.00
Platter, oval, 14″	160.00
Platter, oval, 16 1/2″	200.00
Platter, oval, 18 3/4″	270.00
Ramekin, 3 1/4″	50.00
Roaster, oval, 13 1/8″	200.00
Salt and Pepper Shakers, pair	70.00
Saucer	12.50
Sugar Bowl, covered	80.00
Tankard	75.00

Teapot, covered   170.00
Tureen, covered   450.00
Vegetable, round, 8 1/8″   90.00

Villeroy & Boch, Indian Summer

Creamer, 4 1/8″ $100.00
Cup and Saucer, flat, 2 1/4″   85.00
Lid, vegetable,   215.00
Plate, bread and butter   35.00
Plate, dinner   80.00
Plate, salad   50.00
Salt and Pepper Shakers, pair   100.00
Saucer   30.00

Villeroy & Boch, Le Ballon

Cup and Saucer, flat, 2 1/2″ $50.00
Plate, bread and butter   32.50
Plate, dinner   65.00
Plate, salad   45.00
Sugar Bowl, covered, no lid   80.00

Villeroy & Boch, Petite Fleur, small

Baker, rectangular, 14 1/4″ $120.00
Bowl, cereal, flat, 8″   30.00
Bowl, soup, 4 5/8″   15.00
Bowl, soup, flat, 9″   30.00
Butter Dish, covered, square   75.00
Butter Tray, 7 3/4″   30.00
Cake Plate, square, handled, 9 5/8″   75.00
Candy Box   60.00
Casserole, covered, oval, 8 1/2″   135.00
Casserole, covered, oval, 9 7/8″   140.00
Chop Plate, 12 1/2″   70.00
Coffeepot, covered   110.00
Coffeepot, covered, no lid   70.00
Cream Soup and Saucer   60.00
Cream Soup Saucer   15.00
Creamer   40.00
Cup, demitasse   22.50
Cup and Saucer, demitasse   30.00
Cup and Saucer, flat, 2 3/8″   30.00
Fondue Warmer Stand   65.00
Gravy Boat, attached underplate   85.00
Mug, 3 5/8″   22.50
Napkin Ring   22.50
Pitcher, 4 3/4″   65.00
Plate, bread and butter   20.00
Plate, dinner, 10 1/2″   20.00
Plate, luncheon, 9 5/8″   27.50
Plate, salad   20.00
Platter, oval, 11 1/2″   60.00
Platter, oval, 17 1/8″   105.00
Ramekin, 3 1/4″   27.50
Salt and Pepper Shakers, pair   55.00
Saucer   10.00
Soufflé, 6 1/4″   60.00
Soufflé, 7 3/4″   60.00
Sugar Bowl, covered   40.00
Vegetable, covered, round   150.00
Vegetable, round, 8 1/4″   75.00

In 1759, Josiah Wedgwood established a pottery near Stoke-on-Trent at the former Ivy House works in Burslem, England. By 1761, Wedgwood had perfected a superior quality, inexpensive clear-glazed creamware that proved very successful.

Wedgwood moved his pottery from the Ivy House to the larger Brick House works in Burslem in 1764, and in 1766, upon being appointed "Potter to Her Majesty" by Queen Charlotte, Wedgwood named his creamware "Queen's Ware." The Brick House works remained in production until 1772.

Wedgwood built a new factory in Etruria, which began operating in 1769, the same year he formed a partnership with Thomas Bentley. Wedgwood's most famous set of Queen's Ware, the 1,000-piece "Frog" Service created for Catherine the Great, Empress of Russia, was produced at the Etruria factory in 1774.

By the late 1700s, the Wedgwood product line included black basalt, creamware, jasper, pearlware, and redware. Moonlight luster was made from 1805 to 1815. Bone China was produced from 1812 to 1822, and revived in 1878. Fairyland luster was introduced in 1915. All luster production ended in 1932.

In 1906, a museum was established at the Etruria pottery. A new factory was built at nearby Barlaston in 1940, and the museum was moved to and expanded at this location. The Etruria works was closed in 1950.

During the 1960s and 1970s, Wedgwood acquired many English potteries, including William Adams & Sons, Coalport, Susie Cooper, Crown Staffordshire, Johnson Brothers, Mason's Ironstone, J. & G. Meakin, Midwinter Companies, Precision Studios, and Royal Tuscan. Today, the Wedgwood Group is one of the largest fine china and earthenware manufacturers in the world.

Wedgwood, Portrait, Josiah Wedgwood I (1730–1795). *Photo courtesy of Wedgwood.*

Wedgwood, Agincourt, Contour Shape, Bone China

Bowl, cereal, coupe, 6″	$75.00
Bowl, fruit, 5″	60.00
Bowl, soup, flat, 8 1/4″	100.00
Cream Soup and Saucer	150.00
Cream Soup Saucer	50.00
Creamer	110.00
Cup, demitasse	85.00
Cup, footed, 3″	60.00
Cup and Saucer, demitasse	90.00
Cup and Saucer, footed, 3″	70.00
Gravy Boat, attached underplate	300.00
Lid, sugar bowl	75.00
Plate, bread and butter, 6″	35.00
Plate, dinner, 11″	90.00
Plate, salad, 8 1/8″	50.00
Platter, oval, 13 3/4″	300.00
Platter, oval, 15 3/8″	350.00
Sugar Bowl, covered	150.00
Teapot, covered	300.00
Vegetable, oval, 10″	200.00

Wedgwood, American Clipper, York Shape, Queen's Ware

Cream Soup Bowl	$75.00
Cup, demitasse	40.00
Cup, flat, 2 5/8″	45.00
Cup and Saucer, demitasse	45.00
Cup and Saucer, flat, 2 5/8″	50.00
Gravy Boat, attached underplate	160.00
Plate, bread and butter, 6″	20.00
Plate, dinner	50.00
Plate, salad	30.00
Vegetable, covered, octagonal	250.00
Vegetable, oval, 9 1/2″	100.00

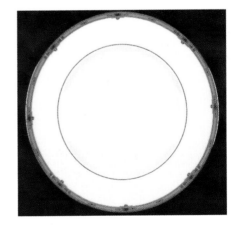

Wedgwood, Amherst, grey band

Bowl, cereal, coupe, 6 1/8″	$30.00
Bowl, fruit, 5 1/8″	32.50
Bowl, soup, flat, 9″	40.00
Chop Plate, 13 1/2″	125.00
Coffeepot, covered, 7″	145.00
Cream Soup and Saucer	80.00
Cream Soup Bowl	60.00
Creamer, 2 3/8″	45.00
Creamer, 3 3/4″	45.00

THE WEDGWOOD GROUP

Historically, individuals leaving the family firm to start a competing business enterprise, apprentices and/or journeymen striking out on their own, partners agreeing to go their separate ways, and consolidation or absorption of firms has been a fact of life in the British pottery industry for more than two centuries. After working for five years with Thomas Whieldon, Josiah Wedgwood left to start his own pottery in 1759 at the Ivy House Works. Tracing the history of many firms is virtually impossible without created pottery "family trees."

From a family firm with some 2,000 employees in 1966, The Wedgwood Group has become a public company, comprising eight factories employing approximately 5,500 people in the United Kingdom and overseas. The Wedgwood Group accounts for 25 percent of the British ceramic tableware industry's output and 25 percent of its exports.

In 1986, Waterford and Wedgwood merged. The Wedgwood Group, now a division of Waterford Wedgwood, consists of six major divisions:

1. **Wedgwood**—The Wedgwood factory, one of the most modern of its type in the world, is located in Barlaston, Staffordshire, England. Wedgwood manufactures high-quality tableware and ornamental wares in fine bone china, Jasper ware, and Black Basalt. Wedgwood's fine earthenware (Queen's Ware) and oven-to-tableware are produced in a dedicated manufacturing unit in Stoke-on-Trent.

2. **Coalport**—Coalport China, established as the Caughley China Works in 1750, is one of England's most famous manufacturers of fine bone china. Its other products range from collectors' plates to figurines and hand-painted ornamental wares.

3. **Johnson Brothers**—Johnson Brothers produces a wide range of earthenware tableware utilizing three world-renowned brand names: Johnson Brothers (established in 1883), Unicorn (established in 1935), and Franciscan (established in 1875).

4. **Mason's Ironstone**—Mason's, founded in 1795, manufactures a wide selection of richly decorated earthenware tableware and ornamental ware. The company's famous "Ironstone" was first made in 1813. Many of the original patterns and shapes continue to be manufactured today.

5. **Wedgwood Hotelware**—This company manufactures fine bone china tableware and is designed especially to cater to the needs of hotels, restaurants, airlines, and related travel industries. It is manufactured in the hi-tech Royal Tuscan unit.

6. **Wedgwood Jewelry**—The Wedgwood jewelry factory produces Jasper cameos in a wide variety of shapes and designs that are hand-mounted in gold-plated and precious metals.

Prior mergers linked the Wedgwood Group with the lineage of many famous pottery manufacturers, among them, William Adams and Sons, Aristocrat Floral & Fancies, Susie Cooper, Crown Staffordshire, J. & G. Meakin, Newport Pottery, and Precision. Many of these trademarks have been retired. William Adams, a leading manufacturer of earthenwares, joined the Wedgwood Group in 1966. Although there is no longer an Adams manufacturing unit, the Wedgwood Group still uses the backstamp on certain images.

Wedgwood's marketing strength centers on the breadth of its wares—in style, type, and price range, varying from luxurious fine bone china tableware to inexpensive earthenware and oven-to-tableware. Design is an essential factor. Wedgwood Group companies are served by a large, highly qualified, and experienced team of designers and modelers, supplemented by contributions from eminent contemporary artists. The company prides itself on the fact that its continuing success is based upon skilled craftsmanship that is allied to advanced technology, coupled with imaginative design, and supported by energetic marketing.

Wedgwood's high sales volume overseas, about 60 percent of the company's total output, continues at an encouraging rate. Traditional overseas markets include Australia, Canada, and the United States. Since 1983, Wedgwood has made major inroads into the Japanese market. Sales of fine bone china tableware to Japan are now virtually level with those to the United States, previously Wedgwood's leading export market for this product. Britain's membership in the European Economic Community (EEC) has strengthened the company's business connections with European member countries. Over the years, Wedgwood has received eleven Queen's Awards to industry for export achievement.

Cup, demitasse, 2 1/4″	32.50
Cup, footed, 2 5/8″	35.00
Cup and Saucer, demitasse, 2 1/4″	35.00
Cup and Saucer, footed, 2 5/8″	40.00
Plate, bread and butter, 6″	12.50
Plate, dessert, 7″	15.00
Plate, dinner, 10 3/4″	32.50
Plate, luncheon, 9″	30.00
Plate, salad, 8 1/8″	17.50
Plate, torte, 12 1/2″	120.00
Platter, oval, 14 1/8″	115.00
Platter, oval, 17 1/4″	195.00
Saucer	12.50
Sugar Bowl, covered, 4 1/8″	65.00
Teapot, covered	145.00
Tureen, covered	410.00
Vegetable, oval, 10 7/8″	110.00

Bowl, salad, serving, 9 1/2″	200.00
Bowl, soup, flat, 8″	65.00
Bowl, soup, flat, 9″	75.00
Chop Plate, 13 1/4″	200.00
Coffeepot, covered, mini	200.00
Cream Soup and Saucer, 4 5/8″	90.00
Cream Soup Saucer	30.00
Creamer, flat	75.00
Creamer, mini	50.00
Cup and Saucer, demitasse	50.00
Cup and Saucer, footed, 2 1/8″	60.00
Cup and Saucer, oversized, 2 3/8″	60.00
Eggcup, single, 2 3/8″	60.00
Gravy Boat, attached underplate	210.00
Gravy Boat Underplate	70.00
Lid, vegetable	150.00
Pickle Dish, 7 7/8″	95.00
Plate, bread and butter, 6″	30.00
Plate, dinner, 10 3/4″	65.00
Plate, luncheon, 9″	50.00
Plate, salad, 8″	35.00
Platter, oval, 13 5/8″	200.00
Platter, oval, 14 1/8″	230.00
Platter, oval, 15 1/4″	250.00
Saucer	20.00
Saucer, demitasse	15.00
Saucer, oversized	20.00
Sugar Bowl, covered, flat	100.00
Sugar Bowl, covered, footed	100.00
Sugar Bowl, open, mini	50.00
Teapot, covered	250.00
Vegetable, covered, round	300.00
Vegetable, oval, 9 3/4″	130.00
Vegetable, oval, 10 5/8″	140.00

Wedgwood, Appledore, Leigh Shape, Bone China, gold trim, W3257

Ashtray, 4 1/2″	$25.00
Bowl, fruit, 5 1/8″	40.00

Wedgwood, Belle Fleur, Leigh Shape, Bone China, R4356

Bowl, fruit, 5 1/8"	$35.00
Coffeepot, covered	200.00
Cream Soup and Saucer	90.00
Cream Soup Bowl	75.00
Creamer, 3"	65.00
Cup, demitasse	45.00
Cup and Saucer, demitasse	50.00
Cup and Saucer, footed, 2 5/8"	50.00
Lid, sugar bowl, 3 1/4"	40.00
Lid, teapot	115.00
Napkin Ring	35.00
Plate, bread and butter, 6"	22.50
Plate, dinner, 10 3/4"	55.00
Plate, luncheon, 9"	50.00
Plate, salad, 8 1/8"	32.50
Platter, oval, 13 3/4"	200.00
Saucer	15.00
Sugar Bowl, covered, 3 1/4"	80.00
Sugar Bowl, open, 3 1/8"	60.00
Vegetable, covered, no lid	240.00

Wedgwood, Bianca, Windsor Shape, Bone China, gold trim, R4499

Creamer, mini, 2 1/8"	$40.00
Cup and Saucer, demitasse	65.00
Cup and Saucer, footed, 2 5/8"	55.00
Plate, bread and butter	20.00
Plate, dinner	50.00
Plate, salad	30.00
Tureen, covered	810.00

Wedgwood, Blue Print, Midwinter

Bowl, cereal, coupe, 5 5/8"	$25.00
Casserole, covered, round, 8 1/4"	135.00
Chop Plate, 12 3/8"	70.00
Coffeepot, covered	110.00
Cup, flat, 2 1/2"	20.00
Cup and Saucer, flat, 2 1/2"	25.00
Gravy Boat and Underplate	90.00
Lid, coffeepot	55.00
Plate, bread and butter, 7"	15.00
Plate, dinner, 10 5/8"	30.00
Plate, salad	17.50
Platter, oval, 11 7/8"	60.00
Vegetable, round, 8 1/4"	55.00

Wedgwood, Bullfinch

Ashtray, 4 3/8″	$25.00
Bowl, fruit, 5 1/2″	32.50
Bowl, soup, flat, 8 5/8″	60.00
Cream Soup and Saucer	90.00
Cream Soup Saucer	30.00
Creamer	60.00
Cup, demitasse	50.00
Cup and Saucer, demitasse	50.00
Cup and Saucer, footed, 2 3/4″	85.00
Eggcup, double, 3 3/4″	60.00
Gravy Boat Underplate	55.00
Lid, sugar bowl	40.00
Lid, teapot	100.00
Plate, bread and butter, 6 3/4″	20.00
Plate, dessert, 7 1/2″	25.00
Plate, dinner, 10 3/4″	50.00
Plate, luncheon, 9 1/2″	50.00
Plate, salad	30.00
Saucer	15.00

Wedgwood, Cavendish, R4680

Bowl, cereal, coupe, 6 1/8″	$35.00
Bowl, fruit, 5″	35.00
Bowl, soup, flat, 9″	50.00

Cake Plate, square, handled, 11 1/8″	110.00
Chop Plate, 13 1/2″	140.00
Coffeepot, covered	200.00
Cream Soup Saucer	30.00
Creamer, 3 3/4″	70.00
Cup, demitasse	45.00
Cup and Saucer, demitasse	50.00
Cup and Saucer, footed, 2 5/8″	55.00
Gravy Boat and Underplate	200.00
Mug, 3 1/2″	45.00
Plate, bread and butter, 6″	25.00
Plate, dessert, 7″	25.00
Plate, dinner, 10 3/4″	45.00
Plate, luncheon, 9″	40.00
Plate, salad, 8 1/8″	30.00
Plate, torte, 12 1/2″	205.00
Platter, oval, 14 1/8″	140.00
Platter, oval, 15 1/2″	205.00
Platter, oval, 17 1/4″	250.00
Saucer	17.50
Sugar Bowl, covered, 4 1/8″	90.00
Teapot, covered	200.00
Teapot, covered, no lid	140.00
Tray, sandwich, 14 1/2″	100.00
Tureen, covered	480.00
Tureen Underplate	190.00
Vegetable, covered, round	260.00
Vegetable, oval, 10 1/8″	115.00

Wedgwood, Charnwood, Peony Shape, Bone China, gold trim

Ashtray, 4 1/2″	$25.00
Bowl, fruit, 5″	35.00
Bowl, soup, flat, 8″	65.00
Bud Vase, 5 1/4″	70.00
Cake Plate, square, handled, 10 7/8″	150.00
Coaster, 4″	25.00
Coffeepot, covered	250.00
Coffeepot, covered, mini	170.00

Cream Soup and Saucer	100.00	Cream Soup Saucer	27.50
Cream Soup Bowl	90.00	Cup and Saucer, demitasse	45.00
Creamer, flat	70.00	Cup and Saucer, footed, 3″	40.00
Cup and Saucer, demitasse	50.00	Gravy Boat, attached underplate	150.00
Cup and Saucer, footed, 2 1/8″	55.00	Gravy Boat and Underplate	150.00
Gravy Boat, attached underplate	220.00	Gravy Boat, no underplate	120.00
Gravy Boat and Underplate	220.00	Plate, bread and butter	17.50
Gravy Boat, no underplate	180.00	Plate, dinner, 10 3/8″	45.00
Lid, coffeepot, mini	85.00	Plate, salad, 8 3/8″	25.00
Lid, teapot	125.00	Platter, oval, 15 1/2″	160.00
Plate, bread and butter, 6″	22.50	Saucer	12.50
Plate, dinner	65.00	Vegetable, covered, round	200.00
Plate, luncheon, 9″	50.00	Vegetable, oval, 9 3/4″	80.00
Plate, salad, 8 1/8″	35.00		
Platter, oval, 10 7/8″	145.00		
Platter, oval, 13 5/8″	180.00		
Platter, oval, 14 1/4″	200.00		
Platter, oval, 15 3/8″	220.00		
Saucer	17.50		
Saucer, demitasse	15.00		
Sugar Bowl, covered, flat	90.00		
Sugar Bowl, covered, flat, no lid	65.00		
Teapot, covered	250.00		
Tray, silver, 4 1/2″	45.00		
Tray, silver, 5″	45.00		
Vegetable, covered, round	300.00		
Vegetable, oval, 9 3/4″	130.00		
Vegetable, oval, 10″	140.00		

Wedgwood, Chinese Tigers, Windsor Shape, Bone China

Bowl, cereal, coupe, 5 7/8″	$65.00
Bowl, soup, flat, 8″	90.00
Coffeepot, covered	300.00
Cream Soup and Saucer	130.00
Cream Soup Bowl	100.00
Cup and Saucer	80.00
Cup and Saucer, demitasse, 2 1/4″	80.00
Flower Pot, 3 3/4″	150.00
Plate, bread and butter, 6″	35.00
Plate, dinner	85.00
Plate, salad	50.00
Saucer	25.00

Wedgwood, Chinese Teal, Queen's Shape, Queen's Ware

Coffeepot, covered	$200.00
Coffeepot, covered, no lid	180.00

The Columbia pattern is based on early Victorian period decorations and was designed by Thomas Allen, art director at Etruria in 1880. The pattern is entirely hand-decorated by three separate processes—transferring, enameling, and lining—and receives four firings.

Wedgwood, Columbia Enameled, Peony Shape with Leigh cup, Bone China

Ashtray, 4 3/8″	$40.00
Bowl, cereal, coupe, 6 1/8″	80.00
Bowl, fruit, 5″	70.00
Bowl, salad, serving, 9 5/8″	300.00
Bowl, soup, flat, 8 7/8″	90.00
Cake Plate, square, handled, 11″	130.00
Chop Plate, 13 3/8″	270.00
Coffeepot, covered	270.00
Cream Soup and Saucer	130.00
Cream Soup Bowl	120.00
Creamer	95.00
Cup, demitasse	75.00
Cup, footed, 2 5/8″	70.00
Cup and Saucer, demitasse	80.00
Cup and Saucer, footed, 2 5/8″	75.00
Gravy Boat and Underplate	270.00
Gravy Boat Underplate	90.00
Plate, bread and butter, 6″	35.00
Plate, dinner, 10 3/4″	70.00
Plate, luncheon, 8 7/8″	65.00

Plate, salad, 8″	40.00
Platter, oval, 13 7/8″	220.00
Platter, oval, 14 1/8″	300.00
Platter, oval, 15 1/2″	310.00
Sugar Bowl, covered, 2 3/4″	130.00
Sugar Bowl, covered, 2 3/4″, no lid	95.00
Teapot, covered	270.00
Tureen, covered	800.00
Vegetable, covered, round	400.00
Vegetable, covered, round, no lid	300.00
Vegetable, oval, 9 7/8″	160.00
Vegetable, oval, 10 7/8″	200.00

Wedgwood, Columbia Sage Green, Peony Shape

Bowl, cereal, coupe, 6 1/8″	$80.00
Bowl, fruit, 5″	65.00
Bowl, soup, flat	110.00
Cake Plate, square, handled, 10 7/8″	240.00
Chop Plate, 13 3/8″	350.00
Coffeepot, covered	270.00
Cream Soup and Saucer	180.00
Cream Soup Bowl	175.00
Creamer, 2 3/8″	135.00
Cup, demitasse	100.00
Cup, footed	105.00
Cup and Saucer, demitasse	105.00
Cup and Saucer, footed	110.00
Gravy Boat and Underplate	350.00
Gravy Boat, no underplate	280.00
Lid, coffeepot	135.00
Lid, sugar bowl	105.00
Lid, teapot	160.00
Plate, bread and butter, 6″	40.00
Plate, dessert, 7″	50.00
Plate, dinner, 10 3/4″	100.00
Plate, luncheon, 8 7/8″	95.00
Plate, salad, 8″	60.00
Platter, oval, 13 3/4″	350.00
Platter, oval, 14 1/8″	400.00
Platter, oval, 15 3/8″	425.00
Platter, oval, 17 1/4″	525.00
Sugar Bowl, covered	210.00
Sugar Bowl, open	135.00
Teapot, covered	320.00
Vegetable, covered, round	405.00
Vegetable, oval, 10″	240.00
Vegetable, oval, 9 3/4″	195.00

Wedgwood, Conway, Edme Shape

Bowl, cereal, coupe, 6 1/2″	$22.50
Bowl, fruit, 5 1/4″	20.00
Bowl, soup, flat, 8 1/8″	40.00
Cream Soup and Saucer	50.00
Cream Soup Saucer	15.00
Cup and Saucer, bouillon	33.50
Cup and Saucer, footed, 2 3/4″	35.00
Eggcup, double	30.00
Lid, coffeepot	70.00
Lid, teapot	70.00
Plate, bread and butter, 6 3/8″	12.50
Plate, dinner, 10 1/2″	35.00
Plate, luncheon, 9 1/8″	30.00
Plate, salad, 8 1/8″	17.50
Platter, oval, 11 5/8″	80.00
Platter, oval, 13 7/8″	100.00
Platter, oval, 14 3/4″	110.00
Platter, oval, 18″	190.00
Saucer	12.50
Saucer, demitasse	10.00
Vegetable, oval, 10 1/2″	80.00

Wedgwood, Countryside, blue

Bowl, cereal, coupe, 6 1/2"	$17.50
Bowl, fruit, 4 7/8"	12.50
Creamer	30.00
Cup and Saucer, demitasse	27.50
Cup and Saucer, flat, 2 3/4"	17.50
Gravy Boat and Underplate	90.00
Gravy Boat, no underplate	70.00
Mug, 3 3/4"	25.00
Plate, bread and butter, 5 7/8"	10.00
Plate, dinner, 10"	20.00
Plate, salad, 7"	15.00
Platter, oval, 11 3/4"	60.00
Salt Shaker	27.50
Saucer	5.00
Sugar Bowl, covered	40.00
Sugar Bowl, covered, no lid	30.00
Vegetable, covered, round	120.00
Vegetable, covered, round, no lid	90.00
Vegetable, round, 8 3/4"	35.00

**Wedgwood, Cream Color on Cream Color,
Plain Edge, Queen's Ware**

Ashtray, 3 3/8"	$15.00
Ashtray, 4 1/4"	15.00
Ashtray, 5 3/4"	15.00
Bowl, cereal, coupe, 6 1/4"	35.00
Bowl, fruit, 5 1/4"	27.50
Bowl, soup, flat, 8 3/8"	55.00
Candlestick, single light, 1 1/2"	45.00
Cigarette Holder	40.00
Coffeepot, covered	180.00
Compote, 3 7/8"	60.00
Cream Soup and Saucer	70.00
Cream Soup Saucer	22.50
Creamer, 3 3/8"	50.00
Cup, bouillon, 2 1/2"	40.00
Cup and Saucer, bouillon, 2 1/2"	45.00
Cup and Saucer, demitasse	40.00
Cup and Saucer, footed, 2 5/8"	45.00
Gravy Boat Underplate	50.00
Lid, coffeepot	90.00
Lid, coffeepot, mini	70.00
Lid, sugar bowl, mini	20.00
Lid, teapot	90.00
Lid, vegetable	120.00
Plate, bread and butter, 6 1/8"	15.00
Plate, dessert, 7 "	22.50
Plate, dinner, 10 3/8"	45.00
Plate, luncheon, 9 1/4"	35.00
Plate, salad, 8 1/8"	25.00
Saucer	15.00
Saucer, demitasse	12.50
Sugar Bowl, covered, 2 7/8"	60.00
Sugar Bowl, covered, 2 7/8", no lid	40.00
Teapot, covered	180.00
Teapot, mini, covered, no lid	85.00
Vase, 6 5/8"	110.00

THE TOP FIVE PATTERNS
COLOR SCHEME—WHITE

ADAMS, WM. & SONS, EMPRESS WHITE
LENOX, MOONSPUN
SPODE, JEWEL EMBOSSED IMPERIAL
WEDGWOOD, CREAM COLOR ON CREAM COLOR
WEDGWOOD, WELLESLEY

Wedgwood, Cream Color on Cream Color,
Shell Edge, Queen's Ware

Wedgwood, Cream Color on Lavender,
Plain Edge, Queen's Ware

Ashtray, 3 3/4″	$25.00	Ashtray, 3 3/8″	$15.00
Bowl, cereal, coupe, 6 1/8″	45.00	Ashtray, 4 1/2″	15.00
Bowl, fruit, 5 1/4″	32.50	Ashtray, 5 5/8″	15.00
Bowl, soup, flat, 8 1/8″	60.00	Bowl, cereal, coupe, 6 1/4″	40.00
Coffeepot, covered	230.00	Bowl, fruit, 5 1/8″	32.50
Coffeepot, covered, no lid	180.00	Bowl, salad, serving	190.00
Cream Soup and Saucer	110.00	Bowl, soup, flat, 8 1/4″	55.00
Cream Soup Saucer	30.00	Cake Plate, square, handled, 10 5/8″	110.00
Creamer	75.00	Candlestick, single light, 1 1/2″	65.00
Cup, bouillon	55.00	Candy Box	100.00
Cup, demitasse, footed, 2 1/4″	40.00	Chop Plate, 12 1/2″	170.00
Cup and Saucer, bouillon	60.00	Cigarette Box	70.00
Cup and Saucer, demitasse,		Cigarette Holder	40.00
footed, 2 1/4″	45.00	Coffeepot, covered, 5 1/2″	190.00
Cup and Saucer, footed, 2 1/2″	55.00	Compote, 3 3/4″	70.00
Gravy Boat, attached underplate	200.00	Cream Soup and Saucer	90.00
Plate, bread and butter, 6 1/2″	22.50	Cream Soup Bowl	80.00
Plate, dinner	60.00	Creamer, 2 1/4″	65.00
Plate, luncheon, 9″	50.00	Cup and Saucer, bouillon	50.00
Plate, salad, 8 1/4″	35.00	Cup and Saucer, demitasse, flat	45.00
Platter, oval, 14 3/8″	210.00	Cup and Saucer, demitasse, footed	45.00
Saucer	17.50	Cup and Saucer, footed, 2 5/8″	55.00
Saucer, demitasse	15.00	Gravy Boat, attached underplate	190.00
Sugar Bowl, covered	90.00	Gravy Boat Underplate	65.00
Sugar Bowl, covered, no lid	60.00	Lid, sugar bowl	40.00
Teapot, covered	230.00	Lid, sugar bowl, mini	27.50
Vegetable, covered, round	300.00	Lid, teapot	100.00
Vegetable, covered, no lid	200.00	Plate, bread and butter	22.50
Vegetable, oval, 9 5/8″	110.00	Plate, dinner	55.00
		Plate, luncheon, 9 1/8″	50.00
		Plate, luncheon, square, 8 1/2″	55.00
		Plate, salad	30.00
		Plate, service, 11 1/4″	85.00
		Platter, oval, 10 1/2″	120.00
		Platter, oval, 12 3/4″	140.00
		Platter, oval, 14 1/2″	190.00
		Platter, oval, 16 1/2″	300.00
		Salt and Pepper Shakers, pair	125.00

Saucer	20.00
Sugar Bowl, covered, 3″	80.00
Sugar Bowl, covered, 3″, no lid	65.00
Sugar Bowl, open	65.00
Teapot, covered, 3 ½″	200.00
Vase, 6 ½″	100.00
Vase, 8 ½″	100.00
Vegetable, covered, round	280.00
Vegetable, covered, round, no lid	195.00
Vegetable, oval, 9 ⅞″	105.00

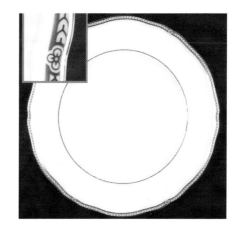

Wedgwood, Cream Color on Lavender, Shell Edge, Queen's Ware

Bowl, soup, flat, 8 ⅛″	$55.00
Chop Plate, 12 ¾″	170.00
Coffeepot, covered	200.00
Cream Soup and Saucer	90.00
Cream Soup Saucer	30.00
Creamer	70.00
Cup, demitasse	45.00
Cup and Saucer, demitasse	50.00
Cup and Saucer, footed, 2 ⅝″	55.00
Lid, teapot	100.00
Plate, bread and butter, 6 ⅜″	20.00
Plate, dinner, 10 ½″	60.00
Plate, luncheon, 9 ¼″	50.00
Plate, salad, 8 ⅛″	30.00
Platter, oval, 14 ⅜″	200.00
Platter, oval, 16 ¼″	250.00
Saucer	17.50
Sugar Bowl, covered	80.00
Vegetable, covered, round, no lid	200.00
Vegetable, oval, 9 ¾″	110.00

Wedgwood, Crown Gold, gold trim

Bowl, cereal, coupe, 6 ⅛″	$40.00
Bowl, fruit, 5 ¼″	40.00
Bowl, soup, flat, 9″	75.00
Cake Plate, square, handled, 10 ¼″	100.00
Coffeepot, covered	230.00
Cream Soup and Saucer	80.00
Cream Soup Bowl	65.00
Creamer	90.00
Cup and Saucer, footed, 3″	60.00
Gravy Boat and Underplate	225.00
Plate, bread and butter, 6 ⅛″	25.00
Plate, dinner, 10 ⅞″	55.00
Plate, luncheon, 9 ¼″	40.00
Plate, salad, 8″	35.00
Platter, oval, 14″	190.00
Platter, oval, 15 ¼″	240.00
Saucer	20.00
Saucer, demitasse	15.00
Sugar Bowl, covered	130.00
Teapot, covered	230.00
Vegetable, covered, round	320.00
Vegetable, oval, 9 ⅞″	160.00

Wedgwood, Devon Sprays, W4076

Ashtray, 4 ¹/₂″	$30.00
Bowl, fruit, 5″	35.00
Bowl, soup, flat, 8″	65.00
Cake Plate, square, 9 ³/₄″	140.00
Cake Plate, square, handled, 10 ³/₄″	140.00
Chop Plate, 13 ¹/₈″	200.00
Cigarette Box	90.00
Coffeepot, covered	200.00
Coffeepot, covered, mini	155.00
Cream Soup and Saucer	100.00
Cream Soup Saucer	35.00
Creamer, 2 ³/₈″	70.00
Creamer, mini	50.00
Cup and Saucer, demitasse	55.00
Cup and Saucer, footed, 2 ³/₄″	60.00
Eggcup, single, 2 ³/₈″	70.00
Gravy Boat, attached underplate	200.00
Gravy Boat Underplate	65.00
Lid, vegetable, round	150.00
Plate, bread and butter, 6″	27.50
Plate, dessert, 7″	35.00
Plate, dinner	70.00
Plate, luncheon, 9″	60.00
Plate, salad, 8 ¹/₈″	35.00
Platter, oval, 13 ³/₈″	190.00
Platter, oval, 15 ¹/₄″	230.00
Saucer, demitasse	20.00
Sugar Bowl, covered, 2 ⁵/₈″	100.00
Sugar Bowl, covered, 4″	100.00
Sugar Bowl, open, 2 ¹/₂″	70.00
Teapot, covered	200.00
Teapot, covered, no lid	160.00
Teapot, covered, mini	170.00
Vegetable, covered, round	300.00
Vegetable, oval, 9 ⁷/₈″	130.00
Vegetable, oval, 11″	170.00

The Edme shape reflects the Georgian tradition of early Wedgwood and was designed by John E. Goodwin in 1908.

Wedgwood, Edme, Edme Shape, Queen's Ware, plain white

Bowl, cereal, coupe, 6 1/4″	$10.00
Bowl, fruit, 5 3/8″	7.50
Bowl, fruit, flat, 7 1/4″	7.50
Bowl, salad, serving, footed, 8 7/8″	60.00
Bowl, soup, flat, 8 1/8″	12.50
Butter Dish, covered, square	27.50
Cake Plate, square, handled, 9 7/8″	22.50
Candlestick, 8″	25.00
Candlestick, single light, 2 1/8″	25.00
Casserole, covered, round, 5 3/8″	65.00
Casserole, covered, round, 6 ″, no lid	65.00
Chop Plate, 12 5/8″	45.00
Coffeepot, covered, 6 7/8″	70.00
Coffeepot, covered, no lid, 6 7/8″	50.00
Cream Soup and Saucer	40.00
Cream Soup Bowl	30.00
Creamer, 3 3/4″	22.50
Cup, footed, 2 5/8″	10.00
Cup and Saucer, bouillon, 3 1/4″	15.00
Cup and Saucer, breakfast, 2 3/4″	27.50
Cup and Saucer, chocolate, 3 1/8″	27.50
Cup and Saucer, demitasse	22.50
Cup and Saucer, footed, 2 5/8″	12.50
Eggcup, double, 4 3/8″	15.00
Eggcup, single, 2 1/4″	12.50
Fish Dish, 14 1/2″	65.00
Gravy Boat and Underplate	70.00
Gravy Boat Underplate	15.00
Lid, butter dish, square	15.00
Lid, coffeepot	35.00
Lid, soup bowl	10.00
Mug, 4 1/4″	10.00
Pitcher, 4 1/2″	35.00
Plate, bread and butter, 6 3/8″	5.00
Plate, dinner, 10 1/2″	12.50
Plate, luncheon, 9″	10.00
Plate, luncheon, square, 8 5/8″	12.50
Plate, salad, 8 1/8″	10.00
Plate, torte, 13″	70.00
Platter, oval, 13 3/4″	40.00
Platter, oval, 15 5/8″	50.00
Ramekin, 3 1/4″	15.00
Ramekin and Saucer, 4 1/8″	25.00
Roaster, oval, 9 1/4″	30.00
Salt and Pepper Shakers, pair	15.00
Saucer, bouillon	5.00
Saucer, chocolate	10.00
Saucer, demitasse	7.50
Saucer, ramekin, 4 1/8″	7.50
Soufflé, 7 1/4″	27.50
Sugar Bowl, covered, footed	30.00
Sugar Bowl, covered, mini, no lid	15.00
Teapot, covered, no lid	50.00
Vase, 6 5/8″	27.50
Vase, 8 3/4″	50.00
Vase, 10 1/2″	65.00
Vegetable, covered, round	120.00
Vegetable, covered, round, no lid	85.00
Vegetable, oval, 10 1/4″	30.00
Vegetable, oval, 11 1/8″	35.00

WEDGWOOD, FLORENTINE

A border design of mythical griffins and winged lions reminiscent of the renaissance style provides the basis for this century-old pattern. It is recorded in a pattern book from 1865 as a design for cream-colored earthenware. Since that time, some eighty versions have been made in a wide variety of colors. It is believed that the original was created by Thomas Allen, Wedgwood's art director in the late nineteenth century.

The first version to decorate bone china was produced in 1924 and printed in brown. Most variations were introduced between 1924 and the outbreak of World War II. While all of the variations were popular, turquoise and cobalt were outstanding and survived the changing taste of the post-war period. Florentine Gold was introduced circa 1953 and Florentine Black in 1961.

Wedgwood, Florentine Black, Peony Shape with Leigh cup, Bone China

Ashtray, 4 1/2″	$25.00
Bowl, cereal, coupe, 6 1/8″	60.00
Bowl, fruit, 5″	60.00
Bowl, salad, serving, 8″	180.00
Bowl, soup, flat, 8″	55.00
Cigarette Holder, 2 3/8″	50.00
Cup, footed, 2 1/8″	55.00
Cup, oversized, 2 1/2″	55.00
Cup and Saucer, demitasse	50.00
Cup and Saucer, footed, 2 1/8″	55.00
Eggcup, single, 2 3/8″	45.00
Gravy Boat and Underplate	165.00
Gravy Boat Underplate	55.00
Lid, teapot	95.00
Plate, bread and butter, 6 1/8″	20.00
Plate, dinner, 10 3/4″	50.00
Plate, luncheon, 9″	45.00

Plate, salad, 8″	30.00
Platter, oval, 14 1/4″	190.00
Saucer	20.00
Saucer, demitasse	17.50
Sugar Bowl, covered	85.00
Teapot, covered	185.00

Wedgwood, Florentine Cobalt, Peony Shape, Bone China

Creamer, 2 3/8″	$100.00
Cup, demitasse, 2 3/8″	70.00
Cup, footed, 2 3/4″	70.00
Cup and Saucer, demitasse, 2 3/8″	80.00
Cup and Saucer, footed, 2 3/4″	80.00
Cup and Saucer, oversized	95.00
Gravy Boat Underplate	100.00
Lid, cigarette box	65.00
Lid, coffeepot	150.00

Plate, bread and butter, 6″	35.00
Plate, dinner, 10 ³/₄″	90.00
Plate, salad, 8″	50.00
Platter, oval, 13 ⁷/₈″	250.00
Platter, oval, 15 ³/₈″	300.00
Sugar Bowl, covered	150.00
Sugar Bowl, open, 3″	100.00
Vegetable, covered, round	430.00

Cup and Saucer, demitasse	100.00
Cup and Saucer, footed, 2 ³/₄″	100.00
Gravy Boat, attached underplate	370.00
Gravy Boat and Underplate	370.00
Plate, bread and butter, 6″	40.00
Plate, dinner, 10 ³/₄″	110.00
Plate, luncheon, 8 ⁷/₈″	95.00
Plate, salad, 8 ¹/₈″	60.00
Platter, oval, 13 ³/₄″	350.00
Platter, oval, 14″	400.00
Platter, oval, 15 ³/₈″	420.00
Sugar Bowl, covered, 2 ³/₄″	200.00
Teapot, covered	350.00
Vegetable, covered, round	530.00
Vegetable, oval, 10″	250.00

Wedgwood, Florentine Gold, Peony Shape, Bone China

Ashtray, 4 ¹/₂″	$40.00
Bowl, fruit, 5″	65.00
Cigarette Holder, 2 ¹/₄″	80.00
Cigarette Lighter	100.00
Coffeepot, covered	350.00
Cream Soup and Saucer	160.00
Creamer, 2 ³/₈″	130.00
Cup, demitasse	90.00
Cup, footed, 2 ³/₄″	90.00

Wedgwood, Florentine Turquoise, Peony Shape, Bone China

Ashtray, 4 ¹/₂″	$30.00
Bowl, cereal, coupe, 6 ¹/₈″	60.00

Wedgwood, Florentine Turquoise. *Photo courtesy of Wedgwood.*

Bowl, fruit, 5″	50.00
Bowl, soup, flat, 8″	75.00
Chop Plate, 13 3/8″	200.00
Coffeepot, covered, 8″	240.00
Coffeepot, covered, mini	170.00
Cream Soup and Saucer	100.00
Cream Soup Bowl	90.00
Creamer, 2 3/8″	90.00
Cup, demitasse	60.00
Cup, footed, 2 1/4″	55.00
Cup and Saucer, demitasse	65.00
Cup and Saucer, footed, 2 1/4″	60.00
Gravy Boat, attached underplate	210.00
Gravy Boat Underplate	70.00
Plate, bread and butter, 6″	25.00
Plate, dessert, 7″	35.00
Plate, dinner, 10 3/4″	65.00
Plate, luncheon, 9″	65.00
Plate, salad, 8″	35.00
Platter, oval, 13 1/2″	190.00
Platter, oval, 14 1/4″	200.00
Platter, oval, 15 5/8″	220.00
Saucer	20.00
Sugar Bowl, covered, 2 3/4″	110.00
Sugar Bowl, open	90.00
Sugar Bowl, open, mini	60.00
Teapot, covered	240.00
Teapot, covered, mini	170.00
Tureen, covered	700.00
Tureen Underplate, 11 3/4″	180.00
Vegetable, covered, round	340.00
Vegetable, oval, 10 5/8″	140.00

Wedgwood, Flying Cloud, York Shape, Queen's Ware

Ashtray, 7 1/4″	$40.00
Bowl, fruit, 5 3/4″	25.00
Bowl, soup, flat, 7 3/4″	55.00
Coffeepot, covered, no lid	140.00
Cream Soup and Saucer	75.00
Cream Soup Saucer	25.00
Cup and Saucer, demitasse, 2 3/8″	45.00
Cup and Saucer, flat, 2 5/8″	45.00
Egg Coddler, 2 1/2″	45.00
Gravy Boat, attached underplate	150.00
Lid, sugar bowl	30.00
Lid, teapot	95.00
Lid, tureen	190.00
Lid, vegetable, octagonal	125.00
Plate, bread and butter	15.00
Plate, dessert, 7 1/4″	20.00
Plate, dinner	45.00
Plate, salad	25.00
Saucer, demitasse	15.00
Saucer, jumbo	30.00
Vegetable, oval, 9 5/8″	90.00

The design known as "Kutani Crane" first appeared in Wedgwood's earliest pattern books as number 1007, suggesting a date of introduction around 1815. The origins of the design are somewhat obscure, but it is most likely that its name derives from seventeenth-century Japanese porcelain from Kutani, the Kaga province.

The Kutani Crane pattern may be found on Queen's Ware, Pearl Ware, and stone china. It has been reintroduced several times with a variety of different decorative finishes. Known as "Bideford" during the nineteenth century, it was at that time a combination print and enamel pattern. Today, it is purely lithograph.

Wedgwood, Kutani Crane, Peony Shape with Leigh cup, Bone China, R4464

Ashtray, round, 4″	$20.00
Ashtray, square, 4″	20.00
Bell	45.00
Bowl, fruit, 5″	35.00
Bowl, soup, flat, 7 7/8″	50.00
Box, covered, heart shape	30.00
Box, covered, round	40.00
Bud Vase, 5 1/2″	40.00
Cachepot	60.00
Cake Plate, square, handled, 11 1/8″	75.00
Chop Plate, 13 1/4″	140.00
Coaster, 4″	17.50
Coffeepot, covered, 8 1/8″	165.00
Cream Soup and Saucer	85.00
Cream Soup Bowl	65.00

Creamer, 2 1/2″	65.00
Creamer, 3 3/4″	65.00
Cup, footed, 2 5/8″	32.50

Wedgwood, Kutani Crane. *Photo courtesy of Wedgwood.*

Cup and Saucer, demitasse, 2 1/4″	50.00	Cigarette Box	60.00
Cup and Saucer, footed, 2 5/8″	35.00	Cigarette Holder	40.00
Gravy Boat Underplate	50.00	Coffeepot, covered	200.00
Jam, covered, no lid	55.00	Compote, 4″	80.00
Lid, teapot	70.00	Cream Soup and Saucer	70.00
Lid, vegetable, round	100.00	Cream Soup Bowl	60.00
Mug, 4 1/8″	40.00	Creamer, 2 3/8″	60.00
Murray Dish, 4 3/8″	80.00	Cup and Saucer, bouillon	50.00
Napkin Ring	22.50	Cup and Saucer, demitasse	45.00
Plate, bread and butter, 6″	15.00	Cup and Saucer, footed, 2 5/8″	50.00
Plate, dessert, 7″	25.00	Lid, coffeepot	100.00
Plate, dinner, 10 3/4″	40.00	Lid, sugar bowl	40.00
Plate, luncheon, 9″	40.00	Lid, teapot	100.00
Plate, salad, 8″	25.00	Lid, vegetable, round	120.00
Plate, torte, 12 5/8″	120.00	Plate, bread and butter, 6 1/8″	15.00
Platter, oval, 14″	140.00	Plate, dessert, 7″	25.00
Platter, oval, 17 1/4″	235.00	Plate, dinner, 10 1/2″	50.00
Posey Pot, 3 5/8″	60.00	Plate, luncheon, 9 1/8″	45.00
Saucer, demitasse	20.00	Plate, salad, 8 3/4″	25.00
Sugar Bowl, covered, 2 3/4″	90.00	Platter, oval, 12 3/4″	140.00
Sugar Bowl, covered, 4 1/8″, no lid	50.00	Salt and Pepper Shakers, pair	110.00
Teapot, covered	160.00	Salt Shaker	55.00
Tray, silver, 5 1/8″	20.00	Saucer	17.50
Trinket Box, covered	50.00	Saucer, demitasse	15.00
Vase, 5″	90.00	Sugar Bowl, covered, 3″	80.00
Vase, 7″	90.00	Sugar Bowl, covered, 3″, no lid	50.00
Vegetable, covered, round	240.00	Vase, 6 1/2″	125.00
Vegetable, oval, 9 3/4″	120.00	Vase, 7 3/4″	125.00
		Vegetable, covered, round	240.00
		Vegetable, oval, 9 3/4″	110.00

**Wedgwood, Lavender on Cream Color,
Plain Edge, Queen's Ware**

Ashtray, 3 3/8″	$20.00
Ashtray, 4″	20.00
Ashtray, 5 5/8″	20.00
Bowl, cranberry, 5″	85.00
Bowl, fruit, 5 1/4″	32.50
Bowl, soup, flat, 8 3/8″	50.00
Cake Plate, square, handled, 10 3/4″	130.00

**Wedgwood, Lavender on Cream Color,
Shell Edge, Queen's Ware**

Ashtray, 3 7/8″	$20.00
Bowl, cereal, coupe, 6 1/4″	40.00
Bowl, fruit, 5 1/8″	32.50
Bowl, soup, flat, 8 1/4″	50.00
Cake Plate, square, handled, 10 7/8″	130.00

Chop Plate, 12 7/8"	190.00
Cream Soup and Saucer	70.00
Cream Soup Bowl	60.00
Cup, demitasse, footed	40.00
Cup and Saucer, bouillon	50.00
Cup and Saucer, demitasse, flat	45.00
Cup and Saucer, demitasse, footed	45.00
Cup and Saucer, footed, 2 5/8"	50.00
Gravy Boat, attached underplate	170.00
Gravy Boat and Underplate	170.00
Lid, vegetable, round	120.00
Plate, bread and butter, 6 1/4"	15.00
Plate, dessert, 7"	25.00
Plate, dinner, 10 3/8"	50.00
Plate, luncheon, 9 1/4"	45.00
Plate, salad, 8 1/4"	25.00
Platter, oval, 14 1/4"	170.00
Platter, oval, 16 3/8"	250.00
Saucer	17.50
Saucer, demitasse	15.00
Sugar Bowl, covered	80.00
Vegetable, covered, round	240.00
Vegetable, oval, 9 3/4"	110.00
Vegetable, oval, 10"	130.00

Wedgwood, Mirabelle, R4537

Bowl, fruit, 5"	$32.50
Bowl, salad, serving, 9 7/8"	200.00
Bowl, soup, flat, 8"	50.00
Bud Vase, 4 7/8"	70.00
Cake Plate, square, handled, 11"	110.00
Chop Plate, 13 1/4"	170.00
Coffeepot, covered	190.00
Cream Soup and Saucer, peony	100.00
Creamer, 4"	60.00
Cup and Saucer, demitasse	45.00
Cup and Saucer, footed, 2 3/4"	55.00
Gravy Boat and Underplate	170.00
Lid, vegetable	125.00
Plate, bread and butter, 6 1/8"	20.00
Plate, dinner, 10 3/4"	50.00
Plate, luncheon, 9"	45.00
Plate, salad, 8 1/8"	30.00
Platter, oval, 14 1/8"	170.00
Platter, oval, 15 1/2"	200.00
Sugar Bowl, covered, 4 1/4"	80.00
Teapot, covered	170.00
Tureen, covered	450.00
Vegetable, covered, round	270.00
Vegetable, oval, 9 3/4"	100.00
Vegetable, oval, 10 1/8"	110.00

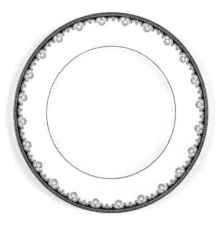

Wedgwood, Medici, R4588

Cup and Saucer, footed, 2 3/4"	$80.00
Plate, bread and butter, 6"	32.50
Plate, dinner, 10 3/4"	75.00
Plate, salad, 8 1/8"	45.00
Sugar Bowl, covered	135.00

Wedgwood, Nantucket

Bowl, cereal, coupe, 7 1/8″	$25.00
Bowl, fruit, 6 1/4″	25.00
Bowl, fruit, serving, 10 1/4″	130.00
Bowl, salad, serving, 8 1/4″	85.00
Bowl, soup, flat, 9″	40.00
Cachepot, 5 1/2″	65.00
Cake Plate, square, handled, 10 1/4″	30.00
Chop Plate, 13 3/8″	90.00
Coffeepot, covered	120.00
Cream Soup and Saucer	60.00
Cream Soup Saucer	17.50
Creamer	45.00
Cup, demitasse	27.50
Cup and Saucer, demitasse	40.00
Cup and Saucer, flat, 2 5/8″	35.00
Gravy Boat and Underplate	105.00
Mug, 3 1/2″	20.00
Plate, bread and butter, 6″	10.00
Plate, dinner, 10 3/4″	27.50
Plate, salad, 8 1/8″	20.00
Platter, oval, 14 1/8″	95.00
Sugar Bowl, covered	50.00
Vegetable, covered, round	185.00
Vegetable, oval, 9 3/4″	80.00

Wedgwood, Napolean Ivy, Traditional Shape, Oven-To-Table

Cream Soup Saucer	$17.50
Cup, demitasse, flat	30.00
Cup and Saucer	40.00
Cup and Saucer, demitasse, footed	35.00
Cup and Saucer, oversized, 2 3/4″	32.50
Lid, coffeepot	50.00
Lid, teapot	50.00
Lid, vegetable	75.00

Plate, bread and butter, 5 3/4″	12.50
Plate, dinner, 10″	32.50
Plate, salad	15.00
Saucer	12.50
Saucer, demitasse	10.00
Saucer, oversized	12.50

Wedgwood, Osborne, R4699

Bowl, cereal, coupe, 6″	$50.00
Bowl, salad, serving, 8″	100.00
Bowl, soup, flat, 8″	50.00
Chop Plate, 13 3/8″	150.00
Coffeepot, covered	165.00
Cream Soup and Saucer	80.00
Cream Soup Saucer	25.00
Creamer	65.00
Creamer, mini	40.00
Cup, demitasse, 2 1/4″	35.00
Cup and Saucer, demitasse, 2 1/4″	55.00
Cup and Saucer, footed, 2 5/8″	50.00
Gravy Boat and Underplate	160.00
Plate, bread and butter, 6″	15.00
Plate, dessert, 7″	20.00
Plate, dinner, 10 7/8″	40.00
Plate, luncheon, 9″	45.00

Plate, salad, 8 1/8″	25.00		Plate, luncheon, 9″	30.00
Plate, torte, 12 1/2″	165.00		Plate, salad, 8″	25.00
Platter, oval, 14 1/8″	140.00		Platter, oval, 14 1/8″	140.00
Platter, oval, 15 1/2″	170.00		Platter, oval, 15 3/4″	170.00
Salt and Pepper Shakers, pair	100.00		Sugar Bowl, covered, 2 3/4″	80.00
Saucer, demitasse	20.00		Sugar Bowl, covered, 4 1/8″	80.00
Sugar Bowl, covered	165.00		Tureen, covered	405.00
Sugar Bowl, covered, mini	70.00		Vegetable, covered, round	230.00
Teapot, covered	165.00		Vegetable, oval, 9 3/4″	110.00
Teapot, covered, mini	110.00			
Tray, sandwich	115.00			
Tureen, covered	535.00			
Vegetable, covered, round	240.00			
Vegetable, oval, 10 1/8″	100.00			

Wedgwood, Patrician, Patrician Shape, plain

Bowl, cereal, coupe, 6 1/2″	$30.00
Bowl, fruit, 5 1/2″	25.00
Bowl, soup, flat, 8 3/8″	55.00
Coffeepot, covered	200.00
Cream Soup and Saucer	75.00
Cream Soup Saucer	22.50
Creamer, 3 5/8″	50.00
Cup and Saucer, demitasse	40.00
Cup and Saucer, footed, 2 1/2″	40.00
Eggcup, double, 4 1/8″	50.00
Gravy Boat, attached underplate	140.00
Lid, teapot	100.00
Lid, vegetable, round, footed	115.00
Plate, bread and butter, 6 1/2″	15.00
Plate, dinner, 10 1/2″	35.00
Plate, luncheon, 9 1/4″	35.00
Plate, salad, 8 3/8″	20.00
Platter, oval, 13 7/8″	150.00
Platter, oval, 16 1/8″	180.00
Platter, oval, 18 3/8″	220.00
Saucer	12.50
Saucer, 2 1/2″	12.50
Saucer, demitasse	12.50
Sugar Bowl, covered	70.00
Sugar Bowl, covered, no lid	50.00
Vegetable, covered, round, footed	230.00
Vegetable, oval, 10 1/2″	90.00

Wedgwood, Palatia, gold trim, 4700

Bowl, cereal, coupe, 6 1/8″	$35.00
Bowl, fruit, 5″	32.50
Bowl, salad, serving, 8″	135.00
Bowl, soup, flat, 8″	50.00
Cake Plate, square, handled, 11″	70.00
Chop Plate, 13 3/8″	150.00
Coffeepot, covered	160.00
Cream Soup and Saucer	80.00
Creamer, 2 1/2″	60.00
Creamer, 3 3/4″	60.00
Cup, demitasse, 2 1/4″	30.00
Cup, footed, 2 5/8″	30.00
Cup and Saucer, demitasse, 2 1/4″	45.00
Cup and Saucer, footed, 2 5/8″	40.00
Gravy Boat and Underplate	155.00
Lid, sugar bowl, 2 3/4″	40.00
Lid, teapot	160.00
Lid, vegetable	80.00
Mug, 3 3/8″	50.00
Plate, bread and butter, 6″	15.00
Plate, dessert, 7″	30.00
Plate, dinner, 10 3/4″	35.00

Wedgwood, Quince, fruits, Oven-To-Table

Baker, rectangular, 10 $\frac{1}{2}$″	$200.00
Bowl, soup, coupe, 7 $\frac{3}{8}$″	50.00
Casserole, covered, oval, 9 $\frac{1}{4}$″	210.00
Casserole, covered, oval, 9 $\frac{1}{4}$″, no lid	170.00
Casserole, covered, round, 6 $\frac{1}{4}$″	200.00
Casserole, covered, round, 6 $\frac{1}{4}$″, no lid	160.00
Casserole, covered, round, 7 $\frac{1}{4}$″	210.00
Casserole, individual, 4 $\frac{1}{8}$″	60.00
Coffeepot, covered, 8″	160.00
Creamer, 2 $\frac{1}{4}$″	45.00
Creamer, 4″	45.00
Cup and Saucer, flat, 2 $\frac{3}{4}$″	40.00
Egg Coddler, 3 $\frac{1}{4}$″	40.00
Gravy Boat and Underplate	130.00
Gravy Boat Underplate	45.00
Lid, casserole, individual, 4 $\frac{1}{8}$″	30.00
Lid, casserole, round, 6 $\frac{1}{4}$″	100.00
Lid, coffeepot, 8″	80.00
Mustard	60.00
Plate, bread and butter, 6 $\frac{3}{8}$″	17.50
Plate, dinner	45.00
Plate, salad	27.50
Platter, oval, 13 $\frac{3}{8}$″	140.00
Quiche Dish, 7 $\frac{5}{8}$″	70.00
Roaster, narrow, 10 $\frac{1}{2}$″	90.00
Salt and Pepper Shakers, pair	90.00
Saucer, 2 $\frac{3}{4}$″	12.50
Soufflé, 7 $\frac{1}{2}$″	115.00
Sugar Bowl, covered	60.00
Tray, hors d'oeuvre, 6 $\frac{1}{2}$″	50.00
Vegetable, oval, 9 $\frac{3}{8}$″	85.00

Wedgwood, Richmond, Catherine Shape, Queen's Ware

Bowl, soup, flat, 8 $\frac{1}{8}$″	$50.00
Chop Plate, 12 $\frac{1}{2}$″	150.00
Coffeepot, covered	170.00
Cream Soup and Saucer	70.00
Cream Soup Saucer	25.00
Creamer	55.00
Cup, demitasse	40.00
Cup and Saucer, demitasse	45.00
Cup and Saucer, footed, 2 $\frac{3}{8}$″	45.00
Gravy Boat, attached underplate	140.00
Gravy Boat and Underplate	140.00
Jam, covered, no lid	60.00
Plate, bread and butter, 6 $\frac{1}{4}$″	15.00
Plate, dinner, 10″	45.00
Plate, luncheon, 9 $\frac{3}{8}$″	35.00
Plate, salad, 8 $\frac{1}{4}$″	25.00
Platter, oval, 11 $\frac{3}{4}$″	100.00
Platter, oval, 14″	130.00
Platter, oval, 15 $\frac{7}{8}$″	170.00
Saucer	15.00
Sugar Bowl, covered	70.00
Sugar Bowl, covered, no lid	50.00
Teapot, covered	170.00
Vegetable, covered, round	200.00
Vegetable, oval, 9 $\frac{7}{8}$″	80.00

Wedgwood, Rosedale, R4665

Cream Soup and Saucer	$90.00
Cream Soup Bowl	80.00
Creamer	70.00
Cup, footed, 2 5/8″	50.00
Cup and Saucer, demitasse	55.00
Cup and Saucer, footed, 2 5/8″	55.00
Gravy Boat and Underplate	170.00
Gravy Boat Underplate	55.00
Lid, coffeepot	115.00
Plate, bread and butter, 6 1/8″	22.50
Plate, dinner	55.00
Plate, salad, 8 1/4″	32.50
Saucer, demitasse	17.50
Sugar Bowl, covered	90.00

Wedgwood, Runnymede Dark Blue, Peony Shape with Leigh cup, Bone China

Bowl, cereal, coupe, 6″	$75.00
Bowl, fruit, 5″	60.00
Bowl, salad, serving, 9 3/4″	195.00
Bowl, soup, flat, 8 7/8″	75.00
Cake Plate, square, handled, 11″	140.00
Chop Plate, 13 1/2″	170.00
Coffeepot, covered	240.00

Coffeepot, covered, no lid	170.00
Cream Soup and Saucer	125.00
Cream Soup Bowl	95.00
Creamer, 2 3/8″	70.00
Cup, demitasse	45.00
Cup and Saucer, demitasse	65.00
Cup and Saucer, footed, 2 5/8″	45.00
Gravy Boat and Underplate	220.00
Mug, 3 3/8″	40.00
Plate, bread and butter, 6″	17.50
Plate, dessert, 7″	30.00
Plate, dinner, 10 3/4″	45.00
Plate, salad, 8 1/8″	25.00
Platter, oval, 14 1/8″	160.00
Platter, oval, 15 3/8″	250.00
Tureen, covered	810.00
Tureen Underplate	195.00
Vegetable, covered, round	310.00
Vegetable, oval, 9 7/8″	150.00

Wedgwood, Silver Ermine, Contour Shape, Bone China, platinum trim, R4452

Bowl, fruit, 5″	$32.50
Bowl, soup, flat, 8 1/8″	55.00
Cream Soup and Saucer	90.00
Creamer	60.00
Cup, demitasse, 2 3/8″	40.00
Cup, footed, 3″	45.00
Cup and Saucer, demitasse, 2 3/8″	45.00
Cup and Saucer, footed, 3″	50.00
Lid, coffeepot	95.00
Lid, vegetable	125.00
Plate, bread and butter, 6 1/8″	20.00
Plate, dinner	50.00
Plate, luncheon, 9″	40.00
Plate, salad, 8 1/8″	27.50
Platter, oval, 13 7/8″	180.00
Platter, oval, 15 1/2″	200.00

Sugar Bowl, covered	80.00
Sugar Bowl, covered, no lid	55.00
Teapot, covered	190.00

Wedgwood, Strawberry Hill

Bowl, fruit, 5 1/8″	$50.00
Cake Plate, 9 1/2″	160.00
Coffeepot, covered	250.00
Cream Soup and Saucer	120.00
Creamer	90.00
Cup and Saucer, demitasse	70.00
Cup and Saucer, footed, 2 5/8″	70.00
Gravy Boat, attached underplate	250.00
Gravy Boat and Underplate	250.00
Gravy Boat Underplate	85.00
Lid, coffeepot	125.00
Plate, bread and butter, 6″	25.00
Plate, dinner	80.00
Plate, luncheon, 9″	70.00
Plate, salad, 8 1/8″	40.00
Platter, oval, 13 3/4″	200.00
Platter, oval, 15 1/4″	260.00
Sugar Bowl, covered	120.00
Sugar Bowl, covered, no lid	90.00
Vegetable, covered, round	350.00
Vegetable, oval, 10 ″	160.00

Wedgwood, Swallow, Contour Shape, Bone China

Cream Soup Saucer	$55.00
Creamer	130.00
Cup, demitasse	80.00
Cup, footed, 3 1/8″	70.00
Cup and Saucer, demitasse	100.00
Cup and Saucer, footed, 3 1/8″	80.00
Lid, coffeepot	150.00
Lid, sugar bowl	90.00

Plate, bread and butter, 6 1/8″	40.00
Plate, dessert, 7″	50.00
Plate, dinner	95.00
Plate, salad, 8 1/8″	55.00
Platter, oval, 14″	300.00
Platter, oval, 15 1/2″	400.00
Sugar Bowl, covered	170.00

Wedgwood, Wellesley, off white

Bowl, fruit, 5 1/2″	$20.00
Bowl, fruit, serving, 9 1/8″	150.00
Bowl, soup, flat, 8 5/8″	45.00
Cake Plate, square, handled, 11 3/8″	90.00
Chop Plate, 13″	130.00
Coffeepot, covered	190.00
Cream Soup and Saucer, 5 5/8″	60.00
Cream Soup Bowl, 5 5/8″	50.00
Cream Soup Saucer	20.00
Creamer, 3 1/2″	50.00
Cup, demitasse	32.50
Cup and Saucer, demitasse	35.00
Cup and Saucer, footed, 2 3/4″	40.00
Eggcup, double, 4″	35.00
Gravy Boat, attached underplate	120.00
Gravy Boat and Underplate	120.00
Lid, muffin dish	90.00

Lid, teapot	95.00
Plate, bread and butter, 6 3/4″	15.00
Plate, dessert, 7 1/2″	20.00
Plate, dinner, 10 3/4″	45.00
Plate, luncheon, 9 1/2	35.00
Plate, salad, 8 1/2″	20.00
Platter, oval, 12″	110.00
Platter, oval, 13 3/4″	120.00
Platter, oval, 18 1/8″	200.00
Saucer	15.00
Sugar Bowl, covered, 3 1/2″	60.00
Vegetable, covered, round	200.00
Vegetable, oval, 10 5/8″	90.00

Wedgwood, White Dolphins, blue

Coffeepot, covered	$200.00
Cream Soup and Saucer	100.00
Cream Soup Saucer	35.00
Creamer, 2 1/2″	70.00
Creamer, 3 3/4″	70.00
Cup, demitasse	45.00
Cup, footed, 2 3/4″	55.00
Cup and Saucer, demitasse	50.00
Cup and Saucer, footed, 2 3/4″	60.00
Plate, bread and butter, 6″	25.00
Plate, dinner, 10 3/4″	60.00
Plate, luncheon, 9″	45.00
Plate, salad, 8 1/8″	32.50
Platter, oval, 14″	180.00
Platter, oval, 15 1/4″	200.00
Sugar Bowl, covered, 2 3/4″	100.00
Sugar Bowl, covered, 4 1/4″	100.00
Vegetable, oval, 10 3/4″	160.00

Wedgwood, Westbury, Leigh Shape, Bone China, green, platinum trim

Bowl, fruit, 5″	$27.50
Bowl, soup, flat, 8″	50.00
Coffeepot, covered	180.00
Cream Soup and Saucer	70.00
Creamer, 3″	50.00
Cup, demitasse, 2 1/4″	40.00
Cup, footed, 2 5/8″	40.00
Cup and Saucer, demitasse, 2 1/4″	40.00
Cup and Saucer, footed, 2 5/8″	40.00
Gravy Boat	140.00
Plate, bread and butter, 6″	15.00
Plate, dinner, 10 3/4″	40.00
Plate, luncheon, 9″	40.00
Plate, salad, 8 1/8″	25.00
Platter, oval, 13 3/4″	140.00
Platter, oval, 14″	160.00
Platter, oval, 15 3/8″	170.00
Sugar Bowl, covered, 3 1/4″	70.00
Sugar Bowl, covered, 3 1/4″, no lid	50.00
Teapot, covered	180.00
Vegetable, covered, round	200.00
Vegetable, oval, 10″	110.00
Vegetable, round, 8″	85.00

Wedgwood, Wild Oats

Ashtray, 4 1/2″	$15.00
Bowl, cereal, coupe, 6 1/8″	30.00

Bowl, fruit, 5″	25.00	Lid, teapot	100.00
Bowl, soup, coupe, 7 7/8″	40.00	Lid, vegetable, oval	75.00
Chop Plate, 13 1/2″	120.00	Plate, bread and butter, 6″	15.00
Cigarette Box	40.00	Plate, dinner, 10 1/4″	40.00
Coffeepot, covered	200.00	Plate, luncheon, 9″	30.00
Coffeepot, covered, mini	140.00	Plate, salad, 8″	22.50
Cream Soup and Saucer	60.00	Platter, oval, 13 3/4″	100.00
Cream Soup Saucer	20.00	Platter, oval, 15 1/4″	140.00
Creamer	40.00	Saucer	15.00
Cup, demitasse	35.00	Sugar Bowl, covered, flat	60.00
Cup and Saucer, demitasse	40.00	Sugar Bowl, open	40.00
Cup and Saucer, flat, 2″	40.00	Teapot, covered	200.00
Gravy Boat, attached underplate	130.00	Vegetable, covered, oval	150.00
Gravy Boat and Underplate	130.00	Vegetable, covered, round	150.00
Lid, cigarette box	20.00	Vegetable, oval, 10″	90.00

Strawberries were featured in the first pattern books of Josiah Wedgwood, dating back to 1760. The Wild Strawberry pattern was introduced in 1965.

Wedgwood, Wild Strawberry, Peony Shape, Bone China

Ashtray, 4″	$20.00
Bonbon, 8 7/8″	70.00
Bowl, cereal, coupe, 6 1/8″	35.00
Bowl, fruit, 5″	17.50
Bowl, fruit, serving, 9 3/4″	150.00
Bowl, salad, serving, 8″	110.00
Bowl, soup, flat, 8″	50.00
Box, covered, round, 1 1/4″	40.00
Bud Vase, 4″	40.00
Bud Vase, 5 1/2″	40.00
Candlestick, single light, 1 1/2″	35.00
Candy Jar, covered	70.00
Casserole, individual, 4 1/4″	25.00
Chop Plate, 13 1/2″	120.00
Chop Plate, square, 11″	120.00
Cigarette Holder	40.00
Coaster, 4″	20.00
Coffeepot, covered	160.00
Cream Soup and Saucer	75.00
Cream Soup Bowl	55.00
Creamer, 2 3/8″	60.00
Cup and Saucer, demitasse, 2 1/4″	40.00
Cup and Saucer, footed, 2 1/4″	40.00
Egg Box, covered, 4″	50.00
Ginger Jar, covered, 9 1/4″	195.00
Gravy Boat	110.00

Gravy Boat, attached underplate	150.00
Gravy Boat and Underplate	150.00
Gravy Boat Underplate	50.00
Mug, 3 1/2″	50.00
Murray Dish	85.00
Mustard, oven	75.00
Plate, bread and butter, 6″	15.00
Plate, dessert, 7″	22.50
Plate, dinner, 10 5/8″	35.00
Plate, luncheon, 9″	35.00
Plate, salad, 8 1/8″	22.50
Plate, torte, 12 3/4″	155.00
Platter, oval, 13 3/8″	115.00
Platter, oval, 14″	140.00
Platter, oval, 15 1/2″	170.00
Platter, oval, 17 1/4″	185.00
Posey Pot, 3 1/2″	50.00
Ramekin, 2″	15.00
Saucer	15.00
Saucer, demitasse	15.00
Soufflé, 6 3/4″	60.00
Sugar Bowl, covered	85.00
Sugar Bowl, open	60.00
Teapot, covered	160.00
Tray, hors d'oeuvre, 6 3/8″	35.00

Wedgwood, Wild Strawberry. *Photo courtesy of Wedgwood.*

Tray, silver, 4 1/2″	35.00
Tray, silver, 5 1/8″	35.00
Tureen, covered	405.00
Vase, 7″	100.00
Vase, 8 1/4″	100.00
Vase, globe, 8″	60.00
Vegetable, covered, round	230.00
Vegetable, oval, 10 1/4″	110.00

Tureen covered	500.00
Vegetable, oval, 9 3/4″	80.00
Vegetable, oval, 10″	90.00

Wedgwood, Williamsburg Potpourri, Queen's Shape, Queen's Ware

Bowl, cereal, coupe, 6 1/4″	$20.00
Bowl, fruit, 5 1/4″	15.00
Bowl, salad, serving, 9 3/8″	95.00
Bowl, soup, flat, 8 1/8″	20.00
Cake Plate, square, handled, 10 3/8″	35.00
Coffeepot, covered	90.00
Creamer	27.50
Cup, footed, 2 7/8″	12.50
Cup and Saucer, demitasse	20.00
Cup and Saucer, footed, 2 7/8″	17.50
Gravy Boat	65.00
Gravy Boat and Underplate	80.00
Gravy Boat Underplate	25.00
Lid, vegetable	70.00
Plate, bread and butter, 6 5/8″	7.50
Plate, dinner, 10 1/2″	17.50
Plate, salad, 8 1/4″	10.00
Platter, oval, 13 5/8″	60.00
Platter, oval, 15 5/8″	70.00
Saucer	7.50
Sugar Bowl, covered	45.00
Sugar Bowl, covered, no lid	32.50
Teapot, covered	90.00
Vegetable, covered, round	135.00
Vegetable, oval, 9 3/4″	40.00
Vegetable, round, 8 1/2″	75.00

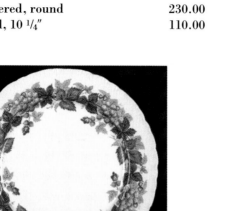

Wedgwood, Wildbriar

Bowl, fruit, 5″	$25.00
Bowl, soup, flat, 8 1/4″	40.00
Chop Plate, 12 3/4″	140.00
Coffeepot, covered	170.00
Cream Soup and Saucer	70.00
Cream Soup Saucer	20.00
Creamer	50.00
Cup and Saucer, demitasse	40.00
Cup and Saucer, flat, 2 1/8″	40.00
Gravy Boat, attached underplate	130.00
Pitcher, 4 1/4″	130.00
Plate, bread and butter, 6 3/8″	15.00
Plate, dinner, 10 3/8″	40.00
Plate, luncheon, 9″	35.00
Plate, salad, 8 1/4″	22.50
Platter, oval, 11 1/2″	100.00
Platter, oval, 14 1/2″	130.00
Platter, oval, 16 1/2″	180.00
Platter, oval, 17 3/4″	200.00
Sauce Boat, 5 1/8″	140.00
Saucer	15.00
Sugar Bowl, covered	60.00

III

APPENDIX:
THE TOP PATTERNS

Top 25 China Patterns (Alphabetically)

Apple by Franciscan (American Backstamp)
Appleblossom by Haviland (New York)
Autumn by Lenox #S1 (Newer, Gold Backstamp)
Azalea by Noritake #19322–252622
Blue Garland by Johann Haviland (Bavarian
  Backstamp)
Botanic Garden by Portmeirion
Brookdale by Lenox #H500
Buttercup by Spode #2/7873 (Older Backstamp)
Christmas Tree by Spode #S3324 (Green Trim)
Desert Rose by Franciscan (USA Backstamp)
Eternal by Lenox
Garden Club by Mikasa/Narumi #EC400
Holiday by Lenox
Ivy by Franciscan
Lace Point by Lenox
Moonspun by Lenox
Old Britain Castles—Pink by Johnson Brothers
Old Country Roses by Royal Albert
Patrician—Plain by Wedgwood
Rosalinde by Haviland (New York, Louis XV)
Rose Chintz—Pink by Johnson Brothers
Savannah by Noritake #2031 (Rim Shape/
  Platinum Trim)
Sunnyvale by Castleton
Weatherly by Lenox #D517
Windsong by Lenox

Top 26–50 China Patterns (Alphabetically)

Adagio by Noritake #7237
America by Pfaltzgraff
Ancestral—Rust/Pink/Aqua by Minton #S376
Blue Danube by Japan
Calico—Blue by Staffordshire
California Provincial by Metlox
Castle Garden by Lenox
Charleston by Lenox
Charnwood by Wedgwood #WD3984
Colburn by Noritake #6107
Currier & Ives—Blue by Royal China
Desert Rose by Franciscan (England Backstamp)
Fairmont by Noritake #6102 (Platinum Trim)
Friendly Village by Johnson Brothers
Heather by Noritake #7548
Indies—Blue by Johnson Brothers
Kingsley by Lenox #X445
Lexington by Oxford—Lenox
Margaux by Mikasa #D1006, Tivoli
Montclair by Lenox #B501
Moss Rose by Rosenthal (Pompadour Shape)
Quince by Wedgwood
Rhodora by Lenox #P471
Terrace Blossoms by International
White and Gold by Noritake

Top 51–100 China Patterns (Alphabetically)

Ariana by Gorham China
Belle Fleur by Wedgwood #R4356
Belvidere by Lenox #S314
Billingsley Rose—Pink by Spode #2/8867 (Older Backstamp)
Buckingham by Noritake #6438
Carlyle by Royal Doulton #H5018
Coaching Scenes—Blue by Johnson Brothers
Coronet by Royal Doulton #H4947
Cream Color on Cream Color by Wedgwood
  (Shell Edge)
Cream Color on Lavender by Wedgwood
  (Plain Edge)
Cream Color on Lavender by Wedgwood
  (Shell Edge)
Dewdrops by Lenox
Evesham Gold by Royal Worcester
Fiesta—Cobalt Blue by Homer Laughlin (Older)
Fiesta—Red by Homer Laughlin (Older)
Fiesta—Yellow by Homer Laughlin (Older)
Flying Cloud—Rust by Wedgwood
Gallery by Noritake #7246
Glenwood by Noritake #5770/5770M
Hearts & Flowers by Johnson Brothers
Lace by Castleton
Lenox Rose by Lenox #J300
Liberty Blue by Staffordshire
Madeira by Franciscan
Miramont by Royal Doulton #TC1022
Morning Blossom by Lenox
October by Franciscan
Olympia—Platinum by Lenox #X303P
Pembroke—Gold Trim by Aynsley
Poppies on Blue by Lenox (For The Blue)
Ranier by Noritake #6909
Revere by Hutschenreuther/Pasco #8045
Rosalinde by Haviland (France)
Rothschild by Noritake #7293
Runnymede—Blue by Wedgwood #W4472
Sculptured Grape by Metlox/Poppytrail
Shenandoah by Noritake #9729
Sherwood by Syracuse
Singapore Bird by Adams (Newer Backstamp)
Snow Lily by Lenox
Solitaire by Lenox
Somerset by Noritake #5317
Springdale by Lenox (Platinum Trim)
Tulane by Noritake #7562
Vista—Brown by Mason's
Wheat by Lenox #R442
Whitebrook by Noritake #6441
Whitehall by Noritake #6115
Whole Wheat by Mikasa #E8000/DX100
Willow Blue by Johnson Brothers

Top 101–200 China Patterns (Alphabetically)

Acapulco by Villeroy/Boch (Older)
Affection by Noritake #7192
Amherst by Wedgwood (Platinum Trim)
Anticipation by Noritake #2963
Apple by Franciscan (England Backstamp)
Asian Song by Noritake #7151
Athena by Johnson Brothers
Autumn Leaf by Hall
Barrymore by Noritake #9737
Blue Haven by Noritake #9004
Blue Hill by Noritake #2482
Blue Nordic by J. & G. Meakin
Blue Tree by Lenox #B300 (Gold Backstamp)

Bryn Mawr by Oxford—Lenox
Burgundy by Royal Doulton (Platinum Trim)
Buttercup by Spoke #2/7873 (Newer Backstamp)
Christmas Heirloom by Pfaltzgraff
Coralbel by Syracuse
Cornwall by Royal Doulton #LS1015 (Rim Shape, Double
    Green Trim)
Cowslip by Spode #S713
Crest by Noritake (Platinum Trim)
Crestmont by Noritake #6013
Cretan by Lenox #0316
Delaware by Haviland
Dolly Madison by Castleton
Dresden Rose by Mikasa/Narumi #L9009
Edgewood by Noritake #5807
Edme by Wedgwood
Empress Dresden Flowers by Schumann/Bavaria (Scal-
    loped)
English Chippendale—Red by Johnson Brothers
English Renaissance by Royal Doulton #H4972
Essex Maroon—Smooth by Lenox #0351R
Fiesta—Chartreuse by Homer Laughlin (Older)
Fiesta—Cream (Old Ivory) by Homer Laughlin (Older)
Fiesta—Dark Green by Homer Laughlin (Older)
Fiesta—Light Green by Homer Laughlin (Older)
Fiesta—Medium Green by Homer Laughlin (Older)
Fiesta—Rose by Homer Laughlin (Older)
Fiesta—Turquoise by Homer Laughlin (Older)
Fireglow by Royal Doulton #TC1080
Florentine Gold by Wedgwood
Fresh Fruit by Franciscan
Gloria by Castleton
Golden Wreath by Lenox #0313
Hacienda Gold by Franciscan
Harvest by Lenox #R441
Heartland by International #SY7774
Heirloom by Pfaltzgraff
Henley by Minton
Homecoming by Noritake #9002
Imperial by Lenox #P338
Indian Tree—Orange/Rust by Spode
Just Flowers by Mikasa/Narumi #A4182
Kilkee Keltcraft by Noritake #9109
Kutani Crane by Wedgwood #R4464

Lavender on Cream Color by Wedgwood (Shell Edge)
Lorelei by Noritake #7541
Magnificence by Noritake #9736
Marywood by Noritake #2181/2556
Mayflower by Spode #2/8772
Medici by Wedgwood #R4588
Merriment by Lenox
Merry Christmas by Johnson Brothers
Ming Rose by Coalport
Mirano by Noritake #6878
Morning Jewel by Noritake #2767
Moss Rose by Johann Haviland
Musette by Lenox #F507
Noblesse by Lenox
Painted Desert by Noritake #8603
Pasadena by Noritake #6311
Pine by Lenox #W331
Princess by Lenox #X516
Princeton by Noritake
Randolph by Noritake #9721
Reina by Noritake #6450Q/6450
Renaissance Platinum by Franciscan
Repertoire by Lenox
Richelieu by Hutschenreuther/Pasco #7658
Rosay by Noritake #6216
Rosebud Chintz by Spode #2/8401
Rutledge by Lenox #P303
Sculptured Daisy by Metlox/Poppytrail
Singapore Bird by Adams (Older Backstamp)
Stansbury by Syracuse
Strawberry Fair by Johnson Brothers
Suzanne by Syracuse
Tango by Mikasa/Narumi #EJ702
Temptation by Noritake #2752
Tonkin by Royal Doulton #TC1107
Tuxedo by Lenox #J33 (Gold Backstamp)
Veruschka by Adams
Victoria by Syracuse
Village by Pfaltzgraff
Wedding Ring by Syracuse
Westwind by Lenox #X407
Wicker Dale by Spode #2/4088/C1891
Wild Oats by Wedgwood
Williamsburg Potpourri by Wedgwood

General References

Bagdade, Susan and Al. *Warman's American Pottery and Porcelain*. Radnor, PA: Wallace-Homestead Books, 1994.

Bagdade, Susan and Al. *Warman's English & Continental Pottery & Porcelain*. 2nd ed. Radnor, PA: Wallace-Homestead Books, 1991.

Chefetz, Sheila. *Antiques for the Table: A Complete Guide to Dining Room Accessories for Collecting and Entertaining*. New York: Viking Studio Books, 1993.

Chipman, Jack. *Collector's Encyclopedia of California Pottery*. Paducah, KY: Collector Books, 1992.

Cooper, Emmanuel. *A History of World Pottery*. Radnor, PA: Chilton Trade Book Publishing, 1972.

Cunningham, Jo. *The Best of Collectible Dinnerware*. Atglen, PA: Schiffer Publishing, 1995.

Cunningham, Jo. *The Collector's Encyclopedia of American Dinnerware*. Paducah, KY: Collector Books, 1982.

Derwich, Jenny B., and Mary Latos. *Dictionary Guide to United States Pottery & Porcelain: 19th & 20th Century*. Franklin, MI: Jenstan, 1984.

Eberle, Linda, and Susan Scott. *The Charlton Standard Catalogue of Chintz*. 1st ed. Toronto, Ontario, Canada: Charlton, 1996.

Field, Rachael. *MacDonald Guide to Buying Antique Pottery & Porcelain*. Radnor, PA: Wallace-Homestead Books, 1987.

Godden, Geoffrey. *Godden's Guide to English Porcelain*. Radnor, PA: Wallace-Homestead Books, 1992.

Haggar, Reginald G. *The Concise Encyclopedia of Continental Pottery and Porcelain*. 2 vol. New York: Hawthorn Books, 1960.

Jasper, Joanne. *Turn of the Century American Dinnerware: 1880s to 1920s*. Paducah, KY: Collector Books, 1996.

Lehner, Lois. *Complete Book of American Kitchen and Dinner Wares*. Des Moines, IA: Wallace-Homestead Books, 1980.

Mankowitz, Wolf, and Reginald G. Haggar. *The Concise Encyclopedia of English Pottery and Porcelain*. New York: Hawthorn Books, n.d.

Replacements, Ltd. *China Identification Kit*. Greensboro, NC: Replacements, 1996.

Marks References

Chaffers, William. *Marks & Monograms on European and Oriental Pottery and Porcelain*. 14th rev. ed. Los Angeles: Borden Publishing, n.d.

Danckert, Ludwig. *Directory of European Porcelain: Marks, Makers and Factories*. 4th ed. 1981. Reprint. Colchester, Essex, UK: N. A. G. Press, 1990.

Gates, William C., Jr., and Dana E. Ormerod. *The East Liverpool, Ohio, Pottery District: Identification of Manufacturers and Marks*. Historical Archaeology, Vol. 16, Nos. 1–2. California, PA: The Society for Historical Archaeology, 1982.

Godden, Geoffrey A. *Encyclopaedia of British Pottery and Porcelain Marks*. Exton, PA: Schiffer Publishing, 1964.

Kovel, Ralph and Terry. *Kovel's New Dictionary of Marks*. New York: Crown Publishers, 1986.

Lehner, Lois. *Lehner's Encyclopedia of U. S. Marks on Pottery, Porcelain & Clay*. Paducah, KY: Collector Books, 1988.

Röntgen, Robert E. *Marks on German, Bohemian and Austrian Porcelain: 1710 to the Present*. Exton, PA: Schiffer Publishing, 1981.

Company Histories

Aupperle, Eldon R. *A Collector's Guide for Currier & Ives Dinnerware by Royal China Company*. Toulon, IL: Eldon R. Aupperle, 1996.

Buten, Harry M. *Wedgwood ABC But Not Middle E*. Merion, PA: Buten Museum of Wedgwood, 1964.

Enge, Delleen. *Franciscan*. Ojai, CA: Delleen Enge, 1992.

Enge, Delleen. *Franciscan Ware*. Paducah, KY: Collector Books, 1981.

Finegan, Mary J. *Johnson Brothers Dinnerware: Pattern Directory & Price Guide*. Boone, NC: Marfine Antiques, 1993.

Gibbs, Carl, Jr. *Collector's Encyclopedia of Metlox Potteries: Identification and Values*. Paducah, KY: Collector Books, 1995.

Jacobson, Gertrude Tatnall. *Haviland China: A Pattern Identification Guide*. 2 vol. Des Moines, IA: Wallace-Homestead Books, 1979.

Jasper, Joanne. *The Collector's Encyclopedia of Homer Laughlin China: Reference & Value Guide*. Paducah, KY: Collector Books, 1993.

Morin, Richard E. *Lenox Collectibles*. Tulsa, OK: Sixty-Ninth Street Zoo, 1993.

Villa Terrace Decorative Arts Museum. *Celebrating 150 Years of Haviland China 1842–1992*. Milwaukee, WI: Villa Terrace Decorative Arts Museum, 1992. [Limited edition catalog from exhibition at Villa Terrace Decorative Arts Museum held June 28–October 4, 1992.]

Whitmyer, Margaret and Ken. *The Collector's Encyclopedia of Hall China*. 2nd ed. Paducah, KY: Collector Books, 1994.

Williams, Peter. *Wedgwood: A Collector's Guide*. Radnor, PA: Wallace-Homestead Books, 1992.

REPLACEMENTS, LTD.

The World's Largest Retailer of Discontinued and Active China, Crystal, Flatware and Collectibles

In 1981, Bob Page, an accountant-turned-flea-marketer, founded Replacements, Ltd. Since then, the company's growth and success can only be described as phenomenal.

Today, Replacements, Ltd. locates hard-to-find pieces in over 80,000 patterns - some of which have not been produced for more than 100 years. Now serving over 2 million customers, with an inventory of 4 million pieces, they mail up to 250,000 inventory listings weekly to customers seeking additional pieces in their patterns.

The concept for Replacements, Ltd. originated in the late 1970's when Page, then an auditor for the state of North Carolina, started spending his weekends combing flea markets buying china and crystal. Before long, he was filling requests from customers to find pieces they could not locate.

"I was buying and selling pieces primarily as a diversion," Page explains. "Back when I was an auditor, no one was ever happy to see me. And, quite frankly, I wasn't thrilled about being there either."

Page began placing small ads in shelter publications and started building a file of potential customers. Soon, his inventory outgrew his attic, where he had been storing the pieces, and it was time to make a change. "I reached the point where I was spending more time with dishes than auditing," Page says. "I'd be up until one or two o'clock in the morning. Finally, I took the big step: I quit my auditing job and hired one part-time assistant. Today I'm having so much fun, I often have to remind myself what day of the week it is!"

Replacements, Ltd. continued to grow quickly. In fact, in 1986, Inc. Magazine ranked Replacements, Ltd. 81st on its list of fastest-growing independently-owned companies in the U.S. "Our growth has been incredible," says Page, who was named 1991 North Carolina Entrepreneur of the Year. "I had no idea of the potential when I started out."

Clear standards of high quality merchandise and the highest possible levels of customer service are the cornerstones of the business, resulting in a shopping experience unparalleled in today's marketplace. Page also attributes much of the success of Replacements, Ltd. to a network of nearly 1,500 dedicated suppliers from all around the U.S. The company currently employs about 500 people in an expanded 225,000 square foot facility (the size of four football fields).

Another major contributor to the company's fast growth and top-level customer service is the extensive computer system used to keep track of the inventory. This state-of-the-art system also maintains customer files, including requests for specific pieces in their patterns. It is maintained by a full-time staff of over 20 people and is constantly upgraded to ensure customers receive the information they desire quickly and accurately.

For those who are unsure of the name and/or manufacturer

Greensboro, North Carolina Facility

Some of the 50,000 shelves in the 225,000 square foot warehouse

of their patterns, Replacements, Ltd. also offers a free pattern identification service. In addition, numerous books and publications focusing on pattern identification have been published by Replacements, Ltd. for both suppliers and individuals.

Replacements, Ltd. receives countless phone calls and letters from its many satisfied customers. Some need to replace broken or lost items while others want to supplement the sets they have had for years. A constant in the varied subjects customers write about is their long and fruitless search - a search that ended when they learned what Replacements, Ltd. could offer. "Since many patterns are family heirlooms that have been handed down from generation to generation, most customers are sentimental about replacing broken or missing pieces," Page says. "It's a great feeling to help our customers replace pieces in their patterns and to be able to see their satisfaction. Like our logo says - *we replace the irreplaceable.*"

Another growing area that Replacements, Ltd. has developed for its customers is the collectibles market. The company now offers a wide range of collectibles from companies such as Bing and Grondahl, Royal Copenhagen, Boehm, Hummel, Lladro and many more. "It was a natural progression of our business," says Page, "and something our customers had been requesting."

The Replacements, Ltd. Showroom and Museum in Greensboro, NC is a 12,000 square-foot retail facility located in front of the massive warehouse. It is decorated with turn of the century hand-carved showcases, 20-foot ceilings and classic chandeliers. Inside, one can view an incredibly varied selection of merchandise - from figurines, mugs and ornaments to the china, crystal and flatware that made the company famous.

The fascinating Replacements, Ltd. Museum, adjacent to the retail Showroom, is the home for over 2,000 rare and unusual pieces that Page has collected over the years. It includes a special section dedicated to one of Page's first loves - early 20th century glass from companies like Tiffin, Fostoria, Heisey, Imperial and Cambridge.

FOR MORE INFORMATION

- Call **1-800-REPLACE** (1-800-737-5223 from 8 am to 10 pm Eastern Time, 7 days a week)

- Write to: 1089 Knox Road, PO Box 26029 Greensboro, NC 27420

- Fax: 910-697-3100

- Visit the Replacements, Ltd. Showroom and Museum, at exit 132 off I-85/40 in Greensboro, NC. The Showroom and Museum are open 7 days a week, from 8 am to 9 pm.

A view of Replacements' 12,000 square foot Showroom

REPLACEMENTS, LTD.
We Replace The Irreplaceable®

1-800-REPLACE (1-800-737-5223)